LECTURES
on
REVIVALS
of
RELIGION

Register This New Book

Benefits of Registering*

- ✓ FREE **replacements** of lost or damaged books

- ✓ FREE **audiobook** – *Pilgrim's Progress,*
  audiobook edition

- ✓ FREE information about new titles
  and other **freebies**

www.anekopress.com/new-book-registration

*See our website for requirements and limitations.

LECTURES
on
REVIVALS
of
RELIGION

A Call to Holiness, Prayer, and the Work of Revival

CHARLES G. FINNEY

We enjoy hearing from our readers. Please contact us at
www.anekopress.com/questions-comments with
any questions, comments, or suggestions.

Lectures on Revivals of Religion

© 2025 by Aneko Press

All rights reserved. First edition 1835.

Revisions copyright 2025.

Scripture quotations from The Authorized (King James) Version. Rights in the Authorized Version in the United
Kingdom are vested in the Crown. Reproduced by permission of the Crown's patentee, Cambridge University Press.

Cover Designer: J. Martin

Cover Images: Adobe Firefly, iStock/Yes, and Shutterstock/sumkinn

Editor: P. Miller

Aneko Press

www.anekopress.com

Aneko Press, Life Sentence Publishing, and our logos are trademarks of

Life Sentence Publishing, Inc.
203 E. Birch Street
P.O. Box 652
Abbotsford, WI 54405

RELIGION / Christian Ministry / Evangelism

Paperback ISBN: 979-8-88936-489-4

eBook ISBN: 979-8-88936-490-0

10 9 8 7 6 5 4 3 2 1

Available where books are sold

Contents

The Lecturer's Preface

Let it be remembered that these lectures were delivered to my own congregation. They were given without my having previously marked out any plan or outline of them. They have been pursued from week to week as one subject naturally introduced another, and one lecture to another, as I believed the state of our people seemed to require.

I agreed to have the editor of the *Evangelist* report them, upon his own responsibility, because he thought that it might stir up a deeper interest in and extend the usefulness of his paper. And as I am now a pastor and don't have sufficient health to labor as an evangelist, and as it has pleased the Head of the church to give me some experience in revivals of Christianity, I thought it possible that while I was doing the work of a pastor in my own church, I might be of some little service to the churches abroad in this way.

I found a particular motivation to this course in the fact that on my return from the Mediterranean, I learned, with sorrow, that the spirit of revival had greatly declined in the United States, and that a spirit of discord and controversy alarmingly prevailed.

The specific circumstances of the church and the state of revivals unavoidably led me to discuss some points that I would gladly have avoided if the omission had been consistent with my main intent to reach and awaken the church when it was fast settling down in complacency.

I am far from setting up the claim of infallibility upon this or any other subject. I have given my own views, as far as I have done, without pretending to have exhausted the subject or to have spoken in the best possible manner upon the points I have discussed.

I am too well acquainted with the state of the church, and especially with the state of some of its ministers, to expect to escape without criticism. I have felt obligated to say some things that I fear will not, in all instances, be received as kindly as they were intended. But whatever may be the result of speaking the truth as it respects some, I have reason to believe that the vast majority of praying people will receive and be benefited by what I have said.

I am well aware that what I have said upon the subject of prayer will not be understood and received by a certain portion of the church, and all I can say is, *He that hath an ear to hear, let him hear* (see Matthew 11:15; Mark 4:9).

I did not have the faintest idea until recently that these lectures, in this or any other form, would ever grow into a book; but the urgent call for their publication in a volume, and the fact that I have had repeated assurances that the reading of them in the *Evangelist* has been acknowledged and blessed to have awakened individuals and churches and has resulted in the conversion of many sinners, have led me to agree to their publication in this imperfect form.

The reporter has succeeded, in general, in giving an outline of the lectures as they were delivered. His report, however, would make no more than a full skeleton of what was said on the subject at the time. In justice to the reporter, I would say that on reading his reports in his paper, although there were some mistakes and misunderstandings, yet I have been surprised that he could so nearly report my meaning without stenography.

As for literary merit, they have none – nor do they lay claim to any. It was not part of my intent to deliver elegant lectures. They were my most routine Friday evening discourses, and my main and only objective was to have them understood and felt.

In correcting the lectures for a volume, I have not had time, nor was it thought advisable to remodel them and change the style in which they had been reported. In some few instances, I have changed the phraseology when a thought had been very awkwardly expressed or when the true idea had not been given; but in nearly every instance, I have left the sentences as they were reported when the thought was clearly expressed, although the style might have been improved by alteration.

They were the editor's reports, and as such they must go before the public with such few additions and alterations as I have had time to make. If I could have written them out in full, I do not doubt that they would have been more acceptable to many readers, but this was impossible, and the only alternative was to let the public have them as they are or refuse to let them go out in the form of a volume at all. I am sorry they are not better lectures and in a more attractive form, but I have done what I could under the circumstances; and, as it is the wish of many whom I love, and delight to please and honor, to have them, although in this imperfect form, they must have them.

—C. G. Finney

By reading the above preface, the reader will get a clue to the time and circumstances that led to the delivery and publication of these lectures. In revising them for a new edition, I have done little more than correct the phraseology in a few instances, add a few footnotes, and replace the last two lectures by newly written ones on the same texts, prepared especially for this edition. These lectures are distinct from the course I deliver to my theology class upon the same subject. I may publish that course before my death. These lectures have been translated in the Welsh and French languages and have been very extensively circulated wherever the English or either of those languages is understood. One house in London published eighty thousand copies in English. They are still in type and in market in Europe, and I have the great satisfaction of knowing that they have been made a great blessing to thousands of souls. Consequently, I have not thought it wise to change them for the sake of giving them a more attractive form. God has allowed and blessed the reading of them as they have been, and with the exceptions above noticed, I have given them to the present and future generations. If the reader will read and remember the preceding preface, he will understand what I said of the church and some of the ministers, and why I said it. I urge my brethren not to take wrongly what I have said, but rather to be assured that every sentence has been spoken in love, and often with a sorrowful heart. May God continue to add His blessing to the reading of these lectures.

—The Author

Note by the Reporter

The work of reporting these lectures was undertaken for the purpose of increasing the interest and usefulness of the *New York Evangelist*. The reporter is completely unacquainted with shorthand, and has, therefore, only aimed to give a sketch of the main thoughts of the discourse. It is hardly necessary to mention that Mr. Finney never writes his sermons, but guides his course of argument by a skeleton, or outline, carefully prepared and so compact that it can be written on one side of a card about half as large as one of these printed pages. His manner is direct, his language is colloquial and Saxon, and his illustrations are drawn from the commonest incidents and expressions of life. The reporter has tried to preserve, as much as he could, the style of the speaker, and is thought to have been in some degree successful. If, in any cases, by letting his language run in a colloquial strain, he has made the copy more simple and ordinary than the original, he hopes to be forgiven easily for a fault by no means prevalent.

If anyone would try to criticize the style of these reports, he will assuredly lose his labor, for the only desire of the reporter has been to use such language that would fully convey the meaning and fairly demonstrate the manner of the lecturer. When words have done this, they have done their great work. The notes were taken with a pencil transcribed in great haste, and sent to the printer without revision. In preparing them for publication in this form, Mr. Finney has reviewed them with reference only to the correct expression of the sentiment. The style of an offhand sketch has been preserved partly by choice and partly from necessity. There was no time to modify the work, and the public opinion seemed to be that it was more desirable and more useful in its present condensed form. Therefore, Mr. Finney has done little more than to amend where the reporter misunderstood the meaning or did not express it with sufficient distinctness. He has enlarged in a few places where the illustrations, as given by the reporter, seemed to be incomplete.

My labor with these sketches is now done, and the results are sent forth in this permanent form with the prayer that God would use the book as He has already done the newspaper edition – to awaken, teach, and strengthen His people, and to guide, unite, and encourage zealous Christians of all classes in the great duty of saving sinners.

—J. L.

The Publisher's Preface

Charles Finney approaches the subject of revivals largely from the perspective of our responsibility in the matter. But he is not strictly an Arminian, as accused by some, and if you read this book, you will become keenly aware of how much Finney believes in prayer – in asking the Lord of the harvest for revival. It appears Finney saw both sides of the matter: our responsibility and God's sovereignty, both absolute truths. That said, there may be times when Finney emphasizes our responsibility so much that you may wonder if he truly does believe in God's sovereignty. Regarding this, I merely plead with you to read the entire book in order to take all that he says in the context of the entire volume, and I trust that you will see that Finney is quite balanced.

Does Finney believe in salvation by faith alone? Yes, and I quote from Lecture 17 of this book: "There is, in fact, no other way in which [man] can be freed and saved except to renounce himself and rest in Christ alone." You will find salvation as being by faith repeated many times, in various ways, throughout this book. But you will also find that the author addresses our responsibility to God in as straightforward a fashion as you will find in Christ's own words in the Gospels or in the Apostle Paul's words when he, too, addresses man's responsibility toward God.

Keep in mind that Charles Finney was a lawyer by profession, and this no doubt influenced the way he expounded on Scripture and the way he ministered to people. Finney, in his preaching and writing, is clear, analytical, and thorough in what he says. He endeavored to leave no loophole for his hearers to slip through – as any good lawyer or Christian should also practice. He rightly understood that the heart of man is deceitful and counseled enough individuals in his lifetime to understand that a presentation of the truth must not be sloppy or haphazard but rather as careful as possible in order to be as truly helpful as possible.

It is our belief that this book is needed today, in an age when grace is emphasized over practical, true Christian living. We believe that this book will be beneficial not only to pastors and evangelists but also to each and every Christian individual who is seeking to deny himself, take up his cross daily, and follow Christ, as he ought (Luke 9:23).

Sincerely,
The Publisher
2025

Lecture 1

What a Revival of Christianity Is

*O Lᴏʀᴅ, revive thy work in the midst of the years, in the
midst of the years make known; in wrath remember mercy.*
—Habakkuk 3:2

It is believed that the prophet Habakkuk was a contemporary of
Jeremiah, and that this prophecy was spoken in anticipation of the
Babylonian captivity. Looking at the judgments that were quickly to
come upon his nation, the soul of the prophet was worked up into an
agony, and he cried out in his distress, *O Lᴏʀᴅ, revive thy work*. It is as
if he had said, "O Lord, do not let Your judgments make Israel desolate.
In the midst of these dreadful years, let Your judgments be made the
means of reviving truth among us. In wrath remember mercy."

Religion is the work of man. It is something for man to do and should
consist in obeying God with and from the heart. It is man's duty. It is
true that God prompts him to do it. He influences him by His Spirit
because of man's great wickedness and reluctance to obey. If it were
not necessary for God to influence men, if people were inclined to obey
God, there would be no occasion to pray, *O Lᴏʀᴅ, revive thy work*. The
ground of necessity for such a prayer comes from people being completely reluctant to obey, and unless God introduced the influence of His
Spirit, not a person on earth would ever obey the commands of God.

A "revival of religion" presupposes a decline. Almost all real

Christianity in the world has been produced by revivals. God has found it necessary to take advantage of the enthusiasm in mankind to produce powerful excitement among them before He can lead them to obey. People are so spiritually sluggish, and there are so many things to lead their minds away from Christ and to oppose the influence of the gospel, that it is necessary to raise an excitement among them until the tide rises so high that it sweeps away the opposing obstacles. They must be so excited that they will break these counteracting influences before they will obey God. It is not that excited feeling is true religion, for it is not; but it is excited desire, appetite, and feeling that prevents true religion. The will is, in a sense, enslaved by the carnal and worldly desires. Therefore, it is necessary to awaken people to a sense of guilt and danger, and thus produce an excitement of counter feeling and desire, which will break the power of carnal and worldly desire and leave the will free to obey God.

Look back at the history of the Jews, and you will see that God used to maintain religion among them by special occasions, when there would be a great excitement and people would turn to the Lord. And after they had been thus revived, it would be only a short time before there would be so many counteracting influences brought to bear upon them that their religious fervor would decline, and keep on declining, until God could have time, so to speak, to convict them of sin by His Spirit and rebuke them by His providence, and thus so gain the attention of the people to the great subject of salvation so as to produce a widespread awakening of religious interest, and consequently a revival of religion. Then the counteracting causes would again operate, religion would decline, and the nation would be swept away in the vortex of luxury, idolatry, and pride.

There is so little principle in the church, so little firmness and stability of purpose, that unless the religious feelings are awakened and kept alive, counter worldly feeling and excitement will prevail, and people will not obey God. They have so little knowledge, and their principles are so weak, that unless they are excited, they will go back from the path of duty and do nothing to promote the glory of God. The state of the world is still such, and probably will be until the millennium is fully come, that Christianity must be promoted by means of revivals.

How long and how often has the experiment been tried to bring the church to act steadily for God without this periodic zeal! Many good men have supposed, and still suppose, that the best way to promote Christianity is to go along uniformly and gather in the ungodly gradually and without fervor.

But however sound such reasoning may appear in the abstract, facts demonstrate its futility. If the church were far enough advanced in knowledge and had stability of principle enough to stay awake, such a course would do; but the church is so little enlightened, and there are so many counteracting causes, that it will not go steadily to work without a special interest being awakened. As the millennium advances, it is probable that these periodic exuberances will be unknown. Then the church will be enlightened, the counteracting causes will be removed, and the entire church will be in a state of habitual and steady obedience to God. The entire church will stand and take the infant mind and cultivate it for God. Children will be trained up in the way they should go, and there will be no such torrents of worldliness and fashion and covetousness to carry away the piety of the church as soon as the excitement of a revival is withdrawn.

It is very desirable that it should be so. It is very desirable that the church would go on steadily in a course of obedience without these excitements. Such excitements tend to injure the health. Our nervous system is so strung that any powerful excitement, if long continued, injures our health and ruins us for duty. If Christianity is ever to have a pervading influence in the world, it cannot be this way. This occasional religion must be done away. Then it will be uncalled for. Christians will not sleep the greater part of the time and once in a while wake up, rub their eyes, bluster about, rant a little while, and then go to sleep again. Then there will be no need for ministers to wear themselves out and kill themselves by their efforts to roll back the flood of worldly influence that sets in upon the church.

As yet, however, the state of the Christian world is such that to expect to promote Christianity without excitements is illogical and absurd. The great political and worldly excitements that agitate Christendom are all unfriendly to Christianity and divert the mind from the interests of the soul. These excitements can only be counteracted by Christian enthusiasm.

And until there is Christian principle in the world to put down worldly excitements, it is vain to try to promote Christianity except by counteracting these. This is true in philosophy, and it is a historical fact.

It is improbable that Christianity will ever make progress among heathen nations except through the influence of revivals. The attempt is now being made to do it by education and other cautious and gradual improvements, but as long as the laws of the mind remain what they are, it cannot be done in this way. There must be excitement sufficient to wake up the dormant moral powers and roll back the tide of degradation and sin. And precisely so far as our own land grows more unbelieving, it is impossible for God or man to promote Christianity in such a state of things except by powerful excitements.

This is evident from the fact that this has always been the way in which God has worked. God does not create these excitements and choose this method to promote Christianity for nothing or without reason. Where people are so reluctant to obey God, they will not act until they are stirred up. For example, how many there are who know that they should be religious, but they are afraid that they will be laughed at by their friends if they become pious. Many people are wedded to idols. Others procrastinate repentance until they are settled in life or until they have secured some favorite worldly interest. Such people will never give up their false shame or relinquish their ambitious schemes until they are so stirred up by a sense of guilt and danger that they cannot contain themselves any longer.

These remarks are designed only as an introduction to the discourse. I will now proceed with the main order to show:

    I.   What a revival of religion is not.

    II. What it is.

    III. The means used in promoting it.

I. A Revival of Religion Is Not a Miracle

1. A miracle has been generally defined as a divine interference, setting aside or suspending the laws of nature. A revival is not a miracle in this

sense. All the laws of matter and mind remain in force. They are neither suspended nor set aside in a revival.

2. A revival is not a miracle according to another definition of the term miracle: something above the powers of nature. There is nothing in religion beyond the ordinary powers of nature. It consists entirely in the right exercise of the powers of nature. It is just that and nothing else. When people become religious, it is not that they are not enabled to put forth exertions that they were unable to put forth previously, but they only exert the powers they had before in a different way and use them for the glory of God.

3. A revival is not a miracle, or dependent on a miracle, in any sense. It is a purely philosophical result of the right use of the established means – as much so as any other effect produced by the application of means. There may be a miracle among its former causes, or there may not be. The apostles used miracles simply as a means by which they brought attention to their message and established its divine authority. But the miracle was not the revival. The miracle was one thing; the revival that followed it was quite another thing. The revivals in the apostles' days were connected with miracles, but they were not miracles.

I said that a revival is the result of the right use of the appropriate means. The means that God has appointed for the production of a revival undoubtedly have a natural tendency to produce a revival. Otherwise, God would not have appointed them. However, we all know that means will not produce a revival without the blessing of God. No more will grain, when it is sowed, produce a crop without the blessing of God. It is impossible for us to say that there is not as direct an influence or agency from God to produce a crop of grain as there is to produce a revival.

What are the laws of nature according to which it is believed that grain yields a crop? They are nothing but the constituted manner of the operations of God. In the Bible, the Word of God is compared to grain, preaching is compared to sowing seed, and the results are compared to the springing up and growth of the crop. The result is just as philosophical in the one case as in the other, and it is just as naturally connected with the cause; or more correctly, a revival is as naturally

5

a result of the use of the appropriate means as a crop is of the use of its appropriate means. It is true that true religion does not properly belong to the category of cause and effect, but although it is not caused by means, yet it has its occasion, and may as naturally and certainly result from its occasion as a crop does from its cause.

I want this idea to be impressed on all your minds, for there has long been an idea prevalent that promoting Christianity has something unusual in it that is not to be judged by the ordinary rules of cause and effect. In short, there is no connection of the means with the result, and no tendency in the means to produce the effect. No doctrine is more dangerous than this to the prosperity of the church, and nothing is more absurd.

Suppose a man were to go and preach this doctrine among farmers about their sowing grain. Let him tell them that God is sovereign and will give them a crop only when it pleases Him, and that for them to plow and plant and labor as if they expected to raise a crop is very wrong and takes the work out of the hands of God, that it interferes with His sovereignty and is going on in their own strength, and that there is no connection between the means and the result on which they can depend. And now, suppose the farmers would believe such doctrine. They would starve the world to death.

The same kind of results will follow if the church is persuaded that promoting true Christianity is somehow so mysteriously a subject of divine sovereignty that there is no natural connection between the means and the end. What are the results? Generation after generation has gone down to hell. No doubt more than five thousand million people have gone down to hell while the church has been dreaming and waiting for God to save them without the use of means. It has been the devil's most successful means of destroying souls. The connection is as clear in Christianity as it is when the farmer sows his grain.

There is one fact under the government of God that is worthy of universal notice and of everlasting remembrance, and that is that the most useful and important things are most easily and certainly obtained by the use of the appropriate means. This is evidently a principle in the divine administration. Therefore, all the necessities of life are obtained with great certainty by the use of the simplest means. The luxuries are more difficult to obtain; the means to procure them are more compli-cated and less certain in their results, while things absolutely harmful and poisonous, such as alcohol, are often obtained only by torturing nature and making use of a kind of infernal sorcery to procure the death-dealing abomination.

This principle holds true in moral government, and as spiritual bless-ings are of greatest importance, we should expect their attainment to be connected with great certainty with the use of the appropriate means. We find this to be the fact, and I fully believe that if facts were known, it would be found that when the appointed means have been rightly used, spiritual blessings have been obtained with greater uniformity than temporal ones.

II. What a Revival of Religion Is

A revival is the renewal of the first love of Christians, resulting in the awakening and conversion of sinners to God. In the popular sense, a revival of true Christianity in a community is the stirring up, awak-ening, and reclaiming of the more or less backslidden church and the more or less general awakening of all classes, and ensuring attention to the claims of God.

It presumes that the church is sunk down in a backslidden state, and a revival consists in the return of a church from her backslidings, and in the conversion of sinners.

1. A revival always includes conviction of sin on the part of the church. Backslidden professing Christians cannot wake up and begin right away in the service of God without deep searchings of heart. The fountains of sin need to be broken up. In a true revival, Christians are always brought under such convictions. They see their sins in such a light that they often find it impossible to maintain a hope of their acceptance with God. It does not always go to that extent, but in a genuine revival there are always deep convictions of sin, and often cases of abandoning all hope.

2. Backslidden Christians will be brought to repentance. A revival is nothing else than a new beginning of obedience to God. Just as in the

case of a converted sinner, the first step is a deep repentance, a breaking down of heart, and getting down into the dust before God with deep humility and forsaking of sin.

3. Christians will have their faith renewed. While they are in their back-slidden state, they are blind to the state of sinners. Their hearts are as hard as marble. The truths of the Bible only appear like a dream. They admit that it is all true. Their conscience and their judgment assent to it, but their faith does not see it standing out in bold relief in all the burning realities of eternity.

But when they enter into a revival, they no longer *see men as trees, walking* (Mark 8:24), but they see things in that strong light that will renew the love of God in their hearts. This will lead them to labor zealously to bring others to Him. They will feel grieved that others do not love God, when they love Him so much. They will proceed compassionately to persuade their neighbors to give Him their hearts. Their love to people will be renewed. They will be filled with a tender and burning love for souls. They will have a longing desire for the salvation of the whole world. They will be in an agony for individuals whom they desire to be saved – their friends, their relatives, and even their enemies. They will not only be urging them to give their hearts to God, but they will carry them to God in the arms of faith, and with strong crying and tears they will plead with God to have mercy on them and save their souls from endless burnings.

4. A revival breaks the power of the world and of sin over Christians. It brings them to such vantage ground that they get a fresh impulse toward heaven. They have a new foretaste of heaven and new desires after union with God. The charm of the world is broken, and the power of sin is overcome.

5. When the churches are thus awakened and reformed, the reformation and salvation of sinners will follow, going through the same stages of conviction, repentance, and reformation. Their hearts will be broken down and changed. Very often the most abandoned reprobates are among the subjects. Prostitutes, alcoholics, atheists, and all sorts of

abandoned characters are awakened and converted. The worst among human beings are softened, reclaimed, and made to appear as lovely specimens of the beauty of holiness.

III. The Means Used in Carrying Forward a Revival of Religion

Ordinarily, there are three agents and one instrument employed in the work of conversion. The agents are God, some person who brings the truth to bear on the mind, and the sinner himself. The instrument is the truth. There are always two agents – God and the sinner – employed and active in every case of genuine conversion.

1. The agency of God is twofold: by His providence and by His Spirit.

a) By His providential government, He so arranges events as to bring the sinner's mind and the truth in contact. He brings the sinner where the truth reaches his ears or his eyes. It is often interesting to trace the manner in which God arranges events to bring this about and how He sometimes makes everything seem to favor a revival. The state of the weather, the public health, and other circumstances harmonize to make everything just right to favor the application of truth with the greatest possible effectiveness. How He sometimes sends a minister along at just the time he is needed! How He brings out a particular truth at just the particular time when the individual it is prepared for is ready and able to hear!

b) God's special agency by His Holy Spirit. Having direct access to the mind, and knowing infinitely well the whole history and condition of each individual sinner, He employs the truth that is best adapted to his particular situation, and then sets it home with divine power. He gives it such vividness, strength, and power that the sinner trembles, throws down his weapons of rebellion, and turns to the Lord. Under His influence, the truth burns and cuts its way like fire. He makes the truth stand out in such aspects that it crushes the proudest person down with the weight of a mountain. If people were inclined to obey God, the truth is given with sufficient clearness in the Bible and from preaching that they could learn all that is necessary for them to know. But because they are completely disinclined to obey God's truth, God clears it up before their minds and pours in a blaze of convincing light upon their souls, which they cannot withstand – and they yield to it, obey God, and are saved.

2. The agency of men is commonly employed. Men are not mere instruments in the hands of God. Truth is the instrument. The preacher is a moral agent in the work; he acts. He is not a mere passive instrument, but he is deliberate in promoting the conversion of sinners.

3. The agency of the sinner himself. The conversion of a sinner consists in his obeying the truth. It is therefore impossible for it to take place without his agency, for it consists in his acting right. He is influenced to this by the agency of God and by the agency of men. Men act on their fellow men, not only by language but also by their looks, their tears, and their daily conduct. See that unrepentant man there who has a pious wife. Her very looks, her tenderness, her solemn, compassionate dignity, softened and molded into the image of Christ are a sermon to him all the time. He has to turn his mind away because it is such a reproach to him. He feels a sermon ringing in his ears all day long.

People are accustomed to reading the countenances of their neighbors. Sinners often read the state of a Christian's mind in his eyes. If his eyes are full of levity, or worldly anxiety and ideas, sinners read it. If they are full of the Spirit of God, sinners read it. Sinners are often led to conviction by barely seeing the countenance of Christians.

An individual once went into a factory to see the machinery. His mind was solemn, as he had been where there was a revival. The people who labored there all knew him by sight and knew who he was. A young lady who was at work saw him, whispered some foolish remark to her companion, and laughed. The person stopped and looked at her with a feeling of grief. She stopped, her thread broke, and she was so troubled that she could not join it together. She looked out at the window to compose herself, and then tried again. Again and again she tried to recover her dignity. Eventually she sat down, overcome with her feelings. The person then approached and spoke with her; she soon manifested a deep sense of sin. The feeling spread through the establishment like fire, and in a few hours almost every person employed there was under conviction. The man, though a worldly man, was astounded, and he requested to have the work stop and have a prayer meeting, for he said it was a great deal more important to have these people converted than to have the work go on. In a few days, that man and nearly every person employed in the establishment were hopefully converted. The eye of this individual, his solemn countenance, and his compassionate feeling rebuked the levity of the young woman and brought her under conviction of sin. This whole revival followed, probably in a great measure, from so small an incident.

If Christians have deep feeling on the subject of religion themselves, they will produce deep feeling wherever they go. If they are cold or light and trifling, they inevitably destroy all deep feeling, even in awakened sinners.

I knew a case of an individual who was very anxious about her soul, but one day I was grieved to find that her convictions seemed to be all gone. I asked her what she had been doing. She told me she had been spending the afternoon among some professing Christians, not thinking that it would dissolve her convictions to spend an afternoon with professing Christians. But they were lighthearted and vain, and so her convictions were lost. Undoubtedly, those professing Christians destroyed a soul by their foolishness, for her convictions did not return.

The church is required to use the means for the conversion of sinners. Sinners cannot properly be said to use the means for their own conversion. The church uses the means. What sinners do is to submit to the truth or to resist it. It is a mistake of sinners to think they are using means for their own conversion. The whole direction of a revival, and everything about it, is designed to present the truth to your mind for your obedience or resistance.

Remarks

1. Revivals used to be regarded as miracles, and even in our day, some people refer to them as such. Other people have ideas on the subject so loose and unsatisfactory that if they would only think, they would see their absurdity. For a long time, the church assumed that a revival was a miracle, an intervention of divine power that they had nothing to do with and that they had no more involvement in producing than they

had in producing thunder, or a storm of hail, or an earthquake. It is only recently that ministers generally have learned that revivals were to be promoted by the use of means designed and adapted specifically to that purpose. Even in New England, it has been supposed that revivals came just as showers do – sometimes in one town and sometimes in another – and that ministers and churches could do nothing more to produce them than they could to make rain showers come on their own town when they are falling on a neighboring town.

It used to be thought that a revival would come about once every fifteen years, and all would be converted whom God intended to save, and then they had to wait until another crop came forward on the stage of life. Finally, the time got shortened down to five years, and they supposed there would be a revival about that often.

I have heard a fact in relation to one of these pastors who supposed revivals might come about once every five years. There had been a revival in his congregation. The next year, there was a revival in a neighboring town. He went there to preach, and he stayed several days until he got his soul all engaged in the work. He returned home on Saturday and went into his study to prepare for the Lord's Day. His soul was in agony. He thought how many adults there were in his congregation at enmity with God – so many still unconverted, so many dying every year, and so many of them unconverted. He realized that if a revival did not come for five years, so many adult heads of families would be in hell. He put down his calculations on paper and presented them in his sermon for the next day, with his heart bleeding at the dreadful picture. As I understood it, he did not do this with any expectation of a revival, but he felt deeply and poured out his heart to his people. That sermon awakened forty heads of families, and a powerful revival followed. His theory about a revival once every five years was shattered.

Thus God has generally overthrown the theory that revivals are miracles.

2. Mistaken ideas concerning the sovereignty of God have greatly hindered revivals. Many people have supposed God's sovereignty to be something very different from what it is. They have supposed it to be such an arbitrary disposal of events, particularly of the gift of His Spirit,

as to impede a rational use of means for promoting a revival. But there is no evidence from the Bible that God exercises any such sovereignty as that. There are no facts to prove it. But everything goes to show that God has connected means with the end through all the departments of His government – in nature and in grace. There is no natural event in which He is not concerned. He has not built the creation like a vast machine that will go on alone without His further care. He has not retired from the universe to let it work for itself. This is mere atheism. He exercises a universal superintendence and control, yet every event in nature has been brought about by means. He neither administers providence nor grace with that sort of sovereignty that does away with the use of means. There is no more sovereignty in one than in the other.

Yet some people are terribly alarmed at all direct efforts to promote a revival, and they cry out, "You are trying to get up a revival in your own strength. Be careful; you are interfering with the sovereignty of God. You had better keep to the usual course and let God give a revival when He thinks it is best. God is a sovereign, and it is very wrong for you to attempt to get up a revival just because you think a revival is needed." This is just the kind of preaching that the devil wants. People cannot do the devil's work more effectively than by preaching the sovereignty of God as a reason why we should not put forth efforts to produce a revival.

3. You see the error of those who think that Christianity can be better promoted in the world without revivals and who are inclined to give up all efforts to produce spiritual awakenings. Because there are evils arising in some instances out of great emotions and excitements on the subject of religion, they are of the opinion that it is best to do away with them entirely. This cannot and must not be. It is true that there is danger of abuses. In cases of great religious as well as all other excitements, more or less incidental evils may be expected, of course, but this is no reason that they should be given up. The best things are always liable to abuses. Great and manifold evils have originated in the providential and moral governments of God. However, these expected abuses and evils were not considered a sufficient reason to give them up, for the establishment of these governments was in general the best that could be done for the production of the greatest amount of happiness.

So in revivals of true religion, it is found by experience that in the present state of the world, Christianity cannot be promoted to any considerable extent without revivals. When the evils that are sometimes complained of are real, they are incidental and of small importance when compared to the amount of good produced by revivals. The view should not be recognized by the church for a moment that revivals may be discontinued. It is filled with all that is dangerous to the interests of Zion, is death to the cause of missions, and brings in its train the damnation of the world.

Finally, I have a proposal to make to you. I did not begin this series of lectures on revivals to stir up a curious theory of my own on the subject. I would not spend my time and strength merely to give you instructions, to gratify your curiosity, and to furnish you with something to talk about. I have no intention of preaching about revivals. It is not my plan to preach to have you be able to say at the end, "We understand all about revivals now," while you do nothing. But I want to ask you a question. What do you hear lectures on revivals for? Do you intend that whenever you are convinced what your duty is in promoting a revival, you will go to work and practice it? Will you follow the instructions I will give you from the Word of God and put them in practice in your own lives? Will you apply them with your families, your friends, your neighbors, and throughout the city, or will you spend your time in learning *about* revivals, but do nothing for them?

As quickly as you learn anything on the subject of revivals, I want you to put it into practice and go to work to see if you can promote a revival among sinners here. If you will not do this, I want you to let me know at the beginning so that I do not waste my strength. You should decide now whether you will do this or not. You know that we call sinners to decide on the spot whether they will obey the gospel or not, and we have no more authority to let you take time to deliberate whether you will obey God than we have to let sinners do so. We call on you to unite now in a solemn pledge to God that you will do your duty as soon as you learn what it is, and to pray that He will pour out His Spirit upon this church and upon the entire city.

Lecture 2

When a Revival Is to Be Expected

Wilt thou not revive us again; that thy people may rejoice in thee?
—Psalm 85:6

This psalm seems to have been written soon after the return of the people of Israel from the Babylonian captivity, as you can see from the language at the beginning of this psalm. The psalmist felt that God had been very favorable to the people, and while contemplating the goodness of the Lord in bringing them back from the land where they had been carried away captive, and while looking at the prospects before them, he broke out into a prayer for a revival of religion: *Wilt thou not revive us again, that thy people may rejoice in thee?* Since God in His providence had reestablished the ordinances of His house in Jerusalem, the psalmist prayed that there may be also a revival of religion to crown the work.

In the last lecture I attempted to show what a revival of religion is not, what a revival is, and the means to be used in promoting it. The topics to which I want to call your attention now are:

I. When a revival of religion is needed.

II. The importance of a revival when it is needed.

III. When a revival of religion may be expected.

I. When a Revival of Religion Is Needed

1. When there is a lack of brotherly love and Christian confidence among professing Christians, a revival is needed. Then there is a loud call for God to revive His work. When Christians have sunk into a low and backslidden state, they neither have, nor should have, nor is there a reason to have, the same love and confidence toward each other as when they are all alive, active, and living holy lives. The love of benevolence may be the same, but not the love of delight. God loves all people with the love of benevolence, but He does not feel the love of delight toward any except those who live holy lives. Christians do not and cannot love each other with the love of delight, only in proportion to their holiness. If Christian love is the love of the image of Christ in His people, then it can never be exercised except where that image really or apparently exists. A person must reflect the image of Christ and show the spirit of Christ before other Christians can love him with the love of delight.

It is in vain to call on Christians to love one another with the love of delight, as Christians, when they are sunk down in ignorance. They see nothing in each other to produce this love. It is next to impossible for them to feel otherwise toward each other than they do toward sinners. Merely knowing that they belong to a church, or seeing them occasionally at the communion table, will not produce Christian love unless they see the image of Christ in them.

2. When there are dissensions, jealousies, and evil speaking among professing Christians, then there is great need of a revival. These things show that Christians are far from God, and it is time to think seriously of a revival. Christianity cannot prosper with such things in the church, and nothing can put an end to them like a revival.

3. When there is a worldly spirit in the church, then it is time to seek a revival. It is clear that the church has sunk into a low and backslidden state when you see Christians conform to the world in clothing, entertainment, parties, seeking worldly amusements, and reading novels and other books such as the world reads. It shows that they are far from God, and that there is great need of a revival.

4. When the church finds its members falling into obvious and scandalous sins, then it is time for the church to wake up and cry to God for a revival of religion. When such things are taking place that give the enemies of Christianity an occasion for reproach, it is time for the church to ask God, "What will become of Your great name?"

5. When there is a spirit of controversy in the church or in the land, a revival is needed. The Christian spirit is not the spirit of controversy. There can be no advancement in the Christian religion where the spirit of controversy prevails.

6. When the wicked triumph over the church and revile them, it is time to seek for a revival of religion.

7. When sinners are careless and foolish and are sinking into hell unconcerned, it is time for the church to wake up. It is as much the duty of the church to wake up as it is for the firemen to awake when a fire breaks out during the night in a large city. The church should put out the fires of hell that are laying hold of the wicked. Sleep? Should the firemen sleep and let the whole city burn down? What would be thought of such firemen? Yet their guilt would not compare with the guilt of Christians who sleep while sinners around them are sinking ignorantly into the fires of hell.

II. The Importance of a Revival of Religion in Such Circumstances

1. A revival is the only possible thing that can wipe away the reproach that covers the church and restore Christianity to the place it should have in the opinion of the public. Without a revival, this reproach will cover the church more and more until it is overwhelmed with universal contempt. You may do anything else you please, and you can change the aspects of society in some respects, but you will do no real good; you only make it worse without a revival of true Christianity. You may go and build a splendid new house of worship, line your seats with expensive fabric, put up an elegant pulpit, and get a magnificent organ and everything of that kind to make a show, and in that way you may

acquire a sort of respect for Christianity among the wicked, but it does no good in reality. It rather does harm. It misleads them as to the real nature of Christianity, and so far from converting them, it carries them farther away from salvation. Look wherever they have surrounded the altar of Christianity with splendor, and you will find that the impression produced is contrary to the true nature of Christianity. There must be a waking up of energy on the part of Christians, and an outpouring of God's Spirit, or the world will laugh at the church.

2. Nothing else will restore Christian love and confidence among church members. Nothing except a revival of religion can restore it, and nothing else should restore it. There is no other way to wake up that love of Christians for one another that is sometimes felt when they have such love as they cannot express. You cannot have such love without confidence, and you cannot restore confidence without such evidence of piety as is seen in a revival.

If a minister finds he has lost in any degree the confidence of his people, he should labor for a revival as the only means of regaining their confidence. I do not mean that his motive in laboring for a revival should be to regain the confidence of his people, but that a revival through his instrumentality, and ordinarily nothing else, will restore to him the confidence of the praying part of his people. So if an elder or private member of the church finds his brethren cold toward him, there is only one way to remedy it, and that is by being revived himself and pouring out from his eyes and from his life the splendor of the image of Christ. This spirit will catch and spread in the church, confidence will be renewed, and brotherly love will prevail again.

3. At such a time, a revival of religion is indispensable to avert the judgments of God from the church. This would be strange preaching if revivals are only miracles, and if the church has no more part in producing them than it has in making a thunderstorm. To say to the church, then, that unless there is a revival you may expect judgments, would then be as ridiculous as to say that unless you have a thunderstorm, you may expect judgments.

The fact is that Christians are more to blame for not being revived than sinners are for not being converted. If they are not awakened, they may know assuredly that God will visit them with His judgments. How often God visited the Israelites with judgments because they would not repent and be revived at the call of His prophets! How often have we seen churches, and even whole denominations, cursed with a curse because they would not wake up and seek the Lord and pray, *Wilt thou not revive us again, that thy people may rejoice in thee?*

4. Nothing except a revival can preserve such a church from annihilation. A church declining in this way cannot continue to exist without a revival. If it receives new members, they will for the most part be made up of ungodly people. Without revivals, there will not ordinarily be as many people converted as will die off in a year. There have been churches in this country where the members have died off, and there were no revivals to convert others in their place, until the church has run out and the organization has been dissolved.

A minister told me that he once labored as a missionary in Virginia on the ground where Samuel Davies once flashed and shone like a flaming torch, and that Davies' church was so reduced as to have only one male member. The church had become proud and was all run out.

I have heard of a church in Pennsylvania that was formerly flourishing, but neglected revivals, and it became so reduced that the pastor had to send to a neighboring church for a ruling elder when he administered the communion.

5. Nothing except a revival of religion can prevent the means of grace from doing great harm to the ungodly. Without a revival, their hearts will grow harder and harder under preaching, and they will experience a more horrible damnation than they would if they had never heard the gospel. Your children and your friends will go down to a much more horrible fate in hell, in consequence of the means of grace, if there are no revivals to convert them to God. It would be better for them if there were no means of grace, no sanctuary, no Bible, no preaching, and if they had never heard the gospel than to live and die where there is no revival. The gospel is the savor of death unto death if it is not made a savor of life unto life (see 2 Corinthians 2:16).

6. There is no other way in which a church can be sanctified, grow in grace, and be made ready for heaven. What is growing in grace? Is it hearing sermons and getting some new thoughts about religion? No – no such thing! The Christian who does this, and nothing more, is getting worse and worse, more and more hardened, and every week it is more difficult to stir him up to duty.

III. When a Revival of Religion May be Expected

1. When the providence of God indicates that a revival is at hand, then a revival may be expected. The indications of God's providence are sometimes so plain as to amount to a revelation of His will. There is a conspiring of events to open the way, a preparation of circumstances to favor a revival, so that those who are looking can see that a revival is at hand just as plainly as if it had been revealed from heaven. Cases have occurred in this country in which the providential manifestations were so plain that those who are careful observers felt no hesitation in saying that God was coming to pour out His Spirit and grant a revival of religion. There are various ways for God to indicate His will to a people – sometimes by giving them distinct means, sometimes by strange and alarming events, sometimes by remarkably favoring the use of means by the weather, health, etc.

2. When the wickedness of the wicked grieves and humbles and distresses Christians, then a revival may be expected. Sometimes Christians do not seem to mind anything about the wickedness around them, or if they talk about it, they do so in a cold and callous and unfeeling way, as if they despaired of a reformation. They are inclined to scold sinners, but not to feel the compassion of the Son of God for them. But sometimes the conduct of the wicked drives Christians to prayer, breaks them down, and makes them sorrowful and tenderhearted so that they can weep day and night, and instead of scolding and reproaching the wicked, they pray earnestly for them. Then you may expect a revival. Indeed, this is a revival begun already.

Sometimes the wicked will get up an opposition to biblical religion, and when this drives Christians to their knees in prayer to God with strong crying and tears, you may be certain there is going to be a revival. The prevalence of wickedness is no evidence at all that there is not going to be a revival. That is often God's time to work. *When the enemy shall come in like a flood, the Spirit of the* LORD *shall lift up a standard against him* (Isaiah 59:19).

Often the first indication of a revival is when the devil gets up something new in opposition. It will invariably have one of two effects. It will either drive Christians to God, or it will drive them farther away from God to some carnal policy that will only make things worse. Frequently the most outrageous wickedness of the ungodly is followed by a revival. If Christians are made to feel that they have no hope except in God, and if they have sufficient feeling left to care for the honor of God and the salvation of the souls of the unrepentant, there will certainly be a revival.

Let hell boil over if it will, and spew out as many demons as there are stones in the pavements – if it only drives Christians to God in prayer, they cannot hinder a revival. Let Satan create a disturbance and sound his horn as loud as he pleases – if Christians will only be humbled and pray, they will soon see God's strong arm in a revival. I have known instances when a revival has broken in upon the ranks of the enemy, almost as suddenly as a clap of thunder, and scattered them, taking the very ringleaders as trophies and breaking up their party in an instant.

3. A revival may be expected when Christians have a spirit of prayer for a revival. That is, when they pray as if their hearts were set upon a revival. Sometimes Christians are not engaged in prayer for a revival, not even when they are warm in prayer. Their minds are upon something else that they are praying for, such as the salvation of the heathen, and not for a revival among themselves. But when they feel the lack of a revival, they pray for it. They feel for their own families and neighborhoods, and they pray for them as if they could not be denied.

What constitutes a spirit of prayer? Is it many prayers and warm words? No. Prayer is the condition of the heart. The spirit of prayer is a state of continual desire and anxiety of mind for the salvation of sinners. It weighs them down. It is the same, as far as the philosophy of the mind is concerned, as when a man is anxious for some worldly interest. A Christian who has this spirit of prayer feels concerned for souls. It is the subject of his thoughts all the time, and it makes him look and act as if he had a burden on his mind. He thinks of it by day and dreams of it by night. This is properly praying *without ceasing* (1 Thessalonians 5:17). The person's prayers seem to flow from his heart as liquid as water: *O LORD, revive thy work.* Sometimes this feeling is very deep. People have been bowed down so that they could neither stand nor sit.

I can name men in this state, of firm nerves and who stand high in character, who have been absolutely crushed with grief for the state of sinners. They have had an actual travail of soul for sinners until they were as helpless as children. The feeling is not always as great as this, but such things are much more common than is supposed. In the great revivals in 1826, they were common. This is by no means enthusiasm. It is just what Paul felt when he said, *My little children, of whom I travail in birth* (Galatians 4:19).

I heard of a person in this state who prayed for sinners and finally got into such a state of mind that she could not live without prayer. She could not rest day or night unless there was somebody praying. Then she would be at ease; but if they ceased, she would shriek in agony until there was prayer again. This continued for two days until she prevailed in prayer and her soul was relieved. This travail of soul is that deep agony that people feel when they lay hold on God for such a blessing and will not let Him go until they receive it. I do not mean to be understood that it is essential to a spirit of prayer that the distress should be as great as this, but this deep, continual, earnest desire for the salvation of sinners is what constitutes the spirit of prayer for a revival. It is a revival begun so far as this spirit of prayer extends.

When this feeling exists in a church, unless the Spirit is grieved away by sin, there will infallibly be a revival of Christians generally, and it will involve the conversion of sinners to God. This anxiety and distress increases until the revival begins. A clergyman once told me of a revival among his people that began with a zealous and devoted woman in the church. She became concerned about sinners and began praying for them. She prayed, and her distress increased. She finally went to her minister, talked with him, and asked him to appoint an anxious meeting for those concerned about their souls, for she felt that one was needed. The minister put her off, for he felt nothing of it. The next week she went again and asked him to appoint an anxious meeting. She knew someone would come, for she felt as if God was going to pour out His Spirit. He put her off again. Finally she said to him, "If you do not appoint an anxious meeting, I will die, for there is certainly going to be a revival."

The next Sunday he appointed a meeting, and he said that if there were any who wanted to talk with him about the salvation of their souls, he would meet them on a specified evening. He did not know of one person who would come, but when he went to the place, to his astonishment he found a large number of anxious inquirers. Now do you not think that woman knew there was going to be a revival? Call it what you please – a new revelation, an old revelation, or anything else. I say it was the Spirit of God who taught that praying woman there was going to be a revival. *The secret of the* LORD was with her (Psalm 25:14), and she knew it. She knew that God had been in her heart, and He had filled it so full that she could keep it in no longer.

Sometimes ministers have had this distress about their congregations, and they felt as if they could not live unless they could see a revival. Sometimes elders and deacons, or private members of the church, men or women, have the spirit of prayer for a revival of religion, so that they will hold on and prevail with God until He pours out His Spirit.

The first ray of light that broke in upon the midnight that rested on the churches in Oneida County in the fall of 1825 was from a woman in feeble health who, I believe, had never been in a powerful revival. Her soul was burdened about sinners. She was in an agony for the land. She did not know what troubled her, but she kept praying more and more until it seemed as if her agony would destroy her body. At last she became full of joy and exclaimed, "God has come! God has come! There is no mistake about it – the work has begun and is going over all the region." And sure enough, the work began. Her family members were almost all converted, and the work spread all over that part of the country. Do you think that woman was deceived? I tell you, no. She knew she had prevailed with God in prayer. She had travailed in birth for souls, and she knew it. This was not the only example, by many, that I knew in that region.

Generally, there are only a few professing Christians who know anything about this spirit of prayer that prevails with God. I have been amazed to see such accounts as are often published about revivals, as if the revival had come without any cause – nobody knew why or for what reason. I have sometimes inquired into such cases, when it was explained that nobody knew anything about it until one Sunday when they saw in the face of the congregation that God was there, or they saw it in their conference room or prayer meeting, and were astonished at the mysterious sovereignty of God in bringing in a revival without any apparent connection with means.

Listen. Go and inquire among the little-noticed members of the church, and you will always find that somebody had been praying for a revival and was expecting it. Some man or woman had been agonizing in prayer for the salvation of sinners until they gained the blessing. It may have found the minister and the body of the church fast asleep, and they would wake up all of a sudden like a man rubbing his eyes open, running round the room, pushing things over, and wondering where all this excitement came from. But although few knew it, you may be sure there has been somebody on the watchtower, constant in prayer until the blessing came. Generally, a revival is more or less extensive as there are more or less people who have the spirit of prayer. But I will not dwell on this subject any further at present, as the subject of prayer will come up again in this course of lectures.

4. Another sign that a revival may be expected is when the attention of ministers is especially directed to this particular object and when their preaching and other efforts are aimed particularly at the conversion of sinners. Most of the time, the labors of ministers are, it would seem, directed to other objects. They seem to preach and labor with no particular design to effect the immediate conversion of sinners. Therefore, it does not need to be expected that there will be a revival under their preaching. There will never be a revival until somebody makes particular efforts for this end.

However, when the attention of a minister is directed to the state of the families in his congregation, when his heart is full of feeling the necessity of a revival, and when he puts forth the proper efforts for this end, then you may be prepared to expect a revival. As I explained previously, the connection between the right use of means for a revival and a revival is as philosophically sure as between the right use of means to raise grain and the resulting crop of wheat. I believe it is even more certain, and there are fewer instances of failure. The effect is more certain to follow. The paramount importance of spiritual things makes it reasonable that it should be so.

Take the Bible, the nature of the case, and the history of the church all together, and you will find fewer failures in the use of means for a revival than in farming or in any other worldly business. In worldly business, there are sometimes cases in which counteracting causes annihilate all a person can do. In raising grain, there are cases that are beyond the control of man, such as drought, hard winter, worms, and so on. So in laboring to promote a revival, things may occur to counteract it, such as something turning up to divert the public attention from truth, which may frustrate every effort.

However, I believe there are fewer such cases in the moral world than in the natural world. I have seldom seen an individual fail when he used the means for promoting a revival in earnest – in the manner pointed out in the Word of God. I believe a man may enter on the work of promoting a revival with as reasonable an expectation of success as he can enter on any other work with an expectation of success – with the same expectation that the farmer has of a crop when he sows his grain. I have sometimes seen this tried and succeed under the most forbidding circumstances that can be conceived.

The great revival in Rochester began under the most disadvantageous circumstances that could be imagined. It seemed as though Satan had introduced every possible obstacle to a revival. The three churches were at variance. One church had no minister, and another one was divided and was about to dismiss their minister. An elder of the third Presbyterian church had brought a charge of unchristian conduct against the pastor of the first church, and they were about to have a trial before the presbytery. After the work began, one of the first things to happen was that the great stone church gave way and created a panic. Then one of the churches went ahead and dismissed their minister right in the midst of it. Another church nearly broke down. Many other things occurred, so that it seemed as if the devil was determined to divert the public attention away from the subject of true religion. But there were a few remarkable cases of the spirit of prayer, which assured us that God was there, and we went on. The more Satan opposed, the higher the Spirit of the Lord lifted up the standard, until finally a wave of salvation rolled over the place.

5. A revival of religion may be expected when Christians begin to confess their sins to one another. At other times, they confess in a general manner, as if they were only half sincere. They may do it in eloquent language, but it does not mean anything. However, when there is a sincere breaking down and a pouring out of the heart in making a confession of their sins, the floodgates will soon burst open, and salvation will flow over the place.

6. A revival may be expected whenever Christians are found willing to make the sacrifice necessary to carry it on. They must be willing to sacrifice their feelings, their business, and their time to help forward the work. Ministers must be willing to lay out their strength and jeopardize their health and life. They must be willing to offend the unrepentant by plain and faithful dealing, and perhaps offend many members of the church who will not rise to the work. They must take a decided stand with the revival, no matter what the consequences may be. They must be prepared to go on with the work, even though they could lose the affections of all the unrepentant and of all the cold part of the church. The minister must be prepared, if it is the will of God, to be driven away from the place. He must be determined to go straight forward and leave the entire event with God.

I knew a minister who had a young man laboring with him in a revival. The young man preached plain truth, and the wicked did not like him. They said, "We like our minister, and we want to have him preach."

They finally said so much that the minister told the young man, "Mr. Such-a-one who gives so much toward my support says such-and-such. Mr. A. says this, and Mr. B. says that. They think it will break up the society if you continue to preach, and I think you had better not preach anymore." The young man went away, but the Spirit of God immediately withdrew from the place, and the revival stopped short.

By yielding to the wicked desires of the wicked, the minister drove him away. He was afraid the devil would drive *him* away from his people, and by undertaking to satisfy the devil, he offended God. And God so ordered events that in a short time he had to leave his people after all. He tried to go between the devil and God, and God dismissed him.

The people, also, must be willing to have a revival, no matter what sacrifices must be made. It will not do for them to say, "We are willing to attend so many meetings, but we cannot attend any more," or "We are willing to have a revival if it will not disturb our arrangements about our business or prevent our making money." I tell you, such people will never have a revival until they are willing to do anything and sacrifice anything that God indicates to be their duty. Christian merchants must be willing to lock up their stores for six months if it is necessary to carry on a revival. I do not mean to say that any such thing is called for, or that it is their duty to do so, but if there should be such a state of feeling to call for it, then it would be their duty, and they should be willing to do it. They should be willing to do it if God calls, and He can easily burn down their stores if they do not. In fact, I would not be sorry to see such a revival in New York that would make every merchant in the city lock up his store until spring and say he had sold enough goods, and now he must give up his whole time to lead sinners to Christ.

7. A revival may be expected when ministers and professing Christians are willing to have God promote it by whatever instruments He pleases. Sometimes ministers are not willing to have a revival unless *they* can have the management of it, or unless *their* group can be prominent in promoting it. They want to specify to God what to direct and bless and what men to put forward. They do not want any new measures. They cannot have any of this different kind of preaching or of these evangelists who go around the country preaching. They have a great deal to say about God being a sovereign, and that He will have revivals come in His own way and time, but then He must choose to have it just their way, or they want nothing to do with it. Such men will sleep on until they are awakened by the judgment trumpet, without a revival, unless

they are willing for God to come in His own way – unless they are willing to have anything or anybody used that will do the most good.

8. Strictly, I say that when these above-mentioned things occur, a revival, to the same extent, already exists. In truth, a revival should be expected whenever it is needed. If we need to be revived, it is our duty to be revived. If it is duty, it is possible, and we should set about being revived ourselves. Relying on the promise of Christ to be with us in making disciples always and everywhere, we should labor to revive Christians and convert sinners with confident expectation of success. Therefore, whenever the church needs reviving, they should and may expect to be revived and to see sinners converted to Christ. When those things are seen that are named above, let Christians and ministers be encouraged and know that a good work has already begun. Follow it up.

Remarks

1. Brethren, you can tell from our subject whether or not you need a revival here in this church and in this city – and whether or not you are going to have one. Elders of the church, men, women, any of you, and all of you – what do you say? Do you need a revival here? Do you expect to have one? Do you have any reason to expect one?

You do not need to be uncertain about it, for you know, or can know if you want to, whether you have any reason to look for a revival here.

2. You see why you do not have a revival. It is only because you do not want one – because you are not praying for it, you are not thirsty for it, and you are not putting forth efforts for it. I appeal to your own consciences. Are you making these efforts now to promote a revival? You know, brethren, what the truth is about it. Will you stand up and say that you have made the efforts for a revival and have been disappointed – that you have cried to God, *Wilt thou not revive us?* and God would not do it?

3. Do you desire a revival? Will you have one? If God would ask you this moment in an audible voice from heaven, "Do you want a revival?"

28

would you dare to say yes? If He would ask, "Are you willing to make the sacrifices?" would you answer yes? If He would ask, "When should it begin?" would you answer, "Let it begin tonight. Let it begin here. Let it begin in my heart now"? Would you dare to say so to God if you would hear His voice tonight?

Lecture 3

How to Encourage a Revival

Break up your fallow ground: for it is time to seek the LORD, *till he come and rain righteousness upon you.*
—Hosea 10:12

The Jews were a nation of farmers, and it is therefore a common thing in the Bible to refer for illustrations to their occupation, and to the scenes with which farmers and shepherds are familiar. The prophet Hosea addresses them as a nation of backsliders, reproves them for their idolatry, and threatens them with the judgments of God. I showed you in my first lecture what a revival is not, what it is, and the means to be used in encouraging it. In my second lecture, I discussed when it is needed, its importance, and when it may be expected. My intent in this lecture is to show how to promote or encourage a revival.

A revival consists of two parts: as it respects the church and as it respects the ungodly. This lecture pertains to a revival in the church. Fallow ground is ground that has once been tilled but now lies waste and needs to be broken up and mellowed before it is suited to receive grain. I will show, as it respects a revival in the church:

I.   What it means to break up the fallow ground, in the sense of the text.

II. How it is to be performed.

I. What Does It Mean to Break Up the Fallow Ground?

To break up the fallow ground is to break up your hearts – to prepare your minds to bring forth fruit unto God. The mind of man is often compared in the Bible to ground, the Word of God is compared to seed sown in it, and the fruit represents the actions and affections of those who receive it. To break up the fallow ground, therefore, is to bring the mind into such a state that it is prepared to receive the Word of God. Sometimes your hearts get matted down hard and dry, and all run to waste, until there is no possibility of getting fruit from them until they are all broken up, mellowed down, and prepared to receive the Word of God. It is this softening of the heart, so as to make it feel the truth, that the prophet calls breaking up your fallow ground.

II. How Is the Fallow Ground to Be Broken Up?

It is not by any direct efforts to feel. People make a mistake on this subject by not making the laws of mind the object of thought. There are great errors on the subject of the laws that govern the mind. People talk about spiritual feeling as if they thought they could call forth religious affection by direct effort. But this is not how the mind acts. No man can make himself feel in this way by merely trying to feel. The feelings of the mind are not directly under our control. We cannot call forth religious feelings by willing or by direct volition. We might as well think to call spirits up from the deep. They are purely involuntary states of mind. They naturally and necessarily exist in the mind under certain circumstances calculated to excite them.

However, they can be controlled indirectly. Otherwise there would be no moral character in our feelings if there were not a way to control them. We cannot say, "Now I will feel so-and-so toward such an object," but we can command our attention to it and look at it intently until the involuntary affections arise.

Let a man who is away from his family think about them, and will he not feel? But it is not by saying to himself, "Now I will feel deeply for my family." A man can direct his attention to any object about which he should feel and wants to feel, and in that way he will call into existence the proper emotions. Let a man call up his enemy in his mind, and his feelings of enmity will rise.

In the same way, if a man thinks of God and focuses his mind on any parts of God's character, he will feel – emotions will come up by the very laws of mind. If he is a friend of God, let him contemplate God as a gracious and holy being, and he will have emotions of friendship kindled up in his mind. If he is an enemy of God, only let him get the true character of God before his mind, look at it, and focus his attention on it, and his enmity will rise against God, or he will break down and give his heart to God.

If you want to break up the fallow ground of your hearts and make your minds feel on the subject of true religion, you must go to work just as you would to feel about any other subject. Instead of keeping your thoughts on everything else and imagining that by going to a few meetings you will get your feelings engaged, go the commonsense way to work, just as you would on any other subject. It is just as easy to make your minds feel on the subject of Christianity as it is on any other subject. God has put these states of mind under your control. If people were as unphilosophical about moving their limbs as they are about regulating their emotions, you would never have come to this meeting.

If you intend to break up the fallow ground of your heart, you must begin by looking at your heart. Examine and note the state of your mind and see where you are. Many people never seem to think about this. They pay no attention to their own hearts and never know whether they are doing well in religion or not – whether they are gaining ground or going back, whether they are fruitful or lying waste like the fallow ground. You must take your attention away from other things and look into this. Make a business of it. Do not be in a hurry. Examine thoroughly the state of your heart and see where you are – whether you are walking with God every day or walking with the devil; whether you are serving God or the devil most; whether you are under the dominion of the prince of darkness or under the dominion of the Lord Jesus Christ.

To do all this, you must set yourself to work to consider your sins. You must examine yourselves. By this I do not mean that you must stop and look directly within to see what is the present state of your feelings. That is the very way to put a stop to all feeling. This is just as absurd as it would be for a man to turn his eyes away from the light and try to turn his eyes inward to find out whether there was any image painted on the retina. The man complains that he does not see anything! And why? Because he has turned his eyes away from the objects of sight.

The truth is that our moral feelings are as much an object of consciousness as our sensations. The way to stir them up is to go on taking action and using our minds. Then we can tell our moral feelings by consciousness, just as I could tell my natural feelings by consciousness if I would put my hand in the fire.

Self-examination consists in looking at your lives, in considering your actions, in calling up the past, and in learning its true character. Look back over your past. Take up your individual sins one by one and look at them. I do not mean that you should just cast a glance at your past life and see that it has been full of sins, and then go to God to make a sort of general confession and ask for forgiveness. That is not the way. You must take up your sins individually.

It would be a good thing to take a pen and paper as you go over them, and write them down as they occur to you. Go over them as carefully as a merchant goes over his books. As often as a sin comes before your memory, add it to the list. General confessions of sin will never do. Your sins were committed one by one, and as far as you can recall them, they should be reviewed and repented of one by one. Now begin; take up first what are commonly, but improperly, called sins of omission.

Sins of Omission

1. Ingratitude. Take this sin, for example, and write down all the instances you can remember when you have received blessings from God for which you have never expressed gratitude. How many cases can you remember? It may be some remarkable providence, some wonderful turn of events, that saved you from ruin. Write down the instances of God's goodness to you when you were in sin before your conversion. Then recall the mercy of God in the circumstances of your conversion, for which you have never been half thankful enough, and the numerous mercies you have received since.

How long the list of instances is in which your ingratitude is so dark that you are forced to hide your face in confusion! Now go on your knees and confess them one by one to God, and ask His forgiveness. By the laws of suggestion, the very act of confession will bring up others to your memory. Write these down. Go over these three or four times in this way, and you will find an astonishing amount of mercies for which you have never thanked God. Then move on to another sin.

2. Lack of love to God. Write that down, and go over all the instances you can remember when you did not give to the blessed God that wholehearted love that you should have given to Him.

Think how grieved and alarmed you would be if you discovered any decline of affection for you in your wife, husband, or children – if you saw somebody else captivating their hearts, thoughts, and time. Perhaps in such a case you would nearly die with a just and virtuous jealousy. God calls Himself a jealous God (Exodus 20:5), and have you not given your heart to other loves, played the harlot, and infinitely offended Him?

3. Neglect of the Bible. Write down the times when for days, weeks, or maybe even months you had no pleasure in God's Word. Perhaps you did not read a chapter, or if you read it, it was in a way that was still more displeasing to God. Many people read over a whole chapter in such a way that even if they were put under oath when they were done, they could not tell what they have been reading. They read with so little attention that they cannot remember where they have read from morning until evening unless they put in a bookmark or turn down a corner of a page. This demonstrates that they did not lay to heart what they read, that they did not make it a subject of reflection. If you were reading a novel, or any other book that greatly interested you, would you not remember what you read? The fact that you must fold a page or put in a bookmark to remember demonstrates that you read rather as a task than from love or reverence for the Word of God. The Word of God is the instruction and guide of your duty, and do you pay so little regard to it as not to remember what you read? If so, it is no wonder you live so at random, and that your religion is such a miserable failure.

4. Unbelief. Recall the instances in which you have practically charged

the God of truth with lying by your unbelief of His clear promises and declarations. God has promised to give the Holy Spirit to those who ask Him (Luke 11:13). Have you believed this? Have you expected Him to answer? When you prayed for the Holy Spirit, have you not essentially said in your hearts, "I do not believe that I will receive the Holy Spirit"? If you have not believed nor expected to receive the blessing that God has promised, you have accused Him of lying.

5. Neglect of prayer. Remember the times when you omitted secret prayer, family prayer, and prayer meetings, or have prayed in such a way as to more grievously offend God than when you neglected it entirely.

6. Neglect of the means of grace. When you have allowed little excuses to keep you from attending preaching, you have neglected and poured contempt upon the means of salvation merely from your aversion to spiritual duties.

7. The manner in which you have performed those duties. Your lack of feeling, lack of faith, and worldly frame of mind have made it so your words were nothing but the mere chattering of a wretch who did not deserve that God should feel the least care for him. You have fallen down upon your knees and said your prayers in such an unfeeling and careless manner that if you had been put under oath five minutes after you ended your time of prayer, you could not have told what you had been praying for.

8. Lack of love for the souls of your fellow men. Look around at your friends and relatives, and remember how little compassion you have felt for them. You have stood by and have seen them going right to hell, and it seems as though you did not care if they did. How many days have there been in which you did not make their condition the subject of a single fervent prayer, or even a sincere desire for their salvation?

9. Lack of care for the heathen. Perhaps you have not cared enough for unbelievers to attempt to recognize their condition. Maybe you did not even care to read a missionary newsletter. Look at this, and note how

much you really care for the unbelievers. Write down honestly the real amount of your feelings for them and your desire for their salvation. Measure your desire for their salvation by the self-denial you practice in giving of your substance to send them the gospel.

Do you deny yourself even the simple luxuries of life, such as coffee or other beverages, or entertainment, in order to help reach the lost? Do you reduce your style of living and subject yourself to any inconvenience to save them? Do you daily pray for them in private? Do you pray with other Christians for the lost all around you? Are you setting aside something from month to month to put into the treasury of the Lord when you go up to pray? If you are not doing these things, and if your soul is not agonized for the poor, simple unbelievers, why are you such a hypocrite as to pretend to be a Christian? Your profession is an insult to Jesus Christ!

10. Neglect of family duties. Recall how you have lived before your family, how you have prayed, and what example you have set before them. What direct efforts do you regularly make for their spiritual good? What duty have you not neglected?

11. Neglect of social duties. Do you personally reach the lost in your own community with the true gospel? Are you burdened for their salvation? Do they see your care for their souls and your desire to lead them from death to life through Jesus?

12. Neglect of watchfulness over your own life. What are some instances in which you have hurried over your private duties and have not taken yourself to task nor honestly confessed your sins and neglect and made things right with God? Where did you entirely neglect to watch your conduct and have been off your guard, and have sinned before the world, before the church, and before God?

13. Neglect to watch over your brethren. How often have you broken your covenant that you would watch over them in the Lord? How little do you know or care about the condition of their souls? Yet you are under a solemn oath to watch over them. What have you done to make

yourself acquainted with them? How many of them have you taken an interest in to know their spiritual state?

Go over the list, and wherever you find neglect, write it down. How many times have you seen your brethren growing cold in religion and have not spoken to them about it? You have seen them beginning to neglect one duty after another and did not reprove them in a brotherly way. You have seen them falling into sin and let them go on, yet you pretend to love them. What a hypocrite! Would you see your wife or child going into disgrace or into the fire and hold your peace? No, you would not. What do you think of yourself, then, when you pretend to love Christians, and to love Christ, while you can see them going into disgrace and say nothing to them?

14. Neglect of self-denial. There are many professing Christians who are willing to do almost anything in their religion that does not require self-denial. But when they are called to do something that requires them to deny themselves – oh, that is too much for them! They think they are doing a great deal for God, and doing about as much as He should reasonably ask, when they are only doing what they can do about as well as not; but they are not willing to deny themselves any comfort or convenience whatsoever for the sake of serving the Lord.

They will not willingly suffer reproach for the name of Christ, nor will they deny themselves the luxuries of life, to save a world from hell. So far are they from remembering that self-denial is a condition of discipleship that they do not know what self-denial is. They have never really denied themselves even a ribbon for Christ and for the gospel. Oh, how soon such professing Christians will be in hell! Some give of their abundance, and give much, and are ready to complain that others don't give more – when in truth, they do not give anything that they need or anything that they could enjoy if they kept it. They only give of their surplus wealth, and perhaps that poor woman who put in a couple dollars at the monthly prayer meeting has exercised more self-denial than they have in giving thousands of dollars.

From these we now turn to sins of commission.

Sins of Commission

1. Worldly mindedness. What has been the state of your heart in regard to your worldly possessions? Have you looked at them as really yours – as if you had a right to dispose of them as your own, according to your own will? If you have, write that down. If you have loved property and sought after it for its own sake, or to gratify lust or ambition or a worldly spirit, or to lay it up for your families, you have sinned and must repent.

2. Pride. Remember all the instances you can in which you have detected pride in yourself. Vanity is a particular form of pride. How many times have you detected vanity in yourself about your clothing and appearance? How many times have you thought more, taken more effort, and spent more time in decorating your body to go to church than you have in preparing your mind for the worship of God? You have gone to the house of God caring more about how you appear outwardly in the sight of mortal men than about how your soul appears in the sight of the heart-searching God. You have in fact set yourself up to be worshipped by them rather than prepared to worship God yourself. You came to divide the worship of God's house, to draw away the attention of God's people so they can look at your appearance. It is in vain to pretend now that you don't care about having people look at you. Be honest about it. Would you take all this effort about your looks if everyone were blind?

3. Envy. Look at the cases in which you were envious of those who you thought were above you in any respect. Or perhaps you have envied those who have been more talented or more useful than yourself. Have you not so envied some people that it has pained you to hear them praised? It has been more agreeable to you to dwell upon their faults than upon their virtues, upon their failures than upon their success. Be honest with yourself, and if you have harbored this spirit of hell, repent deeply before God, or He will never forgive you.

4. Criticalness. Have you had instances in which you have had a bitter spirit and have spoken of Christians in a manner entirely devoid of charity and love – charity that requires you to always hope the best

that the situation will allow, and to put the best construction upon any uncertain conduct?

5. Slander. Have you spoken behind people's backs of their faults, real or supposed, about members of the church or others, unnecessarily or without good reason? This is slander. You do not need to lie to be guilty of slander, for to tell the truth with the intent to injure is slander.

6. Levity. How often have you acted frivolously before God, as you would not have dared to do in the presence of an earthly sovereign? You have either been an atheist and forgotten that there was a God, or you have had less respect for Him and His presence than you would have had for an earthly judge.

7. Lying. Do you understand what lying is? Any type of designed deception for a selfish reason is lying. If the deception is not intentional, it is not lying, but if you determine to make an impression contrary to the simple truth, you lie. Write down all those times you can remember. Don't call them by any soft name. God calls them lies and charges you with lying, and you had better charge yourself correctly.

How innumerable are the falsehoods perpetrated every day in business and in social interactions by words, looks, and actions – intended to make an impression on others contrary to the truth for selfish reasons!

8. Cheating. Write down all the times in which you have dealt with an individual and have done to him that which you would not like to have done to you. That is cheating. God has laid down a rule in the case: *All things whatsoever ye would that men should do to you, do ye even so to them* (Matthew 7:12). That is the rule, and if you have not done so, you are a cheat. The rule is not that you should do what you might reasonably expect them to do to you. That is a rule that would allow every degree of wickedness. Rather, it is that you should do as you would want them to do to you.

9. Hypocrisy. Consider this in regard to your prayers and confessions to God. Write down the times in which you have prayed for things you did

not really want. The evidence is that when you had finished praying, you could not tell what you had prayed for. How many times have you confessed sins that you did not intend to stop, and that you had no sincere desire or determination not to repeat? Yes, you have confessed sins when you knew that you as much expected to go and repeat them as you expected to live.

10. Robbing God. Have you misspent your time and squandered hours that God gave you to serve Him and save souls? Have you spent that time in vain amusements or foolish conversation, reading novels or doing nothing? Have there been times when you have misapplied your talents and powers of mind, when you have squandered money on your lusts or spent it for things you did not need or that would not contribute to your health, comfort, or usefulness. Perhaps some have spent God's money on tobacco. I will not speak of alcoholic beverages, for I presume there is no professing Christian who would drink alcohol. I hope there is no one reading this who uses that filthy poison, tobacco. Just imagine a professing Christian using God's money to poison himself with tobacco!

11. Bad temper. Perhaps you have mistreated or wrongly gotten angry with your wife, your children, your family, employees, or neighbors. Write it all down.

12. Hindering others from being useful. Perhaps you have weakened their influence by insinuations against them. You have not only robbed God of your own talents, but you have tied the hands of somebody else. What a wicked employee he is who wastes time at work and hinders others from working! This is done sometimes by taking their time needlessly, sometimes by destroying Christian confidence in them. Thus you have played into the hands of Satan, not only showing yourself an idle thief, but preventing others from working.

If you realize that you have committed a fault against an individual, and that individual is within your reach, go and confess it immediately and get it out of the way. If the individual you have harmed is too far away for you to go and see him, sit down and write him a letter, and confess the wrong. Mail the letter immediately. If you have defrauded anybody, send the money – the full amount and the interest.

Get right to work in all this. Go now. Don't put it off; that will only make the matter worse. Confess to God those sins that have been committed against God; confess to man those sins that have been committed against man. Don't consider avoiding this by going around the stumbling blocks. Take them out of the way. In breaking up your fallow ground, you must remove every obstruction.

Things may be left that you may think are little things, and you may wonder why you do not feel as you want to in your religion – when the reason is that your proud and carnal mind has covered up something that God required you to confess and remove. Break up all the ground and turn it over. Do not merely pass lightly over it. Do not turn aside because of little difficulties. Drive the plow right through them. Go deep and turn the ground all over so that it may all be mellow and soft and prepared to receive the seed and bear fruit a hundredfold.

After you have thoroughly gone over your whole history in this way, if you will then go over the ground a second time and give your sincere and focused attention to it, you will find that the things you have written down will suggest other related things of which you have been guilty. Then go over it a third time, and you will recall other things connected with these. In the end, you will find that you can remember an amount of your history, and specific actions, even in this life, that you did not think you would remember in eternity. Unless you take up your sins in this way and consider them in detail, one by one, you can form no idea of the amount of your sins. You should go over it as thoroughly, carefully, and solemnly as you would if you were preparing yourself for the judgment.

As you go over the list of your sins, be sure to resolve upon present and entire reformation. Wherever you find anything wrong, resolve at once, in the strength of God, to sin no more in that way. It will be of no benefit to examine yourself unless you determine to change in every specific detail that you find wrong in heart, attitude, or conduct.

As you go on with this duty, if you find that your mind is still all dark, search yourself, and you will find there is some reason for the Spirit of God to depart from you. You have not been faithful and thorough. In the progress of such a work, you must aggressively examine yourself and bring yourself as a rational being to this work with the Bible before you; you must try your heart until you do feel.

You do not need to expect that God will work a miracle for you to break up your fallow ground. It is to be done by means. Fasten your attention to the subject of your sins. You cannot look at your sins long and thoroughly and see how bad they are without feeling, and feeling deeply. Experience abundantly proves the benefit of going over our history in this way. Set yourself to the work now. Resolve that you will never stop until you find that you can pray. You will never have the spirit of prayer until you examine yourself, confess your sins, and break up your fallow ground. You will never have the Spirit of God filling you until you have unraveled this whole mystery of iniquity and have spread out your sins before God. Let there be this deep work of repentance and full confession, this breaking down before God, and you will have as much of the spirit of prayer as your body can handle. The reason why so few Christians know anything about the spirit of prayer is that they would never take the effort to examine themselves properly, and so they never knew what it was to have their hearts all broken up in this way.

I have only begun to lay open this subject. I want to open it up before you in the course of these lectures so that if you will begin and go on to do as I say, the results will be just as certain as they are when the farmer breaks up a fallow field, mellows it, and sows his grain. It will be so, if you will only begin in this way and hold on until all your hardened and callous hearts break up.

Remarks

1. It will do no good to preach to you while your hearts are in this hardened, fruitless, and fallow state. The farmer might just as well sow his grain on the rock. It will bring forth no fruit. This is the reason why there are so many fruitless professing Christians in the church. This is why there is so much outside machinery and so little deep-toned feeling in the church. Look at the Sunday school for instance, and see how much machinery there is and how little of the power of godliness. If you continue in this way, the Word of God will continue to harden you, and you will grow worse and worse, just as the rain and snow on an old fallow field makes the turf thicker and the clods stronger.

2. See why so much preaching is wasted, and worse than wasted. It is because the church will not break up her fallow ground. A preacher may wear out his life and do very little good while there are so many stony-ground hearers who have never had their fallow ground broken up. They are only half converted, and their religion is rather a change of opinion than a change of the feeling of their hearts. There is mechanical religion enough, but very little that looks like deep heart work.

3. Professing Christians should never satisfy themselves, or expect a revival, just by waking up from their sleep, blustering about, making a noise, and talking to sinners. They must get their fallow ground broken up. It is entirely unphilosophical to think of engaging in Christianity in this way. If your fallow ground is broken up, then the way to get more feeling is to go out and see sinners on the road to hell, talk to them, and guide inquiring souls; then you will get more feeling. You may get into a more emotional state without this breaking up. You may show a kind of zeal, but it will not last long, and it will not take hold of sinners, unless your hearts are broken up. The reason is that you go about it mechanically and have not broken up your fallow ground.

4. Now, finally, will you break up your fallow ground? Will you enter upon the course of action now pointed out, and will you persevere until you are thoroughly awake? If you fail here, if you do not do this and get prepared, you can go no further with me in this course of lectures. I have gone with you as far as it is of any use to go until your fallow ground is broken up. You must make thorough work upon this point, or all I have further to say will do you little good. No, it will only harden you and make you worse.

If, with the next lecture, your heart remains unbroken, you do not need to expect to be benefited by what I will say. If you do not set about this work immediately, I will take it for granted that you do not intend to be revived – that you have forsaken your minister and intend to let him go up to battle alone. If you do not do this, I charge you with having forsaken Christ, with refusing to repent and do your first work. But if you will be prepared to enter upon the work, I propose, God willing, to lead you in the next lecture into the work of saving sinners.

Lecture 4

Prevailing Prayer

The effectual fervent prayer of a righteous man availeth much.
—James 5:16

The last lecture referred mainly to the confession of sin. This lecture will be primarily confined to the subject of intercession or prayer. There are two approaches required to promote a revival: one to influence people, and the other to influence God.

The truth is used to influence people, and prayer to move God. When I speak of moving God, I do not mean that God's mind is changed by prayer or that His disposition or character is changed. But prayer produces such a change in us and fulfils such conditions that make it consistent for God to do as it would not be consistent for Him otherwise. When a sinner repents, that state of mind makes it proper for God to forgive him. God has always been ready to forgive him on that condition, so when the sinner changes his mind toward God, it requires no change of feeling in God to forgive him. It is the sinner's repentance that renders God's forgiveness proper and is the occasion of God's acting as He does.

So when Christians offer effectual prayer, their state of mind renders it proper for God to answer them. He was always ready to bestow the blessing on the condition that they believed right and offered sincere, heartfelt prayer. Whenever this change takes place in them, and they offer sincere, honest prayer, then God, without any change in Himself, can answer them. When we offer effectual, fervent prayer for others, the fact that we offer such prayer renders it consistent for Him to do what we pray for, when otherwise it would not have been consistent.

Prayer is an essential link in the chain of causes that lead to a revival – as much so as truth is. Some have zealously used truth to convert people and have laid very little stress on prayer. They have preached, talked, and distributed tracts with great zeal, and then wondered why they had such little success. The reason was that they forgot to use the other branch of the means – effectual prayer. They overlooked the fact that truth by itself will never produce the effect without the Spirit of God, and that Spirit is given in answer to earnest prayer.

Sometimes it happens that those who are the most engaged in employing truth are not the most engaged in prayer. This is always unfortunate, for unless they, or some others, have the spirit of prayer, the truth by itself will do nothing but harden people in impenitence. Probably in the day of judgment it will be found that nothing is ever done by the truth, no matter how zealously it is used, unless there is a spirit of prayer somewhere in connection with the presentation of truth.

Others err on the other side. It is not that they lay too much emphasis on prayer, but they overlook the fact that prayer might be offered forever by itself, and nothing would be done, as sinners are not often converted by direct contact of the Holy Spirit, but by the truth used as a means. To expect the conversion of sinners by prayer alone, without the use of truth, is to tempt God.

The subject of this lecture is prevailing prayer:

I.   What effectual or prevailing prayer is.

II. The most essential attributes of prevailing prayer.

III. Reasons God requires this kind of prayer.

IV. Such prayer will avail much.

I. What Prevailing Prayer Is

1. Effectual, prevailing prayer does not consist only in benevolent desires,

which are undoubtedly pleasing to God. Such desires pervade heaven and are found in all holy beings, but they are not prayer. People may have these desires as the angels and glorified spirits have them, but this is not the effectual, prevailing prayer spoken of in the text. Prevailing prayer is something more than this.

2. Prevailing, or effectual prayer, is the prayer that obtains the blessing that it seeks. It is the prayer that effectually moves God. The very idea of effectual prayer is that it effects its purpose.

II. The Most Essential Attributes of Prevailing Prayer

I cannot list in full all the things that go to make up prevailing prayer, but I will mention some things that are essential to it – some things that a person must do in order to prevail in prayer.

1. He must pray for a definite object. He does not need to expect to offer such prayer if he prays at random, without any distinct or definite objective. He must have an objective distinctly in mind. I speak now of private prayer. Many people go away into a private place because they must *say* their prayers. The time of day has come when they are in the habit of going by themselves for prayer – in the morning, at noon, or at whatever time of day it may be. However, instead of having anything to say, any definite object before their mind, they fall down on their knees and pray for whatever comes into their minds. They pray for everything that floats into their imagination at the time, and when they are done, they can hardly tell a word of what they have been praying for. This is not effectual prayer. What would we think of anybody who tried to persuade a legislature by saying, "Now it is winter, and the legislature is in session; it is time to send up petitions," and would go up to the legislature and petition at random without any definite object in mind? Do you think such petitions would move the legislature?

A person must have some definite objective in mind. He cannot pray effectually for a variety of objects at once. The mind of man is so formed that it cannot fasten its desires intensely upon many things at the same time. All the instances of effectual prayer recorded in the

Bible were of this kind. Wherever you see that the blessing sought for in prayer was attained, you will find that the prayer that was offered was prayer for that definite object.

2. To be effectual, prayer must be in accordance with the revealed will of God. To pray for things contrary to the revealed will of God is to tempt God. There are three ways in which God's will is revealed to people for their guidance in prayer:

a) By specific promises or predictions in the Bible, God reveals that He will give or do certain things. These may be specific promises in regard to particular things, or promises in general terms that we may apply to particular things. For instance, there is this promise: *What things soever ye desire, when ye pray, believe that ye receive them, and ye shall have them* (Mark 11:24).

b) Sometimes God reveals His will by His providence. For example, there are times when He makes it clear that certain events are about to take place or that it is His will to grant certain blessings.

c) God reveals His will by His Spirit. When God's people are at a loss what to pray for that is agreeable to His will, His Spirit often instructs them. Where there is no particular revelation, when providence leaves it dark, and when we do not know what to pray for as we should, we are specifically told that *the Spirit also helpeth our infirmities*, and *the Spirit itself maketh intercession for us with groanings which cannot be uttered* (Romans 8:26).

A great deal has been said on the subject of praying in faith for things not revealed. The objection is that this doctrine implies a new revelation. I answer that new or old, it is the very revelation that Jehovah says He makes. It is just as plain here as if it were now revealed by a voice from heaven that the Spirit of God helps the people of God to pray according to the will of God, when they themselves do not know what things they should pray for. *And he that searcheth the hearts knoweth what is the mind of the Spirit, because he maketh intercession for the saints according to the will of God* (Romans 8:27). He leads Christians to pray for just those things *with groanings which cannot be uttered*. When neither the Word nor providence enables them to decide, then let them be filled with the Spirit, as God commands them to be. He says, *Be filled with the Spirit* (Ephesians 5:18). He will lead their minds to such things as God is willing to grant.

3. To pray effectually, you must pray with submission to the will of God. Do not confuse submission with indifference. No two things are more different. I once knew an individual who came to where there was a revival. He himself was cold and did not enter into the spirit of it, and he had no spirit of prayer. When he heard the brethren pray as if they could not be denied, he was shocked at their boldness and kept insisting on the importance of praying with submission, when it was as plain as anything could be that he confused submission with indifference.

So again, do not confuse submission in prayer with a general confidence that God will do what is right. It is proper to have this confidence that God will do what is right in all things, but this is different from submission. By submission in prayer, I mean obedience and submission to the revealed will of God. To submit to any command of God is to obey it. Submission to some supposable or possible, but speculative, decree of God is not submission. To submit to any decree of providence is impossible until it is fulfilled, for we can never know what the event is to be until it takes place.

Here is an example: When David's child was sick, David was distressed, he agonized in prayer, and he refused to be comforted. He took it so much to heart that when the child died, his servants were afraid to tell him that the child was dead. However, as soon as he heard that the child was dead, he laid aside his grief and arose. He asked for food and he ate and drank as usual. While the child was alive, David did not know what the will of God was, so he fasted and prayed and said, *Who can tell whether GOD will be gracious to me, that the child may live?* (2 Samuel 12:22).

He did not know if his prayer and agony would be the very thing that would determine whether the child was to live or not. He thought that if he humbled himself and pleaded with God, perhaps God would spare him this blow. But as soon as God's will appeared, and the child was dead, he bowed like a saint. He seemed not only to submit, but actually to take a satisfaction in it. *I shall go to him, but he shall not return to me* (2 Samuel 12:23).

This was true submission. He reasoned correctly in this situation. While he had no revelation of the will of God, he did not know whether the child's recovery depended on his prayer. But when he had a revelation of the will of God, he submitted. While the will of God is not known, to submit without prayer is tempting God. Perhaps, and for all you know, the fact of your offering the right kind of prayer may be the thing on which the event turns. In the case of an unrepentant friend, the very condition on which he is to be saved from hell may be the fervency and persistence of your prayer for that individual.

4. Effectual prayer for something implies a desire for that object proportionate to its importance. If a person truly desires any blessing, his desires will bear some proportion to the greatness of the blessing. The desires of the Lord Jesus Christ for the blessing He prayed for were amazingly strong, and amounted even to agony. If the desire for an object is strong and is a benevolent desire, and the thing is not contrary to the will and providence of God, the presumption is that it will be granted. There are two reasons for this presumption:

a) We can presume this based upon the general benevolence of God. If it is a desirable object – if it would be an act of benevolence in God to grant it, His general benevolence is presumptive evidence that He will grant it.

b) If you find yourself developing benevolent desires for any object, there is a strong presumption that the Spirit of God is stirring up these very desires and motivating you to pray for that object so that it may be granted in answer to prayer. In such a case, no degree of desire or persistence in prayer is improper.

A Christian may come and take hold of the hand of God. Note the case of Jacob when he exclaimed in an agony of desire, *I will not let thee go, except thou bless me* (Genesis 32:26). Was God displeased with his boldness and perseverance? Not at all. He granted him the very thing he prayed for.

It was the same in the case of Moses. God said to Moses, *Let me alone, that I may destroy them, and blot out their name from under heaven: and I will make of thee a nation mightier and greater than they* (Deuteronomy 9:14). What did Moses do? Did he stand aside and let

God do as He said? No. His mind ran back to the Egyptians, and he considered how they would triumph. *Wherefore should the Egyptians speak, and say, For mischief did he bring them out?* (Exodus 32:12). It seemed as if he took hold of the uplifted hand of God to avert the blow. Did God rebuke him for his interference and tell him he had no business to interfere? No. It seemed as if He was unable to deny anything to such resolve, so Moses stood in the gap and prevailed with God.

It is said of Xavier, the missionary, that he was once called to pray for a man who was sick, and he prayed so fervently that he seemed as it were to do violence to heaven. That is how the writer expressed it. And he prevailed, and the man recovered.

Such prayer is often offered in the present day, when Christians have been worked up to such a pitch of desire and such a holy boldness that afterward, when they looked back, they were frightened and amazed at themselves to think they would dare to exercise such persistence with God. Yet these prayers have prevailed and obtained the blessing. Many of these people, whom I am acquainted with, are among the holiest people I know in the world.

5. To be effectual, prayer must be offered from proper motives. Prayer should not be selfish, but should be dictated by a supreme regard for the glory of God. A great deal of prayer is offered from pure selfishness. Women sometimes pray for their husbands that they may be converted, because they say, "It would be so much more pleasant to have my husband go to the church service with me." They never seem to lift their thoughts above themselves at all. They do not seem to think of how their husbands are dishonoring God by their sins and how God would be glorified in their conversion.

It is very often the same with parents. They cannot bear to think that their children would be lost. They pray for them very earnestly indeed. But if you talk with them, they are very tender, and they tell you how good their children are and how they respect Christianity, and they think they are almost Christians now. They talk as if they were afraid you would hurt their children if you would tell them the truth. They do not think how such kind and lovely children are dishonoring God by their sins; they are only thinking what a dreadful thing it would be for them to go to hell. Unless their thoughts rise higher than this, their prayers will never prevail with a holy God. The temptation to be self-ishly motivated is so strong that there is reason to fear that a great many parental prayers never rise above the yearnings of parental tenderness. That is the reason why so many prayers are not heard, and why so many pious, praying parents have ungodly children.

Much of the prayer for the heathen world seems to be based on no higher principle than sympathy. Missionary agents and others are dwelling almost exclusively upon the six hundred million heathens going to hell, while little is said of their dishonoring God. This is a great evil, and until the church has higher motives for prayer and mission-ary effort than sympathy for the heathen, their prayers and efforts will never amount to much.

6. To be effectual, prayer must be by the intercession of the Spirit. You can never expect to offer prayer according to the will of God without the Spirit. In the first two cases, it is not because Christians are unable to offer such prayer where the will of God is revealed in His Word or indicated by His providence. They are able to do so, just as they are able to be holy. But the fact is that they are so wicked that they never do offer such prayer without being influenced by the Spirit of God. There must be a faith such as that produced by the effectual operation of the Holy Spirit.

7. It must be persevering prayer. As a general rule, Christians who have backslidden and have lost the spirit of prayer will not at once get into the habit of persevering prayer. Their minds are not in a right state, and they cannot focus their minds and hold on until the blessing comes. If their minds were in that state, they would persevere until the answer comes. Effectual prayer could be offered at once, as well as after pray-ing ever so many times for a purpose. Instead, they must pray again and again because their thoughts tend to wander away and are easily diverted from the purpose to something else.

Until their minds get saturated with the spirit of prayer, they will not stay focused on one point and push their petition of an issue on the spot. Do not think you are prepared to offer prevailing prayer if your feelings will let you pray once for something and then dismiss it. Most Christians come up to prevailing prayer by a protracted process. Their minds gradually become filled with concern about an object so that they will even go about their business sighing out their desires to God – just as the mother whose child is sick goes around her house sighing as if her heart would break. And if she is a praying mother, her sighs are breathed out to God all day long. If she goes out of the room where her child is, her mind is still on the child. If the mother is asleep, her thoughts are still on the child; she cringes in her dreams, thinking the child is dying. Her whole mind is absorbed in that sick child. This is the state of mind in which Christians offer prevailing prayer.

What was the reason that Jacob wrestled all night in prayer with God? He knew that he had done his brother Esau a great wrong in stealing the birthright years earlier. Now he was informed that his wronged brother was coming to meet him with an armed force entirely too powerful for him to contend against – and there was great reason to suppose he was coming with a purpose of revenge.

There were two reasons, then, why Jacob would be distressed. The first was that he had done this great wrong of stealing the birthright, and had never made any rectification. The other was that Esau was coming with a force sufficient to crush him. What did Jacob do? He first arranged everything in the best manner he could to meet his brother, sending his present first, then his property, and then his family – putting those he loved most farthest behind. By this time his mind was so distressed that he could not contain himself. He went away alone over the brook and poured out his very soul in an agony of prayer all night.

Just as the day was breaking, the angel of the covenant said, *Let me go*; and his whole being was, as it were, agonized at the thought of giving up. He cried out, *I will not let thee go, except thou bless me* (Genesis 32:26). He obtained the blessing, but he always carried the marks of it and showed that his body had been greatly affected by this mental struggle. This is prevailing prayer.

Do not deceive yourselves by thinking that you offer effectual prayer, unless you have this intense desire for the blessing. Prayer is not effectual unless it is offered with an agony of desire. The apostle Paul speaks of it as a travail of the soul (Galatians 4:19). Jesus Christ, when

He was praying in the garden, was in such an agony that He sweat *as it were great drops of blood falling down to the ground* (Luke 22:44; see also Isaiah 53:11). I have never known a person to sweat blood, but I have known a person pray until the blood came from the nose. I have also known people who prayed until they were all wet with perspiration in the coldest weather in winter. I have known people who prayed for hours until their strength was all exhausted with the agony of their minds. Such prayers prevailed with God.

This agony in prayer was prevalent in President Edwards' day in the revivals that took place. It was one of the great stumbling blocks in those days to people who were opposed to the revival that people prayed until their bodies were overpowered with their feelings. I will read some of what President Jonathan Edwards said on the subject, to let you see that this is not a new thing in the church, but has always prevailed wherever revivals prevailed with power. It is from his *Thoughts on Revivals*:

> We cannot determine that God will never give any person so much of a discovery of himself, not only as to weaken their bodies, but to take away their lives. It is supposed by very educated and wise theologians that Moses' life was taken away after this manner; and this has also been supposed to be the case with some other saints. Yes, I do not see any solid, sure grounds any have to determine that God will never make such strong impressions on the mind by His Spirit that will be an occasion of so impairing the frame of the body, and particularly that part of the body, the brain, that people will be deprived of the use of reason. As I said before, it is too much for us to determine that God will not bring an outward calamity in bestowing spiritual and eternal blessings, so it is too much for us to determine how great an outward calamity He will bring. If God gives a great increase of discoveries of Himself, and of love to Him, the benefit is infinitely greater than the calamity, even if the life would soon after be taken away. . . . We cannot determine how great a calamity distraction is, when considered with all its consequences, and all that might

have occurred if the distraction had not happened; nor indeed whether (thus considered) it is any calamity at all, or whether it is not a mercy, by preventing some great sin or some more dreadful thing, if it had not been.

It would be a great fault in us to limit a sovereign, all-wise God, whose judgments are a great deep, and His ways past finding out, where He has not limited Himself, and in things concerning which He has not told us what His way will be. Considering in what multitudes of instances, and to how great a degree, the frame of the body has been over-powered of late, it is remarkable that people's lives have, nevertheless, been preserved, and that the instances of those that have been deprived of reason have been so very few. . . . A merciful and careful divine hand is very obvious in it, that in so many instances where the ship has begun to sink, yet it has been upheld and has not totally sunk. The instances of those who have been deprived of reason are so few, that certainly they are not enough to cause us to be in any fright, as though this work that has been carried on in the country was likely to be of adverse influence – unless we are disposed to gather up all that we can to darken it and present it negatively.

There is one particular kind of exercise and concern of mind that many have been overpowered by that has been especially stumbling to some, and that is the deep concern and distress that they have been in for the souls of others. I am sorry that any put us to the trouble of doing that which seems so unnecessary as defending such a thing as this. It seems so senseless in such a plain case to enter into a formal and particular debate in order to determine whether there is anything in the greatness and importance of the case that will answer and bear a proportion to the greatness of the concern that some have manifested. People may be allowed, from no higher a principle than common ingenuity and humanity, to be very deeply concerned and greatly exercised in mind at seeing others in great danger of no greater a calamity than drowning or being burned up in a house on fire. And if so, then undoubtedly it will be allowed to be equally reasonable to be still much more concerned if they saw them in danger of a calamity ten times greater, and so much more still, if the calamity was still vastly greater.

Why, then, should it be thought unreasonable, and looked upon very suspiciously, as if it must come from some bad cause when people are extremely concerned at seeing others in very great danger of suffering the fierceness and wrath of Almighty God to all eternity? And besides, it will undoubtedly be recognized that those who have very great degrees of the Spirit of God – that is, a spirit of love – may well be supposed to have vastly more love and compassion to their fellow creatures than those who are influenced only by common humanity. Why should it be thought strange that those who are full of the Spirit of Christ should be proportionately, in their love to souls, similar to Christ? Christ Jesus had so strong a love to them and concern for them as to be willing to drink the dregs of the cup of God's fury for them; and at the same time that He offered up His blood for souls, He offered up also, as their high priest, strong crying and tears, with an extreme agony, when the soul of Christ was, as it were, in travail for the souls of the elect (Hebrews 5:7); and therefore, in saving them, He is said to *see of the travail of his soul* (Isaiah 53:11). As such a spirit of love to and concern for souls was the spirit of Christ, so it is the spirit of the church; and therefore, the church, in desiring and seeking that Christ might be brought forth in the world and in the souls of men, is represented as a woman crying, *travailing in birth, and pained to be delivered* (Revelation 12:2).

The spirit of those who have been in distress for the souls of others, as far as I can discern, seems not to be different from that of the apostle, who travailed for souls, and was ready to wish himself accursed from Christ for others (Romans 9:3). It was also that of the psalmist: *Horror hath taken hold upon me because of the wicked that forsake the law* (Psalm 119:53), and *Rivers of waters run down mine eyes, because they keep not thy law* (Psalm 119:136). It was also the spirit of the prophet Jeremiah: *My bowels, my bowels! I am pained at my very heart; my heart maketh a noise in me: I cannot hold my peace, because thou hast heard, O my soul, the sound of the trumpet, the alarm of war* (Jeremiah 4:19; see also Jeremiah 9:1, Jeremiah 13:17, and Isaiah 22:4). We read of Mordecai, when he saw his people in danger of being destroyed with an earthly destruction, that he *rent his clothes, and put on sackcloth with ashes, and went out into the midst of the city, and cried with a loud and bitter cry* (Esther 4:1). Why, then, should people be thought to be unsound when they cannot keep from crying out at the consideration of the misery of those who are going to eternal destruction?

I have provided this from Edwards to show that this was common in the great revivals of those days. It has always been so in all great revivals, and has been more or less common in proportion to the greatness, extent, and depth of the work. It was so in the great revivals in Scotland, and multitudes used to be overpowered, and some almost died, by the depth of their agony.

8. If you desire to pray effectually, you must pray a great deal. It was said of the apostle James that after he was dead, it was learned that his knees, from praying so much, were callous like a camel's knees. Ah, here was the secret of the success of those primitive ministers. They had calloused knees.

9. If you intend prayer to be effectual, it must be offered in the name of Christ. You cannot come to God in your own name. You cannot plead your own merits. Rather, you can come in a name that is always acceptable. You know what it is to use the name of a man. If you go to

the bank with a draft or note endorsed by John Jacob Astor, that would be giving you his name, and you could get the money from the bank just as he could himself.

Jesus Christ gives you the use of His name. When you pray in the name of Christ, the meaning is that you can prevail as well as He could Himself, and you can receive just as much as God's well-beloved Son if He were to pray for the same things. However, you must pray in faith. His name has all the virtue in your lips that it has in His own, and God is just as free to bestow blessings upon you, when you ask in the name of Christ and in faith, as He would be to bestow them upon Christ, if He would ask.

10. You cannot prevail in prayer without renouncing all your sins. You must not only recall them to mind, but you must actually renounce them, leave them, and in the purpose of your heart, renounce them forever.

11. You must pray in faith. You must expect to obtain the things you ask for. You do not need to look for an answer to prayer if you pray without an expectation of obtaining it. You are not to form such expectations without any reason for them. In the cases I have supposed, there is a reason for the expectation. In case the thing is revealed in God's Word, if you pray without an expectation of receiving the blessings, you make God a liar. If the will of God is indicated by His providence, you should depend on it, according to the clearness of the indication, so far as to expect the blessing if you pray for it. If you are led by His Spirit to pray for certain things, you have as much reason to expect the thing to be done as if God had revealed it in His Word.

But some say, "Will not this view of the leadings of the Spirit of God lead people into fanaticism?" I answer that I don't know, but many people may deceive themselves in respect to this matter. Multitudes have deceived themselves in all the other points of religion. If some people should think they are led by the Spirit of God when it is nothing but their own imagination, is that any reason why those who know that they are led by the Spirit should not follow?

Many people suppose themselves to be converted when they are not. Is that any reason we should not cling to the Lord Jesus Christ?

Suppose some people are deceived in thinking they love God; is that any reason why the pious saint who knows he has the love of God shed abroad in his heart (Romans 5:5) should not give vent to his feelings in songs of praise?

I suppose some people may deceive themselves in thinking they are led by the Spirit of God, but there is no need of being deceived. If people follow impulses, it is their own fault. I do not want you to follow impulses. I want you to be sober-minded and follow the sober, rational leadings of the Spirit of God. There are those who understand what I mean and who know very well what it is to give themselves up to the Spirit of God in prayer.

III. Reasons These Things are Essential to Effectual Prayer

Why does God require such prayer, such strong desires, and such agonizing supplications?

1. These strong desires strongly illustrate the strength of God's feelings. They are like the real feelings of God for unrepentant sinners. When I have seen the amazing strength of love for souls that has been felt by Christians, I have been wonderfully impressed with the amazing love of God and His desires for their salvation. The case of a certain woman in a revival made the greatest impression on my mind. She had such an unutterable compassion and love for souls that she actually panted for breath almost to suffocation. What must be the strength of the desire that God feels when His Spirit produces such amazing agony, such distress of soul, such travail! God has chosen the best word to express it – it is travail – travail of the soul!

I have seen a man with as much strength of intellect and muscle as any man in the community fall down prostrate, absolutely overpowered by his unutterable desires for sinners. I know this is a stumbling block to many, and it always will be as long as so many blind and ignorant professing Christians remain in the church, but I cannot doubt that these things are the work of the Spirit of God.

Oh, that the whole church could be so filled with the Spirit as to travail in prayer until a nation is born in a day! It is said in the Word of God that *as soon as Zion travailed, she brought forth* (Isaiah 66:8). What does that mean? I asked a professing Christian this question once. He was taking issue with our ideas of effectual prayer, and I asked him what he thought was meant by Zion's travailing. "Oh," he said, "it means that as soon as the church walks together in the fellowship of the gospel, then it will be said that Zion *travels*! This walking together is called *traveling*." You can see that is not the same term.

2. These strong desires that I have described are the natural results of great benevolence and clear views of the danger of sinners. It is perfectly reasonable that it should be so. If the women here would look up and see a family burning to death in a fire, and hear their shrieks and see their agony, they would feel distressed, and it is very likely that many of them would faint with agony. Nobody would wonder at it or say they were fools or crazy to feel so distressed at such a dreadful sight. They would think it strange if there were not expressions of powerful feeling.

Why is it any wonder, then, if Christians should feel as I have described when they have clear views of the condition of sinners and the dreadful danger they are in? The fact is that those individuals who have never felt that way have never felt much real benevolence, and their piety must be of a very superficial character. I do not mean to judge harshly or to speak unkindly. I state it as a simple matter of fact. People may talk about it as they please, but I know that such piety is superficial. This is not criticism, but plain truth.

People sometimes wonder at Christians having such feelings. What do they wonder at? They wonder at the natural, philosophical, and necessary results of deep piety toward God and deep benevolence toward man in view of the great danger they see sinners to be in.

3. When the soul of a Christian is burdened in this way, it must have relief. God rolls this weight upon the soul of a Christian to bring him near to Himself. Christians are often so unbelieving that they will not exercise proper faith in God until He rolls this burden upon them – so heavy that they cannot live under it, and then they must go to God for relief. It is like the case of many convicted sinners. God is willing

to receive the sinner at once if he will come right to Him with faith in Jesus Christ.

However, the sinner will not come. He hangs back, struggles, and groans under the burden of his sins. He will not throw himself upon God until his burden of conviction becomes so great that he can live no longer. When he is driven to desperation, as it were, and feels as if he is ready to sink into hell, he makes a mighty plunge and throws himself upon God's mercy as his only hope.

It was his duty to come before then. God had no delight in his distress for its own sake. Only the sinner's stubbornness created the necessity for all this distress. He would not come without it. So when professing Christians get loaded down with the weight of souls, they often pray again and again, but the burden is not gone, nor their distress abated, because they have never thrown it all upon God in faith.

They cannot get rid of the burden. As long as their benevolence continues, it will remain and increase, and unless they resist and quench the Holy Spirit, they can get no relief until at last they are driven to extremity, make a desperate effort to roll the burden upon the Lord Jesus Christ, and exercise a childlike confidence in Him. Then they feel relieved. They feel as if the soul they were praying for will be saved. The burden is gone, and in kindness, God seems to sooth the mind to feel a sweet assurance that the blessing will be granted.

Often, after a Christian has had this struggle, this agony in prayer, and has obtained relief in this way, you will find the sweetest and most heavenly affections flow out. The soul rests sweetly and gloriously in God and rejoices *with joy unspeakable and full of glory* (1 Peter 1:8).

Do any of you think that there are no such things in the experience of believers? If I had time, I could show you from President Edwards and others cases and descriptions just like this. Do you ask why we never have such things here in New York? It is not at all because you are so much wiser than Christians are in the country, because you have so much more intelligence or more enlarged views of the nature of Christianity, or that you have a more stable and well-regulated piety. No, for instead of priding yourselves in being free from such extravagances, you should hide your heads because Christians in New York are so worldly and have so much formality, pride, and fashion that they cannot lower themselves to such spirituality as this. I wish it could be so. Oh, that there might be such a spirit in this city and in this church! I know it would make a noise if we had such things done here, but I would not care. Let them say that the folks in Chatham Chapel are getting deranged. We do not need to be afraid of that if we could live near enough to God to enjoy His Spirit in the manner I have described.

4. These effects of the spirit of prayer upon the body are themselves no part of religion. It is only that the body is often so weak that the feelings of the soul overpower it. These bodily effects are not at all essential to prevailing prayer, but are only a natural or physical result of highly excited emotions of the mind. It is not at all unusual for the body to be weakened and even overcome by any powerful emotion of the mind on other subjects besides Christianity. The doorkeeper of Congress in the time of the Revolution fell down dead when he received some highly encouraging intelligence.

I knew a woman in Rochester who was in a great agony of prayer for the conversion of her son-in-law. One morning he was at a meeting for those concerned about their souls, and she remained at home to pray for him. At the close of the meeting, he came home a convert, and she was so joyful that she fell down and died on the spot. It is no more strange that these effects should be produced by religion than by strong feeling on any other subject. It is not essential to prayer, but is the natural result of great effort of the mind.

5. Undoubtedly, one main reason why God requires the exercise of this agonizing prayer is that it forms such a bond between Christ and the church. It creates such a sympathy between them. It is as if Christ came and poured the overflowings of His own benevolent heart into His church and led them to sympathize and cooperate with Him as they never do in any other way. They feel just as Christ feels – so full of compassion for sinners that they cannot contain themselves. It is often the same way with those ministers who are distinguished for their success in preaching to sinners; they often have such compassion, such overflowing desires for their salvation, that it shows itself in their speaking and their preaching, just as though Jesus Christ spoke through them. The

words come from their lips fresh and warm, as if from the very heart of Christ. I do not mean that He dictates their words, but He inspires the feelings that give utterance to them. Then you see a movement in the hearers, as if Christ Himself spoke through lips of clay.

6. This travailing in birth for souls also creates a remarkable bond of union between warmhearted Christians and the young converts. Those who are converted are very dear to the hearts that have had this spirit of prayer for them. The feeling is like that of a mother for her firstborn. Paul expresses it beautifully when he says, *My little children.* His heart was warm and tender to them. *My little children, of whom I travail in birth again.* They had backslidden, and he had all the agonies of a parent over a wandering child. *My little children, of whom I travail in birth again until Christ be formed in you* (Galatians 4:19). *Christ in you, the hope of glory* (Colossians 1:27).

In a revival, I have often noticed how those who have had the spirit of prayer love the young converts. I know this is difficult to understand for those who have never felt it. However, to those who have experienced the agony of wrestling, prevailing prayer for the conversion of a soul, you may depend upon it that after the soul is converted, it appears as dear as a child is to the mother who has brought him forth with pain. He has agonized for it and received it in answer to prayer, and he can present it to the Lord Jesus Christ, saying, "Here I am, Lord, and the children You have given me" (see Isaiah 8:18).

7. Another reason God requires this sort of prayer is that it is the only way in which the church can be properly prepared to receive great blessings without being harmed by them. When the church is prostrated in the dust before God, and is in the depth of agony in prayer, the blessing does them good. While at the same time, if they had received the blessing without this deep prostration of soul, it would have puffed them up with pride. But as it is, it increases their holiness, love, and humility.

IV. Such Prayer Will Avail Much

I want to show that such prayer as I have described will avail much, but time fails me to go into particular detail of the evidence that I intended to bring forward in regard to this. Elijah the prophet mourned over the decline of the house of Israel, and when he saw that no other means were likely to be effectual to prevent a perpetual descent into idolatry, he prayed that the judgments of God might come upon the guilty nation. He prayed that it might not rain, and God shut up the heavens for three years and six months, until the people were driven to the last extremity.

And when he saw that it was time to relent, what did he do? He went up to the mountain and bowed down in prayer. He wanted to be alone, and he told his servant to go seven times, while he was agonizing in prayer. The last time, the servant told him that a little cloud appeared like a man's hand, and Elijah instantly arose from his knees, for he knew that the blessing was obtained. The time had come for the calamity to be turned back.

"Ah, but," you say, "Elijah was a prophet." Do not make this objection. They made it in the apostle's days, and what did the apostle say? He brought forward this very example, and the fact that Elijah was a man of like passions with ourselves, as an example of prevailing prayer, and he insisted that they should pray likewise (James 5:17-18).

John Knox was a man famous for his power in prayer. Bloody Queen Mary used to say that she feared his prayers more than all the armies of Europe. Events showed that she had reason to fear them. He used to be in such an agony for the deliverance of his country that he could not sleep. He had a place in his garden where he used to go to pray. One night as Knox and several friends were praying together, Knox spoke and said that deliverance had come. He could not tell what had happened, but he felt that something had taken place, for God had heard their prayers. What was it? The next news they heard was that Mary was dead!

I once heard a minister say that in a certain town there had been no revival for many years. The church was nearly wasted away. The youth were all unconverted, and desolation reigned unbroken. There lived in a secluded part of the town an aged man, a blacksmith by trade, who stammered so much that it was painful to hear him speak. On one Friday, as he was at work alone in his shop, his mind became concerned about the state of the church and of the unrepentant. His agony became so great that he stopped his work, locked the shop door, and spent the afternoon in prayer.

He prevailed, and on the Lord's Day he called on the minister and asked him to appoint a conference meeting. After some hesitation, the minister consented, observing, however, that he feared that not many would attend. He scheduled it the same evening at a large private house. When evening came, more assembled than could be accommodated in the house. All was silent for a time until one sinner broke out in tears and said that if anyone could pray, to please pray for him. Another followed, and another, and still another, until people from every part of the town were under deep conviction. What was remarkable was that they all dated their conviction to the hour when the old man was praying in his shop. A powerful revival followed. Thus the old stammering man prevailed, and as a prince, had power with God (Genesis 32:28). I could name multitudes of similar cases, but, for lack of time, must conclude with only a few.

Remarks

1. A great deal of prayer is lost, and many people never prevail in prayer, because when they have desires for particular blessings, they do not follow them up. They may have had desires, benevolent and pure, that were inspired by the Spirit of God; and when they have them, they should persevere in prayer, for if they turn their attention to other objects, they will quench the Spirit. We tell sinners not to turn away their minds from the one object, but to keep their attention focused there until they are saved. When you find these holy desires in your minds, take care of two things: do not quench the Spirit, and do not be diverted to other objects. Follow the leadings of the Spirit until you have offered that effectual, fervent prayer that avails much.

2. Without the spirit of prayer, ministers will only do a little good. A minister does not need to expect much success unless he prays for it. Sometimes others may have the spirit of prayer and obtain a blessing on his labors. Generally, however, those preachers are the most successful who have the most of a spirit of prayer themselves.

3. Not only must ministers have the spirit of prayer, but it is necessary for the church to unite in offering that effectual, fervent prayer that can prevail with God. You do not need to expect a blessing unless you ask for it. *I will yet for this be enquired of by the house of Israel, to do it for them* (Ezekiel 36:37).

Now, my brethren, I have only to ask you in regard to what I have said, "Will you do it?" Have you done what I preached to you in the last lecture? Have you examined your sins and confessed them, and got them all out of the way? Can you pray now? And will you join and offer prevailing prayer so that the Spirit of God may come down here?

Lecture 5

The Prayer of Faith

Therefore I say unto you, What things soever ye desire, when ye pray, believe that ye receive them, and ye shall have them.
—Mark 11:24

These words have been thought by some people to refer exclusively to the faith of miracles, but there is not the least evidence of this. The context proves that the text was not intended by our Savior to refer exclusively to the faith of miracles. If you read the chapter, you will see that Christ and His apostles were at this time very engaged in their work and were very prayerful. As they returned from their places of rest in the morning, faint and hungry, they saw a fig tree at a little distance. It looked very beautiful, and doubtless gave signs of having fruit on it, but when they came near, they found nothing on it but leaves. And Jesus said, *No man eat fruit of thee hereafter for ever* (Mark 11:14).

And in the morning, as they passed by, they saw the fig tree dried up from the roots. And Peter calling to remembrance saith unto him, Master, behold, the fig tree which thou cursedst is withered away.

And Jesus answering saith unto them, Have faith in God. For verily I say unto you, that whosoever shall say unto this

*mountain, Be thou removed, and be thou cast into the sea;
and shall not doubt in his heart, but shall believe that those
things which he saith shall come to pass; he shall have whatsoever he saith.* (Mark 11:20-23)

Then follow the words of the text: *Therefore I say unto you, What things
soever ye desire when ye pray, believe that ye receive them, and ye shall
have them* (Mark 11:24).

Our Savior desired to give His disciples instructions about the nature
and power of prayer and the necessity of strong faith in God. He therefore gave a strong example, a miracle – one so great as the removal of
a mountain into the sea. He told them that if they exercised a proper
faith in God, they could do such things. But His remarks are not to be
limited to faith merely in working miracles, for He goes on to say, *And
when ye stand praying, forgive, if ye have aught against any, that your
Father also which is in heaven may forgive you your trespasses. But if ye
do not forgive, neither will your Father which is in heaven forgive your
trespasses* (Mark 11:25-26).

Does that relate to miracles? When you pray, you must forgive. Is
that only required when someone wants to work a miracle? There are
many other promises in the Bible closely related to this and speaking
nearly the same language, which have been inadequately disposed of
as referring to the faith employed in miracles, as if the faith of miracles
was something different from faith in God!

In my last lecture, I dwelt upon the subject of prevailing prayer, and
you will remember that I passed over the subject of faith in prayer very
briefly because I wanted to reserve it for a separate discussion. This
lecture is about the prayer of faith.

I will discuss the following points:

I.   Faith is an indispensable condition of prevailing prayer.

II. What it is that we are to believe when we pray.

III. When we are bound to exercise this faith, or to believe that we
     will receive that which we ask for.

IV. This kind of faith in prayer always obtains the blessing sought.

V. How we are to come into the state of mind in which we can exercise such faith.

VI. Several objections that are sometimes alleged against these views of prayer.

I. Faith Is an Indispensable Condition of Prevailing Prayer

It will not be seriously doubted that faith is an indispensable condition of prevailing prayer. There is such a thing as offering benevolent desires, which are acceptable to God as such, but do not include the exercise of faith in regard to the actual reception of those blessings. But such desires are not prevailing prayer, the prayer of faith. God may see fit to grant the things desired as an act of kindness and love, but it would not be done properly in answer to prayer.

I am speaking now of the kind of faith that ensures the blessing. Do not understand me as saying that there is nothing in prayer that is acceptable to God, or that even obtains the blessing sometimes, without this kind of faith. Rather, I am speaking of the faith that secures the very blessing it seeks. To prove that faith is indispensable to prevailing prayer, it is only necessary to repeat what the apostle James specifically tells us: *If any of you lack wisdom, let him ask of God, that giveth to all men liberally, and upbraideth not; and it shall be given him. But let him ask in faith, nothing wavering. For he that wavereth is like a wave of the sea driven with the wind and tossed* (James 1:5-6).

II. What It Is That We Are to Believe When We Pray

1. We are to believe in the existence of God: *He that cometh to God must believe that he is,* and in His willingness to answer prayer: *and that he is a rewarder of them that diligently seek him* (Hebrews 11:6). There are many people who believe in the existence of God but do not believe in the effectiveness of prayer. They profess to believe in God, but deny the necessity or influence of prayer.

2. We are to believe that we will receive something, but what? Not

something, or anything, as it happens, but some particular thing we ask for. We are not to think that God is such a being that if we ask for a fish, He will give us a serpent, or if we ask for bread, He will give us a stone (Luke 11:11), but He says, *What things soever ye desire, when ye pray, believe that ye receive them, and ye shall have them* (Mark 11:24).

With respect to the faith for miracles, it is plain that they were to believe that they should receive just what they asked for – that the very thing itself would come to pass. That is what they were to believe.

What should people believe in regard to other blessings? Is it a mere loose idea that if a person prays for a specific blessing, God will by some mysterious sovereignty give something or other to him, or something to somebody else somewhere? When a man prays for his children's conversion, is he to believe that either his children will be converted, or somebody else's children, and it is entirely uncertain which? All this is utter nonsense and is highly dishonorable to God. No, we are to believe that we will receive the very things that we ask for.

III. When Are We Bound to Make This Prayer?

When are we bound to believe that we will have the very things we pray for? When we have evidence of it. Faith must always have evidence. A person cannot believe something unless he sees something that he supposes to be evidence. He is under no obligation to believe, and has no right to believe, that a thing will be done unless he has evidence. It is the height of fanaticism to believe without evidence. The kinds of evidence a person may have are the following:

1. Suppose that God has specifically promised the thing. For instance, God says He is more ready to give His Holy Spirit to those who ask Him than parents are to give bread to their children. Here we must believe that we will receive it when we pray for it. You have no right to put in an *if* and say, "Lord, if it is Your will, give us Your Holy Spirit." This is to insult God. To put an *if* into God's promise, where God has put none, is like accusing God of being insincere. It is like saying, "O God, if You are sincere in making these promises, grant us the blessing we pray for."

I heard of a young convert who taught a minister a solemn truth on the subject of prayer. She was from a very wicked family and went to live with a minister. While there, she was hopefully converted, and appeared well. One day she went to the minister's study while he was in it – a thing she was not in the habit of doing. He thought that something must have been wrong, so he asked her to sit down, and he gently inquired into the state of her religious feelings. She said that she was distressed at the manner in which the old church members prayed for the Spirit. They would pray for the Holy Spirit to come and would seem to be very sincere. They would plead the promises of God and then say, "O Lord, if it is Your will, grant us these blessings for Christ's sake." She thought that saying "If it is Your will," when God had specifically promised it, was questioning whether God was sincere in His promises.

The minister tried to reason her out of it, but he only succeeded in confusing her. She was distressed and filled with grief, and she said, "I cannot argue the point with you, sir, but it is impressed on my mind that it is wrong and is dishonoring God." She went away weeping with anguish.

The minister saw that she was not satisfied, and it led him to look at the matter again. Finally he saw that it was putting in an *if* where God had put none, and where He had specifically revealed His will, and that it was an insult to God. He went and told his church that they were bound to believe that God was sincere when He made them a promise. The spirit of prayer came down upon that church, and a most powerful revival followed.

2. Where there is a general promise in the Bible that you may reasonably apply to a particular case before you, you are bound to pray this prayer. If its true meaning includes the particular thing for which you pray, or if you can reasonably apply the principle of the promise to the case, there you have evidence. For instance, suppose it is a time when wickedness greatly prevails, and you are led to pray for God's intervention. What promise do you have? *When the enemy shall come in like a flood, the Spirit of the LORD shall lift up a standard against him* (Isaiah 59:19). This is a general promise laying down a principle of God's administration, which you may apply to the case before you as authorization to exercise faith in prayer. And if the situation comes up to inquire as to the time

71

in which God will grant blessings in answer to prayer, you have this promise: *While they are yet speaking, I will hear* (Isaiah 65:24).

There is a vast amount of general promises and principles laid down in the Bible, which Christians might make use of if they would only think. Whenever you are in circumstances to which the promises or principles apply, there you are to use them. A parent finds this promise: *The mercy of the LORD is from everlasting to everlasting upon them that fear him, and his righteousness unto children's children; to such as keep his covenant, and to those that remember his commandments to do them* (Psalm 103:17-18). This is a promise made to those who possess a certain character. If any parent is aware that this is his character, he has a rightful basis to apply it to himself and his family. If you have this character, you are bound to make use of this promise in prayer, and believe it, even to your children's children.

If I had time, I could go from one end of the Bible to the other and produce an astonishing variety of texts that are applicable as promises – enough to prove that in whatever circumstances a child of God may be placed, God has provided in the Bible some promise, either general or specific, that he can apply that is precisely suited to his situation. Many of God's promises are very broad on purpose in order to cover much ground. What can be broader than the promise in the text: *What things soever ye desire when ye pray. . .?* What praying Christian is there who has not been surprised at the length, breadth, and fullness of the promises of God when the Spirit has applied them to his heart? Who that lives a life of prayer has not wondered at his own blindness in not having before seen and felt the extent of meaning and richness of those promises when viewed under the light of the Spirit of God? At such times he has been astonished at his own ignorance and has found the Spirit applying the promises and declarations of the Bible in a sense in which he had never dreamed of their being applicable before.

The manner in which the apostles applied the promises, prophecies, and declarations of the Old Testament places in a strong light the breadth of meaning, fullness, and richness of the Word of God. He who walks in the light of God's countenance, and is filled with the Spirit of God as he should be, will often make an appropriation of promises to himself, and an application of them to his own circumstances and the circumstances of those for whom he prays, that a blind professing Christian would never dream of.

3. You may pray this prayer when there is any prophetic declaration that the thing prayed for is agreeable to the will of God. When it is plain from prophecy in the Word of God that the event is certain to come, you are bound to believe it and to make it the ground for your special faith in prayer. If the time is not specified in the Bible, and there is no evidence from other sources, you are not bound to believe that it will take place now, or immediately. But if the time is specified, or if the time may be learned from the study of the prophecies, and it appears to have arrived, then Christians are under obligation to understand and apply it by offering the prayer of faith.

For instance, take the case of Daniel in regard to the return of the Jews from captivity. What does he say? *I Daniel understood by books the number of the years, whereof the word of the LORD came to Jeremiah the prophet, that he would accomplish seventy years in the desolations of Jerusalem* (Daniel 9:2). Here he learned from books – that is, he studied his Bible, and in that way understood that the length of the captivity was to be seventy years. What did he do then? Did he sit down upon the promise and say, "God has pledged Himself to put an end to the captivity in seventy years, and the time has expired, and there is no need of doing anything"? No; he said, *And I set my face unto the Lord God, to seek by prayer and supplications, with fasting, and sackcloth, and ashes* (Daniel 9:3). He set himself at once to pray that the thing might be accomplished. He prayed in faith. But what was he to believe? He was to believe what he had learned from prophecy.

There are many prophecies yet unfulfilled in the Bible that Christians are bound to understand, as far as they are capable of understanding them, and then make them the basis of believing prayer. Do not think, as some seem to, that because a thing is foretold in prophecy it is not necessary to pray for it, or that it will come whether Christians pray for it or not. There is no truth in this. God says, in regard to this very class of events, which are revealed in prophecy, *I will yet for this be enquired of by the house of Israel, to do it for them* (Ezekiel 36:37).

4. When the signs of the times or the providence of God indicate that a particular blessing is about to be bestowed, we are bound to believe it, The Lord Jesus Christ blamed the Jews and called them hypocrites because they did not understand the indications of providence (Matthew 16:3). They could understand the signs of the weather, and see when it was about to rain and when it would be fair weather; but they could not see, from the signs of the times, that the time had come for the Messiah to appear and build up the house of God. There are many professing Christians who are always stumbling and hanging back whenever anything is proposed to be done. They always say, "The time has not come. The time has not come," when there are others who pay attention to the signs of the times and who have spiritual discernment to understand them. These people pray in faith for the blessing, and it comes.

5. When the Spirit of God is upon you and stirs up strong desires for any blessing, you are bound to pray for it in faith. You are bound to infer, from the fact that you find yourself drawn to desire such a thing while in the exercise of such holy affections as the Spirit of God produces, that these desires are the work of the Spirit. People are not apt to desire with the right kind of desires unless they are inspired by the Spirit of God. The apostle refers to these desires, excited by the Spirit, in his epistle to the Romans, where he says, *Likewise the Spirit also helpeth our infirmities: for we know not what we should pray for as we ought: but the Spirit itself maketh intercession for us with groanings which cannot be uttered. And he that searcheth the heart knoweth what is the mind of the Spirit, because he maketh intercession for the saints according to the will of God* (Romans 8:26-27). Here, then, if you find yourself strongly drawn to desire a blessing, you are to understand it as an indication that God is willing to bestow that particular blessing, and so you are bound to believe it. God does not trifle with His children. He does not go and stir up in them a desire for one blessing, only to turn them away from it with something else. Instead, He stirs up the very desires He is willing to gratify. When they feel such desires, they are bound to follow them out until they get the blessing.

IV. This Kind of Faith Always Obtains the Object

The text is plain here, showing that you will receive the very thing prayed for. It does not say, "Believe that you shall receive, and you shall either have that or something else equivalent to it." To prove that this faith obtains the very blessing asked, observe the following:

1. If this were not the case, we could never know whether our prayers were answered, and we might continue praying and praying long after the prayer was answered by some other blessing equivalent to the one we ask for.

2. If we are not bound to expect the very thing we ask for, it must be that the Spirit of God deceives us. Why would He stir us up to desire a certain blessing when He intends to grant something else?

3. What is the meaning of this passage: *If his son ask bread, will he give him a stone* (Matthew 7:9)? Does not our Savior rebuke the idea that prayer may be answered by giving something else? What encouragement do we have to pray for anything in particular if we are to ask for one thing and receive another? Suppose a Christian would pray for a revival here, and would be answered by a revival in China. Or he might pray for a revival, and God would send the cholera or an earthquake. All the history of the church shows that when God answers prayer, He gives His people the very thing for which their prayers are offered. God gives other blessings, to both saints and sinners, which they do not pray for at all. He sends His rain both upon the just and the unjust (Matthew 5:45), but when He answers prayer, it is by doing what they ask Him to do. To be sure, He often more than answers prayer. He grants them not only what they ask, but often connects other blessings with it.

4. It is evident that the prayer of faith will obtain the blessing from the fact that our faith rests on evidence that to grant that thing is the will of God. It is not evidence that something else will be granted, but that this particular thing will be granted. How, then, can we have evidence that *this* thing will be granted, if *another* thing is to be granted? People

often receive more than they pray for. Solomon prayed for wisdom, and God granted him riches and honor in addition. A wife sometimes prays for the conversion of her husband, and if she offers the prayer of faith, God may not only grant that blessing, but may also convert her child and her whole family. Blessings sometimes seem to hang together, so that if a Christian gains one, he gets them all.

V. How We Are to Come into This State of Mind in Which We Can Offer Such Prayer

People sometimes ask, "How should I offer such prayer? Should I say, 'Now I will pray in faith for such and such a blessing'?" No, the human mind is not moved in this way. You might just as well say, "Now I will call up a spirit from the bottomless pit." I give the following answer:

1. You must first obtain evidence that God will give the blessing. How did Daniel come to the conclusion to offer the prayer of faith? He searched the Scriptures. You do not need to let your Bible lie on a shelf and expect God to reveal His promises to you. Search the Scriptures and see where you can get either a general or special promise, or a prophecy, on which you can plant your feet when you pray. Go through the Bible, and you will find it full of such things – precious promises that you may plead in faith. You never need to lack objects of prayer if you will do as Daniel did. People are confused on this subject because they never make a proper use of the Bible.

A curious case occurred in one of the towns in the western part of this state. There was a revival there. A certain clergyman visited the place and heard a great deal said about the prayer of faith. He was amazed at what they said, for he had never regarded the subject in the light they did. He inquired about it of the minister who was laboring there. The minister requested him, in a kind spirit, to go home, take his New Testament, look up the passages that refer to prayer, and go around to his most praying people and ask them how they understood these passages. He said he would do it, for although these views were new to him, he was willing to learn. He did it. He went to his praying men and women and read the passages without note or comment, and asked them what they thought. He found that their plain common sense had led them to understand these passages, and to believe that they mean just what they say. This affected him, and then the fact of his going around and presenting the promises before their minds awakened the spirit of prayer in them, and a revival followed.

I could name many individuals who have set themselves to examine the Bible on this subject, and before they got halfway through with it have been filled with the spirit of prayer. They found that God meant by His promises just what a plain, commonsense man would understand them to mean. I advise you to try it. You have Bibles; look them over, and whenever you find a promise that you can use, fasten it in your mind before you go on. I dare to predict that you will not get through the Book without finding out that God's promises mean just what they say.

2. Cherish the good desires you have. Christians very often lose their good desires by not attending to this, and then their prayers are mere words, without any desire or earnestness at all. The slightest longing of desire must be cherished. If your body was likely to freeze, and you had even the least spark of fire, how you would cherish it! In the same way, if you have even the least desire for a blessing, no matter how small, do not waste it away. Do not grieve the Spirit. Do not be distracted. Do not lose good desires by levity, by criticalness, or by worldly mindedness. Watch and pray, and follow it up, or you will never pray the prayer of faith.

3. Entire consecration to God is indispensable to the prayer of faith. You must live a holy life and consecrate all to God – your time, talents, influence – all you have and all you are, to be His entirely. Read the biographies and autobiographies of godly men, and you will be struck with the fact that they used to set apart times to renew their covenant and to dedicate themselves anew to God, and whenever they did so, a blessing always followed immediately. If I had the writings of Jonathan Edwards with me now, I could read passages showing how it was in his days.

4. You must persevere. You are not to pray for something once, and then stop, and call that the prayer of faith. Look at Daniel. He prayed

for twenty-one days, and did not stop until he had obtained the blessing. He set his heart and face unto the Lord, to seek Him by prayer and supplications, with fasting and sackcloth and ashes. He held on for three weeks, and then the answer came. Why did it not come before? God sent an archangel to carry the message, but the devil hindered him all this time. See what Christ says in the parable of the unjust judge (Luke 18:1-8) and the parable of the loaves (Luke 11:5-8). What does He teach us by them? That God will grant answers to prayer when it is urgent. *Shall not God avenge his own elect, who cry day and night unto him?* (Luke 18:7).

5. If you want to pray in faith, be sure to walk every day with God. If you do, He will tell you what to pray for. Be filled with His Spirit, and He will give you objects enough to pray for. He will give you as much of the spirit of prayer as you have strength of body to bear.

A good man said to me, "Oh, I am dying for the lack of strength to pray. My body is crushed, the world is on me, and how can I refrain from praying?" I have known that man to go to bed absolutely sick due to weakness and faintness under the pressure. I have known him to pray as if he would do violence to heaven, and then I have seen the blessing come as plainly in answer to his prayer as if it was revealed, so that no person would doubt it any more than if God had spoken from heaven. Shall I tell you how he died? He prayed more and more, and he used to take the map of the world before him and pray, and look over the different countries and pray for them, until he absolutely died in his room praying. Blessed man! He was the reproach of the ungodly and of carnal, unbelieving professing Christians, but he was the favorite of heaven, and a prevailing prince in prayer.

VI. I Will Now Refer to Some Objections That Are Brought Forward Against This Doctrine

1. "It leads to fanaticism and amounts to a new revelation." Why should this be a stumbling block? They must have evidence to believe before they can offer the prayer of faith. If God gives other evidence besides the senses, where is the objection? It is true that there is a sense in which

this is a new revelation, for it is making known a thing by His Spirit. But it is the very revelation that God has promised to give. It is just the one we are to expect if the Bible is true – that when we do not know what we should pray for, according to the will of God, His Spirit helps our infirmities and teaches us the very thing to pray for (Romans 8:26). Will we deny the teaching of the Spirit?

2. It is often asked, "Is it our duty to pray the prayer of faith for the salvation of all people?" No, for that is not something according to the will of God. It is directly contrary to His revealed will. We have no evidence that all will be saved. We should feel compassionately to all, and, in itself considered, desire their salvation, but God has revealed it to us that many of the human race will be damned. It cannot be a duty to believe that they will all be saved in the face of a revelation to the contrary. In Christ's prayer, in the seventeenth chapter of John, He specifically said, *I pray not for the world, but for them which thou hast given me* (John 17:9).

3. Some people say, "If we were to offer this prayer for all people, would not all people be saved?" Yes, and so they would be saved if they would all repent. But they will not. Neither will Christians offer the prayer of faith for all people because there is no evidence on which to ground a belief that God intends to save all people.

4. But you ask, "For whom are we to offer this prayer? We want to know in what cases, for what people and places, at what times, etc., we are to make the prayer of faith." The answer is, When you have evidence from promises, prophecies, providences, or the leadings of the Spirit that God will do the things you pray for.

5. "How is it that so many prayers of pious parents for their children are not answered? Did you not say there was a promise that pious parents may apply to their children? Why is it, then, that so many pious praying parents have had unrepentant children who died in their sins?" Granted that it is so, but what does it prove? *Let God be true, but every man a liar* (Romans 3:4). Which shall we believe: that God's promise

has failed, or that these parents did not do their duty? Perhaps they did not believe the promise, or did not believe there was any such thing as the prayer of faith. Wherever you find a professing Christian who does not believe in any such prayer, you find, in general, that he has children still in their sins. And it is no wonder, unless they are converted in answer to the prayers of somebody else.

6. "Will not these views lead to fanaticism? Will not many people think they are offering the prayer of faith when they are not?" That is the same objection that the Unitarians make against the doctrine of regeneration – that many people think they have been born again when they have not been. It is an argument against all spiritual religion whatever. Some think they have it when they have not, and are fanatics. However, there are those who *know* what the prayer of faith is, just as there are those who know what true spiritual experience is, though it may stumble coldhearted professing Christians who do not know it. Even ministers often lay themselves open to the rebuke that Christ gave to Nicodemus: *Art thou a master in Israel, and knowest not these things?* (John 3:10).

Remarks

1. People who have not known by experience what the prayer of faith is have great reason to doubt their piety. This is by no means uncharitable. Let them examine themselves. It is to be feared that they understand prayer as Nicodemus did the new birth. They have not walked with God, and you cannot describe it to them any more than you can describe a beautiful painting to a blind man who cannot see colors. Many professing Christians can understand about the prayer of faith just as much as a blind man does of colors.

2. There is reason to believe that millions of people are in hell because professing Christians have not offered the prayer of faith. When they had promises under their eye, they have not had faith enough to use them. In this way, parents let their children, even baptized children, go down to hell because they would not believe the promises of God. Undoubtedly many women's husbands have gone to hell when they

could have prevailed with God in prayer and could have seen them saved. The signs of the times and the indications of providence were favorable, perhaps, and the Spirit of God prompted desires for their salvation, and they had evidence enough to believe that God was ready to grant a blessing; and if they had only prayed in faith, God would have granted it, but God turned it away because they would not discern the signs of the times.

3. You say, "This leaves the church under a great load of guilt." True, it does so, and no doubt multitudes will stand up before God covered all over with the blood of souls that have been lost through their lack of faith. The promises of God, accumulated in their Bibles, will stare them in the face and weigh them down to hell.

4. Many professing Christians live so far from God that to talk to them about the prayer of faith is all unintelligible. Very often the greatest offense possible to them is to preach about this kind of prayer.

5. I want to ask the professing Christians a few questions. Do you know what it is to pray in faith? Did you ever pray in this way? Have you ever prayed until your mind was assured that the blessing would come – until you felt that rest in God, that confidence, as perfectly as if you saw God come down from heaven to give it to you? If not, you should examine your foundation. How can you live without praying in faith at all? How do you live in view of your children while you have no assurance whatsoever that they will be converted? One would think you would go crazy.

I knew a father in the West. He was a good man, but he had erroneous views respecting the prayer of faith. His whole family of children were grown up, and not one of them was converted. His son eventually got sick and seemed about to die. The father prayed, but the son grew worse and seemed to be sinking into the grave without hope. The father prayed until his anguish was unutterable. He went at last and prayed (there seemed no prospect of his son's life), and he poured out his soul as if he would not be denied, until at last he got an assurance that his son would not only live, but would be converted – and not only this one, but that his whole family would be converted to God. He came into the house and told his family that his son would not die. They were astonished at him. "I tell you," he said, "he won't die. And no child of mine will ever die in his sins." That man's children were all converted years ago.

What do you think of that? Was that fanaticism? If you believe so, it is because you do not know or understand the prayer of faith. Do you pray in that way? Do you live in such a manner that you can offer such prayer for your children? I know that the children of professing Christians may sometimes be converted in answer to the prayers of somebody else, but should you live so? Do you dare to trust in the prayers of others when God calls you to sustain this most important relation to your children?

Finally, see what combined effort is made to dispose of the Bible. The wicked are for throwing away the threatenings of the Bible, and the church the promises. And what is there left? Between them, they leave the Bible blank. I say it in love: What are our Bibles good for if we do not lay hold on their precious promises and use them as the ground of our faith when we pray for the blessing of God? It would be better for you to send your Bibles to the heathen, where they will do some good, if you are not going to believe and use them. I have no evidence that there is much of this prayer now in this church or in this city. And what will the result be? What will become of your children, your neighbors, and the wicked?

Lecture 6

The Spirit of Prayer

Likewise the Spirit also helpeth our infirmities: for we know not what we should pray for as we ought: but the Spirit itself maketh intercession for us with groanings which cannot be uttered. And he that searcheth the hearts knoweth what is the mind of the Spirit, because he maketh intercession for the saints according to the will of God.
—Romans 8:26-27

One of my earlier lectures was on the subject of effectual prayer, in which I observed that one of the most important attributes of effectual or prevailing prayer is faith. This was such an extensive subject that I reserved it for a separate discussion. Accordingly, I lectured last on the subject of faith in prayer, or as it is termed, the prayer of faith. It was my intention to discuss the subject in a single lecture, but as I was under the necessity of condensing so much on some points, it occurred to me, and was mentioned by others, that there might be some questions that people would ask that should be answered more fully, especially as the subject is one on which there is so much darkness. One main purpose in preaching is to exhibit the truth in such a way as to answer the questions that would naturally arise in the minds of those who read the Bible with attention, and who want to know what it means so that they can put it into practice. In explaining the text, I propose to show:

I.   What Spirit is here spoken of: *The Spirit also helpeth our infirmities.*

II. What that Spirit does for us.

III. Why He does what the text declares Him to do.

IV. How He accomplishes it.

V.   The degree in which He influences the minds of those who are under His influence.

VI. How His influences are to be distinguished from the influences of evil spirits, or from the suggestions of our own minds.

VII. How we are to obtain this agency of the Holy Spirit.

VIII.Who has a right to expect to enjoy His influences in this matter, or for whom the Spirit does the things spoken of in the text.

I. What Spirit Is It That Is Spoken of in the Text?

Some have supposed that the Spirit spoken of in the text means our own spirit – our own mind. However, a little attention to the text will show plainly that this is not the meaning. *The Spirit helpeth our infirmities* would then read, "Our own spirit helps the infirmities of our own spirit," and "Our own spirit likewise makes intercession for our own spirit." You see you can make no sense of it on that assumption. It is evident from the manner in which the text is introduced that the Spirit referred to is the Holy Spirit.

> *For if ye live after the flesh, ye shall die: but if ye through*
> *the Spirit do mortify the deeds of the body, ye shall live. For*
> *as many as are led by the Spirit of God, they are the sons of*
> *God. For ye have not received the spirit of bondage again to*
> *fear; but ye have received the Spirit of adoption, whereby we*
> *cry, Abba, Father. The Spirit itself beareth witness with our*
> *spirit, that we are the children of God.* (Romans 8:13-16)

The text is plainly speaking of the same Spirit.

II. What the Spirit Does

Answer: He intercedes for the saints. He *maketh intercession for us* and *helpeth our infirmities* when *we know not what to pray for as we ought.* He helps Christians to pray according to the will of God, or for the things that God desires them to pray for.

III. Why Is the Holy Spirit Thus Engaged?

He works in this way because of our ignorance, because we do not know what we should pray for as we should. We are so ignorant both of the will of God, revealed in the Bible, and of His unrevealed will, as we should learn it from His providence. Humans are vastly ignorant both of the promises and prophecies of the Bible, and are blind to the providence of God. They are still more in the dark about those points of which God has said nothing except by the leadings of His Spirit. You recall that I named these four sources of evidence on which to ground faith in prayer: promises, prophecies, providences, and the Holy Spirit. When all other means fail of leading us to the knowledge of what we should pray for, the Spirit does it.

IV. How Does He Make Intercession for the Saints? In What Mode Does He Operate So as to Help Our Infirmities?

1. He does not do so by overriding the use of our abilities. It is not by praying for us while we do nothing. He prays for us by enlivening our own abilities. It is not that He immediately suggests words to us or guides our language, but He enlightens our minds and makes the truth take hold of our souls. He leads us to consider the state of the church and the condition of sinners around us. We cannot tell the manner in which He brings the truth before the mind, and keeps it there until it produces its effect, but we can know that He leads us to a deep consideration of the state of things. The natural and philosophical result of this is deep feeling. When the Spirit brings the truth up before a man's mind, there is only one way in which he can keep from deep feeling, and that is by turning away his thoughts and leading his mind to think of other things.

When the Spirit of God brings the truth before sinners, they must feel. They feel wrong, as long as they remain unrepentant. So if someone is a Christian, and the Holy Spirit brings a subject into warm contact with his heart, it is just as impossible for him not to feel as it is that your hand should not feel anything if you put it into the fire. If the Spirit of God leads him to dwell on things calculated to excite warm and over-powering feelings, and he is not excited by them, it proves that he has no love for souls, nothing of the Spirit of Christ, and knows nothing about Christian experience.

2. The Spirit makes the Christian feel the value of souls, as well as the guilt and danger of sinners in their present condition. It is amazing how dark and ignorant Christians often are about this. Even Christian parents let their children go right down to hell before their eyes, and hardly seem to exercise a single feeling or put forth any effort to save them. And why? Because they are so blind to what hell is, so unbelieving about the Bible, and so ignorant of the precious promises that God has made to faithful parents. They grieve the Spirit of God away, and it is in vain to try to make them pray for their children while the Spirit of God is away from them.

3. He leads Christians to understand and apply the promises of Scripture. It is astonishing that in no age have Christians been able fully to apply the promises of Scripture to the events of life as they go along. This is not because the promises themselves are obscure, for the promises themselves are plain enough. However, there has always been a wonderful disposition to overlook the Scriptures as a source of light respecting the passing events of life.

How astonished the apostles were at Christ's application of so many prophecies to Himself! They seemed to be continually ready to exclaim, "Astonishing! Can it be so? We never understood it before." Who has witnessed the manner in which the apostles, influenced and inspired by the Holy Spirit, applied passages of the Old Testament to gospel times, and has not been amazed at the richness of meaning that they found in the Scriptures? It has been this way with many Christians. While deeply engaged in prayer, they have seen certain passages of Scripture as applicable that they have never thought of before as having any such application.

I once knew an individual who was in great spiritual darkness. He had withdrawn for prayer, resolved that he would not stop until he had found the Lord. He kneeled down and tried to pray. All was dark, and he could not pray. He rose from his knees and stood for a while, but he could not give it up, for he had promised that he would not let the sun go down before he had given himself to God. He knelt again, but it was all dark, and his heart was as hard as before. He was nearly in despair, and said in agony, "I have grieved the Spirit of God away, and there is no promise for me. I am shut out from the presence of God."

He was determined not to give up, and again he knelt down. He had said only a few words when a Bible passage came into his mind as fresh as if he had just read it; it seemed as if he had just been reading the words, *Ye shall seek me, and find me, when ye shall search for me with all your heart* (Jeremiah 29:13). Although this promise was in the Old Testament, and was addressed to the Jews, it was still as applicable to him as to them. It broke his heart, like the hammer of the Lord, in a moment. He prayed and then stood up, happy in God.

This kind of thing often happens when professing Christians are praying for their children. Sometimes they pray, and are in darkness and doubt, feeling as if there were no foundation for faith and no special promises for the children of believers. But while they are pleading, God has shown them the full meaning of some promise, and their soul has rested on it as on the mighty arm of God.

I once heard of a widow who was greatly troubled about her children until this passage was brought powerfully to her mind: *Leave thy fatherless children [with Me], I will preserve them alive* (Jeremiah 49:11). She saw it had an extended meaning, and she was enabled to lay hold on it, as it were, with her hands, and then she prevailed in prayer and her children were converted. The Holy Spirit was sent into the world by the Savior to guide His people and instruct them and bring things to their remembrance, as well as to convince the world of sin.

4. The Spirit leads Christians to desire and pray for things of which nothing is specifically said in the Word of God. Take the case of an individual. It is a general truth that God is willing to save. It is also a general truth that He is willing to answer prayer. But how shall I know

the will of God respecting that individual, whether I can pray in faith according to the will of God for the conversion and salvation of that individual or not? This is where the agency of the Spirit comes in – to lead the minds of God's people to pray for those individuals, and at those times, when God is prepared to bless them.

When we do not know what to pray for, the Holy Spirit leads the mind to dwell on some object, to consider its situation, to realize its value, to feel for it, and to pray and travail in birth until the object is attained. This sort of experience is less common in cities than it is in some parts of the country because of the infinite number of things to divert the attention and grieve the Spirit in cities. I have had much opportunity to know how it has been in some parts of the country.

I was acquainted with an individual who used to keep a list of people whom he was especially concerned for, and I have had the opportunity to know many of these people on his list who were soon converted. I have seen him pray for people on his list when he was literally in an agony for them, and have sometimes known him to call on some other person to help him pray for such a one. I have known his mind to fasten on an individual of hardened, abandoned character, and who could not be reached in any ordinary way.

In a town in the north part of this state, where there was a revival, there was a certain individual who was a most violent and bold opposer. He kept a tavern, and used to delight in swearing at a desperate rate whenever there were Christians within hearing – on purpose to hurt their feelings. He was so bad that one man said he believed he would have to sell his place or give it away and move out of town, for he could not live near a man who swore so. This good man of whom I was speaking was passing through the town and heard of the case, and was very much grieved and distressed for the individual. He added him to his prayer list. The case weighed on his mind when he was asleep and when he was awake. He kept thinking about him and praying for him for days. The next thing we knew, this ungodly man came into a meeting, got up and confessed his sins, and poured out his soul. His tavern immediately became the place where they held prayer meetings. In this manner, the Spirit of God leads individual Christians to pray for things that they would not pray for unless they were led by the Spirit, and so they pray for things according to the will of God.

By some, this may be said to be a revelation from God. I do not doubt that great evil has been done by saying that this kind of influence amounts to a new revelation. Many people will be afraid of it if they hear it called a new revelation, and they will not stop to ask what it means, or whether the Scriptures teach it or not. They suppose it to be a complete answer to the idea. But the plain truth of the matter is that the Spirit leads a person to pray, and if God leads a person to pray for an individual, the inference from the Bible is that God intends to save that individual. If we find by comparing our state of mind with the Bible that we are led by the Spirit to pray for an individual, we have good evidence to believe that God is prepared to bless him.

5. The Spirit leads people to pray in this way by giving to Christians a spiritual discernment respecting the movements and developments of providence. Devoted, praying Christians often see these things so clearly, and look so far ahead, as to greatly astonish others. They sometimes almost seem to prophesy. No doubt people may be deluded, and sometimes are so, by leaning to their own understanding when they think they are led by the Spirit, but there is no doubt that a Christian may be made to see and to discern clearly the signs of the times so as to understand, by providence, what to expect, and thus to pray for it in faith. Thus they are often led to expect a revival, and to pray for it in faith, when nobody else can see the slightest signs of it.

There was a woman in New Jersey, in a place where there had been a revival. She was very positive there was going to be another revival. She insisted upon it that they had had the former rain, and were now going to have the latter rain. She wanted to have conference meetings appointed, but the minister and elders saw nothing to encourage it, and would do nothing. She saw they were blind, so she went forward and got a carpenter to make seats for her, for she said she would have meetings in her own house. There was certainly going to be a revival. She had scarcely opened her doors for meetings before the Spirit of God came down in great power. These sleepy church members found themselves surrounded all at once with convicted sinners. They could only say, "Surely the Lord was in this place, and we knew it not" (see Genesis 28:16). The reason why such people understand the indication of God's will is not because of the superior wisdom that is in them, but because the Spirit of God leads them to see the signs of the times. This is not by revelation, but they are led to see that providential circumstances and events converge to a single point, which produces in them a confident expectation of a certain result.

V. The Degree in Which the Spirit of God Affects the Minds of Believers

The text says that the Spirit *maketh intercession for us with groanings that cannot be uttered*. I understand the meaning of this to be that the Spirit stirs up desires too great to be uttered except by groans. These are something that language cannot utter, making the soul too full to utter its feelings by words, where the person can only groan them out to God, who understands the language of the heart.

VI. How We Are to Know Whether It Is the Spirit of God That Influences Our Minds or Not

1. We do not know this by feeling that some external influence or agency is applied to us. We are not to expect to feel our minds in direct physical contact with God. If such a thing can be, we know of no way in which we can be made aware of it. We know that we exercise our minds freely, and that our thoughts are exercised on something that stirs up our feelings, but we are not to expect a miracle to be worked, as if we were physically led by the hand, or like something whispered in the ear, or any miraculous manifestation of the will of God. People often grieve the Spirit away because they do not embrace Him and cherish His influences.

Sinners often do this ignorantly. They suppose that if they were under conviction by the Spirit, they would have certain mysterious feelings, or a shock would come upon them that they could not mistake. Many Christians are so ignorant of the Spirit's influences, and have thought so little about having His assistance in prayer, that when they have them, they do not know it, and so do not cherish and yield to them and preserve them. We are aware of nothing in the case except the movement of our own minds. There is nothing else that can be felt. We are merely aware that our thoughts are intensely occupied on a certain subject.

Christians are often unnecessarily misled and distressed on this point for fear that they do not have the Spirit of God. They feel intensely, but they do not know what makes them feel. They are distressed about sinners, but why should they not be distressed when they think of their condition? They keep thinking about them all the time, and why shouldn't they be distressed?

The truth is that the very fact that you are thinking about them is evidence that the Spirit of God is leading you. Do you not know that the greater part of the time these things do not affect you so? The greater part of the time you do not think much about the case of sinners. You know their salvation is always equally important, but at other times, even when you are quite at leisure, your mind is entirely reserved and absent of any feeling for them. But now, although you may be busy about other things, you think, you pray, and you feel intensely for them, even while you are about business that at other times would occupy all your thoughts. Now almost every thought you have is, "God have mercy on them."

Why is this? Their case is placed in a strong light before your mind. Do you ask what it is that leads your mind to exercise compassion for sinners and to agonize in prayer for them? What can it be but the Spirit of God? There are no devils that would lead you so. If your feelings are truly compassionate, you are to consider it as the Holy Spirit leading you to pray for things according to the will of God.

2. Try the spirits by the Bible. People are sometimes led away by strange ideas and crazy impulses. If you compare them faithfully with the Bible, you never need to be led astray. You can always know whether your feelings are produced by the Spirit's influences by comparing your desires with the spirit and nature of religion as described in the Bible. The Bible commands you to try the spirits. *Beloved, believe not every spirit, but try the spirits whether they are of God* (1 John 4:1). Observe not only your own feelings in regard to your fellow men, but also, and more especially, observe the teachings of the Spirit within you respecting our Lord Jesus Christ. *Hereby know ye the Spirit of God: Every spirit*

that confesseth that Jesus Christ is come in the flesh is of God: and every spirit that confesseth not that Jesus Christ is come in the flesh is not of God; and this is that spirit of antichrist whereof ye have heard that it should come; and even now already it is in the world (1 John 4:2-3).

VII. How Shall We Get This Influence of the Spirit of God?

1. It must be sought by fervent, believing prayer. Christ says, *If ye then, being evil, know how to give good gifts unto your children, how much more shall your heavenly Father give the Holy Spirit to them that ask him?* (Luke 11:13). Does anyone say, "I have prayed for Him, and He does not come"? It is because you do not pray rightly. *Ye ask, and receive not, because ye ask amiss, that ye may consume it upon your lusts* (James 4:3). You do not pray from right motives.

A professing Christian, and a leading member in a church, once asked a minister what he thought of his situation. He had been praying week after week for the Spirit, and had not received Him. The minister asked him what his motive was in praying. He said he wanted to be happy. He knew that those who had the Spirit were happy, and he wanted to enjoy his mind as they did. What? The minister responded that the devil himself could pray in the same way. That is mere selfishness.

The man turned away in anger. The minister accurately saw that the man had never known what it was to pray. He was convinced that he was a hypocrite and that his prayers were all selfish, dictated only by a desire for his own happiness. David prayed that God would uphold him by His free Spirit so that he could teach transgressors and turn sinners to God (Psalm 51:12-13). A Christian should pray for the Spirit so that he may be more useful and glorify God more – not that he himself may be happier. This man saw clearly where he had been in error, and he was converted. Perhaps many here have been just so. You should examine yourself and see if all your prayers are selfish.

2. Use the means adapted to stir up your minds on the subject and to keep your attention focused there. If a man prays for the Spirit and then diverts his mind to other things, if he uses no other means but goes right away to worldly objects, then he tempts God, he swings loose from his

intention, and it would be a miracle if he would get what he prays for. How is a sinner to get conviction? By thinking of his sins. That is the way for a Christian to obtain deep feeling – by thinking on the object. God is not going to pour these things on you without any effort of your own. You must cherish the slightest impressions. Take the Bible and go over the passages that show the condition and prospects of the world. Look at the world, look at your children and your neighbors, and see their condition while they remain in sin. Then persevere in prayer and effort until you obtain the blessing of the Spirit of God to dwell in you. This was undoubtedly the way that Dr. Isaac Watts came to have the feelings that he has described in the hymn below:

My thoughts on awful subjects roll,
    Damnation and the dead;
What horrors seize the guilty soul
    Upon a dying bed!

Lingering about these mortal shores
    She makes a long delay,
Till like a flood, with rapid force,
    Death sweeps the wretch away.

Then swift and dreadful she descends
    Down to the fiery coast,
Amongst abominable fiends,
    Herself a frightful ghost.

There endless crowds of sinners lie,
    And darkness makes their chains;
Tortured with keen despair they cry,
    Yet wait for fiercer pains.

Not all their anguish and their blood
    For their old guilt atones;
Nor the compassion of a God
    Shall hearken to their groans.

Amazing grace, that kept my breath,
    Nor bid my soul remove,
Till I had learned my Savior's death,
    And well insured His love!

Look, as it were, through a telescope that will bring it up near to you. Look into hell and hear them groan. Then turn the glass upward and look at heaven, and see the saints there in their white robes, with their harps in their hands, and hear them sing the song of redeeming love. Then ask yourself, "Is it possible for me to prevail with God to elevate the sinner there?" Do this, and if you are not a wicked person and a stranger to God, you will soon have as much of the spirit of prayer as your body can sustain.

3. You must watch unto prayer. You must keep a lookout and see if God grants the blessing when you ask Him. People sometimes pray, but never look to see if the prayer is granted. Be careful also not to grieve the Spirit of God. Confess and forsake your sins. God will never lead you as one of His hidden ones, and let you into His secrets, unless you confess and forsake your sins. Do not just be always confessing your sins without forsaking them, but confess and also forsake them. Make things right wherever you have committed a wrong. You cannot expect to get the spirit of prayer first, and then repent. You cannot fight it through so. Professing Christians, who are proud and unyielding and justify themselves, will never force God to dwell with them.

4. Aim to obey perfectly the written Word of God. In other words, have no fellowship with sin. Aim at being entirely above the world. *Be ye therefore perfect, even as your Father which is in heaven is perfect* (Matthew 5:48). If you sin at all, let it be your daily sorrow. The man who does not aim at this intends to live in sin. Such a person does not need to expect God's blessing, for he is not sincere in desiring to keep all His commandments.

VIII. For Whom Does the Spirit Intercede?

He makes intercession for the saints, for all saints, for any who are saints. *Likewise the Spirit also helpeth our infirmities: for we know not what we should pray for as we ought; but the Spirit itself maketh intercession for us with groanings which cannot be uttered. And he that searcheth the hearts knoweth what is the mind of the Spirit, because he maketh intercession for the saints according to the will of God* (Romans 8:26-27).

Remarks

1. Why do you suppose it is that so little emphasis is placed on the influences of the Spirit in prayer when so much is said about His influences in conversion? Many people are amazingly afraid that the Spirit's influences will be left out. They place great emphasis on the Spirit's influences in converting sinners, but how little is said and written about His influence in prayer! How little complaining that people do not make enough of the Spirit's influences in leading Christians to pray according to the will of God! Let it never be forgotten that no Christian ever prays properly unless led by the Spirit. He has natural power to pray, and as far as the will of God is revealed, is able to do it; but he never does unless the Spirit of God influences him, just as sinners are able to repent, but never do, unless influenced by the Spirit.

2. This subject lays open the foundation of the difficulty felt by many people on the subject of the prayer of faith. They object to the idea that faith in prayer is a belief that we will receive the very things for which we ask, and they insist that there can be no foundation or evidence upon which to rest such a belief. In a sermon published a few years ago upon this subject, I brought forward this difficulty and presented it in its full strength. I said that I have no evidence that the thing prayed for will be granted until I have prayed in faith, because praying in faith is the condition upon which it is promised.

Of course, I cannot claim the promise until I have fulfilled the condition. If the condition is that I am to believe that I will receive the very blessing for which I ask, it is evident that the promise is given upon the performance of an impossible condition, and is of course a mere nothing. The promise would amount to just this: you will have whatsoever you ask, upon the condition that you first believe that you will receive it. I must fulfill the condition before I can claim the promise, but I can have no evidence that I will receive it until I have believed that I will receive it. This reduces me to the necessity of believing that I will receive it before I have any evidence that I will receive it – which is impossible.

The whole force of this objection arises out of the fact that the Spirit's influences are entirely overlooked, which He exerts in leading an individual to the exercise of faith. It has been supposed that Mark 11:22-24, and other similar promises on the subject of the prayer of faith, relate exclusively to miracles. But suppose this were true. I would ask what were the apostles to believe when they prayed for a miracle? Were they to believe that the precise miracle would be performed for which they prayed? It is evident that they were. In the verses just alluded to, Christ says, *For verily I say unto you, that whosoever shall say unto this mountain, Be thou removed, and be thou cast into the sea, and shall not doubt in his heart, but shall believe that these things which he saith shall come to pass, he shall have whatsoever he saith. Therefore I say unto you, what things soever ye desire, when ye pray, believe that ye receive them, and ye shall have them.* Here it is evident that the thing to be believed, and which they were not to doubt in their heart, was that they would have the very blessing for which they prayed.

The objection stated above lies in all its force against this kind of faith when praying for the performance of a miracle. If it is impossible to believe this in praying for any other blessing, it was equally so in praying for a miracle. I might ask if an apostle could believe that the miracle would be worked before he had fulfilled the condition. The answer is yes, inasmuch as the condition was that he should believe that he should receive that for which he prayed. Either the promise is void and is a deception, or there is a possibility of performing the condition.

As I have said, the whole difficulty lies in the fact that the Spirit's influences are entirely overlooked, and that the faith that is of the operation of God is left out of the question. If the objection is good against praying for any object, it is as good against praying in faith for the performance of a miracle. The fact is that the Spirit of God could give evidence on which to believe that any particular miracle would be granted. He could lead the mind to a firm reliance upon God and trust that the blessing sought would be obtained.

Even so at the present day He can give the same assurance in praying for any blessing that we need. Neither in the one case nor in the other are the influences of the Spirit miraculous. Praying is the same thing whether you pray for the conversion of a soul or for a miracle. Faith is the same thing in the one case as in the other; it only transpires on a different object – in the one case on the conversion of a soul, and in the other on the performance of a miracle. Nor is faith exercised in the one more than in the other, without reference to a promise, and a general promise may with the same reasonableness be applied to the conversion of a soul as to the performance of a miracle.

It is equally true in the one case as in the other that no one ever prays in faith without being influenced by the Spirit of God. If the Spirit could lead the mind of an apostle to exercise faith in regard to a miracle, He can lead the mind of another Christian to exercise faith in regard to receiving any other blessing by a reference to the same general promise.

When are we under an obligation to believe that we will receive the blessing for which we ask?

a) When there is a particular promise specifying the particular blessing, as when we pray for the Holy Spirit. This blessing is particularly named in the promise, and here we have evidence, and are obligated to believe, whether we have any divine influence or not – just as sinners are obligated to repent whether the Spirit strives with them or not. Their obligation does not rest upon the Spirit's influences, but upon the powers of moral agency that they possess – upon their ability to do their duty. While it is true that not one of them will ever repent without the influences of the Spirit, they still have power to do so, and are under obligation to do so, whether the Spirit strives with them or not. It is the same with the Christian. He is obligated to believe where he has evidence. And although he never does believe without the Spirit of God, even where he has a specific promise, yet his obligation to do so rests upon his ability, and not upon the divine influence.

b) Where God makes a revelation by His providence, we are obligated to believe in proportion to the clearness of the providential indication.

c) So where there is a prophecy, we are also obligated to believe. But in neither of these cases do we, in fact, believe without the Spirit of God.

d) But where there is no promise, providence, or prophecy on which to rest our faith, we are under no obligation to believe unless, as I have shown in this discourse, the Spirit gives us evidence by creating desires and by leading us to pray for a particular object. In the case of those promises of a general nature, where we are honestly at a loss to know in what particular cases to apply them, in many instances it may be considered as our privilege rather than as our duty to apply them to specific cases. However, whenever the Spirit of God leads us to apply them to a particular object, then it becomes our duty to apply them so. In this case, God explains His own promise and shows how He intended it to be applied. Then our obligation to make this application, and to believe in reference to this particular object, remains in full force.

3. Some have supposed that Paul prayed in faith for the removal of the thorn in the flesh, and that it was not granted. But they cannot prove that Paul prayed in faith. The presumption is all on the other side, as I have shown in a former lecture. Paul did not have promise, prophecy, providence, nor the Spirit of God to lead him to believe. The whole objection goes on the ground that the apostle might pray in faith without being led by the Spirit. This is truly a shorthand method of disposing of the Spirit's influences in prayer. Certainly, to assume that he prayed in faith is to assume either that he prayed in faith without being led by the Spirit, or that the Spirit of God led him to pray for that which was not according to the will of God.

I have dwelt longer on this subject because I want to have it made so plain that you will all be careful not to grieve the Spirit. I want you to have high ideas of the Holy Spirit and to feel that nothing good will be done without His influences. No praying or preaching will be of any avail without Him. If Jesus Christ were to come down here and preach to sinners, not one would be converted without the Spirit. Be careful, then, not to grieve Him away by disregarding or neglecting His heavenly influences when He invites you to pray.

4. In praying for an object, it is necessary to persevere until you obtain

it. Oh, with what eagerness Christians sometimes pursue a sinner in their prayers when the Spirit of God has fixed their desires on him! No miser pursues his gold with so fixed a determination.

5. The fear of being led by impulses has done great harm by not being properly considered. A person's mind may be led by a delusion, but we do wrong if we let the fear of impulses lead us to resist the good impulses of the Holy Spirit. No wonder Christians do not have the spirit of prayer if they are unwilling to take the trouble to distinguish, and so reject or resist, all impulses and all leadings of invisible agents. A great deal has been said about extremism, which is very unguarded and causes many minds to reject the leadings of the Spirit of God. *As many as are led by the Spirit of God, they are the sons of God* (Romans 8:14). It is our duty to *try the spirits whether they are of God* (1 John 4:1). We should insist on a close scrutiny and an accurate discernment. There must be such a thing as being led by the Spirit, and when we are convinced it is of God, we should be sure to follow – follow on with full confidence that He will not lead us wrong.

6. We see from this subject the absurdity of using forms of prayer. The very idea of using a form rejects, of course, the leadings of the Spirit. Nothing is more calculated to destroy the spirit of prayer and to entirely darken and confuse the mind as to what constitutes prayer than to use forms. Forms of prayer are not only absurd in themselves, but they are the very device of the devil to destroy the spirit and break the power of prayer. It is of no use to say that the form is a good one. Prayer does not consist in words, and it does not matter what the words are if the heart is not led by the Spirit of God. If the desire is not inflamed, the thoughts directed, and the whole current of feeling produced and led by the Spirit of God, it is not prayer. Set forms are, of all things, best calculated to keep an individual from praying as he should.

7. The subject furnishes a test of character. The Spirit makes intercession – for whom? For the saints. Those who are saints are thus engaged. If you are saints, you know by experience what it is to be thus engaged, or it is because you have grieved the Spirit of God so that He will not

lead you. You live in such a manner that this Holy Comforter will not dwell with you or give you the spirit of prayer. If this is so, you must repent. Whether you are a Christian or not, do not stop to settle that, but repent, as if you never had repented. Do your first works. Do not take it for granted that you are a Christian, but go like a humble sinner and pour out your heart unto the Lord. You can never have the spirit of prayer in any other way.

8. It is important to understand this subject in order to be useful. Without this spirit, there can be no such harmony between you and God that you can either walk with God or work with God. You need to have a strong beating of your heart with His, or you do not need to expect to be greatly useful.

Understanding this subject is as important as your sanctification. Without such a spirit of prayer, you will not be sanctified, you will not understand the Bible, and you will not know how to apply it to your situation. I want you to feel the importance of having God with you all the time. If you live as you should, He says that He will come unto you and make His abode with you (John 14:23), and dine with you, and you with Him (Revelation 3:20).

9. If people do not know the spirit of prayer, they are very inclined to be unbelieving in regard to the results of prayer. They do not see what takes place, they do not see the connection, or they do not see the evidence. They are not expecting spiritual blessings. When sinners are convicted, they think they are only frightened by such dreadful preaching. And when people are converted, they feel no confidence in their conversion, but only say, "We'll see how they turn out."

10. Those who have the spirit of prayer know when the blessing comes. It was this way when Jesus Christ appeared. These ungodly religious doctors did not know Him. Why? Because they were not praying for the redemption of Israel. But Simeon and Anna knew Him. How was that? Notice what they said, how they prayed, and how they lived. They were praying in faith, and so they were not surprised when He came. It is the same with such Christians. If sinners are convicted or converted,

they are not surprised at it. They were expecting just such things. They know God when He comes because they were looking out for His visits.

11. There are three classes of people in the church who are inclined to error, or have left the truth out of view, on this subject.

a) Those who place great reliance on prayer, and use no other means. They are alarmed at any talk about "getting up a revival" or any special means.

b) Over against these are those who use means, and pray, but never think about the influences of the Spirit in prayer. They talk about prayer for the Spirit, and feel the importance of the Spirit in the conversion of sinners, but do not realize the importance of the Spirit in prayer. Their prayers are all cold talk – nothing that anyone can feel or that can take hold of God.

c) Those who have certain strange ideas about the sovereignty of God, and are waiting for God to convert the world without prayer or means.

There must be in the church a deeper sense of the need of the spirit of prayer. The fact is that, generally, those who use means most intensely make the most strenuous efforts for the salvation of men and have the most correct beliefs of the manner in which means should be used for converting sinners. They also pray most for the Spirit of God, and wrestle most with God for His blessing. What is the result? Let facts speak, and say whether these people do or do not pray, and whether the Spirit of God testifies to their prayers and follows their labors with His power.

12. A spirit very different from the spirit of prayer appears to prevail in certain portions of the Presbyterian church at the present time. Nothing will produce an excitement and opposition so quickly as the spirit of prayer. If any person feels burdened in prayer with the case of sinners so as to groan in his prayer, the women are nervous, and he is visited at once with rebuke and opposition.

From my soul, I abhor all pretense of feeling where there is none, and all attempts to work oneself up into feeling by groans. But I feel bound to defend the position that there is such a thing as being in a state of mind in which there is only one way to keep from groaning, and that is by resisting the Holy Spirit. I was once present where this subject was discussed. It was said that groaning should be disapproved of. The question was asked whether God could not produce such a state of feeling that to abstain from groaning was impossible, and the answer was, "Yes, but He never does." If that is true, then the apostle Paul was terribly deceived when he wrote about groanings that cannot be uttered. Then Jonathan Edwards was deceived when he wrote his book about revivals. No one who reviews the history of revival in the church will adopt such a sentiment. I do not like this attempt to shut out, stifle, keep down, or limit the spirit of prayer. I would sooner cut off my right hand than rebuke the spirit of prayer, as I have heard of its being done by saying, "Do not let me hear any more groaning."

I hardly know where to conclude this subject. I would like to discuss it for a month, and until the whole church could understand it so as to pray the prayer of faith. Beloved, I want to ask you if you believe all this. Do you wonder that I should talk in this way? Perhaps some of you have had some glimpses of these things. Will you give yourselves up to prayer and live so as to have the spirit of prayer, and have that spirit with you all the time?

Oh, for a praying church! I once knew a minister who had a revival fourteen winters in succession. I did not know how to account for it until I saw one of his members get up in a prayer meeting and make a confession. "Brethren," he said, "I have been long in the habit of praying every Saturday night until after midnight for the descent of the Holy Spirit among us. And now, brethren," and he began to weep, "I confess that I have neglected it for two or three weeks." The secret was out. That minister had a praying church.

Brethren, in my present state of health, I find it impossible to pray as much as I have been in the habit of doing, and still continue to preach. It overcomes my strength. Should I give myself up to prayer and stop preaching? That will not do. Will not you who are in good health throw yourselves into this work, bear this burden, and give yourselves to prayer until God pours out His blessing upon us?

Lecture 7

On Being Filled with the Spirit

Be filled with the Spirit.
—Ephesians 5:18

Several of my last lectures have been on the subject of prayer and the importance of having the spirit of prayer and the intercession of the Holy Spirit. Whenever the necessity and importance of the Spirit's influences are held forth, there can be no doubt that people are in danger of abusing the doctrine and misconstruing it to their own harm. For instance, when you tell sinners that without the Holy Spirit they will never repent, they are very liable to misconstrue the truth and understand by it that they cannot repent, and therefore are under no obligation to do so until they feel the Spirit. It is often difficult to make them see that the "cannot" is simply their unwillingness, and not their inability. So again, when we tell Christians that they need the Spirit's aid in prayer, they are very inclined to think they are under no obligation to pray the prayer of faith until they feel the influences of the Spirit. They overlook their obligation to be filled with the Spirit, so they wait for the spirit of prayer to come upon them without asking, and thus tempt God.

Before we come to consider the other branch of means for promoting a revival – that is, the means to be used with sinners – I want to show you that if you live without the Spirit, you are without excuse. Obligation to perform duty never rests on the condition that we will first have the influence of the Spirit, but on the powers of moral agency. We, as moral agents, have the power to obey God, and are perfectly obligated to obey. The reason we do not is that we are unwilling. The influences of the Spirit are entirely a matter of grace. If they were indispensable to enable us to perform duty, the bestowment of them would not be a gracious act, but a mere matter of common justice. Sinners are not obligated to repent because they have the Spirit's influence, or because they can obtain it, but because they are moral agents and have the powers that God requires them to exercise.

It is the same in the case of Christians. They are not obligated to pray in faith because they have the Spirit (except in those cases where His influences in promoting desire constitute the evidence that it is God's will to grant the object of desire), but because they have evidence. They are not obligated to pray in faith at all, except when they have evidence as the foundation of their faith. They must have evidence from promises, principle, prophecy, or providence. And where they have evidence independent of His influences, they are obligated to exercise faith whether they have the Spirit's influence or not. They are obligated to see the evidence and to believe. The Spirit is not given to enable them to see or believe, but because without Him they will not look, feel, or act as they should. I intend to show from the text:

I.   Christians may be filled with the Spirit of God.

II. It is their duty to be filled with the Spirit.

III. Why they are not filled with the Spirit.

IV. The guilt of those who do not have the Spirit of God to lead their minds in duty and prayer.

V. The consequences that will follow if they are filled with the Spirit.

VI. The consequences if they are not filled with the Spirit.

I. Christians May Be Filled with the Spirit

This is not because it is a matter of justice for God to give you His Spirit, but because He has promised to give Him to those who ask: *If ye then, being evil, know how to give good gifts unto your children, how much more shall your heavenly Father give the Holy Spirit to them that ask him?* (Luke 11:13). If you ask for the Holy Spirit, God has promised to give Him.

Also, God has commanded you to have Him. He says in the text, *Be filled with the Spirit*. When God commands us to do something, it is the highest possible evidence that we can do it. For God to command is equivalent to an oath that we can do it. He has no right to command unless we have power to obey. There is no stopping short of the conclusion that God is an infinite tyrant if He commands that which cannot be done.

II. It Is Your Duty to Be Filled with the Spirit

1. You have a promise of it.

2. God has commanded it.

3. It is essential to your own growth in grace that you should be filled with the Spirit.

4. It is as important as it is that you should be sanctified.

5. It is as necessary as it is that you should be useful and do good in the world.

6. If you do not have the Spirit of God in you, you will dishonor God, disgrace the church, and die and go to hell.

III. Why Many Do Not Have the Spirit

There are some, even professing Christians, who will say, "I do not know anything about this. I never had any such experience. Either it is not true or I am all wrong." Undoubtedly you are all wrong if you know nothing about the influence of the Spirit. I want to present you with a few of the reasons that may prevent you from being filled with the Spirit.

1. It may be that you live a hypocritical life. Your prayers are not earnest and sincere. Not only is your religion a mere outward show, without any heart, but you are insincere in your interactions with others. Thus you do many things to grieve the Spirit so that He cannot dwell with you.

A minister was once boarding with a certain family, and the lady of the house was constantly complaining that she did not enjoy her mind, and nothing seemed to help her. One day some ladies called to see her, and she protested that she was very much offended because they had not called before, and she urged them to stay and spend the day. She declared that she could not consent to let them go. They excused themselves, however, and left the house. As soon as they were gone, she said to her servant that she wondered how these people had so little sense as to be always troubling her and taking up her time. The minister heard it, and immediately rebuked her, and told her that she could now see why she did not enjoy the Christian religion. It was because she was in the daily habit of insincerity that amounted to downright lying, and the Spirit of truth could not dwell in such a heart.

2. Others have so much levity that the Spirit will not dwell with them. The Spirit of God is solemn and serious, and will not dwell with those who give way to thoughtless levity.

3. Others are so proud that they cannot have the Spirit. They are so fond of expensive clothing, luxury, popularity, wealth, fashion, etc., that it is no wonder they are not filled with the Spirit. Yet such people will pretend to be at a loss to know why it is that they do not enjoy Christianity!

4. Some people are so worldly minded, love possessions so well, and are trying so hard to get rich that they cannot have the Spirit. How can He dwell with them when their thoughts are all on things of the world, and all their powers are absorbed in obtaining wealth? Then when they get it, they hold on to it and are displeased if pressed by conscience to do something for the conversion of the world. They show how much they love the world in all their interaction with others. Little things show it. They will take advantage of a poor man, who is doing a little work for them, to the lowest penny. If they are dealing on a large scale, it is very

likely they will be generous and fair, because it is for their advantage. However, if it is a person they do not care about – such as a laborer, a mechanic, or a housekeeper, they will grind him down to the last penny, no matter what it is really worth; and they actually pretend to make conscience of it that they cannot possibly give any more.

They would be ashamed to deal that way with people of their own rank because it would be known and would damage their reputation. However, God knows it, and has it all written down that they are covetous and unfair in their dealings, and will not do right unless it is for their own interest. How can such professing Christians have the Spirit of God? It is impossible.

There are a multitude of such things by which the Spirit of God is grieved. People call them little sins, but God will not call them little. I was struck with this thought when I saw a little notice in the *Evangelist*. The publishers stated that they were owed many thousands of dollars by subscribers, which was justly due, and that it would cost them as much as it was worth to send an agent to collect it. I suppose it is so with all the other Christian publications, that subscribers either put the publisher to the trouble and expense of sending an agent to collect his due, or else they cheat him out of it.

There are undoubtedly many thousands of dollars held back in this way by professing Christians, just because it is in such small sums, or they are so far off that they cannot be sued. Yet these people will pray and appear very pious and wonder why they cannot enjoy Christianity and have the Spirit of God! It is this looseness of moral principle, this lack of conscience about little matters, prevailing among Christians, that grieves away the Holy Spirit. It would be disgraceful to God to dwell and have communion with such people who will take advantage of and cheat their neighbor out of his dues because they can do it and not be disgraced.

5. Others do not fully confess and forsake their sins, and so cannot enjoy the Spirit's presence. They will confess their sins in general terms, perhaps, and are ready always to acknowledge that they are sinners. They may even partially confess some specific sins, but they do so reservedly, proudly, and cautiously, as if they were afraid that they would say a little

more than is necessary – that is, when they confess the harm they have done to others. They do it in a way that shows that instead of bursting forth from a childlike heart, the confession is wrung from them by the hand of conscience gripping them. If they have harmed anyone, they will make a partial recantation that is hard-hearted, cruel, and hypocritical, and then they will ask, "Now, brother, are you satisfied?" You know it would be very difficult for a person to say that he was not satisfied, even if the confession is cold and heartless.

However, I tell you that God is not satisfied. He knows whether you have gone the full length of honest confession and have taken all the blame that belongs to you. If your confessions have been constrained and wrung from you, do you suppose you can cheat God? *He that covereth his sins shall not prosper: but whoso confesseth and forsaketh them shall have mercy* (Proverbs 28:13). *He that shall humble himself shall be exalted* (Matthew 23:12). Unless you humble yourself and confess your sins honestly, and make amends where you have done harm, you have no right to expect the spirit of prayer.

6. Others are neglecting some known duty, and that is the reason why they are not filled with the Spirit. One person does not pray in his family, although he knows he should, yet he is trying to get the spirit of prayer! There are many young men who feel in their hearts that they should prepare for the ministry, but they do not have the spirit of prayer because they have some worldly object in view, which prevents them from devoting themselves to the work. They have known their duty, and refuse to do it, and now they are praying for direction from the Spirit of God. They cannot have it.

Another person has neglected to make a profession of Christianity. He knows his duty, but he refuses to join the church. He once had the spirit of prayer, but neglecting his duty, he grieved the Spirit away. Now he thinks that if he could once more enjoy the light of God's countenance and have his evidences renewed, he would do his duty and join the church. So he is praying for it again, and trying to bring God over to his terms, to grant him His presence. You do not need to expect it. You will live and die in darkness unless you are first willing to do your duty before God manifests Himself as reconciled to you. It is in vain to say that you will come forward if God will first show you the light of His countenance. He will never do it as long as you live. He will let you die without it if you refuse to do your duty.

I have known women who felt that they should talk to their unconverted husbands, and pray with them, but they have neglected it, and so they get into the dark. They knew their duty and refused to do it. They avoided it, and there they lost the spirit of prayer.

If you have neglected any known duty, and thus lost the spirit of prayer, you must yield first. God has a disagreement with you. You have refused obedience to God, and you must retract it. You may have forgotten it, but God has not, and you must set yourself to recall it to your mind and to repent. God will never yield or grant you His Spirit until you repent. If I had an omniscient eye now, I could call the names of the individuals in this congregation who had neglected some known duty or committed some sin that they have not repented of, and now they are praying for the spirit of prayer, but they cannot succeed in obtaining it.

To illustrate this, I will relate a case. A good man in the western part of this state had been a long time an active Christian, and he used to talk to the sleepy church with which he was connected. Eventually the church was offended and ran out of patience. Many people told him that they wished he would leave them alone, for they did not think he could do them any good. He took them at their word, and they all went to sleep together, and remained so for two or three years.

One day a minister came among them and a revival began, but this elder seemed to have lost his spirituality. He used to be active in a good work, but now he held back. Everybody thought it was strange. Finally, as he was going home one night, the truth of his situation flashed upon his mind, and he went into absolute despair for a few minutes. At last his thoughts were directed back to that sinful resolution to leave the church alone in their sins. He felt that no language could describe the darkness of that sin. He realized that moment what it was to be lost and to learn that God had a disagreement with him. He saw that it was a bad spirit that caused the resolution – the same that caused Moses to say, "You rebels" (Numbers 20:10). He humbled himself on the spot, and God poured out His Spirit on him.

Perhaps some of you are in a similar situation. You have said something provoking or unkind to someone. Perhaps you were irritable with an employee who was a Christian. Maybe you spoke wrongly of a minister or some other person. Perhaps you have been angry because your ideas have not been accepted or your dignity has been encroached upon. Search thoroughly, and see if you cannot find out the sin. Perhaps you have forgotten it, but God has not forgotten it, and He will not forgive your unchristian conduct until you repent. God cannot overlook it. It would do no good if He would. What good would it do to forgive you while the sin is festering in your heart?

7. Maybe you have resisted the Spirit of God. Perhaps you are in the habit of resisting the Spirit. You resist conviction. In preaching, when something has been said that reached your case, your heart has risen up against it and you have resisted. Many people are willing to hear plain and searching preaching as long as they can apply it all to others. A critical spirit makes them take satisfaction in hearing others searched and rebuked, but if the truth touches them, they immediately cry out that it is personal and offensive. Is this your case?

8. The fact is that you do not usually desire the Spirit. This is true in every case in which you do not have the Spirit. Let me not be mistaken here. I want you to carefully differentiate. Nothing is more common than for people to desire a certain thing on some accounts that they do not generally choose. A person may see an item in a store that he desires to purchase, and he goes in and asks the price, and thinks about it a little, and on the whole concludes not to purchase it. He desires the item, but does not like the price or does not want to pay that much for it, so that, upon the whole, he prefers not to purchase it. That is the reason why he does not purchase it.

In the same way, people may desire the Spirit of God on some accounts, from a regard to the comfort and joy of heart that He brings. If you know what it is by previous experience to commune with God, and how sweet it is to melt in repentance and to be filled with the Spirit, you cannot help but desire a return of those joys. You may set yourself to pray earnestly for it, and to pray for a revival of religion, but on the whole you are unwilling for it to come. You have so much to do that you cannot attend to it, or it will require so many sacrifices that you cannot bear to have it. There are some things you are not willing to give up. You find that if you want to have the Spirit of God dwell with you, you must lead a different life, you must give up the world, you must make sacrifices, you must break away from your worldly associates, and you must confess your sins. And so on the whole you do not choose to have Him come unless He will consent to dwell with you and let you live as you please; but He will never do that.

9. Perhaps you do not pray for the Spirit, or you pray and use no other means, or pray and do not act consistently with your prayers. Maybe you even use means calculated to resist them. Maybe you ask, and as soon as He comes and begins to affect your mind, you grieve Him right away and will not walk with Him.

IV. The Great Guilt of Not Having the Spirit of God

1. Your guilt is just as great as the authority of God is great, which commands you to be filled with the Spirit. God commands it, and it is just as much a disobedience of God's commands as it is to swear profanely, or steal, or commit adultery, or break the Sabbath. Think of that. Yet there are many people who do not blame themselves at all for not having the Spirit. They even think they are quite pious Christians because they go to prayer meetings, partake of the sacrament, and all that, although they live year after year without being filled with the Spirit of God.

The same God who says, "Do not get drunk" also says, "Be filled with the Spirit." You all say that if someone is a habitual murderer or thief, he is no Christian. Why? Because he lives in habitual disobedience to God. So if he swears, you have no sympathy for him. You will not allow him to plead that his heart is right and that words do not matter, that God does not care anything about words. You would think it outrageous to have such a man in church, or to have a company of such people pretend to call themselves a church of Christ. Yet they are not a bit more absolutely living in disobedience to God than you are who live without the spirit of prayer and without the presence of God.

2. Your guilt is equal to all the good you might do if you had the Spirit of God in as great a measure as it is your duty to have Him, and as

you could have Him. You elders of this church, how much good you could do if you had the Spirit. And you Sunday-school teachers, how much good you could do, and you church members, too, if you were filled with the Spirit. You could do vast good, infinite good. Well, your guilt is just as great. Here is a blessing promised, and you can have it by doing your duty. You are entirely responsible to the church and to God for all this good that you could do. A person is responsible for all the good he can do.

3. Your guilt is further measured by all the evil that you do as a result of not being filled with the Spirit. You are a dishonor to Christianity. You are a stumbling block to the church and to the world. Your guilt is enhanced by all the various influences you exert, and it will prove so in the day of judgment.

V. The Consequences of Having the Spirit

1. You will be called eccentric, and you will probably deserve it. You will probably really be eccentric. I never knew a person who was filled with the Spirit who was not called eccentric. The reason is that they are unlike other people. This is always a term of comparison. There is therefore the best of reasons why such people appear to be eccentric. They act under different influences, take different views, are moved by different motives, and are led by a different spirit. You are to expect such remarks. How often I have heard the remark respecting such and such a person: "He is a very good man, but he is rather eccentric." I have sometimes asked for the specifics. I ask in what ways he is eccentric. I hear the list, and the conclusion is that he is spiritual. Make up your mind that you will be viewed as eccentric. There is such a thing as affected eccentricity, which is horrible. But there is such a thing as being so deeply filled with the Spirit of God that you must and will act so as to appear strange and eccentric to those who cannot understand the reasons for your conduct.

2. If you have much of the Spirit of God, it is likely that you will be thought deranged by many. We judge people to be deranged when they

act differently from what we think to be prudent and according to common sense, and when they come to conclusions for which we can see no good reasons. Paul was accused of being deranged by those who did not understand the views of things under which he acted. No doubt Festus thought the man was crazy, and that much learning had made him mad. But Paul said, *I am not mad, most noble Festus* (Acts 26:25). His conduct was so strange, so different, that Festus thought it must be insanity. But the truth was that he only saw the subject so clearly that he threw his whole soul into it. They were entirely in the dark in respect to the motive by which he was driven. This is by no means uncommon. Multitudes have appeared to those who had no spirituality as if they were deranged, yet they saw good reasons for doing as they did. God was leading their minds to act in such a way that those who were not spiritual could not see the reasons. You must make up your mind to this, and so much the more, as you live more above the world and walk with God.

3. If you have the Spirit of God, you must expect to feel great distress in view of the church and the world. Some spiritual pleasure-seekers ask for the Spirit because they think it will make them so perfectly happy. Some people think that spiritual Christians are always very happy and free from sorrow.

There never was a greater mistake. Read your Bibles and see how the prophets and apostles were always groaning and distressed in view of the state of the church and the world. The apostle Paul says he was always bearing about in his body the dying of the Lord Jesus. *I protest*, he said, that *I die daily* (1 Corinthians 15:31). You will know what it is to sympathize with the Lord Jesus Christ and to be baptized with the baptism that He was baptized with. Oh, how He agonized in view of the state of sinners! How He travailed in soul for their salvation! The more you have of His Spirit, the more clearly you will see the state of sinners, and the more deeply you will be distressed about them. Many times you will feel as if you could not live in view of their situation. Your distress will be unutterable. Paul said, *I say the truth in Christ, I lie not, my conscience also bearing me witness in the Holy Ghost, that I have great heaviness and continual sorrow in my heart. For I could wish that myself were accursed from Christ for my brethren, my kinsmen according to the flesh* (Romans 9:1-3).

4. You will often be grieved with the state of the ministry. Some years earlier I met a woman belonging to one of the churches in this city. I asked her about the state of Christianity here. She seemed unwilling to say much about it. She made some general remarks, and then choked. Her eyes filled, and she said, "Oh, our minister's mind seems to be very dark."

Spiritual Christians often feel like this, and often weep over it. I have seen much of it, and often found Christians who wept and groaned in secret to see the darkness on the minds of ministers in regard to religion, their worldliness, and fear of man; but they dared not speak of it lest they would be denounced and threatened, and perhaps turned out of the church. I do not say these things censoriously to reproach my brethren, but because they are true.

Ministers should know that nothing is more common than for spiritual Christians to feel burdened and distressed at the state of the ministry. I do not want to stir up any wrong feeling toward ministers, but it is time that it should be known that Christians do often get spiritual views of things, and their souls are kindled up – and then they find that their minister does not enter into their feelings, that he is far below the standard of what he should be, and in spirituality is far below some of the members of his church.

This is one of the most prominent and deeply to be deplored evils of the present day. The piety of the ministry, although real, is so superficial in many instances that the spiritual part of the church feels that ministers cannot and do not understand them. Their preaching does not meet their needs. It does not feed them. It does not meet their experience. The minister does not have enough depth of Christian experience to know how to search and wake up the church, to help those under temptation, to support the weak, to direct the strong, and to lead them through all the labyrinths and mazes with which their path may be troubled.

When a minister has gone with a church as far as his experience in spiritual exercise goes, there he stops; and until he has a renewed experience, until he is awakened, until his heart is broken up anew and he is set forward in the divine life and Christian experience, he is unable to help them anymore. He may preach sound doctrine, and so may an unconverted minister; but, after all, his preaching will lack that searching pungency, that practical bearing, that unction that alone will reach the case of a spiritually minded Christian.

It is a fact over which the church is groaning, that the piety of young men suffers so much in the course of their education that when they enter the ministry, no matter how much intellectual knowledge they may possess, they are in a state of spiritual infancy. They need nursing and to be fed rather than to attempt to feed the church of God.

5. If you are filled with the Spirit of God, you must make up your mind that you will have much opposition, both in the church and the world. It is very likely that the leading men in the church will oppose you. There has always been opposition in the church. It was there when Christ was on earth. If you are far above their state of feeling, church members will oppose you. If any man will live godly in Christ Jesus, he must expect persecution (2 Timothy 3:12). Often the elders, and even the minister, will oppose you if you are filled with the Spirit of God.

6. You must expect very frequent and agonizing conflicts with Satan. Satan has very little trouble with those Christians who are not spiritual, but are lukewarm, slothful, and worldly minded. Such people do not understand what is said about spiritual conflicts. Perhaps they will smile when such things are mentioned, and so the devil leaves them alone. They do not disturb him, nor he them. But he understands spiritual Christians very well. They are doing him much harm, and therefore he sets himself against them. Such Christians often have terrible conflicts. They have temptations that they never thought of before, such as blasphemous thoughts, atheism, suggestions to do deeds of wickedness, to destroy their own lives, and the like. And if you are spiritual, you may expect these terrible conflicts.

7. You will have greater conflicts with yourself than you ever thought of. You will sometimes find your own corruptions making strange headway against the Spirit. *The flesh lusteth against the Spirit, and the*

Spirit against the flesh (Galatians 5:17). Such a Christian is often thrown into consternation at the power of his own corruption. I was told of a high-ranking naval officer who was a spiritual man. His pastor told me that he had known that man to lie on the floor and groan a great part of the night, in conflict with his own corruptions, and to cry to God in agony that he would break the power of the temptation. It seemed as if the devil was determined to ruin him, and his own feelings, for the time being, were almost in league with the devil.

8. You will have peace with God. If the church, and sinners, and the devil oppose you, there will be one with whom you will have peace. Let those who are called to these trials, conflicts, and temptations, and who groan, pray, weep, and break your hearts, remember this consideration: your peace, so far as your feelings toward God are concerned, will flow like a river.

9. You will likewise have peace of conscience if you are led by the Spirit. You will not be constantly aggravated and tortured by a guilty conscience. Your conscience will be calm and quiet, as unruffled as the summer's lake.

10. If you are filled with the Spirit, you will be useful. You cannot help being useful. Even if you were sick and unable to go out of your room, or to converse, and saw nobody, you would be ten times more useful than a hundred of those common type of Christians who have no spirituality. To give you an idea of this, I will relate an anecdote. A pious man in the western part of this state was sick with a consumption. He was a poor man, and was sick for years. An unconverted merchant in the place had a kind heart, and used to send him now and then something for his comfort, or for his family. The man felt grateful for the kindness, but could make no return, as he wanted to do. Eventually he determined that the best return he could make would be to pray for his salvation. He began to pray, and his soul kindled, and he got hold of God. There was no revival there, but eventually, to the astonishment of everyone, this merchant came right out on the Lord's side. The fire kindled all over the place. A powerful revival followed, and multitudes were converted.

This poor man lingered in this way for several years before he died. After his death, I visited the place, and his widow put into my hands his diary. Among other things, he said in his diary: "I am acquainted with about thirty ministers and churches." He then went on to set apart certain hours in the day and week to pray for each of these ministers and churches, and also certain seasons for praying for the different missionary stations. Then followed, under different dates, such facts as these: "Today," naming the date, "I have been enabled to offer what I call the prayer of faith for the outpouring of the Spirit on – – church, and I trust in God there will soon be a revival there." Under another date, "I have today been able to offer what I call the prayer of faith for such a church, and trust there will soon be a revival there." Thus he had gone over a great number of churches, recording the fact that he had prayed for them in faith that a revival might soon prevail among them.

Of the missionary stations, if I remember correctly, he mentions in particular the mission at Ceylon. I believe the last place mentioned in his diary for which he offered the prayer of faith was the place in which he lived. Not long after noticing these facts in his diary, the revival began, and went over the region of country nearly, I believe, if not quite, in the order in which they had been mentioned in his diary. In due time, news came from Ceylon that there was a revival of religion there. The revival in his own town did not begin until after his death. Its commencement was at the time when his widow put into my hands the document to which I have referred. She told me that he was so exercised in prayer during his sickness that she often feared he would pray himself to death.

The revival was exceedingly great and powerful in the entire region, and the fact that it was about to prevail had not been hidden from this servant of the Lord. According to His Word, *the secret of the LORD is with them that fear him* (Psalm 25:14). Thus this man, too feeble in his body to leave his house, was yet more useful to the world and the church of God than all the heartless professing Christians of the country. Standing between God and the desolations of Zion, and pouring out his heart in believing prayer, as a prince he had power with God, and he prevailed (see Genesis 32:28).

11. If you are filled with the Spirit, you will not find yourselves distressed,

irritated, and worried when people speak against you. When I find people irritated and bothered by any little thing that concerns them, I am sure they do not have the Spirit of Christ. Jesus Christ could have everything said against Him that malice could invent, yet not be in the least disturbed by it. If you want to be meek under persecution and exemplify the temper of the Savior, and honor Christianity in this way, you need to be filled with the Spirit.

12. You will be wise in using means for the conversion of sinners. If the Spirit of God is in you, He will lead you to use means wisely, in a way adapted to the purpose, and to avoid doing harm. No man who is not filled with the Spirit of God is fit to be used in directing the measures adopted in a revival. Their hands will be all thumbs, unable to take hold, and they will act as if they had no common sense. However, a man who is led by the Spirit of God will know how to time his measures properly, and how to apportion divine truth, so as to make it count to the best advantage.

13. You will be calm under affliction. You will not be thrown into confusion or fear when you see the storm coming over you. People around you will be astonished at your calmness and cheerfulness under heavy trials, not knowing the inward supports of those who are filled with the Spirit.

14. You will be reconciled in death. You will always feel prepared to die, and not afraid to die – and after death you will be proportionably happier forever in heaven.

VI. Consequences of Not Being Filled with the Spirit

1. You will often doubt, and reasonably doubt, whether you are a Christian. You will have doubts, and you should have them. The children of God are led by the Spirit of God. If you are not led by the Spirit, what reason do you have to think you are His children? You will try to make a little evidence go a great way to bolster up your hopes, but you cannot do it unless your conscience is seared as with a hot iron (1 Timothy 4:2). You

cannot help being plunged often into painful doubt and uncertainty about your condition. *But ye are not in the flesh, but in the Spirit, if so be that the Spirit of God dwell in you. Now if any man have not the Spirit of Christ, he is none of his* (Romans 8:9). *Examine yourselves, whether ye be in the faith; prove your own selves. Know ye not your own selves, how that Jesus Christ is in you, except ye be reprobates?* (2 Corinthians 13:5).

2. You will always be unsettled in your views about the prayer of faith. The prayer of faith is something so spiritual, so much a matter of experience and not of speculation, that unless you are spiritual yourselves, you will not understand it fully. You may talk a great deal about the prayer of faith, and for the time be thoroughly convinced of it, but you will never feel so settled on it as to retain the same position of mind concerning it, and in a little while you will be all uncertainty.

I knew a curious instance in a brother minister. He told me, "When I have the Spirit of God, and enjoy His presence, I believe firmly in the prayer of faith; but when I do not have Him, I find myself doubting whether there is any such thing, and my mind offers objections." From my own experience, I know what this is, and when I hear people raising objections to that view of prayer that I have presented in these lectures, I understand very well what their difficulty is, and have often found it impossible to satisfy their minds while so far from God, when at the same time they would understand it themselves, without argument, when they had experienced it.

3. If you are not filled with the Spirit, you will be very inclined to stumble at those who are. You will doubt the propriety of their conduct. If they seem to feel a good deal more than you do, you will be likely to call it earthly feeling. You will perhaps doubt their sincerity when they say they have such feelings. You will say, "I do not know what to make of brother so-and-so; he seems to be very pious, but I do not understand him. I think he has a great deal of earthly feeling." Thus you will try to censure them for the purpose of justifying yourself.

4. You will have a good reputation with the unrepentant, and with worldly professing Christians. They will praise you as a rational, orthodox,

consistent Christian. You will be in the right frame of mind to walk with them because you are agreed.

5. You will be much troubled with fears about fanaticism. Whenever there are revivals, you will see in them a strong tendency to fanaticism, and you will be full of fears and anxiety, or rather of opposition to them.

6. You will be much disturbed by the measures that are used in revivals. If any measures are adopted that are definite and direct, you will think they are all "new," and you will stumble at them just in proportion to your lack of spirituality. You do not see their appropriateness. You will stand and complain about the measures because you are so blind that you cannot see their usefulness, while all heaven is rejoicing in them as the means of saving souls.

7. You will be a reproach to Christianity. The unrepentant will sometimes praise you because you are so much like themselves, and sometimes laugh about you because you are such a hypocrite.

8. You will know only a little about the Bible.

9. If you die without the Spirit, you will fall into hell. There can be no doubt of this. Without the Spirit, you will never be prepared for heaven.

Remarks

1. Christians are as guilty for not being filled with the Spirit as sinners are for not repenting.

2. They are even more so. As they have more light, they are so much the more guilty.

3. All beings have a right to complain of Christians who are not filled with the Spirit. You are not doing work for God, and He has a right to complain. He has placed His Spirit at your disposal, and if you are not filled with Him, He has a right to look to you and to hold you responsible

for all the good you might do if you were filled with Him. You are sinning against all heaven, for you should be adding to their happy ranks. Sinners, the church, and ministers have a right to complain.

4. You are standing in the way of the work of the Lord. It is in vain for a minister to try to work over your head. Ministers often groan and struggle and wear themselves out in vain, trying to do good where there are members who live without the Spirit of God. If the Spirit is poured out at any time, the church will grieve Him right away. Thus you may tie the hands and break the heart of your minister, and break him down and perhaps kill him, because you will not be filled with the Spirit.

5. You see the reason why Christians need the fulness of the Spirit, and the degree of their dependence. This cannot be too strongly demonstrated.

6. Do not tempt God by waiting for His Spirit while using no means to obtain His presence.

7. If you desire to be filled with the Spirit, you must be childlike and yield to His influences – just as yielding as air. If He is drawing you to prayer, you must leave everything else and yield to His gentle strivings. No doubt you have sometimes felt a desire to pray for something, and you have put it off and resisted, and God left you. If you want Him to remain, you must yield to His softest and gentlest motions, watch to learn what He would have you do, and yield yourself to His guidance.

8. Christians should be willing to make any sacrifice to enjoy the presence of the Spirit. A woman in high life, a professing Christian, said, "I must either give up hearing this minister preach, or I must give up my lighthearted friends." She gave up the preaching and stayed away. How different from another case!

A woman in the same position of life heard the same minister preach, and she went home resolved to abandon her carefree and worldly manner of life. She dismissed most of her attendants, and she changed her whole manner of clothing, of luxury, of living, and of conversation so that her frivolous and worldly friends were soon willing to leave her to the enjoyment of communion with God, and left her free to spend her time in doing good.

9. You see from this that it must be very difficult for those in fashionable life to go to heaven. What a calamity to be in such circles! Who can enjoy the presence of God in them?

10. See how crazy they are who are scrambling to get up to these circles, enlarging their houses, changing their style of living, possessions, etc. It is like climbing up a masthead to be thrown off into the ocean. To enjoy God, you must come down, not go up there. God is not there among all the formality and flattery of high society.

11. Many professing Christians are as ignorant of true spirituality as Nicodemus was of the new birth (John 3). They are ignorant, and I fear unconverted. If anyone talks to them about the spirit of prayer, they do not understand. The case of such professing Christians is dreadful. How different was the character of the apostles! Read the history of their lives and read their letters, and you will see that they were always spiritual and walked daily with God.

But now how little there is of such religion! *When the Son of Man cometh, shall he find faith on the earth?* (Luke 18:8). Set some of these professing Christians to work in a revival, and they do not know what to do. They have no energy, no skill, and make no impression. When will professing Christians set themselves to work, filled with the Spirit? If I could see this church filled with the Spirit, I would ask nothing more to move this whole mighty mass of minds. Not two weeks would pass before the revival would spread all over this city.

Lecture 8

Meetings for Prayer

Again I say unto you, That if two of you shall agree on earth as touching any thing that they shall ask, it shall be done for them of my Father which is in heaven.
—Matthew 18:19

Previously, in dealing with the subject of prayer, I have confined my remarks to secret prayer. I am now to speak about social prayer, or prayer offered in company, where two or more are united in praying. Such meetings have been common from the time of Christ, and even hundreds of years before. It is probable that God's people have always been in the habit of making united supplication whenever they had the privilege. The method of the practice will not be questioned here. I do not need to dwell now on the duty of social prayer, nor is it my plan to discuss the question whether any two Christians agreeing to ask any blessing will be sure to obtain it. My purpose is to make some remarks on meetings for prayer:

I.   The purpose of prayer meetings.

II. The manner of conducting them.

III. Several things that will defeat the design of holding them.

I. The Purpose of Prayer Meetings

1. One purpose of assembling several people together for united prayer is to promote union among Christians. Nothing tends to cement the hearts of Christians more than praying together. Never do they love one another so well as when they witness the outpouring of each other's hearts in prayer. Their spirituality produces a feeling of union and confidence, highly important to the prosperity of the church. It is doubtful whether Christians can ever be otherwise than united if they are in the habit of really praying together. Where they have had hard feelings and differences among themselves, those feelings and differences are all done away by uniting in prayer. The great object is gained if you can bring them to really unite in prayer. If this can be done, the difficulties vanish.

2. A second purpose of social prayer is to extend the spirit of prayer. God has so formed us, and such is the wisdom of His grace, that we are sympathetic beings, and we communicate our feelings to each other. A minister, for example, will often, as it were, breathe his own feelings into his congregation. The Spirit of God who inspires his soul makes use of his feelings to influence his hearers, just as much as he makes use of the words he preaches. In the same way, He makes use of the feelings of Christians. Nothing is more calculated to produce a spirit of prayer than to unite in social prayer with one who has the spirit of prayer himself, unless this person is so far ahead that his prayer will repel the rest. His prayer will awaken them if they are not so far behind as to revolt at it and resist it. If they are anywhere near the standard of his feelings, his spirit will kindle, burn, and spread all around. One individual in a church who obtains a spirit of prayer will often awaken a whole church and extend the same spirit through the whole, and a general revival follows.

3. Another good purpose of social prayer is to move God. Not that it changes the mind and feelings of God, for when we speak of moving God, as I have said in a former lecture, we do not mean that it alters the will of God. But when the right kind of prayer is offered by Christians, they are in

such a state of mind that it becomes proper for God to bestow a blessing. They are then prepared to receive it, and He gives because He is always the same and is always ready and happy to show mercy. When Christians are united and are praying as they should, God opens the windows of heaven and pours out His blessings until there is not room to receive them.

4. Another important purpose of prayer meetings is the conviction and conversion of sinners. When properly conducted, they are particularly calculated to produce this effect. Sinners tend to be solemn when they hear Christians pray. Where there is a spirit of prayer, sinners must feel. An ungodly man, a Universalist, once said about a certain minister, "I can bear his preaching very well, but when he prays, I feel awful; I feel as if God were coming down upon me."

Sinners are often convicted by hearing prayer. A young man of distinguished talents, known to many, said concerning a certain minister whom he had been very much opposed to before his conversion, "As soon as he began to pray, I began to be convicted, and if he had continued to pray much longer, I would not have been able to contain myself." Just as soon as Christians begin to pray as they should, sinners then know that they pray, and they feel awful. They do not understand what spirituality is because they have no experience of it. But when such prayer is offered, they know there is something in it. They know God is in it, and it brings them near to God. It makes them feel exceedingly solemn, and they cannot bear it. Not only is it calculated to impress the minds of sinners, but when Christians pray in faith, the Spirit of God is poured out, and sinners are melted down and converted on the spot.

II. The Manner of Conducting Prayer Meetings

1. It is often good to open a prayer meeting by reading a short portion of the Word of God, especially if the person who takes the lead of the meeting can call to mind any portion that will be applicable to the object or occasion, and that is impactful and to the point. If he has no passage that is applicable, he had better not read any at all. Do not drag in the Word of God to make up part of the meeting as a mere matter of form. This is an insult to God. It is not good to read any more than is

applicable to the subject before the meeting or occasion. Some people think it is always necessary to read an entire chapter, no matter how long it is, and have a variety of subjects. It is just as impressive and judicious to read a whole chapter as it would be for a minister to take a whole chapter for his text when his object was to make some specific truth bear on the minds of his audience. The design of a prayer meeting should be to bring Christians to the point to pray for a definite object. Wandering over a large field hinders and destroys this design.

2. It is proper that the person who leads should make some short and appropriate remarks that are calculated to explain the nature of prayer and the encouragements we have to pray, and to bring the object to be prayed for directly before the minds of the people.

A person can no more pray without having his thoughts concentrated than he can do anything else. The person leading should therefore see to this by bringing up before their minds the object they came to pray for. If they came to pray for any object, he can do this. And if they did not, they had better go home. It is of no use to stay there and mock God by pretending to pray when they have nothing on earth to pray for.

After stating the object, he should bring up some promise or principle as the ground of encouragement to expect an answer to their prayers. If there is any indication of providence, or any promise, or any principle in the divine government that provides a ground of faith, let him call it to mind, and not let them talk out of their own hearts at random without knowing any solid reason to expect an answer.

One reason why prayer meetings generally accomplish so little is because there is so little common sense exercised about them. Instead of looking around for some solid footing on which to rest their faith, they just come together and pour forth their words, and neither know nor care whether they have any reason to expect an answer. If they are going to pray about anything concerning which there can be any doubt or any mistake in regard to the ground of faith, they should be shown the reason there is for believing that their prayers will be heard and answered. It is easy to see that unless something like this is done, three-fourths of them will have no idea of what they are doing, or of the ground on which they should expect to receive what they pray for.

3. In calling on people to pray, it is always desirable to let things take their own course wherever it is safe. If it can be left so with safety, let those pray who are most inclined to pray. It sometimes happens that even those who are ordinarily the most spiritual, and most proper to be called on, are not at the time in a proper frame of mind to pray. They may be cold and worldly, and only freeze the meeting. However, if you let those pray who desire to pray, you avoid this. But often this cannot be done with safety, especially in large cities, where a prayer meeting might be liable to be interrupted by those who have no business to pray, such as some fanatic or crazy person, some hypocrite or enemy, who would only make a noise. In most places, however, this course may be taken with perfect safety.

Give up the meeting to the Spirit of God. Those who desire to pray, let them pray. If the leader sees anything that needs to be set right, let him remark, freely and kindly, and put it right, and then go on again. Only he should be careful to time his remarks so as not to interrupt the flow of feeling, to chill the meeting, or to turn off the minds from the proper subject.

4. If it is necessary to name the individuals who are to pray, it is best to call on those who are most spiritual first. If you do not know who they are, then call on those whom you would naturally suppose to be most alive. If they pray at the beginning, they will be likely to spread the spirit of prayer through the meeting and elevate the tone of the whole. Otherwise, if you call on those who are cold and lifeless at the beginning, they will be likely to diffuse a chill throughout the meeting. The only hope of having an efficient prayer meeting is when at least a part of the church is spiritual, and they infuse their spirit into the rest. This is the very reason why it is often best to let things take their course, for then those who have the most feeling are inclined to pray first and give character to the meeting.

5. The prayers in a public meeting should always be very short. When individuals allow themselves to pray long, they forget where they are, that they are only the mouth of the congregation, and that the congregation cannot be expected to sympathize with them so as to go along

and feel united in prayer if they are long and tedious and go all around the world and pray for everything they can think of. Commonly, those who pray long in a meeting do not do so because they have the spirit of prayer, but because they do not have it. They go around and around because they are not full of prayer. Some people will spin out a long prayer in telling God who and what He is, or they exhort God to do so and so. Some pray out a whole system of theology. Some preach and some exhort the people until everybody wishes they would stop – and God wishes so too, undoubtedly. They should keep to the point and pray for what they came to pray for, and not follow the imagination of their own foolish hearts all over the universe.

6. Each person should pray for some specific object. It is good for every individual to have one object for prayer; two or more people may pray for the same thing, or each for a separate object. If the meeting is convened to pray for some specific thing, let them all pray for that. If its object is more general, let them select their subjects according as they feel interested in them. If one person feels particularly inclined to pray for the church, let him do it. If the next feels inclined to pray for the church, he may do so too. Perhaps the next will feel inclined to pray for sinners, for the youth, or to confess sin. Let him do so, and as soon as he has done so, let him stop. Whenever a person has deep feeling, it is always on some particular point, and if he prays for that, he will speak out of the abundance of his heart, and then he will naturally stop when he is done. Those who feel most will be most ready to confine their prayers to that point, and then stop when they are done and not pray all over the world.

7. If in the progress of the meeting it becomes necessary to change the object of prayer, let the man who leads state that fact and explain it in a few words. If the object is to pray for the church, for backsliders, for sinners, or for the heathen, let him state it plainly, and then turn it over and hold it up before them until he brings them to think and feel deeply before they pray. Then state to them the basis on which they may rest their faith in regard to obtaining the blessings they pray for, if any such statement is needed, and so lead them right up to the throne and let

them take hold of the hand of God. This is according to the philosophy of the mind. People always do it for themselves when they pray in secret, if they really mean to pray to any purpose, and it should be the same in prayer meetings.

8. It is important that the time should be fully occupied so as not to leave long periods of silence. This always makes a bad impression and chills the meeting. I know that sometimes churches have seasons of silent prayer, but in those cases they should be specifically requested to pray in silence so that all may know why they are silent. This often has a most powerful effect, when a few moments are spent by a whole congregation in silence while all lift up their thoughts to God. This is very different from having long intervals of silence because there is nobody to pray, for everyone feels that such a silence is like the cold damp of death over the meeting.

9. It is exceedingly important that he who leads the meeting should urge sinners who may be present to immediate repentance. He should press this firmly, and should urge the Christians present to pray in such a way as to make sinners feel that they are expected to repent immediately. This tends to inspire Christians with compassion and love for souls. The remarks made to sinners are often like pouring fire upon the hearts of Christians so as to awaken them to prayer and effort for their conversion. Let them see and feel the guilt and danger of sinners right among them, and then they will pray.

III. Several Things That May Defeat the Purpose of a Prayer Meeting

1. When there is an unhappy lack of confidence in the leader, there is no hope of any good. Whatever the cause may be, whether he is to blame or not, the very fact that he leads the meeting will cast a cloud over it and prevent all good. I have witnessed it in churches, where there was some offensive elder or deacon, perhaps justly offensive, and perhaps not, set to lead the prayer meeting, and the meeting would die under his influence. If there is a lack of confidence in regard to his piety, his ability, his judgment, or in anything connected with the meeting, everything

he says or does will fall to the ground. The same thing often takes place when the church members have lost their confidence in the minister.

2. Where the leader lacks spirituality, there will be a dryness and coldness in his remarks and prayers, and everything will indicate his lack of unction; his whole influence will be the very reverse of what it should be. I have known churches where a prayer meeting could not be sustained, and the reason was not obvious; but those who understood the state of things knew that the leader was so notorious for his lack of spirituality that he would inevitably freeze a prayer meeting to death. In many Presbyterian churches, the elders are so far from being spiritual men that they always freeze a prayer meeting, and then they are often amazingly jealous for their dignity and cannot bear to have anyone else lead the meeting. If any member who is spiritual takes the lead of a prayer meeting, they will take him to task for it: "You are not an elder, and should not lead a prayer meeting in the presence of an elder." Thus, they stand in the way while the whole church is suffering under their harmful influence.

A man who knows he is not in a spiritual frame of mind has no business conducting a prayer meeting; he will kill it. There are two reasons: First, he will have no spiritual discernment, and will not know what to do or when to do it. A person who is spiritual can see the movements of God and can feel the Spirit of God. He can understand what He is leading them to pray for so as to time his subjects and take advantage of the state of feeling among Christians. He will not overthrow all the feeling in a meeting by introducing other things that are unsuitable or poorly timed. He has spiritual discernment to understand the leading of the Spirit and His working in those who pray, and to follow on as the Spirit leads.

Suppose an individual leads who is not spiritual, and there are two or three prayers, and the spirit of prayer rises, but the leader has no spiritual discernment to see it. He makes some remarks on another point, or reads a piece out of some book that is as far from the feeling of the meeting as the North Pole. It may be just as evident to others what they are called to pray for as if the Son of God Himself had come into the meeting and named the subject, but the leader will overthrow it all because he is so unaware that he does not know the indications of the meeting.

If the leader is not spiritual, he will very likely be dull and dry in his remarks and in all that he does there. He will read a long hymn in an inattentive manner, and then read a long passage of Scripture in a tone so cold and wintry that he will spread a wintry cover over the meeting, and it will be dull as long as his cold heart is placed up in front of the whole thing.

3. A lack of suitable talents in the leader is harmful to a prayer meeting. If he is lacking in those kinds of talents that are appropriate to make a meeting useful, he will harm the meeting. If he can say nothing, or if his remarks are so out of the way as to produce levity or contempt, or if they have nothing in them that will make an impression upon the mind, or are not guided by good sense, or are not appropriate, he will harm the meeting. A man may be pious, but so weak that his prayers do not edify, but rather disgust the people present. When this is so, he had better keep silent.

4. Sometimes the benefit of a prayer meeting is defeated by a bad spirit in the leader. For instance, when there is a revival and great opposition, if a leader gets up in a prayer meeting and speaks of instances of opposition, and comments upon them, and thus diverts the meeting away from the object they came to pray for, he knows not what spirit he is of (Luke 9:55). Its effect is always harmful to a prayer meeting. Let a minister in a revival come out and preach against the opposition, and he will invariably destroy the revival and turn the hearts of Christians away from their proper object. Let the man who is set to lead the church be careful to guard his own spirit lest he should mislead the church and set the wrong tone. The same will be true if anyone who is called upon to speak or pray introduces in his remarks or prayers anything controversial, disrespectful, unreasonable, unscriptural, ridiculous, or irrelevant. Any of these things will quench the tender breathings of the spirit of prayer and destroy the meeting.

5. People coming late to the meeting will cause harm to the prayer

meeting. This is a very great hindrance to a prayer meeting. When people have begun to pray, and their attention is fixed, and they have shut their eyes and closed their ears to keep out everything else from their minds, in the midst of a prayer somebody will come rushing in and walk up through the room. Some people will look up, and all will have their minds interrupted for the moment. Then they all get fixed again, and another comes in, and so on. I suppose the devil would not care how many Christians went to a prayer meeting if they will only go after the meeting has begun. He would be glad to have ever so many go scattering along so, and entering in very piously after the meeting has begun.

6. When people make cold prayers and cold confessions of sin, they are sure to quench the spirit of prayer. When the influences of the Spirit are enjoyed in the midst of the warm expressions that are flowing forth, and an individual comes in who is cold, and pours his cold breath out like the damp of death, it will make every Christian who has any feeling want to get out of the meeting.

7. In some places it is common to begin a prayer meeting by reading a long portion of Scripture. Then the deacon or elder gives out a long hymn. Next, they sing it. Then he prays a long prayer, praying for the Jews and the fullness of the Gentiles, and many other objects that have nothing to do with the occasion of the meeting. After that he might read a long extract from some book or magazine. Then they have another long hymn and another long prayer, and then they go home. I once heard an elder say that they had kept up a prayer meeting for many years, yet there had been no revival in the place. The truth was that the officers of the church had been accustomed to carry on the meetings in just such a dignified way, and their dignity would not allow anything to be altered. No wonder there was no revival. Such prayer meetings are enough to hinder a revival. And if ever so many revivals would begin, the prayer meeting would destroy them.

There was a prayer meeting once in this city, as I have been told, where there appeared to be some feeling, and someone proposed that they should have two or three prayers in succession, without rising from their knees. One dignified man present opposed it and said that they had never done so, and he hoped there would be no innovations. He did not approve of innovations. That was the last of the revival. Such people have their prayer meetings stereotyped, and they are determined not to turn out of their track whether they have the blessing or not. To allow any such thing would be a new measure, and they never like new measures.

8. A great deal of singing often harms a prayer meeting. The agonizing spirit of prayer does not lead people to sing. There is a time for everything. There is a time to sing and a time to pray. But if I know what it is to travail in birth for souls, Christians never feel less like singing than when they have the spirit of prayer for sinners. Singing is the natural expression of feelings that are joyful and cheerful. The spirit of prayer is not a spirit of joy. It is a spirit of travail, of agony of soul, of supplicating and pleading with God with strong cryings and with groanings that cannot be uttered (Romans 8:26). This is more like anything else than it is like singing.

I have known states of feeling where you could not distress the people of God more than to begin to sing. It would be so entirely different from their feelings. If you knew that your house was on fire, would you first stop and sing a hymn before you put it out? How would it look here in New York, if a building was on fire and the firemen were all gathered together, for the fire chief to stop and sing a hymn? It is just about as natural for the people to sing when exercised with a spirit of prayer. When firemen feel like pulling people out of the fire, they do not feel like singing.

I never knew a singing revival to amount to much. Its tendency is to do away with all deep feeling. It is true that singing a hymn has sometimes produced a powerful effect upon sinners who are convicted, but in general it is the perfect contrast between their feelings and those of the happy souls who sing that produces the effect. If the hymn is of a joyful character, it is not directly calculated to benefit sinners, and is highly suitable to relieve the mental anguish of the Christian so as to destroy that travail of soul that is indispensable to his prevailing in prayer.

When singing is introduced in a prayer meeting, the hymns should be short, and so selected as to bring out something solemn – some clear words, such as the Judgment Hymn, and others calculated to produce an effect on sinners, or something that will produce a deep impression on the minds of Christians; but not that joyful kind of singing that makes everybody feel comfortable and takes the mind away from the object of the prayer meeting.

I once heard a celebrated organist produce a remarkable effect in a long meeting. The organ was a powerful one, and the double bass pipes were like thunder. The hymn was given out that has these lines:

> See the storm of vengeance gathering
>   O'er the path you dare to tread;
> Hear the awful thunder rolling,
>   Loud and louder o'er your head.[1]

When he came to these words, we first heard the distant roar of thunder; then it grew nearer and louder, until at the word "louder," there was a crash that seemed almost to overpower the whole congregation. Such things in their proper place do good, but common singing dissipates feeling. It should always be such as not to take away feeling, but to deepen it.

Often a prayer meeting is harmed by calling on the young converts to sing joyful hymns. This is highly improper in a prayer meeting. It is no time for them to let feeling flow away in joyful singing while so many sinners around them, and their own former companions, are going down to hell. A revival is often put down by the church and minister all giving themselves up to singing with young converts. Thus by stopping to rejoice, when they should feel more and more deeply for sinners, they grieve away the Spirit of God, and they soon find that their agony and travail of soul are all gone.

9. Introducing subjects of controversy into prayer will defeat a prayer meeting. Nothing of a controversial nature should be introduced into prayer unless it is the object of the meeting to settle that thing.

---

1   This is from the hymn entitled "The Voice of Mercy" that begins with "Listen, sinner! Mercy hails you," written by Andrew Reed (1782-1862).

Otherwise, let Christians come together in their prayer meetings on the broad ground of offering united prayer for a common object, and let controversies be settled somewhere else.

10. Great effort should be taken, both by the leader and others, to closely watch the motions of the Spirit of God. Let them not pray without the Spirit, but follow His leadings. Be sure not to quench the Spirit for the sake of praying according to the regular custom. Avoid everything calculated to divert attention away from the object. All pretense of feeling that is not real should be especially guarded against. If there is a pretense of feeling, others usually see and feel that it is artificial and not reality. At any rate, the Spirit of God knows it, and will be grieved and will leave the place. On the other hand, all resistance to the Spirit will equally destroy the meeting. It frequently happens that there are some so cold that if anyone should break out in the spirit of prayer, they would call it fanaticism, and perhaps break out in opposition.

11. If individuals refuse to pray when they are called on, it harms a prayer meeting. There are some people who always pretend they have no gifts. Women sometimes refuse to take their turn in prayer and pretend they have no ability to pray. But if anyone else should say so, they would be offended. Suppose they would know that any other person had made such a remark as this: "Do not ask her to pray; she cannot pray; she does not have enough talent"; would they like it? It is the same with a man who pretends he has no gifts; let anyone else report that he does not have enough talent to make a decent prayer, and see if he will like it. The pretense is not sincere; it is all a sham.

Some say they cannot pray in their families, that they have no gift. But a person could not offend them more than to say they cannot pray a decent prayer before their own families. They would say, "The man talks as if he thought nobody else had any gifts but himself." People are not inclined to have such a low opinion of themselves. I have often seen the curse of God follow such professing Christians. They have no excuse. God will take none. The man has got a tongue to talk to his neighbors, and he can talk to God if he has any heart for it. You will see their children unconverted, their son a curse, their daughter – tongue cannot tell. God says He will pour out His fury on the families that do not call on His name (Jeremiah 10:25). If I had time, I could mention a host of facts to show that God marks those individuals with His disapproval and curse who refuse to pray when they should. Until professing Christians will repent of this sin and take up the cross (if they choose to call praying a cross!) and do their duty, they do not need to expect a blessing.

12. Prayer meetings are often too long. They should always be dismissed while Christians have feeling, and not be dragged out until all feeling is exhausted and the Spirit is gone.

13. Heartless confessions harm prayer meetings. People confess their sins and do not forsake them. Every week they make the same confession over again. A long, cold, dull, mindless confession this week, and then the next week another just like it, without forsaking any sins. They have no intention of forsaking their sins! It shows plainly that they do not intend to reform. All their religion consists in these confessions. Instead of getting a blessing from God by such confessions, they will only get a curse.

14. Prayer meetings are harmed when Christians spend all the time in praying for themselves. They should have done this in private. When they come to a prayer meeting, they should be prepared to offer effectual intercession for others. If Christians pray in private as they should, they will feel like praying for sinners. If they pray exclusively in private for themselves, they will not get the spirit of prayer. I have known men who close themselves up for days to pray for themselves, and never get any life because their prayers are all selfish. If they will just forget themselves and throw their hearts abroad and pray for others, it will wake up such a feeling that they can pour forth their hearts. Then they can go to work for souls.

I knew an individual in a revival who closed himself up for seventeen days and prayed as if he wanted God to come to his terms, but it would not do. Then he went out to work, and immediately he had the Spirit of God in his soul. It is good for Christians to pray for themselves and confess their sins, and then throw their hearts abroad until they feel as they should.

15. Prayer meetings are often defeated by the lack of appropriate remarks. The things are not said that are calculated to lead the people to pray. Perhaps the leader has not prepared himself. Maybe he does not have the needed ability to lead the church out in prayer, or he does not lead their minds to dwell on the appropriate topics of prayer.

16. Prayer meetings are hindered when individuals who are quite offensive for any cause are bold in speaking and praying. Such people are sometimes very much set upon taking a part in the meeting. They say it is their duty to get up and testify for God on all occasions. They will say that they know they are not able to edify the church, but that nobody else can do their duty, and they wish to testify. Perhaps the only place they ever testified for God was in a prayer meeting, while their entire life outside of the meeting testifies against God. They had better keep still.

17. It can harm a prayer meeting when people take a leading part who are so coarse and rude in their words that it is impossible for people of tact not to be disgusted. People of intelligence cannot follow them, and their minds are unavoidably diverted. I do not mean that it is necessary for a person to have an advanced education in order to lead in prayer. All people of common education, especially if they are in the habit of praying, can lead in prayer if they have the spirit of prayer. But there are some people who use such absurd and coarse expressions that cannot but disgust every intelligent mind. They cannot help being disgusted. The feeling of disgust is an involuntary thing, and when a disgusting object is before the mind, the feeling is irresistible. Piety will not keep a person from feeling it. The only way is to take away the object. If such people intend to do good, they had better remain silent. Some of them may feel grieved at not being called to take a part, but it is better that they should be kindly told the reason than to have the prayer meeting regularly harmed and rendered ridiculous by their performances.

18. A lack of union in prayer can harm a prayer meeting. When one leads and the others do not follow, but are thinking of something else, their hearts do not unite. They do not say amen, or so be it, in agreement. It is as bad as if someone would make a petition and another

person would oppose it. One person asks God to do something, and the others ask Him not to do it, or to do something else.

19. Neglect of secret prayer can harm public prayer. Christians who do not pray in secret cannot unite with power in a prayer meeting, and cannot have the spirit of prayer.

Remarks

1. A poorly conducted prayer meeting often does more harm than good. In many churches, the general manner of conducting prayer meetings is such that Christians do not have the least idea of the purpose or power of such meetings. These meetings tend to keep down rather than to promote pious feeling and the spirit of prayer.

2. A prayer meeting is an indication of the state of Christianity in a church. If the church neglects the prayer meeting or does not have the spirit of prayer, you know that manner of religion is low. Let me go into the prayer meeting, and I can always see the state of Christianity there.

3. Every minister should know that if the prayer meetings are neglected, all his labors are in vain. Unless he can get Christians to attend the prayer meetings, all he can do will not cultivate the true religion.

4. A great responsibility rests on him who leads a prayer meeting. If the prayer meeting is not what it should be, if it does not elevate the state of Christianity, he should go seriously to work and see what the matter is, get the spirit of prayer, and prepare himself to make such remarks that are calculated to do good and set things right. A leader has no business to lead prayer meetings if he is not prepared, both in head and heart, to do this. I want you who lead the district prayer meetings of this church to notice this point.

5. Prayer meetings are the most difficult meetings to sustain as they should be. They are so spiritual that unless the leader is especially prepared, both in heart and mind, they will dwindle. It is in vain for the

leader to complain that members of the church do not attend. In nine cases out of ten, it is the leader's fault that they do not attend. If he felt as he should, they would find the meetings so interesting that they would attend regularly. If he is so cold and dull and without spirituality as to freeze everything, it is no wonder that people do not come to the meeting. Church officers often complain and scold people because they do not come to the prayer meeting, when the truth is that they themselves are so cold that they freeze everybody to death who comes.

6. Prayer meetings are the most important meetings for the church. It is highly important for Christians to sustain the prayer meetings for the following reasons:

- To promote unity.

- To increase brotherly love.

- To cultivate Christian confidence.

- To promote their own growth in grace.

- To cherish and advance spirituality.

7. Prayer meetings should be so numerous in the church, and be so arranged, as to exercise the gifts of every individual member of the church, both male and female. Everyone should have the opportunity to pray and to express the feelings of his heart, if he has any. The sectional prayer meetings of this church are designed to do this. If they are too large for this, let them be divided so as to bring the entire flock into the work, to exercise all gifts, and to spread unity, confidence, and brotherly love throughout the entire congregation.

8. It is important for unrepentant sinners to always attend prayer meetings. If none come of their own accord, go out and invite them. Christians should take great effort to persuade their unrepentant friends and neighbors to come to prayer meetings. They can pray better for unrepentant sinners when they have them right before their eyes. I have known female prayer meetings to exclude sinners from the meeting. The reason was that they were so proud that they were ashamed to

pray before sinners. What a spirit! Such prayers will do no good. They insult God. You have not done enough, by any means, when you have gone to the prayer meeting yourself. You cannot pray if you have not invited any sinner to go. If everyone in the church has neglected their duty, and has gone to the prayer meeting without having taken any sinners along with them, no subjects of prayer – what have they come for?

9. The great object of all the means of grace is to aim directly at the conversion of sinners. You should pray that they may be converted there. Do not just pray that they may be awakened and convicted, but pray that they may be converted on the spot. No one should either pray or make any remarks as if he expected a single sinner to go away without giving his heart to God. You should all make the impression on his mind that he must submit now. If you do this, while you are yet speaking, God will hear (Isaiah 65:24).

If Christians make it clear that they have really set their hearts on the conversions of sinners, and are intent upon it, and pray as they should, there would rarely be a prayer meeting held without souls being converted, and sometimes every sinner in the room. That is the very time, if ever, when sinners should be converted in answer to those prayers. I do not doubt but that you may have sinners converted in every local prayer meeting if you do your duty. Take them there, take your families, your friends, or your neighbors there with that intent, give them the proper instruction if they need instruction, pray for them as you should, and you will save their souls. Rely upon it, if you do your duty in a right manner, that God will not keep back His blessing, and the work will be done.

Lecture 9

Means to Be Used with Sinners

Ye are my witnesses, saith the LORD, *and*
my servant whom I have chosen.
—Isaiah 43:10

In the text it is affirmed of the children of God that they are His witnesses. In several previous lectures I have been dwelling on the subject of prayer, or that type of means for the promotion of a revival that is intended to move God to pour out His Spirit. I am now to begin discussing the other type: means to be used for the conviction and conversion of sinners.

It is true, in general, that people are affected by the subject of Christianity in proportion to their conviction of its truth. Inattention to true religion is the great reason why so little is felt concerning it. No one can look at the great truths of Christianity, as truths, and not feel deeply concerning them. The devil cannot, for he believes and trembles (James 2:19). Angels in heaven feel in view of these things. God feels. An intellectual conviction of truth is always accompanied with feeling of some kind.

One main purpose why God leaves Christians in the world after their conversion is so they may be witnesses for God. It is so they may call the attention of the thoughtless multitude to the subject and make them see the difference in the character and destiny of those who believe the gospel and those who reject the gospel. This inattention is the great difficulty in the way of promoting true religion. What the Spirit of God does is to awaken the attention of people to the subject of their sin and the way of salvation.

Miracles have sometimes been used to grab the attention of sinners. In this way, miracles may become instrumental in conversion, although conversion is not itself a miracle, nor do miracles themselves ever convert anybody. They may be the means of awakening, but they are not always effectual even in that. If continued or made common, they would soon lose their power. What is needed in the world is something that can be a sort of omnipresent miracle, able not only to grab attention, but also to focus it and keep the mind in warm contact with the truth until it yields.

Therefore we see why God has scattered His children everywhere, in families and among the nations. He never would allow them to be all together in one place, no matter how agreeable it might be to their feelings. He wants them scattered. When the church at Jerusalem herded together, neglecting to go forth as Christ had commanded, to spread the gospel all over the world, God let loose a persecution upon them and scattered them abroad, and then they *went every where preaching the word* (Acts 8:4). In examining the text, I propose to inquire:

I.   To what particular points Christians are to testify for God.

II. The manner in which they are to testify.

I. To What Points Are the Children of God Required to Testify?

Generally, they are to testify to the truth of the Bible. They are competent witnesses to this, for they have experience of its truth. The Christian who has experienced the truth of Christianity has no more need of external evidence to prove the truth of the Bible to his mind than he has to prove his own existence. The whole plan of salvation is so fully spread out and settled in his conviction that to attempt to reason him out of his belief in the Bible would be as impractical as to try to reason him out of the belief in his own existence.

People have tried to awaken a doubt of the existence of the material world, but they cannot succeed. No one can doubt the existence of a material world. To doubt it goes against his own consciousness. You may use arguments that he cannot answer, and you may puzzle and perplex him and close his mouth. He may be no logician or philosopher, and may be unable to detect your fallacies, but what he knows he knows.

It is the same in Christianity. The Christian is aware that the Bible is true. The simplest child in the Christian religion knows by his experience the truth of the Bible. He may hear objections from unbelievers that he never thought of and that he cannot answer, and he may be confounded – but he cannot be driven from his ground. He will say, "I cannot answer you, but I know the Bible is true."

It is as if a man would look in a mirror and say, "That's my face." How do you know it is your face? "Why, by its looks." In the same way, when a Christian sees himself drawn and pictured forth in the Bible, he sees the likeness to be so exact that he knows it is true. But more particularly, Christians are to testify to the following:

1. To the immortality of the soul. This is clearly revealed in the Bible.

2. To the vanity and unsatisfying nature of all earthly good.

3. To the satisfying nature and glorious sufficiency of the Christian religion.

4. To the guilt and danger of sinners. On this point they can speak from experience as well as from the Word of God. They have seen their own sins, and they understand more of the nature of sin and the guilt and danger of sinners.

5. To the reality of hell, as a place of eternal punishment for the wicked.

6. To the love of Christ for sinners.

7. To the necessity of a holy life, if we think of ever getting to heaven.

8. To the necessity of self-denial and living above the world.

9. To the necessity of meekness, heavenly mindedness, humility, and integrity.

10. To the necessity of an entire renovation of character and life for all who would enter heaven.

These are the subjects on which they are to be witnesses for God, and they are obligated to testify in such a way as to persuade others to believe the truth.

II. How Are They to Testify?

They are to testify by precept and example, on every proper occasion, by their lips – but mainly by their lives. Christians have no right to be silent with their lips. They should rebuke, exhort, and entreat with all long-suffering and doctrine. But their main influence as witnesses is by their example.

They are required to be witnesses in this way because example teaches with so much greater force than directives. This is universally known. Actions speak louder than words. But where both precept and example are brought to bear, it brings the greatest amount of influence to bear upon the mind. As to the manner in which they are to testify and the way in which they should bear witness to the truth of the points specified, in general, they should live in their daily walk and conversation as if they believed the Bible.

1. They are to testify as if they believed the soul to be immortal, and as if they believed that death was not the end of their existence, but the entrance into an unchanging state. They should live so as to make this impression strong upon all around them. It is easy to see that precept without example on this point will do no good. All the arguments in the world will not convince mankind that you really believe this unless you live as if you believe it. Your reasoning may be unanswerable, but if you do not live accordingly, your practice will defeat your arguments. They will say you are a clever disputer or a discerning reasoner, and perhaps admit that they cannot answer you; but then they will say that it is evident that your reasoning is all false and that you know it is false

because your life contradicts your theory – or that, if it is true, you do not believe it. So all the influence of your testimony goes to the other side.

2. They are to testify in regard to the vanity and unsatisfying nature of the things of this world. You are to testify this by your life. The failure in this is the great stumbling block in the way of mankind. Here the testimony of God's children is needed more than anywhere else. People are so struck with the physical objects of this world, and so constantly occupied with them, that they are very inclined to shut out eternity from their minds. A small object that is held close to the eye may shut out the distant ocean. In the same way, the things of the world that are near are so magnified in their minds that they overlook everything else. One important purpose in keeping Christians in the world is to teach people on this point, practically, not to labor for the meat that perishes (John 6:27).

But suppose professing Christians teach the vanity of earthly things by their words, but contradict it in practice. Suppose the women are just as fond of the clothing of the world, and just as particular in observing all the fashions, and the men as eager to have fine houses and cars, as the people of the world. Who does not see that it would be quite ridiculous for them to testify with their lips that this world is all vanity and its joys unsatisfying and empty?

People feel this absurdity, and it is this that closes the lips of Christians. They are ashamed to speak to their neighbors while they load themselves down with these trifles, because their daily conduct testifies to everybody the very reverse. How it would look for some of the church members in this city, male or female, to go about among the common people and talk to them about the vanity of the world! Who would believe what they say?

3. They are to testify as to the satisfying nature of Christianity. Christians are obligated to show by their conduct that they are actually satisfied with the enjoyments of the Christian religion without the customs and vanities of the world. They are to testify that the joys of true religion and communion with God keep them above the world. They are to make clear that this world is not their home. Their profession is that heaven is a reality and that they expect to dwell there forever.

But suppose they contradict this by their conduct and live in such a way as to prove that they cannot be happy unless they have a full share of the fashion and entertainment of the world; and that as for going to heaven, they would much rather remain on earth than to die and go there! What does the world think when they see a professing Christian just as much afraid to die as an unbeliever? Such Christians perjure themselves; they swear to a lie, for they testify that there is nothing in Christianity for which a person can afford to live above the world.

4. They are to testify about the guilt and danger of sinners. Christians are obligated to warn sinners of their dreadful condition and exhort them to *flee from the wrath to come* (Matthew 3:7) and lay hold on everlasting life. But who does not know that the manner of doing this is everything? Sinners are often struck under conviction by the very manner of doing a thing.

There was a man once very much opposed to a certain preacher. On being asked to specify some reason, he replied, "I cannot bear to hear him, for he says the word 'hell' in such a way that it rings in my ears a long time afterward." He was displeased with the very thing that constituted the power of speaking that word.

The manner may be such as to convey an idea directly opposite to the meaning of the words. A man may tell you that your house is on fire in such a way as to make directly the opposite impression, and you will take for granted that it is not your house that is on fire. The watchman might sing out "Fire, fire," in such a way that everybody would think he was either asleep or drunk. A certain manner is so usually connected with the announcement of certain things that they cannot be expressed without that manner. The words themselves never alone convey the meaning because the idea can only be fully expressed by a particular manner of speaking.

Go to a sinner and talk with him about his guilt and danger, and if in your manner you make an impression that does not correspond, you basically bear testimony the other way and tell him that he is in no danger of hell. If the sinner believes at all that he is in danger of hell, it is completely on other grounds than your saying so. If you live in such a way as to show that you do not feel compassion for sinners around you; if you show no tenderness by your eyes, your features, and your voice; if your manner is not solemn and earnest, how can they believe you are sincere?

Woman, suppose you tell your converted husband in an easy, laughing way, "My dear, I believe you are going to hell." Will he believe you? If your life is lighthearted and frivolous, you show that either you do not believe there is a hell, or that you desire to have him go there, and are trying to keep off every serious impression from his mind. Do you have children who are unconverted? Suppose you never say anything to them about true religion, or when you do talk to them it is in such a cold, hard, dry way that shows you have no feeling. Do you suppose they believe you? They don't see the same coldness in you in regard to other things.

They are in the habit of seeing all the mother in your eye, and in the tones of your voice, your emphasis, and the like, and feeling the warmth of a mother's heart as it flows out from your lips in regard to all that concerns them. If, then, when you talk to them on the subject of Christianity, you are cold and lighthearted, can they suppose you believe it? If you display before your child this careless, heartless, prayerless spirit, and then you talk to him about the importance of the Christian religion, the child will go away and laugh to think that you would try to persuade him that there is a hell.

5. They are to testify to the love of Christ. You are to bear witness to the reality of the love of Christ by the regard you show for His commandments, His honor, and His kingdom. You should act as if you believed that He died for the sins of the whole world, and as if you blamed sinners for rejecting His great salvation. This is the only legitimate way in which you can impact sinners with the love of Christ. Instead of this, Christians often live so as to make the impression on sinners that Christ is so compassionate that they have very little to fear from Him.

I have been amazed to see how a certain class of professing Christians want ministers to be always preaching about the love of Christ. If a minister preaches about duty and urges Christians to be holy and to labor for Christ, they call it all preaching the law. They say they want to hear the gospel. Well, suppose you present the love of Christ. How will they bear testimony in their lives? How will they show that they believe it? Why, by conformity to the world, they will testify point blank that they do not believe a word of it and that they care nothing at all for the love of Christ except to have it for a cloak so that they can talk about it and so cover up their sins. They have no sympathy with His compassion, no belief in it as a reality, and no concern for the feelings of Christ that fill His mind when He sees the condition of sinners.

6. They are to testify of the necessity of holiness in order to enter heaven. It will not do to depend on just talking about this. They must live holy, and thus testify that people do not need to expect to be saved unless they are holy. The idea has so long prevailed that we cannot be perfect here that many professing Christians do not so much as seriously aim at a sinless life. They cannot honestly say that they ever so much as really meant to live without sin. They drift along before the tide in a loose, sinful, unhappy, and abominable manner, at which the devil undoubtedly laughs, because it is, of all others, the surest way to hell.

7. They are to testify to the necessity of self-denial, humility, and heavenly mindedness. Christians should show by their own example what the religion is that is expected of them. After all, that is the most powerful preaching, and the most likely to have influence on the unrepentant – by showing them the vast difference between them and Christians. Many people are trying to make people Christians by a different course, by copying as closely as possible their present manner of life and conforming to them as much as will possibly do. They seem to think they can make people fall in with Christianity best by bringing it down to their standard, as if the nearer you bring Christianity to the world, the more likely the world would be to embrace it.

Now all this is as wide as the poles from the true philosophy of making Christians, but it is always the policy of carnal professing Christians. And they think they are displaying wonderful wisdom and judgment by taking so much effort not to scare people at the mighty strictness and holiness of the gospel. They argue that if you present Christianity to mankind as requiring such a great change in their manner of life, changes to their sinful habits, separating from their old associates, you will drive them all away. This seems plausible at first glance, but it is not true. Let professing Christians live in this casual and easy way, and sinners say, "It seems that I am about right, or at least so near right, that it is impossible that God would send me to hell for the difference between me and these professing Christians. It is true that they do a little more than I do. They go to the communion table, pray with their families, and a few other little things, but they cannot make any such great difference as heaven and hell."

No, the true way is to present Christianity and the world in strong contrast, or you can never make sinners feel the necessity of a change. Until the necessity of this fundamental change is embodied and held forth in a strong light by example, how can you make people believe they are going to be sent to hell if they are not wholly transformed in heart and life?

This is not only true in philosophy, but it has been proved by the history of the world. Look at the missions of the Jesuits in Japan by Francis Xavier and his associates. See how they lived, what a contrast they showed between their religion and the heathen, and what results followed! I was reading a letter from one of our missionaries in the East, who wrote, I believe, to this effect, that a missionary must be able to rank with the English nobility, and so recommend his religion to the respect of the natives. He must get way up above them so as to show a superiority, and thus impress them with respect! Is this philosophy? Is this the way to convert the world? You can no more convert the world in this way than by blowing a ram's horn. It has no tendency that way. What did the Jesuits do? They went about among the people in the daily practice of self-denial before their eyes, teaching, preaching, praying, and laboring, unwearied and unawed, mingling with every caste and grade, bringing down their instructions to the capacity of every individual. In that way the mission carried idolatry before it like a wave of the sea, and all at once their religion spread over the vast empire of Japan. If they had not meddled with politics and brought themselves in needless collision with the government, no doubt they would have held their ground until this day.

I am not saying anything in regard to the religion they taught, for I am not sure how much truth they preached with it. I speak only of their following the true policy of missions by showing, by their lives, the religion they taught in wide contrast with a worldly spirit and the foolishness of idolatry. This one feature of their policy so commended itself to the consciences of the people that it was irresistible. If Christians contradict this one point, and attempt to accommodate their religion to the worldliness of men, they render the salvation of the world impossible. How can you make people believe that self-denial and separation from the world are necessary unless you practice them?

8. They are to testify in meekness, humility, and heavenly mindedness. The people of God should always show a character like the Son of God, who, when He was reviled, *reviled not again* (1 Peter 2:23). If a professing Christian is irritable and ready to resent an offense, fly into a rage, and take the same measures as the world does to get retaliation or restitution, by going to law and such, how is he to make people believe there is any reality in a change of heart? They cannot recommend Christianity while they have such a spirit. If you are in the habit of resenting hurtful conduct, if you do not bear it meekly and put the best construction that can be on it, you contradict the gospel.

Some people always show a bad spirit, always ready to put the worst construction on what is done, and take aim at any little thing. This shows a great lack of that charity that *believeth all things, hopeth all things, endureth all things* (1 Corinthians 13:7). However, if someone always shows meekness under offenses, it will confound opposition. Nothing makes as solemn an impression upon sinners, and bears down with such a tremendous weight on their consciences, as to see a Christian being Christlike by bearing offenses and insults with the meekness of a lamb. It cuts like a two-edged sword.

I will mention a case to show this. A young man insulted a minister to his face and reviled him in an unprecedented manner. The minister possessed his soul in patience and spoke mildly in reply, telling him the truth directly, yet in a very kind manner. This only made him angrier, and eventually he went away in a rage, declaring that he was not going to stay and bear this admonition, as if it was the minister instead of himself who had been scolding. The sinner went away, but with the arrows of the Almighty in his heart. In less than half an hour, he followed the minister to his lodgings in intolerable agony. He wept, begged for forgiveness, broke down before God, and yielded up his heart to Christ. This calm and mild manner was more overwhelming to him than a thousand arguments.

If that minister had been thrown off his guard and answered harshly, no doubt he would have ruined the soul of that young man. How many of you have defeated every future effort you may make with your unrepentant friends or neighbors in some such way as this? On some occasion you have showed yourself so hostile that you have sealed up your own lips and laid a stumbling block over which that sinner will stumble into hell. If you have ever done so, do not sleep until you have done all you can to repair the damage – until you have confessed the sin and done everything to counteract it as far as possible.

9. They are to testify to the necessity of complete honesty in a Christian. Oh, what a field opens here for comment, but I cannot go over it fully now. It extends to all parts of life. Christians need to show the strictest regard to integrity in every part of business and in all their communication with their fellow men. If every Christian would pay a strict regard to honesty and would always be conscientious to do exactly right, it would make a powerful impression on the minds of people of the reality of Christian principle.

A lady was once buying some eggs in a store, and the clerk miscounted and gave her one more than she requested. She saw it at the time, but said nothing, and after she got home it troubled her. She felt that she had acted wrong, and she hurried back to the young man, confessed it, and paid the difference. The impression of her conscientious integrity went to his heart like a sword. It was a great sin in her to conceal the miscount because the temptation was so small, for if she would cheat him out of an egg, it showed that she would cheat him out of his whole store if she could do it and not be found out. But her prompt and humble confession showed an honest conscience.

I am happy to say that there are some people who deal on this principle of integrity – yet the wicked hate them for it. They criticize them and complain about them in taverns, that they will never buy goods from such and such individuals, that such a hypocrite will never touch a dollar of their money, and all that, and then they will go right away and buy from them because they know they will be honestly dealt with. This is a testimony to the truth of Christianity that is heard from Georgia to Maine. Suppose all Christians did so; what would be the result? Christians would run away with the business of the city. Christians would soon do the business of the world.

The great argument that some Christians use, that if they do not do business upon the common principle of stating one price and taking another, that they cannot compete with people of the world, is all false – false in philosophy and false in history. Only make it your unchanging rule to do right and to do business upon principle, and you control the market. The ungodly will be obliged to conform to your standard. It is perfectly in the power of the church to regulate the commerce of the world if they will only themselves maintain perfect integrity.

If Christians will do the same in politics, they will sway the destinies of nations without involving themselves at all in the unprincipled and corrupting strife of parties. Only let Christians generally determine to vote for no one for any office who is not an honest person and a person of pure morals, and let it be known that Christians are united in this, no matter what their difference in political sentiments may be, and no one would be put up as a candidate who is not such a character.

In three years it would be talked about in taverns and published in newspapers, when any man is set up as a candidate for office, "What a good man he is, how moral, how pious!" and the like. Any political party would no more set up a known Sabbath breaker, or a gambler, or a profane swearer, or someone immoral, or a seller of alcohol as their candidate for office than they would set up the devil himself for president.

The carnal policy of many professing Christians who attempt to correct politics by such means as the wicked use, and who are determined to vote with a party no matter how corrupt and immoral and unprincipled the candidate may be, is all wrong. It is wrong in principle, contrary to philosophy and common sense, and destructive to the best interests of mankind.

The dishonesty of the church is cursing the world. I assure you that I am not going to preach a political sermon, but I want to show you that if you want to impact people favorably to your religion by your lives, you must be honest, strictly honest, in business, in politics, and in everything you do. What do you suppose those ungodly politicians, who know that they are playing a dishonest game in carrying an election, think of your religion when they see you uniting with them? They know you are a hypocrite!

Remarks

1. It is unreasonable for professing Christians to wonder at the thoughtlessness of sinners. Considering everything, the carelessness of sinners is not unusual. We are affected by testimony, and only by that testimony that is received by our minds. Sinners are so taken up with business, pleasure, and the things of the world that they will not examine the Bible to find out what true religion is. Their feelings are only stirred up on worldly subjects because only these are brought into warm contact with their minds. Therefore, the things of the world make a strong impression, but there is so little to make an impression on their minds in respect to eternity, and to bring Christianity home to them, that they do not feel impassioned on the subject.

If they examined the subject, they would feel impassioned, but they do not examine it, nor think about it, nor care about it. And they never will, unless God's witnesses rise up and testify. But inasmuch as the majority of Christians in fact live so as to testify on the other side by their conduct, how can we expect sinners to feel properly on the subject? Nearly all the testimony and all the influence that comes to their minds tends to make them feel the other way. God has left His cause here before the human race, and left His witnesses to testify in His behalf, and behold, they turn around and testify the other way! Is it any wonder that sinners are careless?

2. We see why it is that preaching does so little good and how it is that so many sinners get gospel-hardened. Sinners who live under the gospel are often supposed to be gospel-hardened, but if the church simply wakes up and acts consistently, they will feel. If the church were to live only one week as if they believed the Bible, sinners would melt down before them. Suppose I were a lawyer and would go into court and spread out my client's case. The issue is explained, I make my statements and tell

what I expect to prove, and then call in my witnesses. The first witness takes his oath, and then rises up and contradicts me to my face. What good will all my pleading do? I could address the jury for a month and be as eloquent as Cicero, but as long as my witnesses contradicted me, all my pleading would do no good.

It is the same with a minister who is preaching in the midst of a cold, careless, and God-dishonoring church. In vain does he hold up to view the great truths of Christianity when every member of the church is ready to swear that he lies. In such a church, their very manner of going out of the aisles contradicts the sermon. They leave as cheerful and as easy, bowing to one another and whispering together, as if nothing was the matter. Even if the minister warns every person daily with tears, it will produce no effect. If the devil would come in and see the state of things, he would think he could not improve the business for his interest.

Yet there are ministers who will continue in this way for years, preaching over the heads of such a people who contradict every word they say by their lives, and they think it is their duty to do so. Duty! To preach to a church that is undoing all his work and contradicting all his testimony, and that will not change! No. Let him shake off the dust from his feet for a testimony, and go to the heathen or to the new settlements. The man is wasting his energies, wearing out his life, and just rocking the cradle for a sleepy church, which all testifies to sinners that there is no danger. Their whole lives are a practical testimony that the Bible is not true. Will ministers continue to wear themselves out so? Probably not less than ninety-nine hundredths of the preaching in this country is lost because it is contradicted by the church. Not one truth in a hundred that is preached takes effect, because the lives of professing Christians testify that it is not so.

3. It is evident that the standard of Christian living must be raised or the world will never be converted. If we had as many church members now as there are families, and scattered all over the world, and a minister for every five hundred souls, and every child in a Sunday school, and every young person in a Bible class, you would have all the machinery you want, but if the church contradicts the truth by their lives, it will never produce a revival.

They will never have a revival in any place while the whole church in effect testifies against the minister. It is often the case that where there is the most preaching, there is the least religion, because the church contradicts the preaching. I never knew means to fail of a revival where Christians live consistently. One of the first things needed is to raise the standard of religion so as to express and display in the sight of all people the truth of the gospel. Unless ministers can get the church to wake up and act as if Christianity was true, and back their testimony by their lives, they will attempt to promote a revival in vain.

Many churches depend on their minister to do everything. When he preaches, they will say, "What a great sermon that was! He's an excellent minister. Such preaching must do good. We will have a revival soon, I do not doubt." And all the while they are contradicting the preaching by their lives. I tell you that if they are depending on preaching alone to carry on the work, they will fail. If Jesus Christ were to come and preach, and the church would contradict it, He would fail. It has been tried once. Let an apostle rise from the dead, or an angel come down from heaven and preach (Galatians 1:8), without the church to witness for God, and it would have no effect. The novelty might produce a certain kind of effect for a time, but as soon as the novelty was gone, the preaching would have no saving effect while contradicted by the witnesses.

4. Every Christian makes an impression by his conduct, and witnesses either for one side or the other. His appearance, clothing, and entire demeanor make a constant impression on one side or the other. He cannot help testifying for or against Christianity. He is either gathering with Christ or scattering abroad. Every step you take, you tread on chords that will vibrate to all eternity. Every time you move, you touch keys whose sound will reecho over all the hills and valleys in heaven, and through all the dark caverns and vaults of hell. Every movement of your lives, you are exerting a tremendous influence that will have an effect on the immortal interests of souls all around you. Are you asleep while all your conduct is exerting such an influence?

Are you going to walk in the street? Take care how you dress. What is that on your head? What does that gaudy ribbon and those ornaments upon your dress say to everyone who meets you? It makes the impression that you want to be thought pretty. Take care! You might just as well write on your clothes, "No truth in religion." It says, "Give me clothing, give me fashion, give me flattery, and I am happy."

The world understands this testimony as you walk the streets. You are living epistles, *known and read of all men* (2 Corinthians 3:2). If you show pride, levity, bad temper, and the like, it is like tearing open the wounds of the Savior. How Christ might weep to see professing Christians going about displaying His cause to contempt at the corners of streets. Only let the *women adorn themselves in modest apparel, with shamefacedness and sobriety; not with broidered hair, or gold, or pearls, or costly array, but (which becometh women professing godliness) with good works* (1 Timothy 2:9-10); only let them act consistently, and their conduct will expose the world, heaven will rejoice, and hell will groan at their influence.

But oh, let them display vanity, try to be pretty, bow down to the goddess of fashion, fill their ears with ornaments and their fingers with rings; let them put feathers in their hats and clasps upon their arms and lace themselves up until they can hardly breathe; let them put on their *round tires* (Isaiah 3:18), *walking and mincing as they go* (Isaiah 3:16), and their influence is reversed. Heaven puts on the robes of mourning, and hell may hold a jubilee.

5. It is easy to see why revivals do not prevail in a large city. How can they? Just look at God's witnesses and see what they are testifying to. They seem to be *agreed together to tempt the Spirit of the Lord* and lie to the Holy Spirit (Acts 5:3, 9). They make their vows to God to consecrate themselves wholly to Him, and then go bowing down at the shrine of fashion – and then wonder why there are no revivals. It would be more than a miracle to have a revival under such circumstances.

How can a revival prevail in this church? Do you suppose I have such a vain imagination of my own ability as to think I can promote a revival by preaching over your heads while you live on as some of you do? Do you not know that as far as your influence goes, many of you are right in the way of a revival? Your spirit and conduct and manner produce an influence on the world against Christianity. How will the world believe the Christian religion when the witnesses are not agreed among themselves? You contradict yourselves, you contradict one another, and you contradict your minister, and the sum of the whole testimony is that there is no need to be pious.

Do you believe that the things I have been preaching are true, or are they the ravings of a disturbed mind? If they are true, do you recognize the fact that they have reference to you? You might say, "I wish some of the rich churches could hear it!" I am not preaching to them; I am preaching to you. My responsibility is to you, and my fruits must come from you. Are you contradicting it? What is the testimony on the page of the record that is now sealed for the judgment concerning this day? Have you shown a sympathy with the Son of God when His heart is bleeding in view of the desolations of Zion? Have your children, employees, and friends seen it to be so? Have they seen a solemnity on your countenance and tears in your eyes in view of perishing souls?

Finally, I must close by remarking that God and all moral beings have great reason to complain of this false testimony. There is reason to complain that God's witnesses turn and testify point-blank against Him. They declare by their conduct that there is no truth in the gospel. Heaven might weep and hell rejoice to see this. Oh, how guilty! Here you are, going to the judgment, red all over with blood. Sinners are to meet you there, those who have seen how you live – many of them already dead, and many others you will never see again. What an influence you have exerted! Perhaps hundreds of souls will meet you in the judgment and curse you (if they are allowed to speak) for leading them to hell by practically denying the truth of the gospel. What will become of this city, and of the world, when the church is united in practically testifying that God is a liar? They testify by their lives that if they make a profession of faith and live a moral life, that is religion enough. Oh, what a doctrine of devils that is – enough to ruin the whole human race!

Lecture 10

To Win Souls Requires Wisdom

He that winneth souls is wise.
—Proverbs 11:30

The most common definition of wisdom is that it is the choice of the best end and the selection of the most appropriate means for the accomplishment of that end – the best adaptation of means to secure a desired end. *He that winneth souls*, God says, *is wise*. The object of this lecture is to direct Christians in the use of means for accomplishing their infinitely desirable end – the salvation of souls. I will confine my attention to the private efforts of individuals for the conversion and salvation of men. On another occasion, perhaps I will use the same text in speaking of what is wise in the public preaching of the gospel and the labors of ministers. In giving some directions to aid private Christians in this work, I propose:

    I.   To show Christians how they should deal with careless sinners.

    II. To show how they should deal with awakened sinners.

    III. To show how they should deal with convicted sinners.

I. The Manner of Dealing with Careless Sinners

In regard to the time.

It is important that you should select a proper time to try to make a serious impression on the mind of a careless sinner. Much depends on timing your efforts right. If you fail to select the most proper time, you will very probably be defeated. True, you may say, it is your duty at all times to warn sinners and to try to awaken them to think of their souls, and so it is; yet if you do not pay due regard to the time and opportunity, your hope of success may be very doubtful.

1. It is desirable, if possible, to address a person who is careless when he is disengaged from other employments. In proportion as his attention is taken up with something else, it will be difficult to awaken him to religion. People who are careless and indifferent to religion are often offended, rather than benefited, by being called away from important and lawful business. For instance, a minister perhaps goes to visit the family of a businessman, a mechanic, or a farmer, and finds the man absorbed in his business. He might call him away from his work when it is urgent, and the man is agitated and irritable and feels as if the visit was an intrusion. In such a case, there is little room to expect any good.

Although it is true that Christianity is infinitely more important than all his worldly business, and he should postpone everything to attend to the salvation of his soul, yet he does not feel it, for if he did, he would no longer be a careless sinner. Therefore, he regards such a visit as unjustifiable, and gets offended. You must take him as you find him – a careless, unrepentant sinner, and deal with him accordingly. He is absorbed in other things, and very likely will be offended if you take such a time to interfere and call his attention to Christianity.

2. It is important to take a person, if possible, at a time when he is not strongly excited with any other subject. If that is the case, he is in an unfit condition to be addressed on the subject of true religion. In proportion to the strength of that excitement would be the probability that you would do no good. You may possibly reach him, for people have

had their minds affected and turned to Christ in the midst of a powerful excitement on other subjects, but it is not likely.

3. Be sure that the person is perfectly sober. It used to be more common than it is now for people to drink alcohol every day, and become more or less intoxicated. Precisely in proportion as they are so, they are rendered unfit to be approached on the subject of Christianity. If they have been drinking beer or cider or wine so that you can smell it on their breath, you may know there is but little chance of producing any lasting effect on them. I have had professing Christians bring people to me who were pretending to be under conviction; for you know that people under the influence of alcohol are often very fond of talking about religion; but as soon as I came near them so as to smell their breath, I have asked, "Why do you bring this drunken man to me?" They answer that he is not drunk, but has only had a little to drink. Well, that little has made him a little drunk. He is drunk if you can smell it on his breath, The cases are exceedingly rare when a person has been truly convicted who had any intoxicating liquor in him.

4. If possible, when you want to discuss the subject of salvation with someone, take him when he is in a good mood. If you find him irritable, very probably he will get angry and oppose you. It is better to leave him alone for that time, or you will be likely to quench the Spirit. It is possible that you may be able to talk in such a way as to cool his temper, but it is not likely. The truth is that people hate God, and although their hatred may be repressed, it is easily excited, and if you bring God fully before their minds when they are already excited with anger, it will be so much easier to stir up their enmity to open violence.

5. If possible, always take an opportunity to converse with careless sinners when they are alone. Most people are too proud to be conversed with freely in regard to themselves in the presence of others, even among their own family. A man in such circumstances will brace up all his powers to defend himself, while if he was alone, he would melt down under the truth. He will resist the truth or try to laugh it off for fear that if he would display any feeling, somebody will go and report that he is serious.

In visiting families, instead of calling the family together at the same time to be talked to, the better way is to see them one at a time. There was a case of this kind. Several young ladies of a proud, carefree, and fashionable character lived together in a fashionable family. Two men were strongly desirous to get the subject of Christianity before them, but were at a loss how to accomplish it for fear they would all join together and counteract or resist every serious impression. Eventually they took this course. They called and requested one of the young ladies by name. She came down and they conversed with her on the subject of her salvation, and as she was alone, she not only treated them politely, but seemed to receive the truth with seriousness. A day or two after, they called in the same manner on another, and then another, and so on, until they had conversed with each one separately. In a little while they were all, I believe, each one, hopefully converted. This was as it should be, for then they could not support each other in opposition. Instead, the impression made on one was followed up with the others, so that one was not left to exert a bad influence over the rest.

There was a pious woman who kept a boarding house for young gentlemen. She had twenty one or twenty two of them in her house, and eventually she became very concerned for their salvation. She made it a subject of prayer, but saw no seriousness among them. Eventually she saw that there must be something done besides praying, yet she did not know what to do. One morning after breakfast, as they were getting ready to leave, she asked one of them to stop for a few minutes. She took him aside and tenderly conversed with him on the subject of Christ, and prayed with him. She followed up on the impression made, and pretty soon he was hopefully converted. Then there were two, and they addressed another man and prayed with him, and soon he was prepared to join them. Then another, and so on, taking one at a time, and letting none of the rest know what was going on so as not to alarm them, until every one of these young men was converted to God.

If she had brought the subject before all of them together, very likely they would have turned it all into ridicule, or perhaps they would have been offended and left the house, and then she could have had no further influence over them. But taking one alone, and treating him respectfully and kindly, he had no such motive for resistance as arises out of the presence of others.

6. Try to seize an opportunity to converse with a careless sinner when the events of providence seem to favor your intent. If any particular event should occur that is calculated to make a serious impression, be sure to improve the occasion faithfully.

7. Seize the earliest opportunity to converse with those around you who are careless. Do not put it off from day to day, thinking a better opportunity will come. You must seek an opportunity, and if none arises, make one. Appoint a time and place, and get an interview with your friend or neighbor where you can speak to him freely. Send him a note, go to him on purpose, and make it look like a matter of business, as if you were sincere in wanting to promote his soul's salvation. Then he will feel that it is a matter of importance, at least in your eyes. Follow it up until you succeed or become convinced that nothing can now be done.

8. If you have any feeling for a particular individual about his soul, take an opportunity to converse with that individual while this feeling continues. If it is a truly benevolent feeling, you have reason to believe that the Spirit of God is moving you to desire the salvation of his soul and that God is ready to bless your efforts for his conversion. In such a case, make it the subject of special and persistent prayer, and seek an early opportunity to pour out all your heart to him and bring him to Christ.

In regard to the manner of doing all this.
1. When you approach a careless individual to try to awaken him to his soul's concerns, be sure to treat him kindly. Let him see that you do not speak to him because you seek a quarrel with him, but because you love his soul and desire his best good in time and eternity. If you are harsh and overbearing in your manner, you will probably offend him and drive him farther off from the way of life.

2. Be solemn. Avoid all lightness of manner or language. Levity will produce anything but a right impression. You should feel that you are occupied in a very solemn work that is going to affect the character of your friend or neighbor, and probably determine his destiny for eternity. Who could trifle and use levity in such circumstances if his heart was sincere?

3. Be respectful. Some people seem to suppose it necessary to be abrupt, rude, and coarse in their interaction with the careless and unrepentant. This is a great mistake. The apostle Peter has given us a better rule on the subject where he says, *Be pitiful, be courteous: not rendering evil for evil, or railing for railing, but contrariwise blessing* (1 Peter 3:8-9). A rude and coarse address is only calculated to give an unfavorable opinion of both you and your religion.

4. Be sure to be very plain. Do not allow yourself to cover up any circumstance of the person's character and his relationship to God. Lay it all open, not for the purpose of offending or wounding him, but because it is necessary. Before you can cure a wound, you must probe it to the bottom. Keep back none of the truth, but let it come out plainly before him.

5. Be sure to address his conscience. In public addresses, ministers often get hold of the feelings only, and thus awaken the mind. But in private conversation you cannot do so. You cannot pour out the truth in an impassioned and lively manner, and unless you address the conscience directly, you get no hold of the mind at all.

6. Bring the great and fundamental truths to bear upon the person's mind. Sinners are very apt to run off upon some pretext or some subordinate point, especially some point of denominationalism. For example, if the man is a Presbyterian, he will try to turn the conversation to the points of difference between Presbyterians and Methodists, or he will talk against old school divinity. Do not yield to him or talk with him on any such point; it will do more harm than good. Tell him that the present business is to save his soul, and not to settle disputed questions in theology. Hold him to the great fundamental points by which he must be saved or lost.

7. Be very patient. If he has a real difficulty in his mind, be very patient until you find out what it is, and then clear it up. If what he alleges is a mere frivolous objection, make him see that it is a mere frivolous objection. Do not try to answer it by argument, but show him that he is not

sincere in advancing it. It is not worthwhile to spend your time arguing against a frivolous objection, but make him feel that he is committing sin to plead it, and thus enlist his conscience on your side.

8. Be careful to guard your own spirit. There are many people who do not have enough of a good disposition to converse with those who are much opposed to Christianity. Such a person wants no better triumph than to see you angry. He will go away exulting because he has made one of these saints mad.

9. If the sinner is inclined to firmly set himself against God, be careful not to take his part in anything. If he says he cannot do his duty, do not take sides with him or say anything to accept his falsehood. Do not tell him he cannot, or do not help him maintain himself in the controversy against his Maker. Sometimes a careless sinner will resort to finding fault with Christians. Do not take his part or side with him against Christians. Just tell him he does not have their sins to answer for, and he had better see to his own concerns. If you fall in with him, he feels that he has you on his side. Show him that it is a denouncing and wicked spirit that prompts him to make these remarks, and not a regard for the honor of Christianity or the laws of Jesus Christ.

10. Bring up the individual's specific sins. Talking in general terms against sin will produce no results. You must make a person feel that you are referring to him. A minister who cannot make his hearers feel that he is referring to them specifically cannot expect to accomplish much. Some people are very careful to avoid mentioning the specific sins of which they know the individual to be guilty, for fear of hurting his feelings. This is wrong. If you know his history, bring up his specific sins, kindly but plainly – not to give offense, but to awaken his conscience and give full force to the truth.

11. It is generally best to be direct and not drag out what we have to say. Get the attention as soon as you can to the very point. Say a few things and press them home, and bring the matter to an issue. If possible, get them to repent and give themselves to Christ at the time. This is the

proper issue. Carefully avoid making an impression that you do not expect them to repent now.

12. If possible, when you converse with sinners, be sure to pray with them. If you converse with them and leave them without praying, you leave your work undone.

II. The Manner of Dealing with Awakened Sinners

You should be careful to distinguish between an awakened sinner and one who is under conviction. When you find a person who feels a little on the subject of religion, do not take it for granted that he is convicted of sin, and thus neglect to use means to show him his sin. People are often awakened by some providential circumstance such as sickness, a thunderstorm, pestilence, a death in the family, disappointment, or something similar, or by the Spirit of God, so that their ears are open and they are ready to hear about the subject of the Christian religion with attention and seriousness and some feeling.

If you find a person awakened, no matter by what means, lose no time in pouring light upon his mind. Do not be afraid, but show him the breadth of the divine law and the exceeding strictness of its precepts. Make him see how it condemns his thoughts and life. Search out his heart, find what is there, and bring it up before his mind as far as you can. If possible, melt him down on the spot. Once you have got a sinner's attention, very often his conviction and conversion is the work of a few moments. You can sometimes do more in five minutes than in years or a whole life while he is careless or indifferent.

I have been amazed at the conduct of those cruel parents, and other heads of families, who will let an awakened sinner be in their families for days and weeks and not say a word to him on the subject. They say that if the Spirit of God has begun a work in him, he will certainly carry it on! Perhaps the person is anxious to have a conversation about Christ, and puts himself in the way of Christians as often as possible, expecting them to discuss Christ with him, but they do not say a word. Amazing!

Such a person should be dealt with immediately, as soon as he is awakened, and let a blaze of light be poured into his mind without delay. Whenever you have reason to believe that a person within your reach is awakened, do not sleep until you have poured in the light upon his mind and have tried to bring him to immediate repentance. Then is the time to press the subject with effect. If that favorable moment is lost, it can never be recovered.

I have often seen Christians in revivals who were constantly on the lookout to see if any people appeared to be awakened. As soon as they saw anyone begin to show feeling under preaching, they would mark him, and as soon as the meeting was out, invite him to a room and talk and pray with him – and if possible, not leave him until he was converted.

A remarkable case of this kind occurred in a town in the West. A merchant came to the place from a distance to buy goods. It was a time of powerful revival, but he was determined to keep out of its influence, so he would not go to any meeting at all. Eventually he found everybody so much engaged in Christianity that it met him at every turn, and he got angry and swore he would go home. There was so much religion there, he said, that he could not do any business, and he would not stay.

Accordingly he purchased a ticket for the stagecoach, which was to leave at four o'clock the next morning. As he spoke of going away, a gentleman belonging to the house, who was one of the young converts, asked him if he would go to a meeting once before he left town. He finally consented, and went to the meeting. The sermon took hold of his mind, but not with sufficient power to bring him into the kingdom. He returned to his lodgings and called the landlord to pay his bill.

The landlord, who had himself recently experienced Christianity, saw that he was troubled. He accordingly spoke to him on the subject of Christ Jesus, and the man burst into tears. The landlord immediately called in three or four young converts, and they prayed and exhorted him, and at four o'clock in the morning, when the stagecoach called, he went on his way rejoicing in God! When he got home, he called his family together, confessed to them his past sins, declared his determination to live differently, and prayed with them for the first time. It was so unexpected that it was soon reported all around. People began to inquire, and a revival broke out in the place.

Suppose these Christians had done as some do – been careless and let the man go away slightly affected? It is not probable he ever would have been saved. Such opportunities are often lost forever, when once the favorable moment is passed.

III. The Manner of Dealing with Convicted Sinners

By a convicted sinner, I mean one who feels himself condemned by the law of God as a guilty sinner. He has so much instruction as to understand something of the extent of God's law, and he sees and feels his guilty state and knows what his remedy is. Dealing with these people often requires great wisdom. Some of the most difficult cases occur here when it is extremely difficult to know what to do with them.

When a person is convicted and not converted, but remains in an anxious state, there is generally some specific reason for it. In such cases, it does no good to exhort him to repent or to explain the law to him. He knows all that. He understands all these general points, but still he does not repent. There must be some particular difficulty to overcome. You may preach and pray and exhort until doomsday, and not gain anything.

You must then set yourself to inquire what that particular difficulty is. When a physician is called to a patient and finds him sick with a particular disease, he first administers the general remedies that are applicable to that disease. If they produce no effect, and the disease still continues, he must examine the case and learn the constitution of the individual, and his habits, diet, manner of living, etc., and see what the matter is that the medicine does not take effect. It is the same with the case of a sinner who is convicted but not converted. If your ordinary instructions and exhortations fail, there must be a difficulty. The particular difficulty is often known to the individual himself, although he keeps it concealed. Sometimes it is something that has escaped even his own observations.

1. Sometimes the individual has some idol, something that he loves more than God, which prevents him from giving himself up. You must search out and see what it is that he will not give up. Perhaps it is wealth, perhaps some earthly friend, perhaps fashionable clothing, carefree company, or some favorite amusement or entertainment. At

any rate, there is something on which his heart is so set that he will not surrender to God.

2. Perhaps he has done harm to some individual, that calls for correction, and he is unwilling to confess it or to make a just recompense. Until he will confess and forsake this sin, he can find no mercy. If he has harmed the person in property or character or has mistreated him, he must make it up. If you can find it out, tell him plainly and directly that there is no hope for him until he is willing to confess it and do what is right.

3. Sometimes there is some specific sin that he will not forsake. He pretends it is only a small one, or tries to convince himself that it is no sin. No matter how small it is, he can never get into the kingdom of God until he gives it up. Sometimes an individual has seen it to be a sin to use tobacco, and he can never find true peace until he gives it up. Perhaps he is looking upon it as a small sin.

However, God knows nothing about small sins in such a case. What is the sin? It is damaging your health, setting a bad example, and taking God's money, which you are obligated to use in His service, and spending it on tobacco. What would a merchant say if he found one of his clerks in the habit of going to the money drawer and taking enough money to keep him in cigars? Would he call it a small offense? No. He would say he deserved to be sent to the state prison. I mention this particular sin because I have found it to be one of the things to which people who are convicted will hold on when they know it is wrong, and then wonder why they do not find peace.

4. See if there is not some work of restitution that he is obligated to do. Maybe he has defrauded somebody in trade, or has taken some unfair advantage, contrary to the golden rule of doing as you would be done by, and is unwilling to make things right. This is a very common sin among merchants and businessmen. I have known many sad instances in which people have grieved away the Spirit of God, or else have been driven nearly to absolute despair because they were unwilling to make restitution when they have done such things. It is plain that such people can never have forgiveness until they do so.

5. They may have entrenched themselves somewhere and fortified their minds in regard to some particular point, which they are determined not to yield. For example, they may have taken strong ground that they will not do a particular thing. I knew a man who was determined not to go into a certain grove to pray. Several other people during the revival had gone into the grove, and there, by prayer and meditation, had given themselves to God. His own clerk had been converted there. The lawyer himself was awakened, but he was determined that he would not go into the grove. He had powerful convictions, and went on for weeks in this way with no relief. He tried to make God believe that it was not pride that kept him from Christ, and so, when he was going home from a meeting, he would kneel down in the street and pray. Not only that, but he would look around for a mud puddle in the street in which he might kneel to show that he was not proud. He once prayed all night in his room, but he would not go into the grove. His distress was so great, and he was so angry with God, that he was strongly tempted to do away with himself, and he actually threw away his knife for fear that he would cut his throat. At last he concluded that he would go into the grove and pray, and as soon as he got there he was converted, and he went and poured out his full heart to God.

In the same way, individuals are sometimes entrenched in a determination that they will not go to a particular meeting, perhaps the inquiry meeting or some prayer meeting, or they will not have a certain person pray with them, or they will not take a particular seat, such as the anxious seat. They say that they can be converted just as well without yielding this point, for the Christian religion does not consist in going to a particular meeting, taking a particular attitude in prayer, or sitting in a particular seat. This is true, but by taking this ground they make it the major point, and as long as they are entrenched there and are determined to bring God to their terms, they can never be converted. Sinners will often yield anything else, and do anything in the world, except yield the point upon which they have committed themselves and taken a stand against God. They cannot be humbled until they yield this point, whatever it is. And if without yielding it they get a hope, it will be a false hope.

6. Perhaps he has a prejudice against someone, maybe a member of the church, on account of some faithful dealing with his soul, or something in his business that he did not like, and he hangs on this and will never be converted until he gives it up. Whatever it is, you should search it out and tell him the truth plainly and faithfully.

7. He may feel ill will toward someone, or be angry, and cherish strong feelings of resentment that prevent him from obtaining mercy from God. *And when ye stand praying, forgive, if ye have aught against any: that your Father also which is in heaven may forgive you your trespasses. But if ye do not forgive, neither will your Father which is in heaven forgive your trespasses* (Mark 11:25-26).

8. Perhaps he holds some errors in doctrine, or some wrong ideas respecting the thing to be done, or the way of doing it, that may be keeping him out of the kingdom. Perhaps he is waiting for God. He is convinced that he deserves to go to hell, and that unless he is converted, he must go there; but he is waiting for God to do something to him before he submits. He is in fact waiting for God to do for him what He has required the sinner to do.

He may be waiting for more conviction. People often do not know what conviction is, and think they are not under conviction, when in fact they are under powerful conviction. They often think that nothing is conviction unless they have a great fear of hell. But the fact is that individuals often have strong convictions who have very little fear of hell. Show them what the truth is, and let them see they have no need to wait.

Perhaps he may be waiting for certain feelings that somebody else has had before he obtained mercy. This is very common in revivals, when some of the first converts have told of remarkable experiences. Others who are awakened are very inclined to think they must wait for those same feelings. I knew a young man who was awakened in this way. His friend had been converted in a remarkable way, and this man was waiting for the same feelings and experience. He said he was using the means and praying for them, but finally discovered that he was a Christian, although he had not been through the course of feeling he expected.

Sinners often lay out a plan of the way they expect to feel, and how they expect to be converted, and in fact lay out the work for God, determined that they will go in that path or not at all. Tell them this is all wrong, that they must not lay out any such path beforehand, but must let God lead them as He sees to be best. God always leads the blind by a way they know not. There never was a sinner brought into the kingdom through such a course of feeling as he expected. Very often they are amazed to find that they are in, and have had no such experiences as they expected.

It is very common for people to be waiting to be made subjects of prayer, or for some particular means to be used, or to see if they cannot make themselves better. They are so wicked, they say, that they cannot come to Christ. They want to try, by self-abasement, suffering, and prayer, to ready themselves to come. You will have to hunt them out of all these refuges. It is astonishing into how many corners they will often run to before they will go to Christ. I have known people almost deranged for the lack of a little correct instruction.

Sometimes such people think their sins are too great to be forgiven, or that they have grieved the Spirit of God away, when the Spirit is convicting them the entire time. They pretend their sins are greater than Christ's mercies, thus actually insulting the Lord Jesus Christ.

Sometimes sinners get the idea that they have been given up by God, and that now they cannot be saved. It is often very difficult to pry people off from this ground. Many of the most distressing cases I have ever met with have been of this character, when people would insist upon it that they had been given up, and nothing would change them.

In a place where I was laboring in a revival, I went one day into the meeting, and before the exercises began, I heard a low moaning, distressing, unearthly noise. I looked and saw several women gathered around the person who was making the noise. They said she was a woman in despair. She had been a long time in that condition. Her husband was a drunkard. He had brought her to meeting and had gone himself to the tavern. I conversed with her and saw her condition, and that it was very difficult to reach her case.

As I was going away to begin the service, she said she must go out, for she could not bear to hear praying or singing. I told her she must not go, and told the ladies to detain her, by force if necessary. I felt that if the devil had hold of her, God was stronger than the devil and could deliver her. The service began, and she made some noise at first, but soon she looked up. The topic of the sermon was chosen with special reference to her case, and as I proceeded, her attention was gained and her eyes were fixed. I will never forget how she looked. Her eyes and mouth were open, her head was up, and she almost rose from her seat as the truth poured in upon her mind. Finally, as the truth knocked away every foundation on which her despair had rested, she shrieked out, put her head down, and sat perfectly still until the meeting was over. I went to her and found her perfectly calm and happy in God. I saw her long afterward, and she remained so. Thus the will of God threw her where she never expected to be, and compelled her to hear instruction adapted to her case. You may often do incalculable good by finding out precisely where the difficulty lies, and then bringing the truth to bear right on that point.

Sometimes people will strongly maintain that they have committed the unpardonable sin. When they get that idea into their minds, they will turn everything you say against themselves. In some such cases, it is a good way to take them on their own ground and reason with them in this way: "Suppose you have committed the unpardonable sin; what then? It is reasonable that you should submit to God, be sorry for your sins, break off from those sins, and do all the good you can, even if God will not forgive you. Even if you go to hell, you should do this." Press this thought and turn it over until you see that they understand and consent to it.

It is common for people in such cases to keep their eyes on themselves. They will shut themselves up and keep looking at their own darkness instead of looking away to Christ. If you can take their minds off themselves and get them to think of Christ, you may draw them away from brooding over their own present feelings and get them to lay hold on the hope set before them in the gospel.

In conversing with convicted sinners, be careful not to make any compromise with them on any point in which they have a difficulty. If you do, they will be sure to take advantage of it, and thus get a false hope. Convicted sinners often get into a difficulty in regard to giving up some beloved sin, or yielding some point where conscience and the Holy Spirit are at war with them. If they come across an individual who will yield the point, they feel better and are happy, and think they are converted. The young man who came to Christ was of this character. He had one difficulty, and Jesus Christ knew just what it was. He knew he loved his money, and instead of compromising the matter and thus trying to comfort him, He just put His finger on the very place and told him, "Go sell all that you have, and give to the poor, and come follow Me" (Matthew 19:16-22).

What was the effect? The young man went away sorrowful. Very likely, if Christ had told him to do anything else, he would have felt relieved and would have got a hope. He would have professed himself a disciple, joined the church, and gone to hell.

People are often amazingly anxious to make a compromise. They will ask such questions as whether you think a person may be a Christian and yet do such and such things; or if he may be a Christian and not do such and such things. Do not yield an inch to any such questions. These questions themselves may often show you the very point that is laboring in their minds. They will show you that it is pride, or love of the world, or something of the kind that prevents them from becoming Christians.

Be careful to make thorough work on this point of the love of the world. I believe there have been more false hopes built on wrong instructions here than in any other way. I once heard a doctor of divinity trying to persuade his hearers to give up the world, and he told them that if they would only give it up, God would give it right back to them again, for He wants you to enjoy the world.

That is miserable advice! God never gives back the world to the Christian in the same sense that He requires a convicted sinner to give it up. He requires us to give up the ownership of everything to Him so that we will never again for a moment consider it as our own. A man must not think he has a right to judge for himself how much of his property he will give for God. One man thinks he may spend $20,000 a year to support his family. He says he has a right to do it because he has earned the money. Another thinks he may set aside $500,000.

One man said the other day that he had promised he would never give any of his property to educate young men for the ministry. When he is asked to do so, he just answers, "I have said I will never give to any such purpose, and I never will." Did Jesus Christ ever tell you to do so with His money? Has He laid down any such rule? Remember it is His money you are talking about, and if He wants it to educate ministers, you withhold it at your peril. That man has yet to learn the first principle of Christianity, that he is not his own (1 Corinthians 6:19), and that the money that he possesses is Jesus Christ's.

This is the main reason why the church is so full of false hopes. People have been left to suppose they could be Christians while holding on to their money. This has served as an obstruction to every enterprise. It is an undoubted fact that Christians have enough funds to immediately supply the world with Bibles, tracts, and missionaries. But the truth is that professing Christians do not believe that *the earth is the LORD's, and the fulness thereof* (Psalm 24:1). Every person supposes he has a right to decide how much of his own money he will give, and they have no idea that Jesus Christ will dictate to them on the subject.

Be sure to deal thoroughly on this point. The church is now filled with hypocrites because they were never required to give up the world. They were never made to see that unless they made an entire consecration of all to Christ – all their time, all their talents, all their influence, all their possessions – they would never get to heaven, for they are not His.

Many people think they can be Christians and yet dream along through life and use all their time and property for themselves, only giving a little now and then to try to make a good impression on others when they can do so with perfect convenience. But it is a sad mistake, and they will find it so, if they do not use all their energies for God. When they die, instead of finding heaven at the end of the path they are pursuing, they will find hell there.

In dealing with a convicted sinner, be sure to drive him away from every refuge, and do not leave him an inch of ground to stand on as long as he resists God. This does not need to take a long time to do. When the Spirit of God is at work striving with a sinner, it is easy to drive him from his refuges. You will find the truth to be like a hammer, crushing wherever it strikes. Make clean work with it so that he will give up all for God.

Make the sinner see clearly the nature and extent of the divine law, and emphasize the main question of entire submission to God. Bear down on that point as soon as you have made him clearly understand what you aim at, and do not turn aside upon anything else.

In illustrating the subject, be careful not to mislead the mind so as to leave the impression that a selfish submission will answer, or a selfish acceptance of the atonement, or a selfish giving up to Christ and receiving Him, as if a man was making a good bargain, giving up his sins and receiving salvation in exchange. This is mere barter and is not submission to God. Leave no room in your explanations or illustrations for such a view of the matter. Man's selfish heart will eagerly seize such a view of religion if it is presented, and will very likely grasp it, and thus get a false hope.

Another time I will call your attention to certain things that are to be avoided in dealing with sinners.

Remarks

1. Make it an object of constant study and of daily reflection and prayer to learn how to deal with sinners so as to promote their conversion. It is the great business on earth of every Christian to save souls. People often complain that they do not know how to take hold of this matter. The reason is plain enough: they have never studied it. They never took the proper effort to prepare themselves for the work of saving souls. If people made it no more a matter of attention and thought to equip themselves for their worldly business than they do to save souls, how do you think they would succeed? If you are thus neglecting the main business of life, what are you living for? If you do not make it a matter of study, how you may most successfully act in building up the kingdom of Christ, you are acting a very wicked and absurd part as a Christian.

2. Many professing Christians do more harm than good when they attempt to talk to unrepentant sinners. They have so little knowledge and skill that their remarks divert attention rather than increase it.

3. Be careful to find the point where the Spirit of God is dealing with a sinner, and urge the same point in all your remarks. If you divert his

attention from that point, you will be in great danger of destroying his convictions. Take effort to learn the state of his mind, what he is thinking of, how he feels, and what he feels most deeply upon, and then present that thoroughly, and do not divert his mind by talking about anything else. Do not fear to urge that point for fear of driving him to distraction. Some people fear to press a point to which the mind is tremblingly alive lest they should injure the mind, despite the Spirit of God evidently debating that point with the sinner. This is an attempt to be wiser than God. You should clear up the point, throw the light of truth all around it, and bring the soul to submit – and then the mind will be at rest.

4. Great evils have arisen and many false hopes have been created by not distinguishing between an awakened and a convicted sinner. For the lack of this, people who are only awakened are immediately urged to submit. They are told, "You must repent" and "Submit to God" when they are not in fact convinced of their guilt, nor instructed so far as even to know what submission means. This is one way in which revivals have been greatly harmed – by indiscriminate exhortations to repent, unaccompanied by proper instruction.

5. Anxious sinners are to be regarded as being in a very solemn and critical state. They have in fact come to a turning point. It is a time when their destiny is likely to be settled forever. The Spirit of God will not always strive (Genesis 6:3). Christians should feel deeply for them. In many respects, their circumstances are more solemn than the judgment day. Here their destiny is settled. The judgment day simply reveals it. The particular time when it is done is when the Spirit is striving with them. Christians should remember their tremendous responsibility at such times. The physician, if he knows anything of his duty, sometimes feels himself to be under a very solemn responsibility. His patient is in a critical state where a little error will destroy life, and he hangs quivering between life and death.

If such responsibility is felt in relation to the body, what incredible responsibility should be felt in relation to the soul when it is seen to hang trembling on a point and its destiny is now to be decided! One false impression, one unwise remark, one sentence misunderstood, or one slight diversion of mind may wear him the wrong way, and his soul is lost. Never was an angel employed in a more solemn work than that of dealing with sinners who are under conviction. How solemnly and carefully then should Christians walk, and how wisely and skillfully they should work, if they do not want to be the means of damning a soul!

Finally, if there is a sinner here, let me say to you, abandon all your excuses. You have been told here that they are all vain. Tonight it will be told in hell, and told in heaven, and echoed from the ends of the universe, what you decide to do. This very hour may seal your eternal destiny. Will you submit to God now?

Lecture 11

A Wise Minister Will Be Successful

He that winneth souls is wise.
—Proverbs 11:30

I preached last time from this same text on the method of dealing with sinners by private Christians. My purpose at this time is to take up the more public means of grace, with particular reference to the duties of ministers.

As I observed in my last lecture, wisdom is the choice and pursuit of the best end by the most appropriate means. The great purpose for which the Christian ministry was appointed is to glorify God in the salvation of souls. In speaking on this subject, I propose to show:

I. That the proper discharge of the duties of a minister requires great wisdom.

II. That the amount of success in the discharge of his duties (other things being equal) decides the amount of wisdom employed by him in the exercise of his office.

I. The Proper Discharge of the Duties of a Minister Requires Great Wisdom

1. Great wisdom is required on account of the opposition encountered. The very purpose for which the ministry is appointed is one against which is arrayed the most powerful opposition of sinners themselves. If people were willing to receive the gospel, and there were nothing needed to be done but to tell the story of redemption, a child might convey the news. However, people are opposed to the gospel. They are opposed to their own salvation in this way. Their opposition is often violent and unwavering.

I once saw a madman who had made plans against his own life, and he would exercise the utmost insight and skill to effect his purpose. He would be deceptive and make his keepers believe he had no such intent, that he had given it all up. He would appear mild and calm, and at the instant the keeper was off his guard, he would lay hands on himself. In the same way, sinners often exercise great shrewdness in evading all the efforts that are made to save them. And ministers need a great amount of wisdom to meet this dreadful cleverness and overcome it so as to save men.

2. The particular means appointed to be used in the work show the necessity of great wisdom in ministers. If people were converted by an act of physical omnipotence, creating some new taste, or something like that, and if sanctification were nothing but the same physical omnipotence rooting out the remaining roots of sin from the soul, it would not require so much wisdom and skill to win souls. Nor would there then be any meaning in the text. But the truth is that regeneration and sanctification are to be brought about by moral means – by argument and not by force. There never was and never will be anyone saved by anything except truth as the means.

Truth is the outward means, the outward motive, presented first by man and then by the Holy Spirit. Take into view the opposition of the sinner himself, and you see that nothing, after all, short of the wisdom of God and the moral power of the Holy Spirit, can break down this opposition and bring him to submit to God. Still the means are to be used by men, and means adapted to the end, skillfully used. God has provided that the work of conversion and sanctification will in all cases be done by means of that kind of truth, applied in that connection and relation, that is suited to produce such a result.

3. He has the powers of earth and hell to overcome, and that calls for wisdom. The devil is constantly at work trying to prevent the success of ministers, laboring to divert the attention from the subject of Christianity, and working to get the sinner away from God and lead him down to hell. The whole framework of society, almost, is hostile to the Christian religion. Nearly all the influences that surround a person from his cradle to his grave, in the present state of society, are calculated to defeat the purpose of the ministry. Does not a minister then need great wisdom to conflict with the powers of darkness, and the whole influence of the world, in addition to the sinner's own opposition?

4. The same is seen from the infinite importance of the purpose itself. The goal of the ministry is the salvation of the soul. When we consider the importance of the goal and the difficulties of the work, who will not say with the apostle, *Who is sufficient for these things?* (2 Corinthians 2:16).

5. He must understand how to wake up the church and get them out of the way of the conversion of sinners. This is often the most difficult part of a minister's work, and it requires more wisdom and patience than anything else. Indeed, to do this successfully is a most rare qualification in the Christian ministry. It is a point in which almost all ministers fail. They do not know how to wake up the church and raise the tone of piety to a high standard, and thus clear the way for the work of conversion. Many ministers can preach to sinners very well, but gain little success, while the counteracting influence of the church resists it all, and they do not have enough skill to remove the difficulty.

There is only here and there a minister in the country who knows how to challenge the church when they are in a cold, backslidden state so as to successfully wake them up and keep them awake. The members of the church sin against such light so that when they become cold, it is very difficult to stir them up. They have a form of piety that impedes the truth, while at the same time it is just that kind of piety that has no power or effectiveness. Such professing Christians are the most difficult individuals to awaken from their sleep. I do not mean that they are always more wicked than the unrepentant. They often take part in the workings of religion and pass for very good Christians, but they are of no use in a revival.

I know ministers are sometimes amazed to hear it said that churches are not awake. It is no wonder that such ministers do not know how to wake a sleeping church. There was a young recently ordained man who heard Brother Foote the other day, in this city, pouring out truth and trying to wake up the churches, and he knew so little about it that he thought it was abusing the churches. He was so perfectly blind that he really thought the churches in New York were all awake on the subject of Christianity.

Some years ago there was a great controversy and opposition raised because so much was said about the churches being asleep. It was all truth, yet many ministers knew nothing about it, and were astonished to hear such things said about the churches. When it has come to this, that ministers do not know when the church is asleep, it is no wonder that we have no revivals.

I was once invited to preach at a certain place. I asked the minister what the state of the church was. "Oh," he said, "every person is awake." I was delighted at the idea of laboring in such a church, for it was a sight I had never yet seen, to see every single member awake in a revival. But when I got there, I found the church sleepy and cold, and I doubt whether even one of them was awake.

The great difficulty in keeping up revivals is to keep the church thoroughly awake and engaged. It is one thing for a church to get up from their sleep and wander about and run over each other, and a widely different thing for them to have their eyes open and their senses about them, and be wide awake so as to know how to find God and how to work for Christ.

6. He must know how to set the church to work when they are awake. If a minister attempts to go to work alone, intending to do it all himself, it is like attempting to roll a large stone up a hill alone. The church can do

much to help forward a revival. Churches have sometimes had powerful revivals without any minister, but when a minister has a church that is awake, and knows how to set them to work and how to sit at the helm and guide them, he may feel strong, and oftentimes may find that they do more than he does himself in the conversion of sinners.

7. In order to be successful, a minister needs great wisdom to know how to keep the church to the work. Often the church members seem just like children. You set children to work, and they appear to be all busy, but as soon as your back is turned they will stop and go play. The great difficulty in continuing a revival lies here, and to meet it requires great wisdom. Some of the most difficult things in the world are to know how to break them down again when their heart gets lifted up because they have had such a great revival, to wake them up afresh when their zeal begins to decrease, and to keep their hearts full of zeal for the work. Yet if a minister wants to be successful in winning souls, he must know when they first begin to grow proud or lose the spirit of prayer, when to examine them, how to search them over again, and how to keep the church in the field gathering the harvest of the Lord.

8. He must understand the gospel. But you will ask, Do not all ministers understand the gospel? I answer that they certainly do not all understand it in the same way, for they do not all preach the same.

9. He must know how to divide it so as to bring forward the particular truths, in that order, and to make them consider those points and at such times as are calculated to produce a given result. A minister should understand the philosophy of the human mind so as to know how to plan and arrange his labors wisely. Truth, when brought to bear upon the mind, is in itself calculated to produce corresponding feelings. The minister must know what feelings he desires to produce, and how to bring such truth to bear that is calculated to produce these feelings. He must know how to present truth calculated to humble Christians, or to make them feel for sinners, or to awaken sinners, or to convert them.

Often, when sinners are awakened, the ground is lost for the lack of wisdom in following up the impact. Perhaps a stirring sermon is preached, Christians are moved, and sinners begin to feel, and the next Lord's Day something will be brought forward that has no connection with the state of feeling in the congregation and that is not calculated to lead the mind on to the exercise of repentance, faith, or love. It shows how important it is for a minister to understand how to produce a given impression, at what time it may and should be done, and by what truth, and how to follow it up until the sinner is broken down and brought in.

A great many good sermons preached are all lost for the lack of a little wisdom here. They are good sermons and are intended, if well timed, to do much good, but they have so little connection with the actual state of feeling in the congregation that it would be more than a miracle if they would produce a revival. A minister may preach in this random way until he has preached himself to death, and never produce any great results. He may convert a scattered soul here and there, but he will not move the majority of the congregation unless he knows how to follow up with them and carry out a plan of operations and execute it so as to carry on the work when it has begun. He must not only be able to blow the trumpet so loud as to awaken the sinner from his sleep, but when he is waked, he must lead him by the shortest way to Jesus Christ – and not, as soon as sinners are awakened by a sermon, immediately begin to preach about some distant subject that has no tendency to carry on the work.

10. To reach different classes of sinners successfully requires great wisdom on the part of a minister. For example, a sermon on a specific subject may stir up a particular class of people among his hearers. Perhaps they will begin to look serious, or talk about it, or they might begin to complain about it. If the minister is wise, he will know how to observe those indications and to follow right on with sermons adapted to this class until he leads them into the kingdom of God. Then let him go back and take another class, find out where they are hidden, break down their refuges, and follow them up until he leads them into the kingdom of God. He should in this way seek out every place where sinners hide themselves, as the voice of God followed Adam in the garden – "Adam, where are you?" (Genesis 3:9) – until one class of hearers after another are brought in, and so the whole community is converted. A

minister must be very wise to do this. It will never be done so until a minister sets himself to hunt out and bring in every class of sinners in his congregation – the old and young, male and female, rich and poor.

11. A minister needs great wisdom to get sinners away from their present refuges of lies without forming new hiding places for them. I once sat under the ministry of a man who had sounded a great alarm about heresies, and was constantly employed in refuting them. He used to bring up many such heresies that his people never heard of. He got his ideas mainly from books, and mingled very little among the people to know what they thought. The result of his labors was that the people would often be taken with the heresy more than with the argument against it. The novelty of the error attracted their attention so much that they forgot the answer. In that way, he gave many of his people new objections against the Christian religion that they had never thought of before. If a man does not mingle enough with mankind to know how people think nowadays, he cannot expect to be wise enough to meet their objections and difficulties.

I have heard a great deal of preaching against Universalists that did more harm than good because the preachers did not understand how Universalists of the present day reason. They have never mingled with Universalists, and do not know what they believe and how they argue now, but got all they know of Universalism from books that were written long ago and are now out of date among Universalists themselves. The consequence is that when they attempt to preach against Universalism, they oppose a man of straw, and not Universalist sentiments as they are now found in the community. People either laugh at them or say it is all lies, for they know that Universalists do not hold such ideas as are ascribed to them by the preacher.

When ministers undertake to oppose a present heresy, they should know what it is at present. For instance, almost all those who write and preach against Universalism think they are called upon to oppose the idea that God is all mercy. They think that Universalists hold the doctrine that God is all mercy, and that when they have refuted this doctrine, they have got Universalists down. But this is not true. They do not hold such doctrine. They deny it completely. They reject the idea of mercy in the salvation of men, for they hold that every person is punished in full according to what he deserves. Of what use is it, then, to argue against Universalists that God is a God of justice and not a God of all mercy, when they hold to the justice of God alone as the ground of salvation, and do not acknowledge the idea of mercy at all?

In a similar way, I have heard men preach against the idea that people are saved in their sins, and they supposed they were preaching against Universalist doctrine. Universalists believe no such thing. They believe that all people will be made holy and saved in that way. This shows the importance of knowing what people actually believe before you try to reason them out of their errors. It is of no use to misrepresent a person's doctrines to his face and then try to reason him out of them. You must state his doctrine just as he holds it, and state his arguments fairly. Otherwise, if you state them incorrectly, you either make him angry, or he laughs in his sleeve at the advantage you give him. He will say, "That person cannot argue with me on a fair basis. He has to misrepresent our doctrines in order to try to refute me."

Much harm is done in this way. Ministers do not intend to misrepresent their opponents, but the effect of it is that the poor miserable creatures who hold these errors go to hell because ministers do not take care to inform themselves what their real errors are. Errors are never torn away by such a process. I mention these cases to show how much wisdom a minister must have to meet the cases that occur. He must be acquainted with the real views of people in order to meet them and to do away with their errors and mistakes.

12. Ministers should know what measures are best calculated to aid in accomplishing the great purpose of their office – the salvation of souls. Some measures are plainly necessary. By measures, I mean things that should be done to get the attention of the people and bring them to listen to the truth. Building houses for worship, visiting from house to house, etc., are all "measures," the purpose of which is to get the attention of people to the gospel. Much wisdom is needed to devise and carry forward all the various measures that are adapted to favor the success of the gospel.

What do the politicians do? They organize meetings, circulate flyers and pamphlets, get publicity in the newspapers send their supporters through the streets with flags and pamphlets, and send coaches all over town with flyers to bring people up to the polls – all to gain attention to their cause and elect their candidate. All these are their "measures," and for their end they are wisely calculated. The object is to stir up excitement and bring the people out. They know that unless there is excitement, it is in vain to push their end. I do not mean to say that their measures are pious or right, but only that they are wise in the sense that they are the appropriate application of means to the end.

The purpose of the ministry is to get all the people to feel that the devil has no right to rule this world, but that they should all give themselves to God and vote in the Lord Jesus Christ as the governor of the universe. Now what should be done? What measures will we take? One person says, "Be sure and have nothing that is new." That is strange! The goal of our measures is to gain attention, and you must have something new. As sure as the effect of a measure becomes stereotyped, it ceases to gain attention, and then you must try something new. You do not need to make innovations in everything, but whenever the state of things is such that anything more is needed, it must be something new or it will fail.

A minister should never introduce innovations that are not called for. If he does, they will embarrass him. He cannot change the gospel; that remains the same. But new measures are necessary from time to time to awaken attention and bring the gospel to bear upon the public mind. A minister should then know how to introduce new things so as to create the least possible resistance or reaction. People tend to like form in religion. They love to have their religious duties stereotyped so as to leave them at ease, and they are therefore inclined to resist any new movement designed to stir them up to action and feeling. Therefore it is very important to introduce new things wisely so as not to give needless reason or excuse for resistance.

13. Much wisdom is sometimes needed by a minister to know when to put a stop to new measures. When a measure has freshness enough to secure attention to the truth, ordinarily no other new measure should be introduced. You have secured the great goal of novelty. Anything more will be in danger

of diverting the public mind away from the great object and fixing it on the measures themselves. Then, if you introduce new things when they are not called for, you will go over so large a field, that eventually, when you really need something new, you will have nothing else to introduce without doing something that will give too great a shock to the public mind.

The Bible has laid down no specific course of measures to promote revivals of religion, but has left it to ministers to adopt those that are wisely calculated to secure the end. The more sparing we are of our new things, the longer we can use them to keep public attention awake to the great subject of the Christian religion. By a wise course, this may undoubtedly be done for many years, until our present measures will in time have enough freshness in them again to attract and fix public attention. In this way, we will never lack for something new.

14. In order to win souls, a minister must know how to deal with careless, with awakened, and with anxious sinners so as to lead them right to Christ in the shortest and most direct way. It is amazing to see how many ministers there are who do not know how to deal with sinners, or what to say to them in their various states of mind.

A woman in Albany told me that when she was under conviction, she went to her minister and asked him to tell her what she must do to get relief. He told her that God had not given him much experience on the subject, and he advised her to go to a certain deacon who might be able to tell her what to do. The truth was that he did not know what to say to a sinner under conviction, although there was nothing unusual in her case. If you think this minister is a rare case, you are quite deceived. There are many ministers who do not know what to say to sinners.

A minister once appointed a meeting for those concerned about their souls, and went to attend it. Instead of going around to the individuals, he began to ask them the catechism: "Wherein doth Christ execute the office of a priest?" That was about as helpful to a great many of their minds as anything else he would have said.

I know a minister who held a similar meeting, and he went to attend it with a written discourse that he had prepared for the occasion. That was just as wise as it would be if a physician, going out to visit his patients, would sit down ahead of time and write all the prescriptions before he had seen the patients. A minister needs to know the state of mind of the individuals before he can know what truth will be proper and useful to administer. I do not say these things because I love to do it, but because truth, and the object before me, requires them to be said – and such instances as I have mentioned are by no means rare.

A minister should know how to apply truth to all the situations in which he may find dying sinners going down to hell. He should know how to preach, how to pray, how to conduct prayer meetings, and how to use all the means for bringing the truth of God to bear upon the kingdom of darkness. Does not this require wisdom? *And who is sufficient for these things?* (2 Corinthians 2:16).

II. The Amount of a Minister's Success in Winning Souls (Other Things Being Equal) Invariably Decides the Amount of Wisdom He Has Exercised Carrying Out the Duties of His Office

1. This is plainly asserted in the text: *He that winneth souls is wise.* That is, if a man wins souls, he skillfully adapts means to the end, and he exercises wisdom. The greater the number of sinners he saves, the wiser he is. A blockhead may indeed now and then stumble on such truth or such a manner of exhibiting it as to save a soul. It would be a wonder indeed if any minister did not sometimes have something in his sermons that would meet the case of some individual. But the amount of wisdom is to be decided, other things being equal, by the number of cases in which he is successful in converting sinners.

Take the case of a physician. The greatest quack in New York may now and then stumble upon a remarkable cure, and so increase his reputation with the ignorant; but clearheaded and wise people judge of the skill of a physician by the uniformity of his success in overcoming disease, the variety of diseases he can manage, and the number of cases in which he is successful in saving his patients. The most skillful saves the most. This is common sense. It is truth. It is just as true in regard to success in saving souls, and it is true in just the same sense.

2. This principle is not only asserted in the text, but it is a matter of

fact, a historical truth, that *he that winneth souls is wise.* He has actually used means adapted to the end in such a way as to secure the end.

3. Success in saving souls is evidence that a man understands the gospel and understands human nature, that he knows how to adapt means to his end, that he has common sense, and that he has that kind of tact, that practical discernment, to know how to reach people. If his success is extensive, it shows that he knows how to deal with a great variety of characters, in a great variety of circumstances, who are yet all the enemies of God, and to bring them to Christ. To do this requires great wisdom, and the minister who does it shows that he is wise.

4. Success in winning souls shows that a minister not only knows how to labor wisely for that purpose, but also that he knows where his dependence is. Fears are often expressed about those ministers who are aiming most directly and earnestly at the conversion of sinners. People say, "This man is going to work in his own strength; one would imagine he thinks he can convert himself." How often has the result showed that the man knows very well what he is doing, and knows where his strength is too. He went to work to convert sinners so earnestly, just as if he could do it all himself; but that was the very way he should go about his work. He should so reason with sinners, and plead with them, as faithfully and fully as if he did not expect any intervention by the Spirit of God, or as if he thought there was no Holy Spirit. But whenever a man does this successfully, it shows that, after all, he knows he must depend on the Spirit of God alone for success.

Objection. There are many who feel an objection against this subject, arising out of the view they have taken of the ministry of Jesus Christ. They ask us, "What will you say about the ministry of Jesus Christ? Was He not wise?" I answer, yes, He was infinitely wise. But in regard to His alleged lack of success in the conversion of sinners, you will observe the following things:

1. His ministry was vastly more successful than is generally supposed. We read in one of the sacred writers that after His resurrection and before His ascension He *was seen of above five hundred brethren at once*

(1 Corinthians 15:6). If as many as five hundred brethren were found assembled together at one place, we see there must have been a vast number of them scattered over the country.

2. Another circumstance to be observed is that His public ministry was very short, less than three years.

3. Consider the particular purpose of His ministry. His main purpose was to make atonement for the sins of the world. It was not aimed so much at promoting revivals. The dispensation of the Spirit was not yet given. He did not preach the gospel as fully as His apostles did afterward. The prejudices of the people were so firm and violent that they would not bear it. That He did not is plain from the fact that even His apostles, who were constantly with Him, did not understand the atonement. They did not understand the idea that He was going to die, and consequently, when they heard He was actually dead, they were driven to despair and thought the thing was all over, and their hopes were blown to the winds.

The fact was that He had another object in view, to which everything else was made to yield, and the corrupted state of the public mind, and the obstinate prejudices prevailing, showed why results were not seen any more in the conversion of sinners. The state of public opinion was such that they finally murdered Him for what He did preach.

Many ministers who have little or no success are hiding themselves behind the ministry of Jesus Christ as if He was an unsuccessful preacher, whereas in fact, He was eminently successful, considering the circumstances in which He labored. This is the last place in all the world where a minister who has no success should think of hiding himself.

Remarks

1. A minister may be very educated and not wise. There are many ministers who have great learning. They understand all the sciences – physical, moral, and theological. They may know the dead languages and possess all learning, yet not be wise in relation to the great purpose

about which they are primarily employed. Facts clearly demonstrate this. *He that winneth souls is wise.*

2. An unsuccessful minister may be pious as well as educated, yet not wise. It is unfair to infer that because a minister is unsuccessful, therefore he is a hypocrite. There may be something defective in his education, or in his way of viewing a subject, or of presenting it, or such a lack of common sense as will defeat his labors and prevent his success in winning souls, while he himself may be saved – *yet so as by fire* (1 Corinthians 3:15).

3. A minister may be very wise, even if he is not well educated. He may not understand the dead languages, or theology in its common meaning, yet he may know just what a minister of the gospel needs most to know, without knowing many other things. An educated minister and a wise minister are different things. Facts in the history of the church in all ages prove this. It is very common for churches, when looking for a minister, to aim at getting a very educated man. Do not think I am discouraging learning. The more learning the better, if he is also wise in the great matter he is employed about. If a minister knows how to win souls, the more learning he has the better. But if he has any other kind of learning, and not this, he will invariably fail of the purpose of his ministry.

4. Lack of success in a minister (other things being equal) proves: (1) either that he was never called to preach, and has taken it up out of his own head; (2) that he was poorly educated, and was never taught the very things he needs most to know; or (3) if he was called to preach, and knows how to do his duty, he is too lazy and too wicked to do it.

5. They are the best educated ministers who win the most souls. Ministers are sometimes looked down upon and called very ignorant because they do not know sciences and languages, although they are very far from being ignorant of the great thing for which the ministry is appointed. This is wrong. Learning is important and is always useful, but a minister may know how to win souls to Christ without vast

education, and he has the best education for a minister who can win the most souls to Christ.

6. There is evidently a great defect in the present method of educating ministers. It is a solemn fact to which the attention of the whole church should be distinctly called that the great majority of young ministers who are educated accomplish very little.

When young men come out from the seminaries, are they prepared to go into a revival? Look at a place where there has been a revival in progress and a minister is needed. Let them send to a theological seminary for a minister. Will he enter into the work and sustain it and carry it on? Seldom. Like David with Saul's armor, he comes in with such a load of theological frills that he does not know what to do. Leave him there for two weeks, and the revival is at an end. The churches know and feel that the greater part of these young men do not know how to do anything that needs to be done for a revival, and they are complaining that the young ministers are so far behind the church. You may send all over the United States to theological seminaries and find only a few young ministers capable of carrying forward the work. What a state of things!

There is a big defect in educating ministers. Education should be such as to prepare young men for the specific work to which they are destined. But instead of this, they are educated for anything else. The great mistake is that they direct the mind too much to irrelevant matters that are not necessary to be attended to. In their courses of study, they carry the mind over too wide a field, which diverts their attention from the main thing, and so they get cold in religion; and when they get through, instead of being prepared for their work, they are unprepared for it. Under pretense of disciplining the mind, they in fact scatter the attention, so that when they come to their work they are awkward and know nothing about how to be effective, or how to act, to win souls. This is not universally the case, but too often it is so.

It is common for people to talk loudly and positively about an educated ministry. God forbid that I should say a word against an educated ministry. But what do we mean by an education for the ministry? Do we mean that they should be so educated as to be prepared for the work?

If they are so educated, the more education the better. Let education be of the right kind, teaching a young man the things he needs to know, and not the very things he does not need to know.

Let them be educated for the work. Do not let education be such that when young men come out, after spending six, eight, or ten years in study, they are not worth half as much as they were before they went. I have known young men come out after what they call "a thorough course," who were not fit to take charge of a prayer meeting, and who could not manage a prayer meeting so as to make it profitable or interesting.

An elder of a church in a neighboring city informed me recently of a case in point. A young man, before he went to the seminary, had labored as a layman with them, conducted their prayer meetings, and had been exceedingly useful among them. After he had been to the seminary, they sent for him and desired his help; but oh, how he had changed! He was so completely transformed that he made no impression. The church soon began to complain that they would die under his influence, and he left because he was not prepared for the work.

It is common for those ministers who have been to the seminaries, and are now useful, to affirm that their course of studies there did them little or no good, and that they had to unlearn what they had learned there before they could accomplish much. I do not say this condemningly, but it is a distressing fact, and I must say it in love.

Suppose you were going to make a man a surgeon in the navy. Instead of sending him to the medical school to learn surgery, would you send him to the nautical school to learn navigation? In this way, you might qualify him to navigate a ship, but he is no surgeon. Ministers should be educated to know what the Bible is and what the human mind is, and they should know how to bring one to bear on the other. They should be brought into contact with the mind and made familiar with all the aspects of society. They should have the Bible in one hand and the map of the human mind in the other, and know how to use the truth for the salvation of men.

7. A lack of common sense often defeats the purpose of the Christian

ministry. There are many good men in the ministry who have education and talents of a certain sort, but they have no common sense to win souls.

8. We see one big defect in our theological schools: young men are closed up in their schools, confined to books and shut out from interaction with the common people, or contact with the common mind. Therefore, they are not familiar with the way in which common people think. This accounts for the fact that some plain men who have been brought up in business and are acquainted with human nature are ten times better qualified to win souls than those who are educated on the present principle and are in fact ten times as well acquainted with the proper business of the ministry. These are called "uneducated men." This is a big mistake. They are not educated in science, but they are educated in the very things that they need to know as ministers. They are not ignorant ministers, for they know exactly how to reach the mind with truth. They understand the minds of men and how to adapt the gospel to their case. They are better furnished for their work than if they had all the machinery of the schools.

I want to be understood. I do not say that I would not have a young man go to school, nor would I discourage him from studying the field of science. The more the better, if together with it he also learns the things that the minister needs to know in order to win souls. He needs to understand his Bible, understand human nature, know how to bring the truth to bear, know how to guide and manage minds, and know how to lead them away from sin and lead them to God.

9. The success of any measure designed to promote a revival of religion demonstrates its wisdom with the following exceptions:

A measure may be introduced for effect to produce excitement, yet when it is looked back upon afterward, it will look foolish and will appear to have been a mere trick. In that case, it will cause a reaction, and its introduction will do more harm than good.

Measures may be introduced, the revival may be very powerful, and the success may be attributed to the measures – when in fact other things made the revival powerful, and these very measures may have been a hindrance. The prayers of Christians, and the preaching, and other things may have been so well calculated to carry on the work that it has succeeded despite these measures.

However, when the blessing evidently follows the introduction of the measure itself, the proof is unanswerable that the measure is wise. It is wrong to say that such a measure will do more harm than good. God knows about that. His purpose is to do the greatest amount of good possible, and of course, He will not add His blessing to a measure that will do more harm than good. He may sometimes withhold His blessing from a measure that is calculated to do some good because it will be at the expense of a greater good, but He will never bless a harmful proceeding. There is no such thing as deceiving God in the matter. He knows whether a given measure is, on the whole, wise or not. He may bless a course of labors despite some unwise or harmful measures, but if He blesses the measure itself, it is rebuking God to declare it unwise. He who undertakes to do this, let him look to the matter.

10. It is evident that much fault has been found with measures that have been preeminently and continually blessed by God for the promotion of revivals. We know it is said that the horrid oaths of a profane swearer have been the means of awakening another less hardened sinner, but this is a rare case. God does not usually make such a use of profanity. However, if a measure is continually or usually blessed, let the person who thinks he is wiser than God call it in question. Take care how you find fault with God!

11. Christians should pray for ministers. Brethren, if you felt how much ministers need wisdom to perform the duties of their great office with success, and how ignorant they all are, and how insufficient they are of themselves, to think anything as of themselves, you would pray for them a great deal more than you do – that is, if you cared anything for the success of their labors. People often find fault with ministers, when they do not pray for them. Brethren, this is tempting God, for you should not expect any better ministers unless you pray for them. And you should not expect a blessing on the labors of your minister, or to have your families converted by his preaching, when you do not

pray for him. And it is the same for others – for the waste places and the heathen – instead of praying all the time only that God would sent out more laborers, you have need to pray that God would make ministers wise to win souls, and that those He sends out may be properly educated so that they will be scribes well instructed in the kingdom of God (Matthew 13:52).

12. Those laymen in the church who know how to win souls are to be considered wise. They should not be called "ignorant laymen." And those church members who do not know how to convert sinners, and who cannot win souls, should not be called wise – as Christians. They are not wise Christians; only *he that winneth souls is wise.* They may be knowledgeable in politics or in all sciences, or they may be skilled in the management of business or other things, and they may look down on those who win souls as nothing but plain, simplehearted, ignorant people. If any of you are inclined to do this, and to undervalue those brethren who win souls as being not as wise and skillful as you are, you deceive yourselves. They may not know some things that you know, but they know those things that a Christian is most responsible to know, and you do not.

This may be illustrated by the case of a minister who goes to sea. He may be knowledgeable in science, but he knows nothing at all about how to sail a ship. He begins to ask the sailors about this thing and that, and what this rope is for, and the like. The sailors say, "These are not ropes. We only have one rope in a ship. These are the rigging. The man talks like a fool." And so this educated man might become a laughingstock to the sailors because he does not know how to sail a ship. But if he were to tell them half of what he knows about science, they might think he is a sorcerer to know so much. In the same way, educated students may understand their Latin phrases and Greek words very well, and may laugh at the humble Christian and call him ignorant, although he may know how to win more souls than five hundred of them.

I was once distressed and grieved at hearing a minister bearing down upon a young preacher who had been converted under remarkable circumstances and who was licensed to preach without pursuing a regular course of study. This minister, who was never, or at least rarely, known to convert a soul, bore down upon the young man in a very superior, condescending manner, belittling him because he did not have the advantage of a liberal education, when in fact he was instrumental in converting more souls than any five hundred ministers like himself.

I would say nothing to undervalue, or lead you to undervalue, a thorough education for ministers, but I do not call that a thorough education that they get in our colleges and seminaries. It does not prepare them for their work. I appeal to all experience whether our young men in seminaries are thoroughly educated for the purpose of winning souls. Do they do it? Everybody knows they do not.

Look at the reports of the Home Missionary Society. If I remember right, in 1830, the number of conversions in connection with the labors of the missionaries of that society did not exceed five to each missionary. I believe the number has increased since, but is still exceedingly small to what it would have been had they been prepared by a proper course of training for their work. I do not say this to reproach them, for from my heart I pity them, and I pity the church for being under the necessity of supporting ministers trained in this way, or none at all. They are the best men the missionary society can obtain.

I suppose, of course, that I will be reproached for saying this, but it is too true and too painful to be concealed. Those fathers who have the training of our young ministers are good men, but they are ancient men, men of another age and stamp from what is needed in these days of excitement when the church and world are rising to new thought and action. Those dear fathers will not, I suppose, see this, and will perhaps think negatively of me for saying it, but it is the cause of Christ. Some of them are getting back toward second childhood, and should resign and give place to younger men who are not rendered physically incapable by age of keeping pace with the onward movements of the church.

I will add here that to my own mind, it appears evident that unless our theological professing Christians preach a good deal, mingle much with the church, and sympathize with her in all her movements, it is morally, if not naturally, impossible for them to succeed in training young men to the spirit of the age. It is a shame and a sin that theology professors, who preach only seldom and are withdrawn from the active duties of the ministry, would sit in their studies and write their letters, advisory or dictatorial, to ministers and churches who are in the field, and who are in circumstances to judge what needs to be done. The men who spend all or at least a portion of their time in the active duties of the ministry are the only men who are able to judge what is expedient or inexpedient, prudent or imprudent, as to measures from time to time. It is as dangerous and ridiculous for our theology professors, who are withdrawn from the field of conflict, to be allowed to dictate, in regard to the measures and movements of the church, as it would be for a general to sit in his bedroom and attempt to order a battle.

Two ministers were one day discussing another minister whose labors were greatly blessed in the conversion of thousands of souls. One of them said, "That man should not preach anymore; he should stop and go to [a particular theological seminary] and go through a regular course of study." He said the man had "a good mind, and if he was thoroughly educated, he might be very useful."

The other replied, "Do you think he would be more useful after going to that seminary? I challenge you to show by facts that any men are more useful who have been there. No, sir. The fact is that since this man has been in the ministry, he has been instrumental in converting more souls than all the young men who have come from that seminary during that time."

This is logic! Why stop and go to a seminary to prepare himself for converting souls when he is now converting more than all who come from the seminary?

Finally, I want to ask you, who among you can lay any claim to the possession of this divine wisdom? Who among you, laymen? Who among you, ministers? Can any of you? Can I? Are we at work, wisely, to win souls, or are we trying to make ourselves believe that success is no criterion of wisdom? It is a criterion. It is a safe criterion for every minister to try himself by. The amount of his success, other things being equal, measures the amount of wisdom he has exercised in carrying out the duties of his office.

How few of you have ever had wisdom enough to convert as much as a single sinner! Do not say now, "I cannot convert sinners. How can I convert sinners? God alone can convert sinners." Look at the text: *He that winneth souls is wise* – and do not think you can escape the sentence.

It is true that God converts sinners, but there is a sense, too, in which ministers convert them. And you have something to do – something that requires wisdom – something that, if you do it wisely, will ensure the conversion of sinners in proportion to the wisdom employed. If you have never done this, it is high time to examine yourselves and see whether you have wisdom enough to save even your own souls.

You are obligated to be wise in winning souls. Souls may have already perished. Perhaps a friend or a child is in hell because you have not put forth the wisdom that you could have in saving them. The city is going to hell. Yes, the world is going to hell, and will continue going to hell, until the church finds out what to do to win souls. Politicians are wise. The children of this world are wise. They know what to do to accomplish their goals, while we are merely talking, not knowing what to do, or where to take hold of the work – and sinners are going to hell.

Lecture 12

How to Preach the Gospel

He that winneth souls is wise.
—Proverbs 11:30

One of the last remarks in my last lecture was that the text ascribes conversion to men. Winning souls is converting people. In this lecture I intend to show:

I.   Several passages of Scripture ascribe conversion to men.

II. This is consistent with other passages that ascribe conversion to God.

III. Several further details that are considered important in regard to the preaching of the gospel and that show that great practical wisdom is necessary to win souls to Christ.

I. The Bible Ascribes Conversion to Men

There are many passages that represent the conversion of sinners as the work of men. Daniel 12:3 says, *And they that be wise shall shine as the brightness of the firmament; and they that turn many to righteousness as the stars for ever and ever.* Here the work is ascribed to men. So also in 1 Corinthians 4:15: *For though ye have ten thousand instructors in*

Christ, yet have ye not many fathers: for in Christ Jesus I have begotten you through the gospel. Here the apostle Paul distinctly tells the Corinthians that he made them Christians with the gospel or truth that he preached. Again, in James 5:19-20, we are taught the same thing: *Brethren, if any of you do err from the truth, and one convert him; let him know that he which converteth the sinner from the error of his way shall save a soul from death, and shall hide a multitude of sins.*

I could quote many other passages that are equally plain, but these are abundantly sufficient to establish the fact that the Bible does actually ascribe conversion to men.

II. This Is not Inconsistent with Those Passages in Which Conversion Is Ascribed to God

Let me remark here that to my mind, it often appears very strange that people would ever suppose there was an inconsistency here, or that they would ever have overlooked the plain common sense of the matter. How easy it is to see that there is a sense in which God converts them, and another sense in which men convert them.

The Scriptures ascribe the conversion of a sinner to four different agencies: to men, to God, to the truth, and to the sinner himself. The passages that ascribe it to the truth are the largest class. It is surprising that people would ever have overlooked this distinction, and would have regarded conversion as a work performed exclusively by God. It is also surprising that any difficulty would ever have been felt on the subject, or that people would ever have professed themselves unable to reconcile these various classes of passages.

The Bible speaks on this subject precisely as we speak on common subjects. For example, there is a man who has been very sick. How natural it is for him to say of his physician, "That man saved my life." Does he mean to say that the physician saved his life without reference to God? Certainly not, unless he is an atheist. God made the physician, and He made the medicine too. It can never be shown otherwise than that the agency of God is just as truly concerned in making the medicine take effect to save life as it is in making the truth take effect to save a soul. To affirm the contrary is downright atheism. It is true, then, that the physician saved him, and it is also true that God saved him. It is equally true that the medicine saved his life and that he saved his own life by taking the medicine, for the medicine would have done no good if he had not voluntarily taken it or yielded his body to its power.

In the conversion of a sinner, it is true that God gives the truth the ability to turn the sinner to God. He is an active, voluntary, powerful agent in changing the mind, but He is not the only agent. The one who brings the truth to his notice is also an agent. We tend to speak of ministers and other men as only instruments in converting sinners. This is not exactly correct. Man is something more than an instrument. Truth is the mere unconscious instrument, but man is more; he is a voluntary, responsible agent in the business.

In my printed sermon, No. 1, which some of you may have seen, I have illustrated this idea by the case of an individual standing on the banks of Niagara:

> Suppose you are standing on the banks of Niagara Falls. As you stand upon the verge of the precipice, you behold a man lost in deep daydreaming, approaching its verge unaware of his danger. He approaches nearer and nearer, until he actually lifts his foot to take the final step that will plunge him in destruction. At this moment you lift your warning voice above the roar of the foaming waters and cry out, "Stop!" The voice pierces his ear and breaks the charm that binds him. He turns instantly upon his heel, all pale and shocked. He withdraws, quivering, from the verge of death. He reels and almost faints with horror.
>
> He turns and walks slowly to the public house. You follow him. The clear expression in his countenance attracts the attention of many people around him. On your approach, he points to you and says, "That man saved my life!" Here he ascribes the work to you, and certainly there is a sense in which you had saved him. However, on being further questioned, he says, "*Stop!* – how that word rings in my ears. Oh, that was to me the word of life!" Here he ascribes

it to the word that awakened him and caused him to turn. Then, on conversing still further, he says, "If I had not turned at that instant, I would have been a dead man." Here he speaks of it, and truly, as his own act; but immediately you hear him say, "Oh, the mercy of God! If God had not intervened, I would have been lost."

The only defect in this illustration is that in the situation supposed, the only intervention on the part of God was a providential one, and the only sense in which the saving of the man's life is ascribed to Him is in a providential sense. However, in the conversion of a sinner, there is something more than the providence of God working, for here, not only does the providence of God so order it that the preacher cries, "Stop!" but the Spirit of God urges the truth home upon him with such tremendous power as to cause him to turn.

Not only does the preacher cry, "Stop!" but through the living voice of the preacher, the Spirit cries, "Stop!" The preacher cries, *Turn ye, why will ye die?* (Ezekiel 33:11). The Spirit pours the issue home with such power that the sinner turns. In speaking of this change, it is perfectly proper to say that the Spirit turned him, just as you would say of a man who had persuaded another to change his mind on the subject of politics that he had converted him and won him over. It is also proper to say that the truth converted him, as in a case when the political sentiments of a person were changed by a certain argument, and we would say that argument won him over.

So also with perfect reasonableness we may ascribe the change to the living preacher, or to him who had presented the argument – just as we would say of a lawyer who had prevailed in his argument with a jury that he has presented his case and has converted the jury. With the same reasonableness, it is also ascribed to the individual himself whose heart is changed; we would say that he had changed his mind, he has come over, he has repented. Now it is strictly true, and true in the most absolute and highest sense, that the act is his own act, the turning is his own turning, while God by the truth has caused him to turn. Still it is strictly true that he has turned and has done it himself.

Thus you see the sense in which it is the work of God, and also the sense in which it is the sinner's own work. The Spirit of God, by the truth, influences the sinner to change, and in this sense is the efficient cause of the change. But the sinner actually changes, and is therefore himself, in the most proper sense, the author of the change. There are some who, on reading their Bibles, fasten their eyes upon those passages that ascribe the work to the Spirit of God, and seem to overlook those that ascribe it to man, and they speak of it as the sinner's own act. When they have quoted Scripture to prove it is the work of God, they seem to think they have proved that it is that in which man is passive, and that it can in no sense be the work of man.

Some months ago a tract was written, the title of which was "Regeneration, the Effect of Divine Power." The writer goes on to prove that the work is accomplished by the Spirit of God, and there stops. It would have been just as true, just as philosophical, and just as scriptural, if he had said that conversion was the work of man. It was easy to prove that it was the work of God, in the sense in which I have explained it. The writer, therefore, tells the truth, as far as he goes, but he has only told half the truth. For while there is a sense in which it is the work of God, as he has shown, there is also a sense in which it is the work of man, as we have just seen. The very title to this tract is a stumbling block. It tells the truth, but it does not tell the whole truth. And a tract might be written upon this idea, that "Conversion or Regeneration Is the Work of Man," which would be just as true, just as scriptural, and just as philosophical as the one to which I have alluded.

Thus the writer, in his zeal to recognize and honor God as concerned in this work, by leaving out the fact that a change of heart is the sinner's own act, has left the sinner strongly entrenched, with his weapons in his rebellious hands, vigorously resisting the claims of his Maker and waiting passively for God to make him a new heart. Thus you see the consistency between the requirement of the text and the declared fact that God is the author of the new heart. God commands you to change your heart, He expects you to do it, and if it is ever done, you must do it.

And let me tell you, sinner, that if you do not do it, you will go to hell, and to all eternity you will feel that you deserved to be sent there for not having done it.

III. I Will Now Discuss Several Important Points Connected with Preaching the Gospel, and Show That Great Practical Wisdom Is Indispensable to Win Souls to Christ

First, in regard to the matter of preaching.

1. All preaching should be practical. The proper aim of all doctrine is practice. Anything brought forward as doctrine that cannot be made use of as practical is not preaching the gospel. There is none of that sort of preaching in the Bible. That is all practical. *All Scripture is given by inspiration of God, and is profitable for doctrine, for reproof, for correction, for instruction in righteousness: that the man of God may be perfect, thoroughly furnished unto all good works* (2 Timothy 3:16-17).

A great deal of preaching in the present day, as well as in past ages, is called doctrinal preaching rather than practical preaching. The very idea of making this distinction is a device of the devil, and a more abominable device Satan himself never devised. You sometimes hear certain men tell a wonderful deal about the necessity of "indoctrinating the people." By this they mean something different from practical preaching. They mean teaching them certain doctrines as abstract truths without any particular reference to practice.

I have known a minister in the midst of a revival, while surrounded by concerned sinners, stop laboring to convert souls in order to "indoctrinate" the young converts for fear that somebody else would indoctrinate them before him. And there the revival stops! Either his doctrine was not true, or it was not preached in the right way. To preach doctrines in an abstract way, and not in reference to practice, is absurd. God always brings in doctrine to regulate practice. To bring forward doctrinal views for any other purpose is not only nonsense, but it is wicked.

Some people are opposed to doctrinal preaching. If they are used to hearing doctrines preached in a cold, abstract way, no wonder they are opposed to it. They should be opposed to such preaching. But what can a man preach who preaches no doctrine? If he preaches no doctrine, he preaches no gospel. And if he does not preach it in a practical way, he does not preach the gospel. All preaching should be doctrinal, and all preaching should be practical. The very design of doctrine is to regulate practice. Any preaching that does not have this tendency is not the gospel. A loose, exhorting style of preaching may affect the passions and may produce excitement, but it will never sufficiently instruct the people to secure sound conversions. On the other hand, preaching doctrine in an abstract manner may fill the head with beliefs, but it will never sanctify the heart or life.

2. Preaching should be direct. The gospel should be preached to people, and not about them. The minister must address his hearers. He must preach to them about themselves, and not leave the impression that he is preaching to them about others. He will never do them any good any farther than he succeeds in convincing each individual that he means him. Many preachers seem very much afraid of making the impression that they mean anybody in particular. They are preaching against certain sins, not that they have anything to do with the sinner. It is the sin, and not the sinner, that they are rebuking, and they would by no means speak as if they supposed any of their hearers were guilty of these abominable practices. This is anything but preaching the gospel. This is not what the prophets, Christ, or the apostles did. Nor do any ministers do this who are successful in winning souls to Christ.

3. Another very important thing to be regarded in preaching is that the minister should hunt after sinners and Christians wherever they may have entrenched themselves in inaction. It is not the design of preaching to make people content and quiet, but to make them act. It is not the design of calling in a physician to have him give strong drugs, and so cover up the disease and let it run on until it works death, but to search out the disease wherever it may be hidden, and to remove it. In the same way, if a professing Christian has backslidden and is full of doubts and fears, it is not the minister's duty to calm him in his sins and comfort him, but to hunt him out of his errors and backslidings and show him just where he stands and what it is that makes him full of doubts and fears.

A minister should know the religious opinions of every sinner in his congregation. Indeed, a minister in the country is generally inexcusable if he does not. He has no excuse for not knowing the religious views of everyone in his congregation, and of all who may come under his influence if he has had opportunity to know them. How otherwise can he preach to them? How can he know how to bring forth things new and old and adapt truth to their case? How can he hunt them out unless he knows where they hide themselves? He may keep changing how he presents a few fundamental doctrines, such as repentance and faith, and faith and repentance, until the day of judgment, and never make any impression on many minds.

Every sinner has some hiding place, some entrenchment where he lingers. He is in possession of some darling lie with which he is trying to comfort himself. Let the minister find it out and get rid of it, either in the pulpit or in private, or the person will go to hell in his sins, and his blood will be found in the minister's garment.

4. Another important thing to observe is that a minister should dwell most on those specific points that are most needed. I will explain what I mean. Sometimes he may find people who have been led to place great reliance on their own resolutions. They think they can put it off and seek God in their own time, and eventually they will repent when they get ready, without any concern about the Spirit of God. Let the minister take up these ideas and show that they are entirely contrary to the Scriptures. Let him show that if the Spirit of God is grieved away, no matter how able he may be, it is certain he will never repent, and that eventually, when it will be convenient for him to do it, he will have no inclination to do so. The minister who finds these errors prevailing should expose them. He should hunt them out, understand just how they are held, and then preach the class of truths that will show the fallacy, the folly, and the danger of these ideas.

On the other hand, he may find people who have got such views of election and sovereignty as to think they have nothing to do except to wait for the moving of the waters (see John 5:4). Let him go right over against these people and emphasize to them their ability to obey God, and to show them their obligation and duty, and emphasize that until he brings them to submit and be saved. They have a distorted view of these doctrines, and there is no way to drive them out of the hiding place except to set them right on these points. Wherever a sinner is entrenched, unless you pour light upon him there, you will never move him. It is of no use to emphasize to him those truths that he admits, no matter how plainly they may in fact contradict his wrong beliefs. He thinks they are perfectly consistent, and does not see the inconsistency, and therefore it will not move him or bring him to repentance.

I have been informed about a minister in New England who was settled in a congregation that had long enjoyed little else than Arminian preaching, and the congregation themselves were primarily Arminians. Well, this minister, in his preaching, strongly insisted on the opposite points, such as the doctrine of election, divine sovereignty, predestination, etc. The consequence was, as might have been expected where this was done with ability, there was a powerful revival.

Sometime afterward, this same minister was called to labor in another field, in this state, where the people were all on the other side, and strongly steeped in Antinomianism. They had such distorted views of election and divine sovereignty that they were continually saying they had no power to do anything, but must await God's time.

Now what does this minister do but immediately start preaching the doctrine of election! And when he was asked how he could think of preaching the doctrine of election so much to that people, when it was the very thing that lulled them to a deeper slumber, he replied. "Why, that's the very class of truths by which I had such a great revival in ——," not considering the difference in the views of the people. If I am correctly informed, he is there to this day, preaching away the doctrine of election, and wondering that it does not produce as powerful a revival as it did in the other place. Probably those sinners will never be converted.

You must take things as they are, find out where sinners lie, pour in truth upon them there, and get them out from their refuges of lies. It is of vast importance that a minister should find out where the congregation is, and preach accordingly.

I have been in many places in times of revival, and I have never been able to use exactly the same course of preaching in one place as in another. Some are entrenched behind one refuge, and some behind another. In one place, the church will need to be instructed; in another, sinners will need to be taught. In one place, one set of truths need preached, and another set in another place. A minister must find out where they are, and preach accordingly. I believe this is the experience of all preachers who are called to labor from field to field.

5. If a minister wants to promote a revival, he should be very careful not to introduce controversy. He will grieve away the Spirit of God. In this way, probably, more revivals are put down than in any other. Look back upon the history of the church from the beginning, and you will see that ministers are generally responsible for grieving away the Spirit and causing decline by controversy. It is the ministers who bring forward controversial subjects for discussion, and eventually they get very zealous on the subject. Then they get the church into a controversial spirit, and the Spirit of God is grieved away.

If I had time to go over the history of the church from the days of the apostles, I could show that all the controversies that have taken place, and all the great decline in the Christian religion, too, were due to ministers. I believe the ministers of the present day are responsible for the present state of the church, and it will be seen to be true at the judgment. Who does not know that ministers have been crying out "heresy" and "new measures" and talking about the "evils of revivals" until they have got the church all in confusion?

Look at the poor Presbyterian church, and see ministers getting up their Act and Testimony telling of the division between the Old School and New School Presbyterians, and keeping up a continual war! O God, have mercy on ministers. They talk about their days of fasting and prayer, but are these the men to call on others to fast and pray? They should fast and pray themselves.

It is time for ministers to assemble together and fast and pray over the evil of controversy, for they have caused it. The church itself would never get into a controversial spirit unless led into it by ministers. The body of the church is always reluctant of controversy, and will keep out of it unless they are dragged into it by ministers. When Christians are revived, they are not inclined to meddle with controversy, either to read or hear it. However, they may be told of such and such "damnable heresies" that are around, until they get their feelings enlisted in controversy – and then farewell to the revival. If a minister, in preaching, finds it necessary to discuss particular points about which Christians differ in opinion, let him by all means avoid a controversial spirit and manner of doing it.

6. The gospel should be preached in those proportions so that the whole gospel may be brought before the minds of the people and produce its proper influence. If too much stress is laid on one class of truths, the Christian character will not have its due proportions. Its symmetry will not be perfect. If that class of truths is almost exclusively dwelt upon that requires great exertion of intellect, without being brought home to the heart and conscience, it will be found that the church will be indoctrinated in those views and will have their heads filled with beliefs, but will not be awake, active, and efficient in the promotion of Christianity.

If, on the other hand, the preaching is broad, general, moralistic, and highly emotional, the church will be like a ship with too much sail for her ballast. It will be in danger of being swept away by a tempest of feeling, where there is not sufficient knowledge to prevent their being carried away with every wind of doctrine (Ephesians 4:14). If election and sovereignty are preached too much, there will be Antinomianism in the church, and sinners will hide themselves behind the delusion that they can do nothing. If the other doctrines of ability and obligation are too prominent, they will produce Arminianism in the church, and sinners will be proud and self-confident.

When I entered the ministry, there had been so much said about the doctrines of election and sovereignty that I found it was the universal hiding place, both of sinners and of the church – that they could not do anything, or could not obey the gospel. Wherever I went, I found it indispensable to demolish these refuges of lies. A revival would in no way be produced or carried on except by dwelling on that class of truths that holds up man's ability, obligation, and responsibility. This was the only class of truths that would bring sinners to submission.

It was not so in the days when President Jonathan Edwards and George Whitefield labored. Then the churches in New England had enjoyed little else than Arminian preaching, and they were all resting in themselves and their own strength. These bold and devoted servants of God came out and declared those particular doctrines of grace – divine sovereignty and election – and they were greatly blessed. They did not dwell on these doctrines exclusively, but they preached them very fully. The consequence was that because in those circumstances revivals followed from such preaching, the ministers who followed continued to preach these doctrines almost exclusively. They dwelt on them so long that the church and the world got entrenched behind them, waiting for God to come and do what He required them to do, and so revivals ceased for many years.

Now and for years past, ministers have been engaged in hunting them out from these refuges. It is all important for the ministers of this day to bear in mind that if they dwell exclusively on ability and obligation, they will get their hearers back on the old Arminian ground, and then they will cease to promote revivals. Here are a body of ministers who have preached a great deal of truth, and have had great revivals under God. Now let it be known and remarked that the reason is that they have hunted sinners out from their hiding places. But if they continue to dwell on the same class of truths until sinners hide themselves behind their preaching, another class of truths must be preached. Then if they do not change their methods, another cloud will hang over the church until another class of ministers will arise and hunt sinners out of those new retreats.

A proper view of both classes of truths, election and free will, will do no harm. They are entirely calculated to convert sinners and strengthen saints. It is a distorted view that chills the heart of the church and closes the eyes of sinners in sleep until they sink down to hell. If I had time, I would remark on the manner in which I have sometimes heard the doctrines of divine sovereignty, election, and ability preached. They have been presented in irreconcilable contradiction, the one against the other. Such exhibitions are anything but the gospel, and are calculated to make a sinner feel anything else rather than his responsibility to God.

By preaching truth in proper proportions, I do not mean mingling all things together in the same sermon in such a way that sinners will not see their connection or consistency. A minister once asked another, "Why do you not preach the doctrine of election?"

"Because," said the other, "I find sinners here are entrenched behind inability."

The first then said he once knew a minister who used to preach election in the morning and repentance in the afternoon. Marvelous grace it must be that would produce a revival under such preaching! What connection is there in this? Instead of revealing to the sinner his sins in the morning, and then in the afternoon calling on him to repent, he is first turned to the doctrine of election, and then commanded to repent. What is he to repent of? The doctrine of election?

This is not what I mean by preaching truth in its proportion. Bringing things together that only confound the sinner's mind and overwhelm him with a fog of metaphysics is not wise preaching. When talking about election, the preacher is not talking about the sinner's duty. It has no relation to the sinner's duty. Election belongs to the government of God. It is a part of the exceeding richness of the grace of God. It shows the love of God, not the duty of the sinner. To bring election and repentance together in this way diverts the sinner's mind away from his duty.

It has been customary in many places, for a long time, to bring the doctrine of election into every sermon. Sinners have been commanded to repent, and told that they could not repent, in the same sermon. A great deal of creativity has been exercised in attempting to reconcile a sinner's "inability" with his obligation to obey God. Election, predestination, free will, inability, and duty have all been thrown together in one indiscriminate jumble. With regard to many sermons, it has been too true, as has been objected, that ministers have preached, "You can and you can't, you will and you won't, and you'll be damned if you don't." Such a mixture of truth and error, of light and darkness, has confused the congregation and has been the fruitful source of Universalism and every sort of unbelief and error.

7. It is of great importance that the sinner should be made to feel his guilt and sin, and not left to the impression that he is unfortunate. I think this is a very prevailing fault, particularly with printed books on the subject. They are calculated to make the sinner think more of his sorrows than of his sins, and feel that his state is rather unfortunate than wrong. Most of you may have seen a very lovely little book recently published entitled *Todd's Lectures to Children*. It is very fine, wonderfully fine, and pleasing in some of its illustrations of truth. But it has one very serious fault. Many of its illustrations, I may say most of them,

are not calculated to make a correct impression respecting the guilt of sinners, or to make them feel how much they have been to blame. This is very unfortunate. If the writer had guarded his illustrations on this point so as to make them affect sinners with a sense of their guilt, I do not see how a child could read through that book and not be converted.

Multitudes of the books written for children, and for adults too, within the last twenty years, have run into this mistake to an alarming degree. Mrs. Sherwood's writings have this fault standing out upon almost every page. They are not calculated to make the sinner blame and condemn himself. Until you can do this, the gospel will never take effect.

8. A main goal with the preacher must be to make present duty felt. I have talked, I suppose, with many thousands of anxious sinners, and I have found that they had never before felt the pressure of present obligation. The impression is not commonly made by ministers in their preaching that sinners are expected to repent now. If ministers suppose they make this impression, they deceive themselves. Most commonly, any other impression is made upon the minds of sinners by the preacher than that they are expected now to submit.

But what sort of a gospel is this? Does God authorize such an impression? Is this according to the preaching of Jesus Christ? Does the Holy Spirit, when striving with the sinner, make the impression upon his mind that he is not expected to obey now? Was any such impression produced by the preaching of the apostles? How does it happen that so many ministers now preach so as in fact to make an impression on their hearers that they are not expected to repent now? Until the sinner's conscience is reached on this subject, you preach to him in vain. Until ministers learn how to preach so as to make the right impression, the world can never be converted. Oh, to what an alarming extent does the impression now prevail among the unrepentant that they are not expected to repent now, but must await God's time!

9. Sinners should be made to feel that they have something to do – and that is to repent. They should know that it is something that no other being can do for them, neither God nor man, and it is something that they can do, and can do now. The Christian religion is something to

do, not something to wait for, and they must do it now or they are in danger of eternal death.

10. Ministers should never rest satisfied until they have annihilated every excuse of sinners. The plea of "inability" is the worst of all excuses. It slanders God, charging Him with infinite tyranny in commanding people to do that which they have no power to do. Make the sinner see and feel that this is the very nature of his excuse. Make the sinner see that all pleas in excuse for not submitting to God are an act of rebellion against Him. Tear away the last lie that he grasps in his hand, and make him realize that he is absolutely condemned before God.

11. Sinners should be made to feel that if they now grieve away the Spirit of God, it is very probable that they will be lost forever. There is infinite danger of this. They should be made to understand why they are dependent on the Spirit, and that it is not because they cannot do what God commands, but because they are unwilling; and because they are so unwilling, it is just as certain that they will not repent without the Holy Spirit as if they were now in hell, or as if they were actually unable. They are so opposed and so unwilling that they will never repent in the world unless God sends His Holy Spirit upon them.

Show them, too, that a sinner under the gospel who hears the truth preached, if converted at all, is generally converted at a young age. And if not converted while young, he is commonly given up by God. Where the truth is preached, sinners are either gospel-hardened or converted. I know some old sinners are converted, but they are exceptions, and by no means common.

Secondly, I now want to make a few remarks on the manner of preaching.
1. It should be conversational. In order to be understood, preaching should be colloquial in its style. A minister must preach just as he would talk if he wants to be fully understood. Nothing is more calculated to make a sinner feel that Christianity is some mysterious thing that he cannot understand than this chanting, formal, lofty style of speaking that is so generally used in the pulpit. The minister should do as the

lawyer does when he wants to make a jury understand him perfectly. He uses a style that is perfectly colloquial. This lofty, swelling style will do no good. The gospel will never produce any great effects until ministers talk to their hearers from the pulpit as they talk in private conversation.

2. It must be in the language of common life. Not only should it be colloquial in its style, but the words should be those that are in common use; otherwise, they will not be understood. In the New Testament you will observe that Jesus Christ invariably uses words of the most common kind. You hardly find a word of His instructions that any child cannot understand. The language of the Gospels is the plainest, simplest, and most easily understood of any language in the world.

For a minister to neglect this principle is wicked. Some ministers use language that is purely technical in preaching. They think to avoid trouble by explaining the meaning fully at the beginning, but this will not suffice. It will not produce the desired result of making the people understand what he means. If he uses a word that is not in common use, and that people do not understand, his explanation may be very full, but the difficulty is that people will forget his explanations – and then his words are all Greek to them. Or if he uses a word in common use, but uses it in an uncommon sense, giving his special explanations, it is no better, for the people will soon forget his special explanations, and then the impression actually conveyed to their minds will be according to their common understanding of the word. Therefore, he will never communicate the right idea to his congregation. It is amazing how many people of thinking minds there are in congregations who do not understand the most common technical expressions used by ministers – such as regeneration, sanctification, etc.

Use words that can be perfectly understood. Do not, for fear of appearing unlearned, use language that is half Latin and half Greek, which the people do not understand. The apostle Paul says the man is a barbarian who uses language that the people do not understand (1 Corinthians 14:11). And *if the trumpet give an uncertain sound, who shall prepare himself to the battle?* (1 Corinthians 14:8). In the apostles' days, there were some preachers who were marvelously proud of displaying their command of language and showing off the variety of languages they could speak, which the common people could not understand. The apostle rebukes this spirit sharply, and says, *I had rather speak five words with my understanding, that by my voice I might teach others also, than ten thousand words in an unknown tongue* (1 Corinthians 14:19).

I have sometimes heard ministers preach, even when there was a revival, when I have wondered what that part of the congregation would do who did not have a dictionary. So many phrases were brought in, evidently to adorn the discourse rather than to instruct the people, that I have felt as if I wanted to tell the man, "Sit down, and do not confuse the people's minds with your barbarian preaching that they cannot understand."

3. Preaching should be parabolic. That is, illustrations should be constantly used that are drawn from incidents, real or supposed. Jesus Christ constantly illustrated His instructions in this way. He would either advance a principle and then illustrate it by a parable (a short story of some real or imaginary event) or else He would bring out the principle in the parable. There are millions of facts that can be used to advantage, yet very few ministers dare to use them for fear that somebody will reproach them. "Oh," says somebody, "he tells stories."

Tells stories! That is the way Jesus Christ preached, and it is the only way to preach. Facts, real or supposed, should be used to show the truth. Truths not illustrated are generally just as well calculated to convert sinners as a mathematical demonstration. Is it always to be so? Will it always be matter of reproach that ministers follow the example of Jesus Christ in illustrating truths by facts? Let them do it, and let fools reproach them as storytelling ministers. They have Jesus Christ and common sense on their side.

4. The illustrations should be drawn from common life and the common business of society. I once heard a minister illustrate his ideas by the manner in which merchants transact business in their stores. Another minister who was present made some remarks to him afterward. He objected to this illustration specifically because he said it was too familiar and was letting down the dignity of the pulpit. He said all illustrations in preaching should be drawn from ancient history or from some elevated source that would keep up the dignity of the pulpit.

Dignity indeed! It is just the language of the devil. He rejoices in it. The purpose of an illustration is to make people see the truth, not to uphold pulpit dignity. A minister whose heart is in the work does not use an illustration to make people stare, but to make them see the truth. If he brought forward his illustrations from ancient history, it could not make the people see; it would not illustrate anything. The novelty of the thing might awaken their attention, but then they would lose the truth itself.

If the illustration itself is a novelty, the attention will be directed to this fact as a matter of history, and the truth itself, which it was designed to illustrate, will be lost sight of. If possible, the illustration should be a matter of common occurrence, and the more common the occurrence, the more certain it will be not to fix attention upon itself, but to serve as a means through which the truth is conveyed. I have been pained at the very heart at hearing illustrations drawn from ancient history, of which not one in a hundred of the congregation had ever heard. The very manner in which they were presented was strongly tainted, to say the least, with the appearance of vanity, and an attempt to impress the people with an exhibition of learning.

The Savior always illustrated His instructions by things that were taking place among the people to whom He preached, and with which their minds were familiar. He descended often very far below what is now supposed to be essential to support the dignity of the pulpit. He talked about hens and chickens, children in marketplaces, sheep and lambs, shepherds and farmers, and husbandmen and merchants. When He talked about kings, as in the marriage of the king's son, and the nobleman who went into a far country to receive a kingdom, He had reference to historical facts that were well known among the people at the time. The illustration should always be drawn from things so common that the illustration itself will not attract attention away from the subject, but that people may see through it the truth illustrated.

5. Preaching should be repetitious. If a minister wants to preach with effect, he must not be afraid of repeating whatever he sees is not perfectly understood by his hearers. This is the harm of using notes. The preacher preaches right along just as he has it written down, and cannot

observe whether he is understood or not. If he interrupts his reading and attempts to catch the expressions of his audience and to explain where he sees they do not understand, he gets lost and confused and gives up. If a minister has his eyes on the people he is preaching to, he can commonly tell by their looks whether they understand him. And if he sees that they do not understand any particular point, let him stop and illustrate it. If they do not understand one illustration, let him give another, and make it all clear to their minds before he goes on. But those who write their sermons continue right on, in a regular consecutive progression, just as in any essay or a book, and do not repeat their thoughts until the audience fully comprehends them.

I was conversing with one of the most prominent lawyers in this country. He said that the difficulty preachers find in making themselves understood is that they do not repeat enough. He said, "In addressing a jury, I always expect that whatever I want to impress upon their minds, I will have to repeat at least twice, and often I repeat it three or four times, and even as many times as there are jurymen before me. Otherwise, I do not carry their minds along with me so that they can feel the force of what comes afterward." If a jury under oath, called to decide on the common affairs of this world, cannot understand an argument unless there is so much repetition, how is it to be expected that people will understand the preaching of the gospel without it?

In the same way, the minister should turn an important thought over and over before his audience until even the children understand it perfectly. Do not say that so much repetition will create disgust in cultivated minds. It will not disgust. This is not what disgusts thinking people. They are not weary of the efforts a minister makes to be understood. The fact is that the simpler a preacher's illustrations are, and the plainer he makes everything, the more people of mind are interested. I know that men with the brightest minds often get ideas they never had before from illustrations that were designed to bring the gospel down to the comprehension of a child. Such men are commonly so occupied with the affairs of this world that they do not think much about the subject of Christianity, and they therefore need the plainest preaching, and they will like it.

6. A minister should always deeply feel his subject, and then he will match the action to the word and the word to the action so as to make the full impression that the truth is calculated to make. He should be solemnly earnest in what he says. I recently heard a most sensible criticism on this subject: "How important it is that a minister should feel what he says. Then his actions will of course correspond to his words. If he attempts to make gestures, his arms may go like a windmill, and yet make no impression."

It requires the highest range of art on the stage for the actors to make their hearers feel. The design of elocution is to teach this skill. However, if a man feels his subject fully, he will naturally do this. He will naturally do the very thing that elocution laboriously teaches. See any common man in the streets who is sincere in what he is saying. See with what force he gestures. See a sincere woman or child – how natural. To gesture with their hands is as natural as it is to move their tongue and lips. It is the perfection of eloquence.

Let a minister, then, only feel what he says, and not be tied to his notes to read an essay or to speak a piece, like a schoolboy, first on one foot and then on the other, put out first one hand and then the other. Let him speak as he feels and act as he feels, and he will be eloquent.

It is no wonder that a great deal of preaching produces so little effect. Gestures are of more importance than is generally supposed. Mere words will never express the full meaning of the gospel. The manner of saying it is almost everything. Suppose one of you who is a mother goes home tonight, and as soon as you get into the door, the nurse comes rushing up to you with her whole soul in her expression and tells you that your child is burned to death. You would believe it, and you would feel it too, at once. But suppose she comes and tells it in a cold and careless manner. Would that excite you? No, you would not believe her. It is the earnestness of her manner and the distress of her looks that tells the story and convinces you. You know something is wrong before she speaks a word.

I once heard an instructive remark made in regard to a young minister's preaching. He was uneducated, in the common sense of the term, but well educated to win souls. It was said of him, "The manner in which he comes in, sits in the pulpit, and rises to speak, is a sermon of itself. It shows that he has something to say that is important and solemn." I have known that man's manner of saying some things to move the feelings of a whole congregation, when the same things said in a tiresome way would have produced no effect at all.

A fact that was stated by one of the most distinguished professors of elocution in the United States should affect ministers on this subject. That man was an unbeliever. He said, "I have been employed fourteen years in teaching elocution to ministers, and I know they do not believe the Christian religion. The Bible may be true. I do not pretend to know whether or not it is, but I know these ministers do not believe it. I can demonstrate that they do not. The perfection of my art is to teach them to speak naturally on this subject. I go to their studies and converse with them, and they speak eloquently. I say to them, 'Gentlemen, if you will preach just as you yourselves naturally speak on any other subject in which you are interested, you do not need to be taught. That is just what I am trying to teach you. I hear you talk on other subjects with admirable force and eloquence. I see you go into the pulpit, and you speak and act as if you did not believe what you are saying.' I have told them again and again to talk in the pulpit as they naturally talk to me. I cannot make them do it, and so I know they do not believe the Christian religion."

I have mentioned this to show how universal it is that men will gesture right if they feel right. The only thing in the way of ministers being natural speakers is that they do not deeply feel. How can they be natural in elocution when they do not feel?

7. A minister should aim to convert his congregation. But you will ask, Does not all preaching aim at this? No. A minister always has some goal in preaching, but most sermons were never aimed at converting sinners. And if sinners were converted under them, the preacher himself would be amazed. I once heard a fact on this point. There were two young ministers who had entered the ministry at the same time. One of them had great success in converting sinners, while the other had no such success. One day, the latter inquired of the other what was the reason for this difference. The first man replied, "The reason is that I aim at a different goal than you do in preaching. My object is to convert

sinners, but you aim at no such thing. Then you go and say it is due to the sovereignty of God that you do not produce the same effect, when you never aim at it. Here – take one of my sermons and preach it to your people, and see what the effect will be."

The man did so. He preached the sermon, and it produced the intended effect. He was frightened when sinners began to weep, and when one of them came to him after the meeting to ask what he should do, the minister apologized to him, and said, "I did not intend to wound you. I am sorry if I have hurt your feelings." Oh, how horrible that this minister did not lead the convicted man to Christ!

8. A minister must anticipate the objections of sinners, and answer them. What does the lawyer do when pleading before a jury? Oh, how differently is the cause of Jesus Christ pleaded from human causes! It was remarked by a lawyer that the cause of Jesus Christ had the fewest able advocates of any cause in the world – and I partly believe it. Does a lawyer go along in his argument in a regular order, and not explain anything unclear, or anticipate the arguments of his rival? If he did so, he would lose his case to a certainty; but no. The lawyer, who is pleading for money, anticipates every objection that may be made by his rival, and carefully removes or explains them so as to leave the ground all clear as he goes along so that the jury may be settled on every point.

However, ministers often leave one difficulty and another untouched. Sinners who hear them feel the difficulty, and it is never overcome in their minds. They never know how to remove it, and perhaps the minister never takes the trouble to know that such difficulties exist – yet he wonders why his congregation is not converted and why there is no revival. How can he wonder at it when he has never sought out the difficulties and objections that sinners feel and removed them?

9. If a minister intends to preach the gospel with effect, he must be sure not to be monotonous. If he preaches in a monotonous way, he will preach the people to sleep. Any monotonous sound, great or small, if continued, puts people to sleep. The falls of Niagara, the roaring of the ocean, or any sound however great or small has this effect naturally on the nervous system. You never hear this monotonous manner from

people in conversation. A minister cannot be monotonous in preaching if he feels what he says.

10. A minister should address the feelings enough to secure attention. Then he should deal with the conscience and get to the heart of the matter. Appeals to the emotion alone will never convert sinners. If the preacher deals too much in this, he may stir up an excitement and have wave after wave of feeling flow over the congregation. People may be carried away as with a flood, and rest in false hopes. The only way to secure sound conversions is to deal faithfully with the conscience. If attention decreases at any time, appeal to the feelings again and stir it up; but do your work with the conscience.

11. If he can, it is desirable for a minister to learn the effect of one sermon before he preaches another. Let him find out if it is understood, if it has produced any impression, if any difficulties are felt in regard to the subject that need clearing up, if any objections are raised, and so on. When he learns these things, then he knows what to preach next. What would be thought of the physician who would give medicine to his patient, and then give it again and again, without trying to learn the effect of the medication on the patient, or whether it had produced any effect at all? A minister will never be able to deal with sinners as he should until he can find out whether his instruction has been received and understood, and whether the difficulties in sinners' minds are cleared away, and their path is open to the Savior so that they need not stumble and stumble until their souls are lost.

I had intended to discuss several other points, but time does not allow it.

Remarks

1. We see why so few of the leading minds in many communities are converted. Until the recent revivals, professional men were rarely reached by preaching, and they were almost all unbelievers at heart. People almost understood the Bible to affirm the idea that they could not be converted. The reason is obvious. The gospel had not been entrusted to

the consciences of such men. Ministers had not grappled with the mind, and had not reasoned so as to make that class of mind see the truth of the gospel and feel its power. Consequently, such people had come to regard the Christian religion as something unworthy of their notice.

But of recent years, the situation has changed, and in some places there have been more of this class of people converted, in proportion to their numbers, than of any others. That is because they were made to understand the claims of the gospel. The preacher grappled with their minds and showed them the reasonableness of Christianity. When this is done, it is found that people of this class are more easily converted than any other. They have so much more capacity to receive an argument, and are so much more in the habit of yielding to the force of reason, that as soon as the gospel gets a fair hold of their minds, it breaks them right down and melts them at the feet of Christ.

2. Before the gospel can take general effect, we must have a class of extemporaneous preachers, for the following reasons:

a) No group of men can endure the labor of writing sermons and doing all the preaching that will be required.

b) Written preaching is not calculated to produce the required effect. Such preaching does not present truth in the right shape.

c) It is impossible for a man who writes his sermons to arrange his matter, and turn and choose his thoughts, so as to produce the same effect as when he addresses the people directly and makes them feel that he is referring directly to them. Writing sermons had its origin in times of political difficulty. The practice was unknown in the apostles' days. Undoubtedly, written sermons have done a great deal of good, but they can never give to the gospel its great power.

Many ministers may have been trained so long in the use of notes that they had better not throw them away, for they might not know how to preach without them. The difficulty would not be for the lack of mind, but from wrong training. The bad habit is begun with the school-boy, who is called to "speak his piece." Instead of being set to express his own thoughts and feelings in his own language, and with his own natural manner, such as nature itself inspires, he is made to commit another person's writing to memory, and then mouths it out in a stiff and formal way. And so when he goes to college and to the seminary, instead of being trained to speak extemporaneously, he is set to writing his piece and commit it to memory.

I would pursue the opposite course from the beginning. I would give him a subject and let him first think, and then speak his thoughts. Perhaps he will make mistakes. Very well, that is to be expected in a beginner. But he will learn. Suppose he is not eloquent at first. Very well, he can improve, and he is in the very way to improve. This kind of training alone will ever raise up a class of ministers who can convert the world.

But it is objected to extemporaneous preaching that if ministers do not write, they will not think. This objection will have weight with those men whose habit has always been to write down their thoughts, but to a man of a different habit, it will have no weight at all. Writing is not thinking. And if I would judge from many of the written sermons I have heard preached, the makers of them had been doing anything rather than thinking. The mechanical labor of writing is really a hinderance to direct and rapid thought.

It is true that some extemporaneous preachers have not been men of thought, and it is also true that many men who write sermons are not men of thought. A man whose habits have always been that he has thought only when he has put his mind on the end of his pen will, of course, if he lays aside his pen, at first find it difficult to think; and if he attempts to preach without writing, he will, until his habits are completely changed, find it difficult to throw into his sermons the same amount of thought as if he conformed to his old habits of writing.

But it should be remembered that this is only because he has been trained to write, and has always accustomed himself to it. It is the training and habit that makes it so difficult for him to think without writing. Will anybody pretend to say that lawyers are not men of thought, that their arguments before a court and jury are not thoughtful and well considered? Yet everyone knows that they do not write their speeches. It should be understood, too, that in college they have the same training with ministers, and have the same disadvantage of having been trained to write their thoughts. It is only after they enter upon their profession that they change their habit. If they were educated, as they should be, to extemporaneous habits in the schools, they would be vastly more eloquent and powerful in argument than they are.

I have heard much of this objection to extemporaneous preaching ever since I entered the ministry. It was often said to me then, in answer to my views of extemporaneous preaching, that ministers who preached extemporaneously would not instruct the churches, that there would be a great deal of repetition in their preaching, and they would soon become dull and repetitious for lack of thought. However, every year's experience has increased the conviction on my mind that the opposite of this objection is true. The man who writes least may, if he desires, think most, and will say what he thinks in a manner that will be better understood than if it were written; and that, in the same proportion that he lays aside the labor of writing, his body will be left free to exercise, and his mind to experience vigorous and constant thought.

The main reason why it is supposed that extemporaneous preachers more frequently repeat the same thoughts in their preaching is because what they say is, in a general way, more perfectly remembered by the congregation than if it had been read. I have often known preachers who could repeat their written sermons once every few months without it being recognized by the congregation. But the manner in which extemporaneous sermons are generally delivered makes so much more of an impression that the thoughts cannot in general be soon repeated without being remembered.

We will never have a set of men in our halls of legislation, in our courts of justice, and in our pulpits who are powerful and overwhelming speakers and can carry the world before them until our system of education teaches them to think carefully, swiftly, and continuously, and until all their practice of speaking in the schools is extemporaneous.

The very style of communicating thought, in what is commonly called a good style of writing, is not calculated to leave a deep impression on the mind or to communicate thought in a clear and impressive manner. It is not concise, direct, and relevant. It is not the language of nature. It is impossible that gestures should be suited to the common style of writing, and consequently, when they attempt to gesture while reading an essay or delivering a written sermon, their gestures are a mockery of all public speaking.

In delivering a sermon in this essay style of writing, it is impossible that nearly all the fire of meaning and power of gesture, looks, attitude, and emphasis should not be lost. We can never have the full meaning of the gospel until we throw away our notes.

3. A minister's course of study and training for his work should be exclusively theological. I mean just as I say. I am not now going to discuss the question of whether all education should be theological, but I say that education for the ministry should be exclusively so. But you will ask, should not a minister understand science? I would answer, yes – the more the better. I would be glad if ministers would understand all science, but it should all be in connection with theology. Studying science is studying the works of God, and studying theology is studying God.

Let a scholar be asked, for example, this question: "Is there a God?" To answer it, let him ransack the universe, let him go out into every department of science, to find the proofs of design, and in this way learn the existence of God. Let him next inquire how many gods there are, and let him again ransack creation to see whether there is such a unity of design as shows that there is one God.

In the same way, let him inquire concerning the attributes of God and His character. He will learn science here, but will learn it as a part of theology. Let him search every field of knowledge to bring forward his proofs. What was the design of this plan? What was the intent of that arrangement? See whether everything you find in the universe is not calculated to produce happiness, unless corrupted.

Would the student's heart get hard and cold in study, as cold and hard as the college walls, if science was pursued in this way? Every lesson brings him right up before God, and is in fact communion with God. It warms his heart and makes him more pious, more solemn, and more holy. The very distinction between classical and theological study is a curse to the church and a curse to the world. The student spends four years in college at classical studies, with no God in them, and then three years in the seminary at theological studies; and what then? Poor young man. Set him to work, and you will find that he is not educated for the ministry at all. The church groans under his preaching because he does not preach with unction, nor with power. He has been weakened in training.

4. We learn what revival preaching is. All ministers should be revival ministers, and all preaching should be revival preaching. That is, it should be intended to promote holiness. People say, "It is very good to have some men in the church who are revival preachers and who can go around and promote revivals, but then you must have others to educate the church." Strange! Do they not know that a revival educates the church faster than anything else? And a minister will never produce a revival if he does not teach his hearers. The preaching I have described is full of doctrine, but it is doctrine to be practiced – and that is revival preaching.

5. There are two objections sometimes brought against the kind of preaching that I have recommended.

a) One objection is that it is letting down the dignity of the pulpit to preach in this natural, lawyer-like style. They are shocked at it. But it is only on account of its unusualness, and not because there is any inappropriateness in the thing itself. I heard a remark made by a leading layman in the center of this state in regard to the preaching of a certain minister. He said it was the first preaching he ever heard that he understood, and the first minister he ever heard who spoke as if he believed his own doctrine or meant what he said. When he first heard him preach as if he was saying something that he meant, he thought he was crazy. But eventually, he was made to see that it was all true, and he submitted to the truth as the power of God for the salvation of his soul.

What is the dignity of the pulpit? To see a minister go into the pulpit to sustain its dignity! Sadly, during my foreign tour, I heard an English missionary preach exactly in that way. I believe he was a good man, and out of the pulpit he would talk like a man who meant what he said. But no sooner was he in the pulpit than he appeared like a simple robot – remarking, uttering, and vocalizing enough to put all the people to sleep. And the difficulty seemed to be that he wanted to maintain the dignity of the pulpit.

b) The second objection is that this preaching is theatrical. The bishop of London once asked Garrick, the celebrated play-actor, why it was that actors, in representing a mere fiction, move an assembly even to tears, while ministers, in representing the most solemn realities, could scarcely obtain a hearing. The philosophical Garrick well replied, "It is because we represent fiction as reality, and you represent reality as fiction."

This is telling the whole story. Now what is the intent of the actor in a theatrical representation? It is to so throw himself into the spirit and meaning of the writer as to adopt his sentiments, make them his own, feel them, embody them, and throw them out upon the audience as living reality. Now what is the objection to all this in preaching? The actor matches the action to the word, and the word to the action. His looks, his hands, his attitudes, and everything are designed to express the full meaning of the writer.

This should be the goal of the preacher. If by "theatrical" is meant the strongest possible representation of the beliefs expressed, then the more theatrical a sermon is, the better. And if ministers are too formal, and the people too finicky, to learn even from an actor or from the stage, the best method of persuading minds, of presenting beliefs, and of diffusing the warmth of kindled thought over a congregation, then they must go on with their dull speaking and reading and sanctimonious starch. But let them remember that while they are thus turning away and criticizing the art of the actor, and attempting to support "the dignity of the pulpit," the theaters can be filled every night. The commonsense people will be entertained with that manner of speaking, and sinners will go down to hell.

6. A congregation may learn how to choose a minister. When a church is looking for a minister, there are two main points on which they commonly focus their attention: (1) that he would be popular and (2) that he would be learned. That is very good, but this point should be the first in their inquiries: "Is he wise to win souls?"

No matter how eloquent a minister is or how educated, no matter how pleasing and popular he is in his manners – if it is a matter of fact that sinners are not converted under his preaching, it shows that he does not have this wisdom, and your children and neighbors will go down to hell under his preaching.

I am happy to know that many churches will ask this question about ministers. If they find that a minister is destitute of this vital quality, they will not have him. And if ministers can be found who are wise to win souls, the churches will have such ministers. It is in vain to contend against it or to pretend that they are not well educated or not scholarly or the like. It is in vain for the schools to try to force down the throats of the churches a brand of ministers who are educated in everything except what they most need to know. The churches should pronounce them not made right, and they should not sustain that which is notoriously so inadequate as the present system of theological education.

It is very difficult to say what needs to be said on this subject without being in danger of fostering a wrong spirit in the church toward ministers. Many professing Christians are ready to find fault with ministers when they have no reason, insomuch that it becomes very difficult to say of ministers what is true, and what needs to be said, without its being distorted and misused by this class of professing Christians. I would not for the world say anything to harm the influence of a minister of Christ who is really endeavoring to do good. I desire them to have a hundred times more influence than they now deserve or have.

However, to tell the truth will not damage the influence of those ministers who by their lives and preaching give evidence to the church that their purpose is to do good and to win souls to Christ. This class of ministers will recognize the truth of all that I have said or want to say. They see it all and condemn it. But if there are ministers who are doing no good, who are feeding themselves and not the flock, such ministers deserve no influence. If they are doing no good, it is time for them to take up some other profession. They are but leeches on the very life of the church, sucking out its heart's blood. They are useless, and worse than useless. The sooner they are laid aside, and their places filled with those who will exert themselves for Christ, the better.

Finally, it is the duty of the church to pray for us ministers. Not one of us is such as we should be. Like Paul, we can say, *Who is sufficient for these things?* (2 Corinthians 2:16). But who of us is like Paul? Where will you find such a minister as Paul? They are not here. We have been wrongly educated – all of us. Pray for the schools and colleges and seminaries. Pray for young men who are preparing for the ministry. Pray for ministers, that God would give them this wisdom to win souls. Pray that God would give to the church the wisdom and the means to educate a generation of ministers who will go forward and convert the world.

The church must travail in prayer, and groan and agonize for this. It is now the pearl of price to the church to have a supply of the right kind of ministers. The coming of the millennium depends on having a different type of ministers who are more thoroughly educated for their work. And this we will have as sure as the promise of the Lord holds good.

Such a ministry as is now in the church will never convert the world. But the world is to be converted, and therefore God intends to have ministers who will do it. *Pray ye therefore the Lord of the harvest, that he would send forth laborers into his harvest* (Matthew 9:38).

Lecture 13

How Churches Can Help Ministers

And it came to pass, when Moses held up his hand, that Israel prevailed; and when he let down his hand, Amalek prevailed. But Moses' hands were heavy, and they took a stone, and put it under him, and he sat thereon: and Aaron and Hur stayed up his hands, the one on the one side, and the other on the other side; and his hands were steady until the going down of the sun. And Joshua discomfited Amalek and his people with the edge of the sword.
—Exodus 17:11-13

You who read your Bibles will remember the context in which these verses stand. In subduing their enemies, the people of God came to battle against the Amalekites, and these incidents took place. It is difficult to understand why importance should be attached to the circumstance of Moses holding up his hands, unless the expression is understood to signify the attitude of prayer. Then his holding up his hands, and the success attending it, will teach us the importance of prayer to God for His help in all our conflicts with the enemies of God. The cooperation and support of Aaron and Hur have been generally understood to represent the duty of churches to sustain and assist ministers in their work, and the importance of this cooperation to the success of the preached gospel. I will make this use of it now.

As I have spoken of the duty of ministers to labor for revivals, I will now consider the importance of the cooperation of the church in producing and carrying on a revival.

There are a number of things whose importance in promoting a revival has not been properly considered by churches and ministers, which if not attended to will make it impossible for revivals to expand, or even continue for any considerable time. In my last two lectures, I have been dwelling on the duties of ministers, as it was impossible for me to preach a series of lectures on revivals without entering more or less extensively into that department of means. I have not finished with that part of the subject, but have thought it important here to step aside and discuss some points in which the church must stand by and aid their minister if they expect to enjoy a revival. In discussing the subject, I will propose:

I.   Several things that Christians must avoid if they want to support ministers.

II. Some things to which they must attend.

I. Several Things that Must Be Avoided

1. By all means, keep clear of the idea, both in theory and practice, that a minister alone is to promote revivals. Many people are inclined to take a passive attitude on this subject and feel as if they did not have anything to do. They have employed a minister and paid him to feed them with instruction and comfort, and now they have nothing to do except to sit and swallow the food he gives. They are to pay his salary and attend his preaching, and they think that is doing a great deal. On his part, he is expected to preach good, sound, comfortable doctrine, to encourage them, and to make them feel comfortable, and so they expect to go to heaven. I tell you, they will go to hell if this is their religion. That is not the way to heaven.

Rest assured that where this spirit prevails in the church, no matter how good the minister may be, the church has taken the path to prevent a revival. If he is ever so faithful, ever so much involved, and ever so talented and eloquent, he may wear himself out and perhaps destroy his life, but he will have little or no revival.

Where there is no church, or very few members in the church, a revival may be promoted without any organized effort of the church, because it is not there; and in such a case, God accommodates His grace to the circumstances, as He did when the apostles went out single-handed to plant the gospel in the world. I have seen instances of powerful revivals where such was the case.

However, where there are means, God will have them used. I would rather have no church in a place than to attempt to promote a revival in a place where there is a church that will not work. God will be inquired of by His people to bestow blessings. The counteracting influence of a church that will not work is worse than atheism. There is no possibility of occupying neutral ground in regard to a revival, although some professing Christians imagine they are neutral. If a professing Christian will not expend himself in the work, he opposes it.

Let such a person attempt to take middle ground and say he is going to wait and see how they come out – why, that is the very ground the devil wants him to take. Professing Christians can in this way do his work a great deal more effectually than by open opposition. If they take open ground in opposition, everybody will say they have no religion. But by this middle course, they retain their influence, and thus do the devil's work more effectively.

In employing a minister, a church must remember that they have only employed a leader to lead them on to action in the cause of Christ. People would think it strange if anybody would propose to support a general and then let him go and fight alone! This is no more absurd, or destructive, than for a minister to attempt to go forward alone. The church misunderstands the design of the ministry if they leave their minister to work alone. It is not enough that they should hear the sermons. That is only the word of command, which the church is obligated to follow.

2. Do not complain about your minister because there is no revival – if you are not doing your duty. It is of no use to complain about there being no revival if you are not doing your duty. That alone is a sufficient reason why there should be no revival. It is a most cruel and abominable thing for church members to complain about their minister when they themselves are fast asleep. It is very common for professing Christians

to take much credit for themselves and quiet their own consciences by complaining about their ministers. And when the importance of ministers being awake is spoken of, this type of person is ready to say, "We will never have a revival with such a minister," when the fact is that their minister is much more awake than they are themselves.

Another thing is true in regard to this point, and worthy of notice. When the church is sunk down in a low state, professing Christians are very apt to complain about the church, and about the low state of Christianity among them. That intangible being, the "church," is greatly complained about by them for being asleep. Their complaints of the low condition of Christianity and of the coldness of the church or of the minister are poured out despondently, without their seeming to realize that the church is composed of individuals, and that until each one will take his own case in hand, complain of himself, humble himself before God, and repent and wake up, the church can never have any effectiveness, and there can never be a revival.

If instead of complaining about your minister or about the church, you would wake up as individuals, and not complain about him or them until you can say you are pure from the blood of all men, and are doing your duty to save sinners, he would be inclined to feel the justice of your complaints; and if he would not, God would, and would either wake him up or remove him.

3. Do not let your minister kill himself by attempting to carry on the work alone while you refuse to help him. It sometimes happens that a minister discovers that the ark of the Lord will not move unless he lays out his utmost strength, and he has been so desirous of a revival that he has done this, and has died – and he was willing to die for it. I could mention some cases in this state where ministers have died, and no doubt in consequence of their labors to promote a revival where the church hung back from the work.

I will mention one case. A minister, some years ago, was laboring where there was a revival. He was visited by an elder of a church at some distance who wanted him to go and preach there. There was no revival there, and never had been, and the elder complained about their condition. He said they had had two excellent ministers, but one had worn himself completely out and died, and the other had exhausted himself, got discouraged, and left them. They were a poor and feeble church, and their prospects were very dark unless they could have a revival, so he begged this minister to go and help them.

He seemed to be very sorrowful, and the minister listened to his complaint. The minister at last replied by asking, "Why did you never have a revival?"

"I do not know," said the elder. "Our minister labored hard, but the church did not seem to wake up, and somehow there seemed to be no revival."

"Well, now," said the minister, "I see what you want. You have killed one of God's ministers, and broke down another so that he had to leave you, and now you want to get another there and kill him, and the devil has sent you here to get me to go and rock your cradle for you. You had one good minister to preach to you, but you slept on, and he exerted himself until he absolutely died in the work. Then the Lord let you have another, and still you lay and slept, and would not wake up to your duty. And now you have come here in despair, and want another minister, do you? God forbid that you should ever have another while you do as you have done. God forbid that you should ever have a minister until the church will wake up to duty."

The elder was affected, for he was a good man. The tears came to his eyes, and he said it was no more than they deserved. "And now," said the minister, "will you be faithful, and go home and tell the church what I say? If you will, and they will be faithful and wake up to duty, they will have a minister. I will guarantee them that."

The elder said he would, and he was true to his word. He went home and told the church how cruel it was for them to ask another minister to come among them unless they would wake up. They felt it, confessed their sins, and woke up to duty. A minister was sent to them, and a precious and powerful revival followed.

Churches do not realize how often their coldness and reluctance may be absolutely the cause of the death of ministers. The state of the people, and of sinners, rests upon their mind. They travail in soul night and day, and they labor in season and out of season, beyond the power of the human constitution to bear, until they wear out and die. The church does not know the agony of a minister's heart when he travails for souls and labors to wake up the church to help, and still sees them in the slumbers of death. Perhaps sometimes they will get up the occasional effort for a few days, and then all is cold again. So many faithful ministers wear themselves out and die, and then these heartless professing Christians are the first to blame them for doing so much.

I remember a case of a good minister who went to a place where there was a revival, and while there he heard a powerful sermon to ministers. He received it like a man of God. He did not rebel against God's truth, but he vowed to God that he would not rest until he saw a revival among his people. He returned home and went to work. The church would not wake up, except a few members, and the Lord blessed them and poured out His Spirit, but the minister laid himself down on his bed and died in the midst of the revival.

4. Be careful not to complain of plain, direct preaching, even when its reproofs fasten on you. Churches tend to forget that a minister is responsible only to God. They want to make rules for a minister to preach so as not to have the sermons directed to them. If he bears down on the church and exposes the sins that prevail among them, they call it personal, and they rebel against the truth. Or they say he should not preach so plainly to the church before the world. They say that it exposes the Christian religion, and that he should take them by themselves and preach to the church alone, and not tell sinners how bad Christians are.

However, there are cases where a minister can do no less than to show the house of Jacob their sins. If you ask why we do not do it when we are by ourselves, I answer, that sinners are aware that you sin. I will preach to you by yourselves about your own sins when you will get together by yourselves to sin. But as the Lord lives, if you sin before the world, you will be rebuked before the world. Is it not a fact that sinners know how you live, and that they stumble over you into hell? Then do not blame ministers when they see it is their duty to rebuke the church openly before the world. If you are so proud that you cannot bear this, you do not need to expect a revival. Do not call preaching too plain because it exposes the faults of the church. There is no such thing as preaching too plain.

5. Sometimes professing Christians take alarm lest the minister would offend the ungodly by plain preaching. They will begin to caution him against it and ask him if he had not better change a little to avoid giving offense, and similar comments. This fear is increased, especially if some of the more wealthy and influential members of the congregation are offended, lest they should withdraw their support from the church and no longer give their money to help to pay the minister's salary – and so the burden will be heavier on the rest of the church.

They can never have a revival in such a church. The church should pray, above all things, that the truth may come on the ungodly like fire. So what if they are offended? Christ can get along very well without their money. Do not blame your minister or ask him to change his manner of preaching to please and placate the ungodly. It is of no use for a minister to preach to the unrepentant unless he can preach the truth to them. It will do no good for them to pay for the support of the gospel unless it is preached in such a way that they may be searched out and saved.

Sometimes church members will talk among themselves about the minister's carelessness, and create a division, and get into a very wrong spirit because the wicked are displeased. There was a place where there was a powerful revival and great opposition. The church was alarmed for fear that if the minister was not less plain and direct, some of the unrepentant would go and join some other congregation. One of the leading men in the church was appointed to go to the minister and ask him not to preach quite so hard, for if he continued to do so, such and such people would leave the congregation.

The minister asked, "Is not the preaching true?"

"Yes."

"Does not God bless it?"

"Yes."

"Did you ever see anything like this work before in this place?"

"No, I never did."

"Get thee behind me, Satan. The devil has sent you here on this errand. You see God is blessing the preaching, the work is going on, and sinners are converted every day, and now you come to get me to let down the tone of preaching so as to ease the minds of the ungodly."

The man felt the rebuke and took it like a Christian. He saw his error and submitted, and never again was heard to find fault with the plainness of preaching.

In another town where there was a revival, a woman who had some influence (not pious), complained very much about plain, direct, personal preaching, as she called it. But eventually she herself became a subject of the work. After this, some of her unrepentant friends reminded her of what she used to say against the preacher for "preaching it out so hot." She now said her views were changed, and she did not care how hot the truth was preached, if it was red hot.

6. Do not take part with the wicked in any way. If you do it at all, you will strengthen their hands. If the wicked accuse the minister of being careless, or of being personal, and if the church members, without admitting that the minister does so, only admit that personal preaching is wrong, and talk about the inappropriateness of personal preaching, the wicked will feel themselves strengthened by such remarks. Do not unite with them at all, for they will feel that they have you on their side against their minister. If you adopt their principles and use their language, you are understood as sympathizing with them.

What is personal preaching? No individual is ever benefited by preaching unless he is made to feel that the minister is referring to him. Such preaching is always personal. It often appears so personal to wicked people that they feel as if they were just about to be called out by name before the congregation.

A minister was once preaching to a congregation, and when describing certain characters, he said, "If I was omniscient, I could call out by name the very people who answer to this picture." A man cried out, "Name me!" and he looked as if he was going to sink into the earth. He afterward said that he had no intent of speaking out, but the minister described him so perfectly that he really thought he was going to call him by name. The minister did not know there was such a man in the world.

It is common for people to think that their own conduct is described, and they complain, "Who has been telling him about me? Somebody has been talking to him about me and getting him to preach at me." I suppose I have heard of five hundred or a thousand just such cases. Now if the church members will just admit that it is wrong for a minister to mean anybody in his preaching, how can he do any good? If you are not willing for your minister to mean anybody, or preach to anybody, you had better dismiss him. Whom must he preach to, if not to the people, the individuals, before him? And how can he preach to them when he does not mean them?

7. If you want to stand by your minister in promoting a revival, do not contradict his preaching by your lives. If he preaches that sinners are going to hell, do not act as if it is not true, and smile it all away by your levity and unconcern. I have heard sinners speak of the effect produced on their minds by levity in Christians after a solemn and searching discourse. They feel solemn and tender and begin to be alarmed at their condition, and then they see these professing Christians all lighthearted and carefree instead of weeping over them, as much as to say, "Do not be afraid, sinners. It is not so bad after all. Keep cool and you will do well. Do you think we would laugh and joke if you were going to hell so soon? We would not laugh if only your house was on fire – still less if we saw you burning in it." Of what use is it for a minister to preach to sinners in such a state of things?

8. Do not needlessly take up the time of your minister. Ministers often lose a great deal of time by individuals calling on them to talk when they have nothing of importance to talk about, and no particular errand. Of course, the minister is glad to see his friends, and is often too willing to spend time in conversation with his people, as he loves and esteems them.

Professing Christians should remember that a minister's time is worth more than gold, for it can be used in that which gold can never buy. If the minister is kept from his knees, or from his Bible, or from his study so that they may indulge themselves in his conversation, they do much harm.

When you have a good reason for it, you should never be hesitant to call on him, and even take up all the time that is necessary. But if you have nothing in particular to say that is important, keep away. I knew a man in one of our cities who was out of business, and he used to take up months of the minister's time. He would come to his study and sit for three hours at a time and talk because he had nothing else to do, until finally the minister had to rebuke him plainly and tell him how much sin he was committing.

9. Be sure not to approve of anything that is intended to divert public attention from the subject of Christianity. Often when it comes the time of year to work, when the evenings are long and business is light, and the very time to make an extra effort, at this moment somebody in the church will give a party and invite some Christian friends, so as to call it a religious party. Then some other family must do the same to return the compliment. Then another and another, until it grows into an organized system of parties that consume the whole winter. Abominable! This is the grand device of the devil, because it appears so innocent and so proper to promote good feeling and increase the acquaintance of Christians with each other. And so instead of prayer meetings, they will have these parties.

The evils of these parties are very great. They are often held at great expense, and the most abominable gluttony is practiced in them. It is said that the expense is from one hundred to two thousand dollars. I have been told that in some instances professed Christians have given large parties and provided much entertainment, and excused their ungodly extravagance in the use of Jesus Christ's money by giving what was left, after the feast was ended, to the poor! Thus they make it a virtue to feast and revel, even to overindulgence, on the bounties of God's providence under pretense of benefiting the poor.

This is the same in principle with a splendid ball that was given some years ago in a neighboring city. The ball was held for the benefit of the poor, and each gentleman was to pay a certain amount. After the ball was ended, whatever remained of the funds raised was to be given to the poor. Truly this is strange charity – to eat and drink and dance, and when they have reveled and feasted until they can enjoy it no longer, they hand to the poor the crumbs that have fallen from the table. I do not see why such a ball is not quite as pious as such Christian parties. The evil of balls does not consist simply in the exercise of dancing, but in the waste and overindulgence and temptations connected with them.

But it is said they are Christian parties, and that they are all, or nearly all, professing Christians who attend them. Furthermore, they say, they are often concluded with prayer. I regard this as one of the worst features about them – that after the waste of time and money, the excess in eating and drinking, the empty conversation, and the nameless amusements with which such a time is filled up, an attempt would be made to sanctify it and pass it off upon God by concluding it with prayer. Say what you will, but it would not be more absurd, improper, or impious to end a ball, a theater, or a card party with prayer.

Has it come to this, that professing Christians, claiming to desire the salvation of the world, when such calls are made upon them from the four winds of heaven to send the gospel, to furnish Bibles, tracts, missionaries, and to save the world from death, that they would spend hundreds of dollars in an evening, and then go to the monthly prayer meeting and pray for the heathen!

In some instances, I have been told, they find a salve for their consciences in the fact that their minister attends their parties. This, of course, would give weight to such an example, and if one professing Christian had a party and invited their minister, others must do the same. The next step they take may be for each to give a ball and appoint their minister as manager! Why not? Maybe eventually he will do them the favor of playing the fiddle. In my estimation he might quite as well do it as to go and conclude such a party with prayer.

I have heard with sadness that a circle of parties, I do not know to what extent, has been held in Rochester – that place so highly favored by the Lord. I do not know through whose influence they have been started, or by what particular people they have been supported and attended, but I would advise any congregation that is intending to have a circle of parties, in the meantime to dismiss their minister and let him go and preach where the people would be ready to receive the Word and profit by it, and not have him stay and be distressed and grieved and killed by attempting to promote true Christianity among them while they are engaged heart and hand in the service of the devil.

Professing Christians should never start anything that may divert public attention from Christianity without first having consulted their minister and making it a subject of special prayer. If they find it will have this effect, they should never do it. Subjects will often come up before the public that have this tendency – some course of lectures, or entertainment, or the like. Professing Christians should be wise and understand what they are about, and not give support to any such thing until they see what influence it will have, and whether it will hinder a revival. If it will do that, let them have nothing to do with it. Every such thing should be assessed by its bearing upon Christ's kingdom.

In relation to parties, say what you please about their being an innocent recreation. I appeal to any of you who have ever attended them to say whether they prepare you for prayer, or increase your spirituality, or whether sinners are ever converted in them, or if they cause Christians to agonize in prayer for souls.

II. Several Things That Churches Must Do If They Want to Promote a Revival and Help Their Minister

1. They must attend to his material needs. A minister who gives himself wholly to the work cannot be engaged in worldly employment, and of course is entirely dependent on his people for the supply of his material needs, including the support of his family. I do not need to argue this point here, for you all understand this perfectly. It is the command of God, that *they which preach the gospel should live of the gospel* (1 Corinthians 9:14).

But now look around and see what many churches do in this matter. For instance, when they need a minister, they will search around and see how cheap they can get one. They will calculate to a penny how much his salt will cost, and how much his meal, and then set his salary so low as to subject him to extreme inconvenience to get along and keep his family. A minister must have his mind at ease in order to study and labor with effect, and he cannot haggle about prices, and negotiate, and look out for the best chances to buy to advantage what he needs. If he is forced to do this, his mind is embarrassed. Unless his material needs are so supplied that his thoughts may be removed from them, how can he do his duty?

2. Be honest with your minister. Do not measure out and calculate how much salt and how many bushels of grain he can possibly get along with.

Remember, you are dealing with Christ, and He calls you to place His ministers in such a situation that with ordinary care, material embarrassment is out of the question.

3. Be punctual with him. Sometimes when churches are settling a minister in, they have a great deal of pride about giving a salary, and they will get up a subscription and make out an amount that they never pay, and very likely never expected to pay. And so, after one, two, three, or four years, the society gets thousands of dollars behind in payment to their minister, and then they expect he will give it to them. And all the while they wonder why there is no revival! This may be the very reason – because the church has lied. They have faithfully promised to pay so much, and have not done it. God cannot consistently pour out His Spirit on such a church.

4. Pay him his salary without asking. Nothing is so embarrassing, often, to a minister as to be obliged to continually ask his people for his salary. Often he gets enemies, and gives offense, by being forced to call, and call, and call for his money, and then not get it as they promised. They would have paid it if their credit had been at stake, but when it is nothing but conscience and the blessing of God, they let it pass by. If any one of them had a note at the bank, you would see him careful and prompt to be on the ground before three o'clock. That is because the note will be protested, and they will lose their character.

But they know the minister will not sue them for his salary, and they are careless and let it run out, and he must suffer the inconvenience. This is not as common in the city as it is in the country, but in the country I have known some heartrending cases of distress and misery due to the negligence and cruelty of congregations in withholding that which is due. Churches live in habitual lying and cheating, and then wonder why they have no revival. How can they wonder?

5. Pray for your minister. I mean something by this – and what do you suppose I mean? Even the apostles used to urge the churches to pray for them. This is more important than you imagine. Ministers do not ask people to pray for them simply as men, nor that they may be filled

with an abundance of the Spirit's influences, merely to promote their personal enjoyment. But they know that unless the church greatly desires a blessing upon the labors of a minister, it is tempting God for him to expect it.

How often does a minister go into his pulpit, feeling that his heart is ready to break for the blessing of God, while he also feels that there is no room to expect it, for there is no reason to believe the church desires it! Perhaps he has been two hours on his knees in supplication, yet because the church does not desire a blessing, he feels as if his words would leap back in his face.

I have seen Christians who would be in an agony when the minister was going into the pulpit for fear that his mind would be in a cloud, or his heart cold, or he would have no unction, and so a blessing would not come. I have labored with a man of this sort. He would pray until he got assurance in his mind that God would be with me in preaching, and sometimes he would pray himself sick. I have known the time when he had been in darkness for a while, while the people were gathering, and his mind was full of anxiety – and he would go again and again to pray, until finally he would come into the room with a peaceful face and say, "The Lord has come, and He will be with us." I do not know that I ever found him mistaken.

I have known a church bear their minister on their arms in prayer from day to day, and watch with unutterable anxiety to see that he has the Holy Spirit with him in his labors! When they feel and pray this way, oh, what feelings and what looks are manifest in the congregation! They have felt unutterable anxiety to have the word come with power and take effect, and when they see their prayer answered, and they hear a word or a sentence come warm from the heart and take effect among the people, you can see their whole souls look out of their eyes.

How different is the case where the church feels that the minister is praying, and so there is no need of their praying! They are mistaken. The church must desire and pray for the blessing. God says that He will be inquired of by the house of Israel (Ezekiel 36:37). I want you to feel that there can be no substitute for this.

I have seen cases in revivals where the church was kept in the background in regard to prayer, and people from abroad were called on to pray in all the meetings. This is always sad, even if there would be a revival, for the revival will be less powerful and less beneficial in its influences upon the church. I do not know but I have sometimes offended Christians and ministers from abroad by continuing to call on members of the church in the place to pray, and not on those from abroad. It was not from any disrespect to them, but because the purpose was to get that church that was primarily concerned to desire, and pray, and agonize for a blessing.

In a certain place, a prolonged meeting was held with no good results, and great evils were produced. I was led to ask about the reason. It seemed that in all their meetings, not one member of their own church was called on to pray, but all the prayers were made by people from abroad. No wonder there was no good done. The church was not involved. The leader of the meeting meant well, but he attempted to promote a revival without getting the church there into the work. He let a lazy church lie still and do nothing, and so there could be no good.

Churches should pray for ministers as the agents of breaking down sinners with the Word of Truth. Prayer for a minister is often done in a set and formal way, and is confined to the prayer meetings. They will say their prayers in the old way, as they have always done: "Lord, bless Thy ministering servant, whom Thou hast stationed on this part of Zion's walls," and so on, and it amounts to nothing because there is no heart in it. The proof often is that they never thought of praying for him in private. They have never agonized in their homes for a blessing on his labors. They may not omit it entirely in their meetings. If they do that, it is evident that they care very little indeed about the labors of their minister. But that is not the most important place. The way to present effectual prayer for your minister is to take it to your homes, and when you are in private, wrestle with God for success to attend his labors.

I knew a case of a minister in poor health who became depressed and sunk down in his mind, and was very much in darkness so that he did not feel as if he could preach any longer. An individual of the church was awakened to feel for the minister's situation and to pray that he would have the Holy Spirit attend his preaching. One Sunday morning, this person's mind was very much concerned, and he began to pray as soon as it was light, and he prayed again and again for a blessing that day. The Lord in some way directed the minister within hearing of his prayer. The person was telling the Lord just what he thought of the minister's situation and state of mind, and pleading, as if he would not be denied, for a blessing. The minister went into the pulpit and preached, and the light broke in upon him; the Word was preached with power, and a revival began that very day.

6. A minister should be provided for by the church, and his support guaranteed, regardless of the ungodly. Otherwise he may be forced either to starve his family, or to keep back part of the truth so as not to offend sinners. I once reasoned with a minister who was afraid to come out fully with the truth. I told him I was surprised he did not bear down on certain points. He told me he was so situated that he must please certain men who would be affected there. It was the ungodly who mainly supported him, and that made him dependent and wavering. Yet perhaps that very church that left their minister to depend on the ungodly for his bread will turn around and berate him for his lack of faith and his fear of men. The church should always say to their minister, "We will support you. Go to work. Let the truth pour down on the people, and we will stand by you."

7. See that everything is so arranged that people can sit comfortably in the meeting. If people do not sit comfortably, it is difficult to get or to keep their attention. And if they are not attentive, they cannot be converted. They have come to hear for their lives, and they should be so situated that they can hear with all their souls, and have nothing in their bodily position to call for attention. Churches do not realize how important it is that the place of meeting should be made comfortable. I do not mean showy. All your glare and glory of fancy chandeliers, rich carpets, and ornate pulpits is the opposite extreme, and takes away the attention just as much, and defeats every purpose for which a sinner should come to the meeting. You do not need to expect a revival there.

8. See that the house of God is kept clean. The house of God should be kept as clean as you would want your own house to be kept. Churches are often kept excessively disorderly. I have seen them where people

used so much tobacco, and took so little care about neatness, that it was impossible to preach with comfort.

Once in an extended meeting, the matter was brought before the church, and they had to acknowledge that they paid more money for tobacco than they did for the cause of missions. They could not kneel in their pews, and ladies could not sit without all the time watching their clothes, and they had to be careful where they stepped because the house was so dirty and there was so much tobacco juice running all over the floor.

If people cannot go where they can hear without being annoyed with offensive sights and smells, and where they can kneel in prayer, what good will a prolonged meeting do? There is an importance in these things that is not realized. See that man! What is he doing? I am preaching to him about eternal life, and he is thinking about the dirty pew. And that woman is asking for a footstool to keep her feet out of the tobacco juice. Shame!

9. It is important that the church should be just warm enough, and not too warm. Suppose a minister comes into a church and finds it cold. He sees as soon as he gets in that he might as well have stayed home. The people are shivering, their feet are cold, and they feel as if they will catch a cold. They are uneasy, and he wishes he was at home, for he knows he cannot do anything; but he must preach, or they will be disappointed.

Or he may find the church too warm, and the people, instead of listening to the truth, are fanning and panting for breath. Soon a woman faints and makes a commotion, and the train of thought and feeling is all lost, and so a whole sermon is wasted to no good end. These little things take off the attention of people from the words of eternal life. Very often it is so that if you drop a single link in the chain of argument, you lose the whole thing, and the people are damned, just because the careless church does not see to the proper management of these little matters.

10. The church should be well ventilated. Of all houses, a church should be the most perfectly ventilated. If there is no change of the air, it passes through so many lungs that it becomes bad, and its oxygen is exhausted. The people pant, not knowing why, and feel an almost irresistible desire

to sleep – and the minister preaches in vain. The sermon is lost, and worse than lost.

I have often wondered that this matter would be so little the subject of thought. The elders and trustees will sit and hear a whole sermon while the people are all but ready to die for the lack of air. The minister is wasting his strength in preaching in this room that is so stale and stuffy, and there they sit and never think to do anything to help the matter. They should take it upon themselves to see that this is managed properly, that the church is just warm enough, and the air kept pure. How important it is for the church to be awake to this subject so that the minister may labor to the best advantage, and the people give their undivided attention to the truth, which is to save their souls.

When things are wrong, it is very common to place all the blame on the church custodian. This is not so. Often the custodian is not to blame. If the church is cold and uncomfortable, very often it is because the fuel is not good, or the stoves not suitable, or the church is so open it cannot be warmed. If it is too warm, perhaps somebody has interfered when he was out, and heaped on fuel without discretion. Or, if the custodian is at fault, perhaps it is because the church does not pay him enough for his services, and he cannot afford to give the attention necessary to keep the church in order. Churches sometimes force down the custodian's salary to the lowest point so that he is compelled to slight his work. Or they will select one who is incompetent for the sake of getting him cheap, and then the thing is not done.

The fault is with the church. Let them give an adequate compensation for the work, and it can be done, and done faithfully. If one custodian will not do things properly, another will, and the church is obligated to see it done right, or else let them dismiss their minister and not keep him, and at the same time have other things in a state so out of order that he loses all his work. What frugality! To pay the minister's salary, and then for the lack of fifty dollars added to the custodian's wages, everything is so out of order that the minister's labors are all lost, souls are lost, and your children and neighbors go down to hell!

Sometimes this uncleanliness, negligence, and confusion are chargeable to the minister. Perhaps he uses tobacco and sets the example of defiling the house of God. Perhaps the pulpit will be the filthiest place in the church. I have sometimes been in pulpits that were too disgusting to be occupied by human beings. If a minister has no more piety and decency than this, it is no wonder that things are at loose ends in the congregation. And generally it is even so.

11. People should leave their dogs at home and make sure their children are quiet. I have often known contentions to arise among dogs, and children to cry, just at that stage of the services that would most successfully destroy the effect of the meeting. If children are present and weep, they should instantly be removed. I have sometimes known a mother or a nurse sit and toss her child, while its cries were diverting the attention of the whole congregation. This is cruel. And as for dogs, it would be much better to keep them away from the meetings than to divert attention from the Word of God. Maybe a deacon's dog has destroyed more souls in this way than the deacon will ever be instrumental in saving.

12. The members of the church should help the minister by visiting from house to house and trying to save souls. Do not leave all this to the minister. It is impossible for him to do it, even if he gives all his time and neglects his study and his private time with God. Church members should take efforts and qualify themselves for this duty so that they can be useful in it.

13. They should hold Bible classes. Suitable individuals should be selected to hold Bible classes for the instruction of the young people, and where those who are awakened or affected by the preaching can be received and converted. As soon as anyone is seen to be affected, let them be invited to join the Bible class, where they will be properly treated, and probably they will be converted. The church should select the best men for this service, and all should be on the lookout to fill up the Bible classes. It has been done in this congregation, and it is a very common thing, when people are affected, that they are observed by somebody and invited to join the Bible class. They will usually join, and there they are converted. I do not mean that we are doing all we should do in this way, or all we could do. We need more teachers, able and willing, to take charge of such classes.

14. Churches should sustain Sunday schools, and in this way aid their ministers in saving souls. How can a minister attend to this and also preach? Unless the church will take away these responsibilities, cares, and labors from the minister, he must either neglect them or be crushed. Let the church be wide awake, watch and bring in children to the school, teach them faithfully, and lay themselves out to promote a revival in the school.

15. They should watch over the members of the church. They should visit each other in order to stir each other up, know each other's spiritual condition, and provoke one another to love and good works (Hebrews 10:24). The minister cannot do it; he does not have the time to do so. It is impossible for him to study and prepare sermons, and at the same time visit every member of the church as often as it needs to be done to keep them advancing. The church members are bound to do it. They are under oath to watch over each other's spiritual welfare.

But how is this done? Many do not know each other. They meet and pass each other as strangers, and never ask about their spiritual condition. But if they hear anything bad of anyone, they go and tell it to others. Instead of watching over each other for their good, they look for them to fall. How can they watch for good when they are not even acquainted with each other?

16. The church should watch for the effect of preaching. If they are praying for the success of the preached Word, they will watch for it of course. They should keep a look out, and when any in the congregation give evidence that the Word of God has taken hold of them, they should follow it up. Wherever there are any exhibitions of feeling, those people should be attended to instantly, and not left until their impressions wear off. They should talk to them, or visit them, or get them into the anxious meeting or into the Bible class, or bring them to the minister. If the members of the church do not attend to this, they neglect their duty. If they attend to it, they may do incalculable good.

There was a pious young woman who lived in a very cold and wicked place. She alone had the spirit of prayer, and she had been praying for a blessing upon the Word. Eventually she saw one individual in the congregation who seemed to be affected by the preaching, and as soon as the minister came from the pulpit, she came forward, agitated and trembling, and begged him to go and talk with the person immediately. He did so. The individual was soon converted, and a revival followed.

Many clueless professing Christians would not have seen that individual awakened, and would have stumbled over half a dozen of them without notice and let them go to hell. Professing Christians should watch every sermon and see how it affects the congregation. I do not mean that they should be stretching their necks and staring around the church, but they should observe, as they may, and if they find anyone affected by preaching, they should throw themselves in his way and guide him to the Savior.

17. Beware that you do not give away all the preaching to others. If you do not take your portion, you will starve and become like spiritual skeletons. Christians should take their portion to themselves. If the Word is quite searching to them, they should honestly apply it to themselves. They should lay it alongside their heart and practice it and live by it. Otherwise preaching will do them no good.

18. Be ready to help your minister in carrying out his plans for doing good. When the minister is wise to devise plans for usefulness, and the church is ready to carry them out, they may carry all before them. But when the church hangs back from every enterprise until they are actually dragged into it, when they are opposing every proposal because it will cost something, they are a dead weight upon a minister. If stoves are needed – oh, no, they will cost something. If lamps are called for to prevent preaching in the dark – oh, no, they will cost something. And so they will stick up candles on the posts, or do without evening meetings entirely. If they stick up candles, it soon comes to pass that they either give no light, or someone must run around and crop them – and so the whole congregation is disturbed by the person attending to the candles, their attention is taken away, and the sermon is lost.

I once attended an extended meeting where we were embarrassed because there were no lamps in the church. I urged the people to get them, but they thought it would cost too much. I then offered to get them myself, and was about to do it, but found it would give offense, and we went on without. But the blessing did not come to any great extent. How could it? The church began by calculating to a cent how much it would cost, and they would not spend that amount to save souls from hell.

So where a minister appoints a meeting, such people cannot have it because it will cost something. If they can offer unto the Lord that which costs nothing, they will do it (compare 2 Samuel 24:24). Miserable helpers they are (see Job 16:2)! Such a church can have no revival. A minister might as well have a millstone around his neck as such a church. He had better leave them if they cannot learn any better, and go where he will not be so hindered.

19. Church members should make it a point to attend prayer meetings, and attend on time. Some church members will always attend the preaching because there they have nothing to do except to sit and listen and be entertained; but they will not attend prayer meetings for fear that they will be called on to do something. Such members tie up the hands of the minister and discourage his heart. Why do they employ a minister? Is it to amuse them by preaching, or is it so he may teach them the will of God that they may do it?

20. Church members should study and inquire what they can do, and then do it. Christians should be trained like a band of soldiers. It is the duty and office of a minister to train them for usefulness, to teach them and direct them, and to lead them on in such a way as to produce the greatest amount of moral influence. Then they should stand their ground and do their duty, or else they will be right in the way.

I could write a book as big as this Bible in detailing the various things that should be attended to. There are many other points that I noted and intended to touch upon, but I must move on for now.

Remarks

1. You see that a minister's lack of success may not be entirely on account of a lack of wisdom in the exercise of his office. I am not going to plead

for negligent ministers. I will never spare ministers from the simple truth, nor apply flattering tides to men. If they are blameworthy, let them be blamed. Undoubtedly, they are always more or less to blame when the Word produces no effect. However, it is far from true that they are always the main people to blame.

Sometimes the church is much more to blame than the minister, and if an apostle or an angel from heaven were to preach, he could not produce a revival of religion in that church. Perhaps they are dishonest to their minister, or covetous, or careless about the conveniences of public worship. Alas! What a condition many country churches are in, where, for the lack of a few hundred dollars, everything is inconvenient and uncomfortable, and the labors of the preacher are lost. They live in ceiled houses themselves, and let the house of God lie waste (Haggai 1:4). Maybe the church counteracts all the influence of preaching by their ungodly lives. Perhaps their parties, their games, and their worldly entertainment, as in most of the churches in this city, annihilate the influence of the gospel.

2. Churches should remember that they are exceedingly guilty when they employ a minister, and then do not aid him in his work. The Lord Jesus Christ has sent an ambassador to sinners to turn them from their evil ways, and he fails of his errand because the church refuses to do its duty. Instead of advancing his message, seconding his pleadings, and holding up his hands in all the ways that are proper, they stand right in the way and contradict his message and counteract his influence, and souls perish. No doubt in most of the congregations in the United States, the minister is often hindered so much that he might as well be on a foreign mission a great part of the time as to be there, for he has to preach over the heads of an inactive, careless church to see any effect of his preaching in the conversion of sinners.

Yet these very churches are not willing to have their minister absent a few days to attend an extended meeting. "We cannot spare him; he is *our* minister, and we like to have our minister here." At the same time, though, they hinder all he can do. If he could, he would tear himself right away and go where there is no minister, and where the people would be willing to receive the gospel. But there he must stay, although he cannot get the church into a state to have a revival once in three years, to last three months at a time. It might be good for him to say to the church, "Whenever you are determined to take one of these long naps, I want you to let me know so that I can go and labor somewhere else in the meantime, until you are ready to wake again."

3. Many churches cannot be blessed with a revival because they are sponging off other churches, and out of the treasury of the Lord for the support of their minister, when they are abundantly able to support him themselves. Perhaps they are depending on the Home Missionary Society or on other churches, while they are not exercising any self-denial for the sake of the gospel. I have been amazed to see how some churches live. One church that I was acquainted with actually confessed that they spent more money for tobacco than they gave for missions. Yet they had no minister because they were not able to support one, and they have none now. There is one man in that church who is able to support a minister, and still they have no minister and no preaching.

The churches have not been instructed in their duty on this subject. I stopped in one place last summer where there was no preaching. I inquired of an elder in the church why it was so, and he said it was because they were so poor. I asked him how much he was worth. He did not give me a direct answer, but said that another elder's income was about $5,000 a year, and I finally found out that this man's was about the same. "Here," I said, "are two elders, each of you able to support a minister, and because you cannot get help from outside, you have no preaching. If you had preaching, it would not be blessed while you not doing your part to contribute to the Lord's treasury." Finally, he confessed that he was able to support a minister, and the two together agreed that they would do it.

It is common for churches to ask for help when in fact they do not need any help, and when it would be a great deal better for them to support their own minister. If they get funds from the Home Missionary Society, when they should raise funds themselves, they may expect the curse of the Lord upon them, and this will be a sufficient reason for the gospel's proving to be a curse to them rather than a blessing. It could be said of many churches, "You have robbed God, even this whole church."

I know a church that employed a minister only half the time, and felt unable to pay his salary for that. A society of female workers in a neighboring town appropriated their funds for this purpose, and assisted this church in paying their minister's salary. The result was as might be expected. He did them little or no good. They had no revival under his preaching, nor could they ever expect any while acting on such a principle. There was one man in that congregation who alone could support a full-time minister. I was informed by a member that the church members were supposed to be worth $200,000.

Now if this is true, here is a church with an income (if the people would give even 7 percent) of $14,000 a year, who felt themselves too poor to pay $200 to support a part-time minister, and would allow the females of a neighboring town to work with their own hands to help them in paying this amount. Among the elders of this church, I found that several of them used tobacco, and two of them had signed a covenant, written on the blank leaf of their Bible, in which they had pledged themselves to abandon that sin forever.

It was in a great measure for lack of proper instruction that this church was pursuing such a course. For when the subject was taken up and their duty was laid before them, the wealthy man of whom I am speaking said that he would pay the whole salary himself if he thought it would not be resented by the congregation and do more harm than good, and that if the church would find a minister, and go ahead and raise part of his salary, he would make up the remainder. They can now not only support a part-time minister, but a full-time minister, and they pay his salary themselves. They will find it good and profitable to do so.

As I have gone from place to place laboring in revivals, I have always found that churches were blessed in proportion to their generosity. Where they have manifested a disposition to support the gospel and to pour their substance generously into the treasury of the Lord, they have been blessed both in spiritual and physical things. But where they have been stingy and let the minister preach for them for little or nothing, these churches have been cursed instead of blessed. As a general thing, in revivals of religion, I have found it to be true that young converts are most inclined to join those churches that are most generous in making efforts to support the gospel.

The churches are very much in the dark on this subject. They have not been taught their duty. In many instances, I have found an exceeding readiness to do it when the subject was laid before them. I knew an elder in a church who was talking about getting a part-time minister because the church was poor, although his own income was considerable. I asked him if his income was not sufficient to support a full-time minister himself. He said it was. On being asked what other use he could make of the Lord's money that he possessed that would prove as beneficial to the interest of Christ's kingdom as to employ a minister in his own town, he concluded to set himself about it. A minister has been accordingly obtained, and I believe they find no difficulty in paying him his full salary.

The fact is that a minister can do only a little by preaching only half the time. If on one Sunday an impression is made, it is lost before two more Sundays come around. As a matter of prudence, a church should endeavor to support the gospel all the time. If they get the right sort of minister and keep him steadily at work, they may have a revival, and thus the ungodly will be converted and come in and help them. And thus in one year they may have a great addition to their strength. But if they employ a minister only half the time, year after year may roll away while sinners are going to hell, and no addition is made to their strength from the ranks of the ungodly.

The fact is that professing Christians have not been made to feel that all their possessions are the Lord's. Therefore, they have talked about giving their property for the support of the gospel. They talk as if the Lord Jesus Christ was a beggar, and they are called upon to support His gospel as an act of charity!

A merchant in one of the towns in this state was paying a large part of his minister's salary. One of the members of the church was relating the fact to a minister from abroad, and speaking of the sacrifice that this merchant was making. At this moment, the merchant came in. "Brother," said the minister, "you are a merchant. Suppose you employ a clerk to sell goods, and a schoolmaster to teach your children. You order your clerk to pay your schoolmaster out of the store a certain amount for his services in teaching. Now suppose your clerk would say that he had to pay this schoolmaster his salary, and would speak of the sacrifices that he was making to do it. What would you say to this?"

"Well," said the merchant, "I would say it was ridiculous."

"Well," said the minister, "God employs you to sell goods as His clerk, and He employs your minister to teach His children, and requires you to pay his salary out of the income of the store. Do you call this your sacrifice, and say that you are making a great sacrifice to pay this minister's salary? No, for you are just as much obligated to sell goods for God as he is to preach for God. You have no more right to sell goods for the purpose of laying up money than he has to preach the gospel for the same purpose. You are obligated to be just as pious, and to aim as solely at the glory of God in selling goods as he is in preaching the gospel. Thus you are as absolutely to give up your whole time for the service of God as he does. You and your family may lawfully live out of the profits of this store, and so may the minister and his family just as lawfully.

"If you sell goods from these motives, selling goods is just as much serving God as preaching. A man who sells goods upon these principles, and acts in conformity to them, is just as pious, and just as much in the service of God, as he is who preaches the gospel. Every man is obligated to serve God in his calling – the minister by teaching, the merchant by selling goods, the farmer by tilling his fields, and the lawyer and physician by carrying out the duties of their profession.

"It is just as unlawful for any of these people to labor for the meat that perishes. All they do is to be for God, and all they can earn, after comfortably supporting their families, is to be dedicated to the spread of the gospel and the salvation of the world."

It has long enough been supposed that ministers must be more pious than other men – that they must not love the world, that they must labor for God, that they must live as frugally as possible and give their whole time, health, strength, and life to build up the kingdom of Jesus Christ. This is true. But although other people are not called to labor in the same field and to give up their time to public instruction, yet they are just as absolutely obligated to consider their whole time as God's, and they have no more right to love the world, or accumulate wealth, or store it up for their children, or spend it upon their desires, than ministers have.

It is time that the church was acquainted with these principles.

The Home Missionary Society may labor until the day of judgment to convert the people, and they will never succeed until the churches are led to understand and feel their duty in this respect. The very fact that they are asking and receiving aid in supporting their minister from the Home Missionary Society while they are able to support him themselves is probably the very reason why his labors among them are not more blessed.

I wish that the American Home Missionary Society possessed a hundred times the means that it now does of aiding weak churches that are unable to help themselves, but it is neither good frugality nor piety to give their funds to those who are able but unwilling to support the gospel. It is in vain to attempt to help them while they are able but unwilling to help themselves.

If the missionary society had a ton of gold, it would not be charity to give it to such a church; but let the church bring in all the tithes to God's storehouse, and God will open the windows of heaven and pour down a blessing (Malachi 3:10). Let the churches know assuredly that if they are unwilling to help themselves to the extent of their ability, they will know the reason why such small success attends the labors of their ministers. Here they are sponging their support from the Lord's treasury. How many churches are spending their money for tea and coffee and tobacco, and then come and ask aid from the Home Missionary Society! I will protest against helping a church that uses tea and tobacco and lives without the least self-denial, and who wants to offer God only that which costs nothing.

Finally, if they want to be blessed, let them do their duty – all their duty. Let them put their shoulder to the wheel, gird on the gospel armor, and come up to the work. Then, if the church is in the field, the vehicle of salvation will move on, though all hell oppose, and sinners will be converted and saved. However, if a church will leave all the labor for the minister, and will sit still and look on while he is laboring, and will do nothing themselves but complain of him, they will not only fail of a revival of religion, but if they continue slothful and critical, they will eventually find themselves in hell for their disobedience and unprofitableness in the service of Christ.

Lecture 14

Measures to Promote Revivals

These men, being Jews, do exceedingly trouble our city, and teach customs which are not lawful for us to receive, neither to observe, being Romans.
—Acts 16:20-21

These men here spoken of were Paul and Silas, who went to Philippi to preach the gospel, and very much disturbed the people of that city because they supposed the preaching would interfere with their worldly gains. Therefore, they brought the preachers of the gospel before the magistrates of the city, as criminals, and accused them of teaching doctrines, and especially using measures, that were not lawful.

In speaking from these words, I intend to show that:

I. Under the gospel dispensation, God has established no particular system of measures to be used and always adhered to in promoting the Christian religion.

II. Our present forms of public worship, and everything, as far as measures are concerned, have been arrived at by degrees, and by a succession of new measures.

I. Under the Gospel, God Has Established No
Particular Measures to Be Used

Under the Jewish dispensation, there were particular forms required and prescribed by God Himself, from which it was not lawful to depart. But these forms were all typical, and were designed to shadow forth Christ, or something connected with the new dispensation that Christ was to introduce. Therefore, they were fixed, and all their details specifically prescribed by divine authority.

But it was never so under the gospel. When Christ came, the ceremonial or typical dispensation was set aside because the design of those forms was fulfilled, and therefore they were of no further use. Since Christ was the antitype, the types were of course done away at His coming. The gospel was then preached as the appointed means of promoting the Christian religion, and it was left to the discretion of the church to determine, from time to time, what measures would be adopted, and what forms pursued, in giving the gospel its power.

We are left in the dark as to the measures that were pursued by the apostles and early preachers, except so far as we can gather it from occasional hints in the book of Acts. We do not know how many times they sung and how many times they prayed in public worship, nor even whether they sung or prayed at all in their ordinary meetings for preaching. When Jesus Christ was on earth laboring among His disciples, He had nothing to do with forms or measures. He did from time to time in this respect just as it would be natural for any man to do in such cases, without anything like a set form or mode of doing it.

The Jews accused Him of disregarding their forms. His purpose was to preach and teach mankind the true religion. When the apostles preached afterward, with the Holy Spirit sent down from heaven, we hear nothing about their having a particular system of measures to carry on their work, or one apostle doing something in a specific way because others did it in that way. Their commission was, "Go and preach the gospel, and disciple all nations." It did not prescribe any forms. It did not acknowledge any. No person can pretend to get any set of forms or specific instructions as to measures out of this commission.

Do it – the best way you can. Ask wisdom from God. Use the abilities

He has given you. Seek the direction of the Holy Spirit. Go forward and do it. This was their commission. Their goal was to make known the gospel in the most effectual way, to make the truth stand out vividly so as to obtain the attention and secure the obedience of the greatest number possible. No one can find any form of doing this laid down in the Bible. It is preaching the gospel that stands out prominently there as the great thing. The form is left out of the question.

It is evident that in preaching the gospel, there must be some kind of measures used. The gospel must be gotten before the minds of the people, and measures must be taken so that they can hear it, and to persuade them to attend to it. This is done by building churches, holding announced or other meetings, and so on. Without some measures, it can never be made to take effect among people.

II. As Far as Measures Are Concerned, Our Present Forms of Public Worship, and Everything, Have Been Arrived at by Degrees, and by a Succession of New Measures

1. I will mention some things in regard to the ministry. Many years ago, ministers were accustomed to wear specific clothing. It is so now in Catholic countries. It used to be so here. Ministers had specific attire as much as soldiers. They used to wear a cocked hat, bands instead of a cravat or stock, small clothes, and a wig. No matter how much hair a man had on his head, he must cut it off and wear a wig. He also had to wear a gown. All these things were customary, and every clergyman was obligated to wear them. It was considered improper for him to officiate without them. All these had doubtless been introduced by a succession of innovations, for we have no good reason to believe that the apostles and early ministers dressed differently from other men.

But now all these things have been given up, one by one, by a succession of innovations or new measures, until now in many churches a minister can go into the pulpit and preach without being noticed, although dressed like any other man. And when it was done in regard to each one of them, the church complained as much as if a divine institution had been given up. It was denounced as an innovation. When ministers began to lay aside their cocked hats, and wear hats like other men, it grieved the elderly people very much. It looked so undignified, they said, for a minister to wear a round hat. When in 1827 I wore a fur cap, a minister said, "That was too bad for a minister."

When ministers first began to wear white hats a few years ago, it was thought by many to be a sad and very undignified innovation. Even now, they are so bigoted in some places that a clergyman told me just a few days ago that in traveling through New England last summer with a white hat, he could see that it hindered his influence. This spirit should not be looked upon as harmless. I have good reason to know that it is not harmless. Thinking people see it to be mere bigotry, and are exceedingly in danger of viewing everything about Christianity in the same light on this account. This has been the result in many instances. There is at this day hardly a minister in the land who does not feel himself obligated to wear a black coat, as much as if it were a divine institution. The church is still filled with a kind of superstitious reverence for such things. This is a great stumbling block to many minds.

In a similar manner, when ministers laid aside their bands and wore cravats or stocks, it was said they were becoming secular, and many found fault. Even now, in some places, a minister would not dare to be seen in the pulpit in a cravat or stock. The people would feel as if they had no clergyman if he had no bands. A minister in this city asked another, only a few days ago, if it would be acceptable to wear a black stock in the pulpit. He wore one in his ordinary interaction with his people, but doubted whether it would be acceptable to wear it in the pulpit.

It is the same in regard to short clothes or cloaks. They used to be thought essential to the ministerial character. Even now, in Catholic countries, every priest wears small clothes. Even the little boys there who are training for the priest's office wear their cocked hats, black stockings, and small clothes. This would look ridiculous among us, but it used to be practiced in this country.

The time was when good people would have been shocked if a minister had gone into the pulpit with pantaloons on. They would have thought he was certainly going to ruin the church by his innovations. I have been told that some years ago in New England, a certain elderly clergyman was so opposed to the new measure of a minister's wearing pantaloons that he would on no account allow them in his pulpit. A young man was going to preach for him who had no small clothes, and the old minister would not let him officiate in pantaloons. "Why," said he, "my people would think I had brought someone obsessed with fashion into the pulpit, to see a man there with pantaloons on, and it would produce an excitement among them." Finally, the young man had to borrow a pair of the old gentleman's clothes, which were too short for him, and made a ridiculous figure enough, but anything was better than such a terrible innovation as preaching in pantaloons. However, reason has since triumphed.

It was the same in regard to wigs. I remember one minister who, although he was quite a young man, used to wear an enormous white wig. The people talked as if there was a divine right about it, and it was almost as hard to give it up as to give up the Bible itself. Gowns also were considered essential to the ministerial character. Even now, in many congregations in this country, the people will not tolerate a minister in the pulpit unless he has a flowing silk gown with enormous sleeves as big as his body. Even in some of the Congregational churches in New England, they cannot bear to give it up.

How did people come to suppose that a minister must have a gown or a wig in order to preach with effect? Why was it that every clergyman was to feel obligated to use these things? How is it that not one of these things has been given up in the churches without producing a shock among them? They have all been given up, one by one, and many congregations have been distracted for a time by the innovation. But will anyone pretend that the cause of Christianity has been harmed by it? People felt as if they could hardly worship God without them, but plainly their attachment to them was no part of their religion – that is, no part of the Christian religion. It was mere superstition. When these things were taken away, they complained, as Micah did, *Ye have taken away my gods* (Judges 18:24). But no doubt their religious character was improved by removing these objects of superstitious reverence, and the church in general has greatly benefited by the innovations. Thus you see that the present manner of a minister's attire has been gained by a series of new measures.

2. In regard to the order of public worship, the same difficulties have been met in implementing every change because the church has felt as if God had established the specific mode that they were used to.

a) Psalm books. Formerly it was customary to sing David's psalms. In time, a version of the Psalms in rhyme was introduced. This was very bad, to be sure. When ministers tried to introduce them, the churches were distracted, people strongly opposed, and much trouble was created by the innovation. But the new measure triumphed.

Afterward, another version was brought forward in a better style of poetry, and its introduction was opposed with much contention as a new measure. Finally, Isaac Watts' version came along, which is still opposed in many churches. No longer ago than 1828, when I was in Philadelphia, I was told that a minister there was preaching a course of lectures on psalmody to his congregation for the purpose of bringing them to use a better version of psalms and hymns than the one they were accustomed to. Even now, in a great many congregations, there are people who will leave a church if a psalm or hymn is sung from a new book. If Watts' *Psalms* would be adopted, they would secede and form a new congregation rather than tolerate such an innovation.

The same sort of feeling has been excited by introducing the "Village Hymns" in prayer meetings. In one Presbyterian congregation in this city, within the past few years, the minister's wife wanted to introduce the Village Hymns into the female prayer meetings, not daring to go any further. She thought she was going to succeed, but some of the careful souls found out that it was made in New England, and refused to allow it. "It is a Hopkinsian thing, I dare say."[2]

b) Lining the hymns. Formerly, when there were not many hymn-books, it was the custom to line the hymns, as it was called. The deacon used to stand up before the pulpit and read off the psalm or hymn a line at a time, or two lines at a time, and then sing, and the rest would all join in. Eventually, they began to introduce more books and let everyone sing from his book. What an innovation! Alas, what confusion and disorder it made! How could the good people worship God in singing without having the deacon to line off the hymn in his holy tone, for the holiness of it seemed to consist very much in the tone, which was such that you could hardly tell whether he was reading or singing.

c) Choirs. Afterward, another innovation was brought forth. It was

---

2   Samuel Hopkins (1721-1803) was a New England minister credited for helping to develop
     a form of Calvinist doctrine that was named after him.

thought best to have a select choir of singers sit by themselves and sing so as to give an opportunity to improve the music. But this was bitterly opposed. Oh, how many congregations were torn and rent asunder by the desire of ministers and some leading individuals to bring about an improvement in the cultivation of music by forming choirs of singers. People talked about innovations and new measures, and they thought that great evils were coming to the churches because the singers were seated by themselves and cultivating music and learning new tunes that the old people could not sing. It did not used to be so when they were young, and they would not tolerate such new lights and novelties in the church.

d) Pitch pipes. When music was cultivated and choirs were seated together, then the singers wanted a pitch pipe. Formerly, when the lines were given out by the deacon or clerk, he would strike off into the tune, and the rest would follow as well as they could. But when the leaders of choirs began to use pitch pipes for the purpose of pitching all their voices on precisely the same key, what vast confusion it made! I heard a clergyman say that an elder in the town where he used to live would get up and leave the house whenever he heard the chorister blow his pipe. "Away with your whistle," he said. "What! Whistle in the house of God!" He thought it was profane.

e) Instrumental music. Eventually, in some congregations, various instruments were introduced for the purpose of aiding the singers and improving the music. When the bass viol was first introduced, it made a great commotion. People insisted they might just as well have a fiddle in the house of God. "It is a fiddle. It is made just like a fiddle, only a little larger, and who can worship where there is a fiddle? Soon you will want to dance in the meeting house."

Who has not heard these things talked about as matters of the most vital importance to the cause of Christianity and the purity of the church? Ministers in serious ecclesiastical assemblies have spent days discussing them. In a synod in the Presbyterian church only a few years ago, it was seriously talked of by some as a matter worthy of discipline in a certain church that they had an organ in the house of God. This was within the past few years. There are many churches now that would not tolerate an organ. They would not be half as much excited to be told that sinners are going to hell as to be told that there is going to be an organ in the meeting house.

Oh, in how many places can you more easily get the church to do anything else than to come along in an easy and natural way to do what is needed and wisest and best for promoting Christianity and saving souls! They act as if they had a "Thus saith the Lord" for every custom and practice that has been handed down to them, or that they have long followed themselves, no matter how absurd or harmful.

f) Extemporary Prayers. How many people there are who talk just as if the Prayer Book was of divine institution! I suppose multitudes believe it is. In some parts of the church, a man would not be allowed to pray without his book before him.

g) Preaching without notes. A few years ago, a lady in Philadelphia was invited to hear a certain minister preach, and she refused because he did not read his sermons. She seemed to think it would be profane for a man to go into the pulpit and talk, just as if he was talking to the people about some interesting and important subject – as if God had demanded the use of notes and written sermons. They do not know that notes themselves are an innovation, and a modern one, too. They were introduced in a time of political difficulties in England. The ministers were afraid they would be accused of preaching something against the government unless they could show what they had preached by having it all written down beforehand. And with a time-serving spirit, they yielded to political considerations and imposed a yoke of bondage upon the church. Now in many places, they cannot tolerate extemporaneous preaching.

h) Kneeling in Prayer. This has made a great disturbance in many parts of the country. There was a time in the Congregational churches in New England when a man or woman would be ashamed to be seen kneeling at a prayer meeting for fear of being taken for a Methodist. I have prayed in families where I was the only person who would kneel. The others all stood lest they would imitate the Methodists, I suppose, and thus support innovations upon the established form. Others talk as if there was no other posture except kneeling that could be acceptable in prayer.

3. Labors of laymen is another area in which the varying and changing methods have caused controversy.

a) Lay Prayers. Much objection was formerly made against allowing any man to pray or to take a part in managing a prayer meeting unless he was a clergyman. It used to be said that a layman praying in public was interfering with the dignity of ministers and was not to be tolerated. A minister in Pennsylvania told me that a few years ago he appointed a prayer meeting in the church, and the elders opposed it and rejected it. They said they would not have such work. They had hired a minister to do the praying, and he should do it, and they were not going to have common men praying.

Ministers and many others have very extensively objected against a layman's praying in public, especially in the presence of a minister. That would let down the authority of the clergy and was not to be tolerated. At a synod held in this state, there was a synodical prayer meeting appointed. The committee of arrangements, as it was to be a formal thing, designated beforehand the people who were to take part, and named two clergymen and one layman. The layman was a man of talent and information equal to most ministers. However, one doctor of divinity got up and seriously objected to a layman's being asked to pray before that synod. It was not usual, he said. It infringed upon the rights of the clergy, and he wanted no innovations. What a state of things!

b) Lay exhortation. This has been made a question of vast importance, one that has agitated all New England and many other parts of the country, whether laymen should be allowed to exhort in public meetings. Many ministers have labored to close the mouths of laymen entirely. They overlooked the practice of the early churches. So much opposition was made to this practice nearly a hundred years ago that President Jonathan Edwards actually had to take up the subject and write a labored defense of the rights and duties of laymen.

However, the opposition has not entirely ceased to this day. "What! A man who is not a minister – to talk in public! It will create confusion. It will lower the respect of the ministry. What will people think of us ministers if we allow common men to do the same things that we do?" Astonishing!

But now, all these things are gone by in most places, and laymen can pray and exhort without the least objection. The evils that were feared from the labors of laymen have not been realized, and many ministers are glad to have them exercise their gifts in doing good.

4. Female prayer meetings have caused dissension in churches. Within the last few years, female prayer meetings have been extensively opposed in this state. What dreadful things! A minister, now dead, said that when he first attempted to establish these meetings, he had all the clergy around opposed to him. "Set women to praying? Why, the next thing, I suppose, will be to set them to preaching." Serious apprehensions were entertained for the safety of Zion if women would be allowed to get together to pray. Even now, they are not tolerated in some churches.

So it has been in regard to all the active movements of the church. Missions, Sunday schools, and everything of the kind have been opposed and have gained their present hold in the church only by a succession of struggles and a series of innovations. A Baptist association in Pennsylvania, some years ago, disclaimed all fellowship with any minister who had been widely educated, or who supported missions, Bible societies, Sunday schools, temperance societies, etc. All these were denounced as new measures not found in the Bible, and that would necessarily lead to distraction and confusion in the churches.

The same thing has been done by some among the German churches. And in many Presbyterian churches, there are found those who will take the same ground and denounce all these things, with the exception, perhaps, of an educated ministry, as innovations, new measures, new lights, going in their own strength, and the like, and as calculated to do great evil.

5. I will now mention several men who have in divine providence been set forward as prominent in introducing these innovations.

a) The apostles were great innovators, as you all know. After the resurrection, and after the Holy Spirit was poured out upon them, they set out to overhaul the church. They broke down the Jewish system of measures and rooted it out so as to leave scarcely a trace.

b) Martin Luther and the Reformers. You all know what difficulties they had to contend with, and the reason was that they were trying to introduce new measures – new ways of performing the public duties of the Christian religion, and new strategies to bring the gospel with power to the hearts of men. All the strange and ridiculous things of the Roman Catholics were held to in the church with unrelenting obstinacy, as if they were of divine authority. And such an excitement was raised by the attempt to change them that involved nearly all of Europe in blood.

c) John Wesley and his colleagues. Wesley did not at first break away from the Established Church in England, but formed little classes everywhere that grew into a church within a church. He remained in the Episcopal Church, but he introduced so many new measures as to fill all England with excitement and uproar and opposition, and he was everywhere denounced as an innovator, a stirrer up of sedition, and a teacher of new things that were not lawful to receive (see Acts 16:21).

George Whitefield was a man of the same school, and like Wesley, he was an innovator. I believe he and several of his associates were expelled from college for getting up such a new measure as a social prayer meeting. They would pray together and expound the Scriptures, and this was such a daring novelty that it could not be tolerated. When Whitefield came to this country, what an astonishing opposition was raised! Often he nearly lost his life, and barely escaped by the skin of his teeth. Now everybody looks upon him as the glory of the age in which he lived. Many of our own denomination have so far divested themselves of prejudice as to consider Wesley not only a good man but a wise and preeminently useful man. Then, however, almost the entire church viewed them with animosity, fearing that the innovations they introduced would destroy the church.

d) President Jonathan Edwards. This great man was famous in his day for new measures. Among other innovations, he refused to baptize the children of unrepentant parents. The practice of baptizing the children of the ungodly had been introduced in the New England churches in the preceding century, and had become nearly universal. President Edwards saw that the practice was wrong, and he refused to do it. The refusal shook all the churches of New England. A hundred ministers joined and determined to bring him down. He wrote a book on the subject and defeated them all. It produced one of the greatest excitements there ever was in New England. Nothing, unless it was the Revolutionary War, ever produced an equal excitement in the church.

The General Association of Connecticut refused to accept Whitefield because he was such an innovator. "Why, he will preach out of doors and anywhere!" How awful! What a terrible thing that a man should preach in the fields or in the streets! Cast him out!

All these were devoted men, seeking out ways to do good and save souls. Precisely the same kind of opposition was experienced by all the ecclesiastical bodies, obstructing their path and trying to destroy their character and influence. A book, still around, was written in President Edwards' time by a doctor of divinity, and signed by a multitude of ministers, against Whitefield and Edwards, as well as against their associates and their measures.

A letter was published in this city by a minister against Whitefield that brought up the same objections against innovations that we hear now. In the time of the late opposition to revivals in the state of New York, a copy of this letter was taken to the editor of a religious periodical with a request that he would publish it. He refused, and gave for a reason that if published, many would apply it to the controversy that is going on now. I mention it merely to show how identical the opposition is that is raised in different ages against all new measures designed to advance the cause of true Christianity.

6. In the present generation, many things have been introduced that have proved useful, but have been opposed on the ground that they were innovations. Since many people are still unsettled in regard to them, I have thought it best to make some remarks concerning them. There are three things in particular that have primarily attracted notice, and therefore I will speak of them. They are anxious meetings, protracted meetings, and the anxious seat. These are all opposed, and are called new measures.

a) Anxious Meetings. The first anxious meeting that I ever heard of under that name was in New England, where the meetings were appointed for the purpose of holding personal conversation with anxious sinners and to adapt instruction to the cases of individuals so as to lead them immediately to Christ. The design of them is evidently philosophical, but they have been opposed because they were new. There are two modes of conducting an anxious meeting, either of which may bring about the intended result:

(1) By spending a few moments in personal conversation and learning the state of mind of each individual, and then in an address to the whole group, taking up all their errors and removing their difficulties together.

(2) By going around to each person and taking up each individual case, and going over the whole ground with each person separately, and getting them to promise to give up their hearts to God.

Either way, they are important, and have been found most successful in practice. But multitudes have objected to them because they were new.

b) Protracted Meetings. These are not new, but have always been practiced in some form or other ever since there was a church on earth. The Jewish festivals were nothing else but protracted meetings. In regard to the manner, they were conducted differently from what they are now, but the purpose was the same: to devote a series of days to religious services in order to make a more powerful impression of divine things upon the minds of the people.

All denominations of Christians, when religion prospers among them, hold protracted meetings. In Scotland they used to begin on Thursday at all their communion seasons, and continue until after the Lord's Day. The Episcopalians, Baptists, and Methodists all hold protracted meetings. Yet now in our day they have been opposed, particularly among Presbyterians, and called new measures, and regarded as full of all manner of evil, even though they have been so manifestly and so extensively blessed. I will suggest a few things that should be considered in regard to them.

(1) In appointing them, regard should be had to the circumstances of the people – whether the church is able to give its attention and devote its time to carry on the meeting. In some instances, this rule has been neglected. Some have thought it right to break in upon the necessary business of the community. In the country, they would appoint the meeting during harvest time, and in the city during the height of the business season, when all the people were necessarily occupied and pressed with their worldly labors.

In defense of this course, it is said that our business should always be made to yield to God's business, that eternal things are of so much more importance than temporal things, and that worldly business of any kind, and at any time, should be made to yield and give place to a protracted meeting. However, the worldly business in which we are engaged is not our business. It is as much God's business, and as much our duty, as our prayers and protracted meetings are. If we do not consider our business in this light, we have not yet taken the first lesson in Christianity. We have not learned to do all things to the glory of God.

With this view of the subject, separating our business from Christianity, we are living six days for ourselves and the seventh for God. Real duties never interfere with each other. Weekdays have their appropriate duties, and the Lord's Day has its appropriate duties, and we are to be equally pious on every day in the week and in the performance of the duties of every day. We are to plow and sow and sell our goods and attend to our various callings with the same singleness of view to the glory of God that we have when we go to church on Sunday and pray with our families and read our Bibles. This is a first principle in the Christian religion. He who does not know and act on this principle has not learned the basics of piety as yet.

There are particular seasons of the year in which God in His providence calls upon people to attend to business, because worldly business at the time is particularly urgent and must be done at that season, if it is to be done at all – for example, seed time and harvest for the farmer, and the business seasons for the merchant. We have no right to say in those particular seasons that we will quit our business and have a protracted meeting.

The fact is that the business is not ours, and unless God, by some special indication of His providence, shows it to be His will that we should turn aside and have a protracted meeting at such times, I look upon it as tempting God to appoint them. It is saying, "O God, this worldly business is our business, and we are willing to lay it aside for Your business." Unless God has indicated it to be His pleasure to pour out His Spirit and revive His work at such a season, and has thus called upon His people to quit, for the time being, their ordinary employments and attend especially to a protracted meeting, it appears to me that God might say to us in such circumstances, *Who hath required this at your hand?* (Isaiah 1:12).

God has a right to dispose of our time as He pleases. He has a right to require us to give up any portion of our time, or all of our time, to duties of instruction and devotion. When circumstances plainly call for it, it is our duty to lay aside every other business and make direct and continuous efforts for the salvation of souls. If we transact our business upon right principles and from proper motives, and wholly for the glory of God, we will never object to go aside to attend a protracted meeting whenever there appears to be a call for it in the providence of God.

A man who considers himself a steward or a clerk does not consider it a hardship to rest from his labors on the Lord's Day, but a privilege. The selfish owner may feel unwilling to suspend his business on the Lord's Day, but the clerk, who transacts business not for himself but for his employer, considers it a privilege to rest upon that day. In the same way, if we do our business for God, we will not think it hard if He makes it our duty to suspend our worldly business and attend a protracted meeting. We would rather consider it in the light of a holiday.

Whenever, therefore, you hear a man pleading that he cannot leave his business to attend a protracted meeting, that it is his duty to attend to business – there is reason to fear that he considers the business as his own, and the meeting as God's business. If he felt that the business of the store or farm was as much God's business as attending a protracted meeting, he would undoubtedly be very willing to rest from his worldly toils and go up to the house of God and be refreshed whenever there was an indication, on the part of God, that the community was called to that work. It is highly worthy of remark that the Jewish festivals were appointed at those seasons of the year when there was the least pressure of indispensable worldly business.

In some instances, such meetings have been appointed at the very height of the business seasons, and have been followed with no good results, evidently for the lack of attention to the rule laid down here. In other cases, meetings have been appointed in seasons when there was much pressure of worldly business, and have been remarkably blessed. But in those cases, the blessing followed because the meeting was appointed in obedience to the indications of the will of God by those who had spiritual discernment and understood the signs of the times. And in many cases, undoubtedly, individuals have attended who really supposed themselves to be giving up their own business to attend to God's business, and in such cases they made what they supposed to be a real sacrifice, and God in mercy granted them the blessing.

(2) Ordinarily, a protracted meeting should be conducted through, and the labor primarily performed by, the same minister, if possible. Sometimes protracted meetings have been held and dependence placed on ministers coming in from day to day, and they would have no blessing. The reason was obvious: they did not come in a state of mind to enter into the work, and they did not know the state of people's minds so as to know what to preach. Suppose a person who was sick would call in a different physician every day. The physician would not know what the symptoms had been, nor what was the course of the disease or of the treatment, nor what remedies had been tried, nor what the patient could bear. He would certainly not be able to help the patient much. It is the same way in a protracted meeting that is carried on by a succession of ministers. None of them get into the spirit of it, and generally they do more harm than good.

Ordinarily, a protracted meeting should not be appointed unless they can secure the right kind of help and get a minister or two who will agree to stay on the ground until the meeting is done. Then they will probably secure a rich blessing.

(3) There should not be so many public meetings as to interfere with the duties of private and family devotions. Otherwise, Christians will lose their spirituality and let go of their hold of God, and the meeting will run down.

(4) Families should not put themselves out so much in entertaining strangers as to neglect prayer and other duties. It is often the case that when a protracted meeting is held, some of the principal families in the church – I mean those who are principally relied on to sustain the meetings – do not get into the work at all. And the reason is that they are burdened with much serving (see Luke 10:39-40). They often take needless trouble to provide for guests who come from a distance to the meeting, and lay themselves out very foolishly to entertain them,

not only comfortably but luxuriously. It should always be understood that it is the duty of families to have as little working and fanfare as possible, and to get along with their hospitality in the easiest way, so that they may all have time to pray, go to the meeting, and attend to the things of the kingdom.

(5) By all means, guard against unnecessarily keeping late hours. If people keep late hours night after night, they will inevitably wear out the body, their health will fail, and there will be a reaction. They sometimes allow themselves to get so excited as to lose their sleep and become irregular in their meals until they break down and their bodies react. Unless there is the greatest effort taken to keep a regular pattern, the excitement will get so great that nature will give way, their bodies will run down, and the work will stop.

(6) All division and denominationalism should be carefully avoided. If a sectarian spirit breaks out either in the preaching, praying, or conversation, it will counteract all the good of the meeting.

(7) Be watchful against placing dependence on a protracted meeting, as if that of itself would produce a revival. This is a point of great danger, and has always been so. This is the main reason why the church in successive generations has always had to give up her measures – because Christians had come to rely on them for success.

It has been this way in some places in regard to protracted meetings. They have been so blessed that in some places the people have thought that if they would only have a protracted meeting, they would have a blessing, and sinners would certainly be converted. And so they have appointed their meeting without any preparation in the church, and just sent abroad for some minister of note, and set him to preaching, as if that would convert sinners. It is obvious that the blessing would be withheld from a meeting put together in this way.

(8) Avoid adopting the idea that a revival cannot be enjoyed without a protracted meeting. Some churches have got into an unhealthy state of feeling on this subject. Their zeal has become all unsteady and emotional

so that they never think of doing anything to promote a revival except in that way. When a protracted meeting is held, they will seem to be wonderfully zealous, and then sink down to a lethargic state until another protracted meeting produces another spasm. Multitudes in the church now think it is necessary to give up protracted meetings because they are misused in this way. This should be guarded against in every church so that they may not be driven to give them up and lose all the benefits that protracted meetings are intended to produce.

c) The Anxious Seat. By this I mean the appointment of some particular seat in the place of meeting where those who are anxious, or concerned about their souls, may come and be addressed specifically, and be made subjects of prayer, and sometimes be conversed with individually. Lately, this measure has met with more opposition than any of the others. What is the great objection? I cannot see it. The design of the anxious seat is undoubtedly philosophical and according to the laws of mind. It has two significances:

1. When a person is seriously troubled in mind, everybody knows that there is a powerful tendency to conceal it. When a person is weighed down with a sense of his condition, if you can get him willing to have it known, if you can get him to break away from the chains of pride, you have gained an important point toward his conversion. This is agreeable to the philosophy of the human mind. How many thousands there are who will bless God to eternity that when weighed down by the truth, they were ever brought to take this step by which they threw off the idea that it was a dreadful thing to have anybody know that they were serious about their souls.

2. Another significance of the anxious seat is to detect deception and delusion, and thus prevent false hopes. It has been opposed on the ground that it was intended to create delusion and false hopes, but this objection is unreasonable. The truth is the other way. Suppose I were preaching on the subject of temperance, and that I should first show the evils of intemperance, and bring up the drunkard and his family, showing the various evils produced until every heart is beating with emotion. Then I portray the great danger of moderate drinking and

show how it leads to intoxication and ruin, and that there is no safety except in total abstinence, until a hundred hearts are ready to say, "I will never drink another drop of alcohol in the world; if I do, I will expect to find a drunkard's grave."

Then I stop short and let the temperance pledge be circulated, and everyone who is fully resolved is ready to sign it. But how many will begin to draw back and hesitate when you begin to call on them to sign a pledge of total abstinence? One says to himself, "Shall I sign it or not? I thought my mind was made up, but this signing a pledge never to drink again, I do not know about that." Thus you see that when a person is called upon to give a pledge, if he is found not to be decided, he makes it evident that he was not sincere. That is, he never came to that resolution on the subject that could be relied on to control his future life.

It is the same with the awakened sinner. Preach to him, and at the moment he thinks he is willing to do anything. He thinks he is determined to serve the Lord. However, bring him to the test, call on him to do one thing, to take one step that will identify him with the people of God, or counter his pride – his pride comes up, and he refuses. His delusion is brought out, and he finds himself a lost sinner still. Whereas, if you had not done it, he might have gone away flattering himself that he was a Christian. If you say to him, "There is the anxious seat; come out and declare your determination to be on the Lord's side," and if he is not willing to do such a small thing as that, then he is not willing to do anything; and there he is, brought out before his own conscience. It uncovers the delusion of the human heart and prevents a great many false conversions by showing those who might otherwise imagine themselves willing to do anything for Christ, when in fact they are willing to do nothing.

The church has always felt it necessary to have something of the kind to answer this very purpose. In the days of the apostles, baptism answered this purpose. The gospel was preached to the people, and then all those who were willing to be on the side of Christ were called on to be baptized. It held the precise place that the anxious seat does now, as a public manifestation of their determination to be Christians.

In modern times, those who have been strongly opposed to the anxious seat have been obliged to adopt some substitute, or they could not get along in promoting a revival. Some have adopted the means of inviting the people who were concerned for their souls to stay for conversation after the rest of the congregation had left. But what is the difference? This is as much setting up a test as the other. Others, who would be much ashamed to use the anxious seat, have asked those who have any feeling on the subject to sit still in their seats as the rest leave. Others have called the anxious to go to the lecture room. The purpose of all these is the same, and the principle is the same – to bring people out from the refuge of false shame.

One man I heard of who was very far gone in his opposition to new measures requested in one of his meetings for all those who were willing to submit to God, or who desired to be made subjects of prayer, to signify it by leaning forward and putting their heads down upon the pew before them. Who does not see that this was a mere evasion of the anxious seat, that it was intended to answer the purpose in its place, and that he adopted this because he felt that something of the kind was important?

Now what objection is there against taking a specific seat, or standing up, or going into the lecture room? They all mean the same thing when properly conducted, and they are not new in principle at all. The thing has always been done in substance. In Joshua's day, he called on the people to decide what they would do, and they spoke right out in the meeting: *We will serve the LORD. . . . The LORD our God will we serve, and his voice will we obey* (Joshua 24:15, 24).

Remarks

1. If we examine the history of the church, we will find that there has never been an extensive reformation except by new measures. Whenever the churches get settled down into a form of doing things, they soon start relying upon the outward doing of it, and so retain the form of religion while they lose the substance. Then it has always been found impossible to awaken them so as to bring about a reformation of the evils, and produce a revival of religion, by simply pursuing that established form.

Perhaps it is not too much to say that it is impossible for God

Himself to bring about reformations except by new measures. At least it is a fact that God has always chosen this way as the wisest and best that He could devise or adopt. And although it has always been the case that the very measures that God has chosen to use, and which He has blessed in reviving His work, have been opposed as new measures and have been denounced, yet He has continued to act upon the same principle. When He has found that a certain method has lost its influence by having become a form, He brings up some new measure that will break in upon their lazy habits and wake up a slumbering church. And great good has resulted.

2. The same distinctions in substance that now exist have always existed in all seasons of reformation and revival of religion. There have always been those who particularly adhered to their forms and beliefs and precise way of doing things, as if they had a "Thus saith the Lord" for every one of them. They have called those who differed from them, who were trying to roll the ark of salvation forward, Methodists, New Lights, Radicals, New School, New Divinity, and various other derogatory names. The decline that has followed has been uniformly due to two causes, which should by no means be overlooked by the church:

a) The Old School, or Old Measure party, has persevered in its opposition and has eagerly seized hold of any real or apparent indiscretion in the friends of the work. In such cases, the churches have gradually lost their confidence in the opposition to new measures, and the cry of "New Divinity" and "Innovation" has ceased to alarm them. They see that the blessing of God is with those who are thus accused of new measures and innovation, and the continued opposition of the Old School, together with the continued success of the New School, have destroyed their confidence in the opposition, and they get tired of hearing the incessant cry of "New Lights," "New Divinity," and "New Measures." Thus the scale has turned, and the churches have pronounced a verdict in favor of the New School and of condemnation against the Old School.

b) But now, right here in this state of things, the devil has, again and again, taken the advantage. Individuals have risen up, and being sustained by the confidence of the churches in the New Measure party, and finding them sick of opposition and ready to do anything that would promote the interests of Christ's kingdom, they have driven headlong themselves, and in some instances have carried the churches into the very vortex of those difficulties that have been predicted by their opposers. Thus, when the battle had been fought and the victory gained, the careless zeal of some well-meaning but headlong individuals has brought about a reaction that has spread a dark cloud over the churches for years.

This was the case, as is well known, in the days of President Edwards. Here is a rock upon which a lighthouse is now built, and upon which if the church now runs aground, both parties are entirely without excuse. It is now well known, or should be known, that the decline that followed the revivals in those days, together with the declines that have repeatedly occurred, were due to the combined influence of the continued and unyielding opposition of the Old School, and the ultimate bad spirit and recklessness of some individuals of the New School.

And here the note of alarm should be distinctly sounded to both parties, lest the devil would prevail against us at the very point, and under the very circumstances, where he has so often prevailed. Will the church never learn wisdom from experience? How often – oh, how often must these scenes be acted over before the millennium will come! When will it once be that the church may be revived and Christianity prevail without exciting such opposition in the church as to eventually bring about a reaction?

3. The present cry against new measures is highly ridiculous when we consider the quarter from which it comes and all the circumstances in the case. It is truly astonishing that sincere ministers would really feel alarmed at the new measures of the present day, as if new measures were something new under the sun, and as if the present form and manner of doing things had descended from the apostles and were established by a "Thus saith the Lord" – especially when the truth is that every step of the church's advance from the dreadful darkness of Roman Catholicism has been through the introduction of one new measure after another.

We now look with astonishment, and are inclined to look almost with contempt, upon the cry of "Innovation" that has preceded our day. As we review the fears that multitudes in the church have entertained in previous days with respect to innovation, we find it difficult to account for what appear to us the groundless and absurd, at least, if not ridiculous, objections and difficulties that they made. But, my hearers, is it not astonishing that at this late day, after the church has had so much experience in these matters, that solemn and pious men would seriously feel alarmed at the introduction of the simple, the philosophical, and the greatly prospered measures of the last ten years? It is as if new measures were something not to be tolerated, that they were of highly disastrous tendency, and that they would wake the notes and echoes of alarm in every nook and corner of the church.

4. We see why it is that those who have been making the commotion about new measures have not been successful in promoting revivals. They have been taken up with the evils, real or imaginary, that have attended this great and blessed work of God. No one will pretend to deny that there have not been evils, but I do believe that no revival ever existed since the world began of such great power and extent as the one that has prevailed for the last ten years that has not been attended with as great or greater evils. Still, a large portion of the church has been frightening themselves and others by giving constant attention to the evils of revivals.

One of the professors in a Presbyterian theological seminary felt it was his duty to write a series of letters to Presbyterians, which were extensively circulated, the purpose of which seemed to be to sound the note of alarm throughout all the borders of the church in regard to the evils attending revivals. While men are taken up with the evils instead of the excellencies of a blessed work of God, how can it be expected that they will be useful in promoting it? I would say all this in great kindness, but still it is a point upon which I must not be silent.

5. Without new measures, it is impossible for the church to succeed in gaining the attention of the world to the Christian religion. There are so many exciting subjects constantly brought before the public mind, such a running to and fro, so many who cry "Lo here!" and "Lo there!" (see Luke 17:21), that the church cannot maintain her ground and cannot command attention without very exciting preaching and sufficient novelty in measures to get the public ear.

The measures of politicians, of atheists and heretics, the scrambling after wealth, the increase of luxury, and the ten thousand exciting and counteracting influences that bear upon the church and upon the world will gain their attention and turn all people away from the sanctuary and from the altars of the Lord unless we increase in wisdom and piety and wisely adopt such new measures that are calculated to get the attention of people to the gospel of Christ.

I have already said in the course of these lectures that changes should be introduced no faster than they are really called for. They should be introduced with the greatest wisdom, caution, and prayerfulness, and in a manner calculated to excite as little opposition as possible. But we must have new measures. May God prevent the church from settling down in any set of forms and getting the present or any other edition of its measures stereotyped.

6. It is evident that we must have more exciting preaching to meet the character and needs of the age. Ministers are generally beginning to find this out. Some of them complain about it and suppose it is because of new measures, as they call them. They say that such ministers that our fathers would have been glad to hear now cannot be heard and cannot get a position or collect an audience. They think that new measures have polluted the taste of the people. But this is not the difficulty. The character of the age is changed, and these men have not conformed to it, but retain the same stiff, dry, dull style of preaching that satisfied half a century ago.

Look at the Methodists. Many of their ministers are uneducated in the common sense of the term. Many of them are taken right from the shop or the farm, yet they have gathered congregations, pushed their way ahead, and won souls everywhere. Wherever the Methodists have gone, their plain, pointed, and simple, but warm and animated, mode of preaching has always gathered congregations. Few Presbyterian ministers have gathered such large assemblies or won so many souls. Are we to be told that we must pursue the same old, formal mode of doing things amid all these changes? The North River might as well be rolled back as the world converted under such preaching. Those who adopt a different style of preaching, as the Methodists have done, will run away from us. The world will escape from under the influence of this old-fashioned, or rather, new-fashioned, ministry. It is impossible for the public mind to be held by such preaching.

We must have exciting, truly biblical preaching or the devil will have the people, except those whom the Methodists can save. It is impossible for our ministers to continue to do good unless we have innovations in regard to the style of preaching. Many ministers are finding out already that a Methodist preacher, without the advantages of a broad education, will draw a congregation around him that a Presbyterian minister, with perhaps ten times as much learning, cannot equal because he does not have the fervent manner of the other, and does not pour out fire upon his hearers when he preaches.

7. We see the importance of having young ministers obtain proper views of revivals. In a multitude of cases, I have seen that great efforts are taken to frighten our young men who are preparing for the ministry about the evils of revivals, new measures, and the like. Young men in some theological seminaries are taught to look upon new measures as if they were the very inventions of the devil. How can such men have revivals? When they come out, they look around and watch and jump as if the devil was there.

A few years ago, some young men in Princeton came out with an essay about the "evils of revivals." I would like to know now how many of those young men have enjoyed revivals among their people since they have been in the ministry; and if any have, I would like to know whether they have not repented of that essay about the evils of revivals.

If I had a voice so loud as to be heard at Princeton, I would speak to those young men on this subject. It is about time to talk plainly on this point. The church is groaning in all its borders for the lack of suitable ministers. Good men are laboring and are willing to labor day and night to assist in educating young men for the ministry and to promote revivals of religion; and when they come out of the seminary, some of them are as lacking of all the measures that God blesses as they are of Roman Catholicism itself.

Will it be so always? Must we educate young men for the ministry and have them come out frightened to death about new measures, as if there had never been any such thing as new measures? They should know that new measures are not a new thing in the church. Let them go along, keep at work themselves, and not be frightened about new measures. I have been grieved to see that some men, in giving accounts of revivals, have evidently felt themselves obligated to be specific in detailing the measures used in order to avoid the inference that new measures were introduced – evidently feeling that even the church would undervalue the revival unless it appeared to have been promoted without new measures.

Besides, this caution in specifying the measures to demonstrate that there was nothing new looks like admitting that new measures are wrong because they are new, and that a revival is more valuable because it was not promoted by new measures. In this way, I perceive that much evil has been done already, and if the practice is to continue, it must come to this – that a revival must be judged of by the fact that it occurred in connection with new or old measures. I will never accept such a spirit, nor condescend to judge an account of a revival based upon the impu- tation of new or old measures. I believe new measures are right – that is, that it is no objection to a measure simply because it is new or old.

Let a minister enter fully into his work and pour out his heart to God for a blessing, and whenever he sees the lack of any measure to bring the truth more powerfully before the minds of the people, let him adopt it and not be afraid – and God will not withhold His blessing. If ministers will not go forward, and will not preach the gospel with power and passion, and will not turn out of their tracks to do anything new for the purpose of saving souls, they will grieve the Holy Spirit away, and God will visit them with His curse and will raise up other ministers to do His work in the world.

8. It is the right and duty of ministers to adopt new measures for pro- moting revivals. In some places, the church has opposed their minister when he has attempted to use those measures that God has blessed for a revival, and have gone so far as to give up their prayer meetings, and give up laboring to save souls, and stand distant from everything because their minister has adopted what they call new measures. No matter how reasonable the measures are in themselves, nor how seasonable, nor

how much God may bless them, it is enough that they are called new measures, and they will not have anything to do with new measures, nor tolerate them among the people. And so they fall out by the way, grieve away the Spirit of God, and put a stop to the revival when the world around them is going to hell.

Finally, this zealous adherence to particular forms and modes of doing things, which has led the church to resist innovations in measures, savors strongly of fanaticism. What is not a little remarkable is that fanatics of this stamp are always the first to cry out "fanaticism." What is that except fanaticism in the Roman Catholic Church that causes them to adhere with such stubbornness to their particular modes, forms, ceremonies, and ideas? They act as if all these things were established by divine authority, as if there were a "Thus saith the Lord" for every one of them.

We rightly call this a spirit of fanaticism and esteem it worthy of rebuke. However, it is just as absolutely fanatical for the Presbyterian church, or any other church, to be insistent on its particular forms, and to act as if they were established by divine authority. The fact is that God has established in no church any particular form or manner of worship for promoting the interests of Christianity. The Bible is entirely silent on these subjects under the gospel dispensation, and the church is left to exercise its own discretion in relation to all such matters. I hope it will not be thought unkind when I say again that it appears to me that the unkind, angry zeal for a certain mode and manner of doing things, and the overbearing, exterminating cry against new measures, savors strongly of fanaticism.

The only thing insisted upon under the gospel dispensation in regard to measures is that there should be decency and order: *Let all things be done decently and in order* (1 Corinthians 14:40). We are required to guard against all confusion and disorderly conduct, but what is decency and order? Will it be pretended that an anxious meeting, or a protracted meeting, or an anxious seat is inconsistent with decency and order? I would most sincerely reprove and most firmly resist whatever was indecent and disorderly in the worship of God's house, but I do not suppose that by "order" we are to understand any particular set mode in which any church may have been accustomed to perform its service.

Lecture 15

Hindrances to Revivals

I am doing a great work, so that I cannot
come down. Why should the work cease,
whilst I leave it, and come down to you?
—Nehemiah 6:3

This servant of God had come down from Babylon to rebuild the temple and reestablish the worship of God at Jerusalem, the city of his fathers' sepulchers. When it was discovered by Sanballat and certain individuals, his allies, who had long enjoyed the desolations of Zion, that now the temple and the holy city were about to be rebuilt, they raised much opposition. Sanballat and the other leaders tried in several ways to divert Nehemiah and his friends and prevent them from going forward in their work.

At one time they threatened them, and then complained that they were going to rebel against the king. They insisted that their intent was not pious but political, to which Nehemiah replied by a simple and prompt denial: *There are no such things done as thou sayest, but thou feignest them out of thine own heart* (Nehemiah 6:8). Finally, Sanballat sent a message to Nehemiah, requesting him to meet in the plain of Ono to discuss the whole matter politely and have the difficulty adjusted, but he intended to do him harm. They had found that they could not frighten Nehemiah, and now they wanted to get to him by deceit and fraud and take him away from the vigorous performance of his work. But he replied, *I am doing a great work, so that I cannot come down: why should the work cease, whilst I leave it, and come down to you?* (Nehemiah 6:3).

Whenever any of the servants of God do anything in His cause, and there appears to be a probability that they will succeed, it has always been the case that Satan, by his agents, regularly attempts to divert their minds and nullify their labors. It has been like this during the last ten years, during which there have been such remarkable revivals through the length and breadth of the land. These revivals have been very great and powerful and extensive. It has been estimated that no fewer than two hundred thousand people have been converted to God during that time.

The devil has been busy in his devices to divert and distract the people of God, and turn off their energies from pushing forward the great work of salvation. In remarking on the subject, I propose to show the following:

I.   A revival of religion is a great work.

II.   There are several things that may put a stop to it.

III. What must be done for the continuance of this great revival.

I. A Revival of Religion Is a Great Work

It is a great work because there are great interests involved in it. A revival of religion involves both the glory of God, as far as it respects the government of this world, and the salvation of men. Two things that are of infinite importance are involved in it. The greatness of a work is to be estimated by the greatness of the consequences depending on it, and this is the measure of its importance.

II. There Are Several Things That May Put a Stop to a Revival

Some people have talked very foolishly on this subject, as if nothing could harm a genuine revival. They say, "If your revival is a work of

God, it cannot be stopped; can any created being stop God?" Now I ask if this is common sense. It used to be the established belief that a revival could not be stopped because it was the work of God, and so they supposed it would go on, no matter what might be done to hinder it, in the church or out of it. But the farmer might just as well reason so, and think he could go and cut down his wheat and not hurt the crop because it is God that makes grain grow. A revival is the work of God, and so is a crop of wheat – and God is as much dependent on the use of means in one case as the other. Therefore, a revival is as likely to be harmed as a wheat field.

1. A revival will stop whenever the church believes it is going to cease. The church is the instrument with which God carries on this work, and Christians are to work in it voluntarily and with their hearts. Nothing is more fatal to a revival than for its friends to predict that it is going to stop, no matter what the enemies of the work may say about it, predicting that it will all run out and come to nothing, and the like. They cannot stop it in this way, but the friends must labor and pray in faith to carry it on. It is a contradiction to say they are laboring and praying in faith to carry on the work, and yet believe that it is going to stop.

If they lose their faith, it will stop, of course. Whenever the friends of revivals begin to prophecy that the revival is going to stop, they should be instantly rebuked in the name of the Lord. Once the idea begins to prevail, and if you cannot counteract it and root it out, the revival will infallibly cease; for it is indispensable to the work that Christians should labor and pray in faith to promote it, and it is a contradiction to say that they can labor in faith for its continuance while they believe that it is about to cease.

2. A revival will cease when Christians consent that it should cease. Sometimes Christians see that the revival is in danger of ceasing, and that if something productive is not done, it will come to a stop. If this fact distresses them and drives them to prayer and to fresh efforts, the work will not cease. When Christians love the work of God and the salvation of souls so well that they are distressed at the mere thought of a decline, it will drive them to an agony of prayer and effort.

If it does not drive them to agony and effort to prevent its ceasing, if they see the danger and do not try to prevent it or to renew the work, they agree that it should stop. There are at this time many people all over the country who see revivals declining, and realize that they are in great danger of ceasing altogether, yet they do not show much distress, and seem to care but little about it. Entire churches see their condition, and see what is coming unless there can be a waking up, yet they are at ease and do not groan and agonize in prayer that God would revive His work. Some are even predicting that there is now going to be a great reaction, and that a great dearth will come over the church as there was after Whitefield's and Edwards' day. Yet they are not startled at their own forebodings. They are calm about it and turn directly away to other things. They consent to it. It seems as if they were the devil's trumpeters, sent out to scatter dismay throughout the ranks of God's elect.

3. A revival will cease whenever Christians become mechanical in their attempts to promote it. When their faith is strong, their hearts are warm and tender, their prayers are full of holy emotion, and their words are full of power, then the work goes on. But when their prayers begin to be cold and without emotion, when their deep-toned feeling is gone, and when they begin to labor mechanically and to use words without feeling, then the revival will cease.

4. The revival will cease whenever Christians get the idea that the work will go on without their aid. Christians are coworkers with God in promoting a revival, and the work can be carried on just as far as the church will carry it on, and no farther. For eighteen hundred years, God has been trying to get the church into the work. He has been calling and urging, commanding, entreating, pressing, and encouraging to get them to take hold. He has stood all this time ready to make bare His arm to carry on the work with them (Isaiah 52:10).

But the Christians have been unwilling to do their part. They seem determined to leave it to God alone to convert the world, and say, "If He wants the world converted, let Him do it." They should know that this is impossible. As far as we know, neither God nor man can convert the world without the cooperation of the church. Sinners cannot be converted without their own involvement, for conversion consists in their voluntary turning to God. No more can sinners be converted without the appropriate moral influences to turn them – that is, without truth and the reality of things brought full before their minds either by direct revelation or by men. God cannot convert the world by physical omnipotence, but He is dependent on the spiritual influence of the church.

5. The work will cease when the church prefers to attend to its own concerns rather than God's business. I do not say that people have any business that is properly their own, but they think so, and in fact prefer what they consider as their own rather than to work for God. They begin to think that they cannot afford sufficient time from their worldly employments to carry on a revival. They pretend that they are forced to give up attending to Christianity and to let their hearts go out again after the world. And the work must cease, of course.

6. When Christians get proud of their great revival, it will cease. I am referring to those Christians who have before been instrumental in promoting it. It is almost always the case in a revival that a part of the church is too proud or too worldly to take any part in the work. They are determined to stand aside and wait and see what it will come to and how it will come out. The pride of this part of the church cannot stop the revival, for the revival never rested on them. It began without them, and it can go on without them. They may fold their arms and do nothing except look on and find fault, and still the work may go on.

But when that part of the church that works begins to think what a great revival they have had, how they have labored and prayed, how bold and how zealous they have been, and how much good they have done, then the work will be likely to decline. Perhaps it has been published in the newspapers what a revival there has been in the church and how engaged the members have been, and they think how high they must stand in the esteem of other churches all over the land because they have had such a great revival. So they get puffed up and vain. Then they can no longer enjoy the presence of God, the Spirit withdraws from them, and the revival ceases.

7. The revival will stop when the church gets exhausted by labor. Multitudes of Christians commit a great mistake here during times of revival. They are so thoughtless and have so little judgment that they will break up all their habits of living, neglect to eat and sleep at the proper hours, and let the excitement run away with them so that they overwork their bodies. They are so careless that they soon become exhausted, and it is impossible for them to continue in the work. Revivals often cease and decline follows from negligence and carelessness in this respect on the part of those engaged in carrying them on.

8. A revival will cease when the church begins to speculate about abstract doctrines that have nothing to do with practice. If the church turns away its attention from the things of salvation, and begins studying or disputing about abstract points, the revival will cease, of course.

9. A revival will cease when Christians begin to convert people to their own denomination. When the Baptists are so opposed to the Presbyterians, or the Presbyterians to the Baptists, or both against the Methodists, or Episcopalians against the rest, that they begin to make efforts to get the converts to join their church, you soon see the last of the revival. Perhaps a revival will go on for a time, and all sectarian difficulties are banished until somebody circulates a book, privately, to gain converts to their own church.

Perhaps some overzealous deacon, or some mischief-making woman, or some denominational minister cannot keep still any longer, and begins to work the work of the devil by attempting to gain converts, and so stirs up bitterness, raises a selfish strife, grieves away the Spirit, and drives Christians all into divisions and parties. No more revival there.

10. A revival will cease when Christians refuse to render to the Lord according to the benefits received (Psalm 116:12). This is a fruitful source of spiritual decline. God has opened the windows of heaven to a church and poured out a blessing upon them, and then He reasonably expects them to bring in the tithes into His storehouse and devise and execute generous things for Zion (Malachi 3:10). Sadly, they have refused. They have not laid themselves out accordingly to promote the cause of Christ,

and so the Spirit has been grieved and the blessing withdrawn, and in some instances a great reaction has taken place because the church would not be generous when God has been so bountiful. I have known churches that were evidently cursed with barrenness for such a course. They had a glorious revival, and afterward perhaps their meetinghouse needed repairing, or something else was needed that would cost a little money, and they refused to do it, and so for their miserly spirit God gave them up.

11. When the church in any way grieves the Holy Spirit, a revival ceases.

a) When they do not feel their dependence on the Spirit. Whenever Christians get strong in their own strength, God curses their blessings. In many instances, Christians sin against their own mercies because they get lifted up with their success, take the credit to themselves, and do not give to God all the glory. As He says, *If ye will not hear, and if ye will not lay it to heart, to give glory unto my name, saith the* LORD *of hosts, I will even send a curse upon you, and I will curse your blessings: yea, I have cursed them already, because ye do not lay it to heart* (Malachi 2:2).

There has been a great deal of this in this country, undoubtedly. I have seen many things that looked like it, in the newspapers, where there seemed to be a tendency in men to take credit for success in promoting revivals. There is certainly a great temptation to this, and it requires the utmost watchfulness on the part of ministers and churches to guard against it, and not grieve the Spirit away by vaingunrying in men.

b) The Spirit may be grieved by a spirit of boasting about the revival. Sometimes, as soon as a revival begins, you will see it proclaimed in the newspapers. Most commonly, this will kill the revival. There was a case in a neighboring state where a revival began, and instantly there came out a letter from the pastor telling that he had a revival. I saw the letter and said to myself, "That is the last we will hear of this revival." And so it was. In a few days, the work totally ceased. And such things are not uncommon. I could mention cases and places where people have published such things as to puff up the church and make them so proud that little or nothing more could be done for the revival.

Some people, under pretense of publishing things to the praise and glory of God, have published things that savored so strongly of a disposition to exalt themselves and have made their own efforts stand out so obviously that seemed to be evidently calculated to make an unhappy impression.

At the protracted meeting held in this church a year ago last fall, there were five hundred hopefully converted, whose names and places of residence we knew. A considerable number of them joined this church. Many of them united with other churches. Nothing was said about this in the newspapers. I have been asked several times why we were so silent upon the subject. I could only reply that there was such a tendency to self-exaltation in the churches that I was afraid to publish anything on the subject. Perhaps I erred, but I have so often seen harm done by poorly timed publications that I thought it best to say nothing about it.

In the revival in this city four years ago, so much was said in the newspapers that appeared like self-exaltation that I was afraid to publish anything about it myself. I am not speaking against the practice itself, of publishing accounts of revivals, but the manner of doing it is of vast importance. If it is done so as to excite pride, it is always fatal to the revival.

c) The Spirit is also grieved by saying or publishing things that are calculated to undervalue the work of God. When a blessed work of God is spoken lightly of, not giving to God the glory due to His name, the Spirit is grieved. If anything is said about a revival, give only the plain and simple facts just as they are, and let them pass for what they are worth.

12. A revival may be expected to cease when Christians lose the spirit of brotherly love. Jesus Christ will not continue with people in a revival any longer than they continue in the exercise of brotherly love. When Christians are in the spirit of a revival, they feel this love, and then you will hear them call each other brother and sister, very affectionately. But when they begin to get cold, they lose this warmth and glow of affection for one another, and then this calling of brother and sister will seem silly and trivial and they will stop. In some churches they never call each other so, but where there is a revival, Christians naturally do it. I never saw a revival, and probably there never was one, in which they did not do it. But as soon as this begins to cease, the Spirit of God is grieved and departs from among them.

13. A revival will decline and cease unless Christians are frequently reconverted. By this I mean that Christians, in order to keep in the spirit of a revival, commonly need to be frequently convicted, humbled, broken down before God, and "reconverted." This is something that many do not understand – when we talk about a Christian's being reconverted. But the fact is that in a revival, the Christian's heart tends to get crusted over and lose its refined desire for divine things. His unction and habitualness in prayer decreases, and then he must be converted over again. It is impossible to keep him in such a state as not to do harm to the work unless he passes through such a process every few days.

I have never labored in revivals in company with anyone who would remain in the work and be fit to manage a revival continually who did not pass through this process of breaking down as often as once every two or three weeks. Revivals commonly decline because it is found impossible to make the church feel its guilt and its dependence so as to break down before God. It is important for ministers to understand this and learn how to break down the church, and break down themselves when they need it, or else Christians will soon become mechanical in their work and lose their fervor and their power of prevailing with God.

This was the process through which Peter passed when he had denied the Savior, and by which breaking down, the Lord prepared him for the great work on the day of Pentecost. I was surprised, a few years ago, to find that the phrase "breaking down" was a stumbling block to certain ministers and professing Christians. They laid themselves open to the rebuke administered to Nicodemus: *Art thou a master of Israel, and knowest not these things?* (John 3:10). I am confident that until some of them know what it is to be broken down, they will never do much more for the cause of revivals.

14. A revival cannot continue when Christians will not practice self-denial. When the church has enjoyed a revival and begins to grow fat upon it and run into self-indulgence, the revival will soon cease. Unless they sympathize with the Son of God, who gave up all to save sinners, unless they are willing to give up their luxuries and their ease and lay themselves out in the work, they do not need to expect the Spirit of God to be poured out upon them. This is undoubtedly one of the main causes

of personal spiritual decline. Let Christians in a revival beware when they first find an inclination creeping upon them to draw back from self-denial and to give in to one form of self-indulgence after another. It is the device of Satan to bait them off from the work of God, to make them dull and coarse and lazy and fearful and useless and worldly, and to drive away the Spirit and destroy the revival.

15. A revival will be stopped by controversies about new measures. Nothing is more certain to overthrow a revival than this. But as my last lecture was on the subject of new measures, I do not need to dwell longer on the subject now.

16. Revivals can be put down by the continued opposition of the Old School, combined with a bad spirit in the New School. If those who do nothing to promote revivals continue their opposition, and if those who are laboring to promote them allow themselves to get impatient and get into a bad spirit, the revival will cease. When the Old School writes their letters in the newspapers against revivals or revival men, and the New School writes letters back again against them in an angry, contentious, bitter spirit, and they get into a clattering controversy, revivals will cease. Let them keep about their work and not talk about the opposition, nor preach or print about it. If others choose to publish their insults and nonsense, let the Lord's servants keep to their work, and all the writings and slander will not stop the revival while those who are engaged in it mind their business and keep to their work. It is astonishing how far this holds true in fact.

In one place where there was a revival, certain ministers formed together against the pastor of the church, and a plan was set about to ruin him. They actually got him prosecuted before his presbytery. They had a trial that lasted six weeks, right in the midst of the revival, and the work still went on. The praying members of the church laid themselves out so in the work that it continued triumphantly throughout the whole scene. The pastor was called away to attend his trial, but there was another minister who labored among the people, and the members did not even go to the trial, generally, but kept praying and laboring for souls – and the revival rode out the storm. In many other places, opposition has risen up in the church, but a few humble souls have kept at their work, and a gracious God has stretched out His bare arm and made the revival go forward in spite of all opposition.

But whenever those who are actively engaged in promoting a revival get excited at the unreasonableness and tenacity of the opposition and feel as if they could not have it so, and they lose their patience and feel as if they must answer their complaints and refute their slanders, then they get down into the plains of Ono, and the work must cease (Nehemiah 6:2).

17. Any diversion of the public mind will hinder a revival. Anything that succeeds in diverting public attention will put a stop to a revival. In the case I have specified, where the minister was put on trial before his presbytery, the reason why it did not ruin the revival was that the praying members of the church would not allow themselves to be diverted. They did not even attend the trial, but kept praying and laboring for souls, and so public attention was kept to the subject, in spite of all the efforts of the devil.

But whenever he succeeds in engaging public attention on any other subject, no matter what the subject is, he will put an end to the revival. If an angel from heaven were to come down and preach, or walk about the streets, it might be the worst thing in the world for a revival, for it would turn sinners away from the topic of their own sins and would turn the church away from praying for souls in order to follow this glorious being and gaze upon him, and the revival would cease.

18. Resistance to the temperance reformation will put a stop to revivals in a church. The time has come that it can no longer be innocent in a church to stand aside from this glorious reformation. The time was when this could be done ignorantly. The time has been when ministers and Christians could enjoy revivals, notwithstanding if alcohol was used among them. But since light has been thrown upon the subject, and it has been found that the use is only harmful, no church member or minister can be innocent and stand neutral in the cause. They must speak out and take sides. If they do not take ground on one side, their influence is on the other. Show me a minister who has taken ground

against the temperance reformation who has had a revival. Show me one who now stands apart from it who has a revival. Show me one who now hesitates upon this point who does not come out and take a stand in favor of temperance who has a revival. It did not used to be so. But now that the subject has come up and has been discussed and is understood, no man can shut his eyes to the truth. The man's hands are red with blood who stands aside from the temperance cause. And can he have a revival?

19. Revivals are hindered when ministers and churches take wrong ground in regard to any question involving human rights. Take the subject of slavery, for instance. The time was when this subject was not before the public mind. John Newton continued in the slave trade after his conversion. His mind had been so perverted, and his conscience was so completely seared in regard to this most nefarious traffic, that the sinfulness of it never occurred to his thoughts until some time after he had become a child of God. If light had been poured upon his mind previously to his conversion, he never could have been converted without previously abandoning this sin. And after his conversion, when convinced of its iniquity, he could no longer enjoy the presence of God without abandoning the sin forever.

So undoubtedly, many slave dealers and slaveholders in our own country have been converted, notwithstanding their participation in this abomination, because the sinfulness of it was not apparent to their minds. So ministers and churches, to a great extent throughout the land, have held their peace and have given no testimony against this abominable abomination that exists in the church and in the nation.

But recently, the subject has come up for discussion, and the providence of God has brought it distinctly before the eyes of all people. Light is now shed upon this subject, as it has been upon the cause of temperance. Facts are exhibited, principles are established, and light is thrown in upon the minds of men – and this monster is dragged from his horrid den and exhibited before the church, and it is demanded of them, "Is this sin?" Their testimony must be given on this subject. They are God's witnesses. They are sworn to tell "the truth, the whole truth, and nothing but the truth." It is impossible that their testimony should not be given on one side or the other. Their silence can no longer be accounted for upon the principle of ignorance, and that they have never had their attention turned to the subject.

Consequently, the silence of Christians upon the subject is virtually saying that they do not consider slavery to be a sin. The truth is that it is a subject upon which they cannot be silent without guilt. The time has come, in the providence of God, when every southern breeze is loaded down with the cries of lamentation, mourning, and woe. Two million degraded people in our own land stretch their hands, all shackled and bleeding, and send forth to the church of God the agonizing cry for help. Will the church, in its efforts to reclaim and save the world, deafen its ears to this voice of agony and despair? God forbid. The church cannot turn away from this question. It is a question for the church and for the nation to decide, and God will push it to a decision.

It is in vain for the churches to resist it for fear of distraction, contention, and strife. It is in vain to consider it an act of piety to turn away the ear from hearing this cry of distress.

The church must testify, and testify "the truth, the whole truth, and nothing but the truth" on this subject, or she is perjured, and the Spirit of God departs from it. The church is under oath to testify, and ministers and churches who do not pronounce it sin bear false testimony for God. It is undoubtedly true that one of the reasons for the low state of Christianity at the present time is that many churches have taken the wrong side on the subject of slavery, have allowed prejudice to prevail over principle, and have feared to call this abomination by its true name.

20. Another thing that hinders revivals is neglecting the claims of missions. If Christians do not feel for the heathen, if they neglect the prayer meeting, confine their attention to their own church, do not read missionary news or use any other means to inform themselves on the subject of the claims of the world, reject the light that God is throwing before them, and will not do what God calls them to do in this cause, the Spirit of God will depart from them.

21. When a church rejects the calls of God upon them for educating young men for the ministry, they will hinder and destroy a revival. Look

at the Presbyterian church. Look at the two hundred thousand souls converted within ten years, and means enough to fill the world with ministers, yet the ministry is not increasing as fast as the population of our own country. Unless something more can be done to provide ministers, we will become heathen ourselves.

The churches do not urge upon young men the duty of going into the ministry. God pours His Spirit on the churches and converts hundreds of thousands of souls, and if the laborers do not then come forth into the harvest, what can be expected but that the curse of God will come upon the churches, His Spirit will be withdrawn, and revivals will cease? Upon this subject, no minister and no church should be silent or inactive.

22. Slandering revivals will often put them down. The great revival in the days of President Edwards suffered greatly by the conduct of the church in this respect. It is to be expected that the enemies of God will revile, misrepresent, and slander revivals. But when the church itself engages in this work, and many of her most influential members are aiding and abetting in maligning and misrepresenting a glorious work of God, it is reasonable that the Spirit would be grieved away. It cannot be denied that this has been done to a grievous and God-dishonoring extent.

It has been estimated that in one year, since this revival began, one hundred thousand souls were converted to God in the United States. This was perhaps the greatest number ever converted in one year since the world began. It could not be expected that in an excitement of this extent among human beings, there should be nothing to deplore. To expect perfection in such a work as this, of such extent, and carried on by human instrumentality, is entirely unreasonable and absurd. Evils doubtless did exist and have existed. They were to be expected, of course, and guarded against, as far as possible. I do not believe that the world's history can furnish one instance in which a revival, approaching to this in extent and influence, has been attended with so few evils and so little that is honestly to be deplored.

But how has this blessed work of God been treated? Even if we accept all the evils complained of to be real, which is far from being true, they would only be like spots upon the disc of the glorious sun – things hardly to be thought of in comparison to the infinite greatness and excellence of the work. Yet how has a great portion of the Presbyterian Church received and treated this blessed work of God? At the General Assembly, that solemn body of men who represent the Presbyterian Church in the midst of this great work, instead of appointing a day of thanksgiving, instead of praising and glorifying God for the greatness of His work, we hear from them the voice of rebuke.

From the reports that were given of the speeches made there, it appears that the house was filled with complaining. Instead of devising measures to forward the work, their attention seemed to be taken up with the comparatively trifling evils that were incidental to it. After much complaining, they eagerly appointed a committee and sent forth a "Pastoral Letter" to the churches, intended to excite suspicions, quench the zeal of God's people, and turn them from giving glory to God for the greatness of the blessing to finding fault and criticizing the evils. When I heard what was done at that General Assembly, when I read their speeches, when I saw their pastoral letter, my soul was sick. An unutterable feeling of distress came over my mind, and I felt that God would "visit" the Presbyterian Church for conduct like this. Ever since, the glory has been departing, and revivals have been becoming less and less frequent and less and less powerful.

I wish it could be known whether those ministers who poured out those complaints on the floor of the General Assembly, and who were instrumental in writing that pastoral letter, have since been blessed in promoting revivals of religion – whether the Spirit of God has been upon them, and whether their churches can witness that they have an unction from the Holy One.

23. Ecclesiastical difficulties are calculated to grieve away the Spirit and destroy revivals. It has always been the policy of the devil to turn away the attention of ministers from the work of the Lord to disputes and ecclesiastical disputes. President Edwards was forced to be taken up for a long time in disputes before ecclesiastical councils; and in our days, and in the midst of these great revivals of religion, these difficulties have been alarmingly and shamefully multiplied. Some of the most

efficient ministers in the church have been called away from their direct efforts to win souls to Christ in order to attend day after day, and in some instances week after week, to charges presented against them or their fellow laborers in the ministry, which could never be sustained.

Look at Philadelphia: what endless and disgraceful discord has distracted and grieved the church of God in that city, and through the length and breadth of the land. In the Presbyterian church in general, these ecclesiastical difficulties have produced evils enough to make creation weep. Brother Beman was shamefully and wickedly called away from promoting revivals in order to attend a trial before his own presbytery, upon charges which, if true, were most of them ridiculous, but which could never be sustained.

Since that time, a great portion of his time has, it would seem necessarily, been taken up with the adjustment of ecclesiastical difficulties. Brother Duffield of Carlisle, Brother Barnes of Philadelphia, and others of God's most successful ministers have been hindered a considerable part of their time for years by these difficulties. Oh, *tell it not in Gath* (2 Samuel 1:20)! When will those ministers and professing Christians who do little or nothing themselves let others alone and let them work for God?

24. Another thing by which revivals may be hindered is criticism on either side, and especially in those who have been engaged in carrying forward a revival. It is to be expected that the opposers of the work will watch for the faltering of its friends, and be sure to condemn them for all that is wrong, and not infrequently for that which is right in their conduct. It is especially to be expected that many critical and unchristian remarks will be made about those who are the most prominent instruments in promoting the work.

This criticism on the part of the opposers of the work, whether in or out of the church, will not, however, of itself put a stop to the revival. While its promoters remain humble and in a prayerful spirit, while they do not retaliate but possess their souls in patience, while they do not allow themselves to be diverted, to criticize, and to grieve away the spirit of prayer, the work will go forward. In the case referred to, where a minister was on trial for six weeks in the midst of a revival, the people there remained in the dust and prayed, not so much for their minister, for they had left him with God, but with strong crying and tears pleading with God for sinners. God heard and blessed them, and the work went on.

Criticism in those who are opposed to the work is but little to be dreaded, for they do not have the Spirit, nothing depends on them, and they can hinder the work only just as far as they themselves have influence personally. But the others have the power of the Holy Spirit, and the work depends on their keeping in a right disposition. If they get wrong and grieve away the Spirit, there is no help and the work must cease.

Whatever provocation, therefore, the promoters of this blessed work may have had, if it ceases, the responsibility is theirs. One of the most alarming facts in regard to this matter is that in many instances, those who have been engaged in carrying forward the work appear to have lost the Spirit. They are diverted. They begin to think that the opposition is no longer to be tolerated and that they must come out and reply in the newspapers to what they say. It should be known and universally understood that whenever the friends and promoters of this greatest of revivals allow themselves to be called aside to newspaper brawls to attempt to defend themselves and reply to those who write against them, the spirit of prayer will be entirely grieved away, and the work will cease.

Nothing is more detrimental to revivals of religion, and so it has always been found, than for the promoters of it to listen to the opposition and begin to reply. This was found to be true in the days of President Edwards, as you who are acquainted with his book on revivals are well aware.

III. Some Things That Should Be Done to Continue This Great and Glorious Revival of Religion That Has Been in Progress for the Last Ten Years

1. There should be great and deep repentings on the part of ministers. We, my brethren, must humble ourselves before God. It will not do for us to suppose that it is enough to call on the people to repent. We must repent. We must take the lead in repentance, and then call on the churches to follow.

They especially must repent who have taken the lead in producing the feelings of opposition and distrust in regard to revivals. Some ministers have confined their opposition against revivals and revival measures to their own congregations, and have created such suspicions among their own people as to prevent the work from spreading and prevailing among them. Such ministers would do well to consider the remarks of President Edwards on this subject:

> If ministers preach never so good doctrine, and are never
> so arduous and laborious in their work, yet, if at such a day
> as this, they show to their people that they are not well-
> affected to this work, but are very doubtful and suspicious
> of it, they will be very likely to do their people a great deal
> more harm than good; for the very fame of such a great and
> extraordinary work of God, if their people were allowed to
> believe it to be His work, and the example of other towns,
> together with what preaching they might hear occasion-
> ally, would be likely to have a much greater influence upon
> the minds of their people to awaken and encourage them
> in the Christian religion, than all their labors with them.
> Besides, their minister's opinion would not only produce in
> them a suspicion of the work they hear of abroad, whereby
> the mighty hand of God that appears in it loses its influ-
> ence upon their minds, but it will also tend to create a
> suspicion of everything of a similar nature that will appear
> among them as being something of the same ailment that
> has become such an epidemic in the land, and that is, in
> effect, to create a suspicion of all true and living religion
> and to get the people talking against it and discouraging it
> wherever it appears, and knocking it in the head as fast as
> it rises. And we who are ministers, by looking on this work
> from year to year with a displeased countenance, will effec-
> tually keep the sheep from their pasture instead of doing
> the part of shepherds to them by feeding them; and our
> people would be a great deal better off without any settled
> minister at all at such a day as this.

Others have been more public and aimed at exerting a wider influence. Some have written articles for the public newspapers. Some men in high standing in the church have circulated letters that were never printed. Others have had their letters printed and circulated. There seems to have been a system of letter writing around the country calculated to create distrust. In the days of President Edwards, substantially the same course was pursued, in view of which he says in his work on revivals:

> Great care should be taken that the press should be improved to no purpose contrary to the interest of this work. We read that when God fought against Sisera for the deliverance of His oppressed church, *they that handle the pen of the writer* came to the help of the Lord in that cause (Judges 5:14). Whatever sort of men in Israel they were who were intended, yet as the words were authored by a Spirit that had a perfect view of all events to the end of the world, and had a special eye in this song, to that great event of the deliverance of God's church in the latter days, of which this deliverance of Israel was a type, it is not unlikely that they have respect to authors – those who would fight against the kingdom of Satan with their pens.

> Those therefore who publish pamphlets to the disadvantage of this work, and tending either directly or indirectly to bring it under suspicion, and to discourage or hinder it, would do well to thoroughly consider whether this is not indeed the work of God, and whether, if it is, it is not likely that God will go forth as fire to consume all who stand in His way, and so burn up those pamphlets; and whether there is not danger that the fire that is kindled in them will scorch the authors.

All these people must repent. God will never forgive them, nor will they ever enjoy His blessing on their preaching or be honored to labor in revivals until they repent. President Edwards pressed this duty upon ministers in his day in the most powerful terms. There undoubtedly have been now, as there were then, faults on both sides, and there must be deep repentance and mutual confessions of faults on both sides. President Edwards wrote:

> There must be a great deal done at confessing of faults on both sides; for undoubtedly many and great are the faults that have been committed in the noise and confusions, and mixtures of light and darkness, that have been of late. There is hardly any duty more contrary to our corrupt dispositions, and mortifying to the pride of man, but it must be done.

> Repentance of faults is, in a peculiar manner, a proper duty when the kingdom of heaven is at hand, or when we especially expect or desire that it should come, as appears by John the Baptist's preaching. And if God does now loudly call upon us to repent, then He also calls upon us to make proper manifestations of our repentance. I am convinced that those who have openly opposed this work, or have from time to time spoken lightly of it, cannot be excused in the sight of God without openly confessing their fault therein, especially if they are ministers. If they have either directly or indirectly opposed the work in any way, or have so behaved in their public performances or private conversation as to have prejudiced the minds of their people against the work, if in the future they are convinced of the goodness and divinity of what they have opposed, they should by no means condone the matter and excuse themselves and pretend that they always thought so, and that it was only certain carelessness that they objected against, but they should openly declare their conviction and condemn themselves for what they have done; for it is Christ whom they have spoken against in speaking lightly of and prejudicing others against this work; yes, worse than that, it is the Holy Spirit. And although they have done it ignorantly and in unbelief, yet when they find out who it is whom they

have opposed, undoubtedly God will hold them obligated to publicly confess it.

And on the other side, if those who have been zealous to promote the work have in any of the previously mentioned instances openly gone much out of the way, and have done that which is contrary to Christian rules whereby they have openly hurt others, or greatly violated good order, and so done that which has harmed the Christian religion, they must publicly confess it and humble themselves, as they would gather out the stones, and prepare the way of God's people. They who have laid great stumbling blocks in others' way by their open transgression are bound to remove them by their open repentance.

There are ministers in our day, I say it not in unkindness but in faithfulness, and I wish that I had them all here before me while I say it, who seem to have been engaged much of their time for years in doing little else than acting and talking and writing in such a way as to create suspicion in regard to revivals. I cannot doubt that their churches would, as President Edwards says, be better with no minister at all, unless they will repent and regain God's blessing.

2. Those churches that have opposed revivals must humble themselves and repent. Churches that have stood distant or hindered the work must repent of their sin, or God will not go with them. Look at those churches now that have been throwing suspicion upon revivals. Do they experience revivals? Does the Holy Spirit descend upon them to enlarge them and build them up?

There is one church in this city where the session has been publishing in the newspapers what they call their "Act and Testimony," calculated to excite an unreasonable and groundless suspicion against many ministers who are laboring successfully to promote revivals. And what is the state of that church? Have they had a revival? It appears from the official report to the General Assembly that it has dwindled 27 percent in one year. And all such churches will continue to dwindle, in spite of everything else that can be done, unless they repent and have a revival. They may pretend to be quite pious and jealous for the honor of God, but God will not believe they are sincere. He will manifest His displeasure by not pouring out His Spirit.

If I had a voice loud enough, I would like to make every one of these churches and ministers that have slandered revivals hear me when I say that I believe they have helped to bring the cloud of death over the church, and that the curse of God is on them already, and will remain unless they repent. God has already sent leanness into their souls (Psalm 106:15), and many of them know it.

3. Those who have been engaged in promoting the work must also repent. Whatever they have done that was wrong must be repented of, or revivals will not return as in days past. Whenever a wrong spirit has been manifested, or they have gotten irritated and provoked at the opposition and have lost their temper or have mistaken Christian faithfulness for harsh words and a wrong spirit, they must repent. Those who are opposed could never stop a revival alone unless those who promote it get wrong. So we must repent if we have said things that were critical, proud, arrogant, or severe. Such a time as this is no time to stand justifying ourselves. Our first call is to repent. Let each one repent of his own sins, and not argue and quarrel about who is most to blame.

4. The church must take right ground in regard to politics. Do not suppose that I am going to preach a political sermon, or that I want to have you join or start a Christian party in politics. No, I do not believe in that. However, the time has come for Christians to vote for honest men and take consistent ground in politics, or the Lord will curse them. They must be honest men themselves, and instead of voting for a person because he belongs to their party, they must find out whether he is honest and upright and fit to be trusted. They must let the world see that the church will uphold no man in office who is known to be a lawbreaker, an adulterer, a gambler, a drunkard, does not love the Lord, or keep the Lord's Day holy.

Such is the spread of intelligence and the ease of communication in our country that every person can know for whom he gives his vote. If he will give his vote only for honest men, the country will be compelled to have upright rulers. All parties will be compelled to put up honest people as candidates. Christians have been exceedingly guilty in this matter, but the time has come when they must act differently, or God will curse the nation and withdraw His Spirit.

As on the subject of slavery and temperance, so on this subject – the church must act right or the country will be ruined. God cannot sustain this free and blessed country, which we love and pray for, unless the church will take right ground. Politics are a part of religion in such a country as this, and Christians must do their duty to the country as a part of their duty to God. It seems sometimes as if the foundations of the nation were becoming rotten, and Christians seem to act as if they thought God did not see what they do in politics. But I tell you, He does see it, and He will bless or curse this nation according to the course they take.

5. The churches must take right ground on the subject of slavery. And here the question arises, what is right ground? I will first state some things that should be avoided.

a) First of all, a bad spirit should be avoided. Nothing is more calculated to harm religion, and to hurt the slaves themselves, than for Christians to get into an angry discussion on the subject. It is a subject upon which there needs to be no angry argument among Christians. Slaveholding professing Christians, like rum-selling professing Christians, may endeavor to justify themselves, and may be angry with those who trouble their consciences and call upon them to give up their sins. Those proud professing Christians who think a person is to blame, or think it is a shame to have black skin, may allow their prejudices so far to prevail as to shut their ears and be ready to quarrel with those who urge the subject upon them. But I repeat that the subject of slavery is a subject upon which Christians, praying people, need not and must not differ.

b) Another thing to be avoided is an attempt to take neutral ground on this subject. Christians can no more take neutral ground on this subject, since it has come up for discussion, than they can take neutral ground on the subject of the sanctification of the Lord's Day. It is a great national sin. It is a sin of the church. The churches by their silence, and by permitting slaveholders to belong to their communion, have been consenting to it. All denominations have been more or less guilty, although the Quakers have of recent years washed their hands of it.

It is in vain for the churches to pretend it is merely a political sin. I repeat that it is the sin of the church, to which all denominations have consented. They have virtually declared that it is lawful. The very fact of quietly permitting slaveholders to remain in good standing in their churches is the strongest and most public expression of their views that it is not sin. For the church, therefore, to pretend to take neutral ground on the subject, is perfectly absurd. The fact is that the church is not on neutral ground at all. While the church tolerates slaveholders in her communion, it justifies the practice. An enemy of God might just as well pretend that he was neither saint nor sinner, that he was going to take neutral ground and pray "good Lord and good devil" because he did not know which side would be the most popular.

c) Great care should be taken to avoid a denunciatory spirit on both sides. It is a subject on which there has been, and probably will be for some time to come, a difference of opinion among Christians as to the best method of disposing of the question, and it should be treated with much patience on both sides. A denunciatory spirit, impeaching each other's motives, is unchristian, calculated to grieve the Spirit of God and to put down revivals, and is harmful both to the church and to the slaves themselves.

In the second place, I will mention several things that in my judgment the church is necessarily called upon to do on this subject:

a) Christians of all denominations should lay aside prejudice and inform themselves on this subject without any delay. Vast multitudes of professing Christians have indulged prejudice to such a degree as to be unwilling to read and hear and come to a right understanding of the subject. However, Christians cannot pray in this state of mind. I defy anyone to possess the spirit of prayer while he is too prejudiced to examine this or any other question of duty.

If the light did not shine, Christians might remain in the dark upon this point and still possess the spirit of prayer. But if they refuse to come to the light, they cannot pray. Now I call upon all of you who are here present, and who have not examined this subject because you were reluctant to examine it, to say whether or not you have the spirit of prayer. Where ministers, individual Christians, or entire churches resist truth upon this point now, when it is so extensively spread before the public mind, I do not believe they will or can enjoy a revival of the Christian religion.

b) Writings that contain sensible and wise discussions on this subject, and such developments of facts as are before the public, should be quietly and extensively circulated and should be carefully and prayerfully examined by the whole church. I do not mean by this that the attention of the church should be so absorbed by this as to neglect the main question of saving souls in the midst of them.

I do not mean that such premature movements on this subject should be made as to stun the Christian community and involve them in a brawl, but that praying men should act wisely, and that as soon as sufficient information can be dispersed through the community, the churches should meekly but firmly take decided ground on the subject and express before the whole nation and the world their abhorrence of this sin.

The anti-masonic excitement that prevailed a few years ago made such desolations in the churches, and produced for a time so much alienation of feeling and ill will among ministers and people, and the first introduction of this subject has been attended with such commotions, that many good ministers who are themselves entirely opposed to slavery dread to introduce the subject among their people through fear that their churches do not have religion enough to take it up and consider it calmly and decide upon it in the spirit of the gospel.

I know there is danger of this, but still the subject must be presented to the churches. If introduced with discretion and with much prayer, there are very few churches that have enjoyed revivals, and that are at the present time anywhere near a revival spirit, that may not be brought to receive the truth on this subject. Let there be no mistake here. William Morgan's exposé of Freemasonry was published in 1826. The consequent excitement and discussion continued until 1830. In the meantime, the churches had very generally borne their testimony against Freemasonry and resolved that they could not fellowship with practicing masons. As a consequence, the Masonic lodges generally disbanded and gave up their charters. There was a general stampede of professed Christians from the lodges. This prepared the way, and in 1830, the greatest revival the world had then ever seen commenced in the center of the anti-masonic region, and spread over the whole field where the church action had been taken until its converts numbered one hundred thousand souls.

Perhaps no church in this country has had a more severe trial upon this subject than this. They were a church of young and for the most part inexperienced Christians. Many circumstances conspired, in my absence, to produce confusion and wrong feeling among them. But so far as I am now acquainted with the state of feeling in this church, I know of no ill will among them on this subject. The Lord has blessed us, the Spirit has been distilled upon us, and considerable numbers have been added to our communion every month since my return.

There are undoubtedly in this church those who feel on this subject in very different degrees, yet I can honestly say that I am not aware of the least difference in sentiment among them. We have from the beginning, previous to my going on my foreign tour, taken the same ground on the subject of slavery that we have on temperance. We have excluded slaveholders and all concerned in the traffic from our communion. Some people in this church have criticized this course as unwarrantable and uncharitable, and I would by no means make my own judgment, or the example of this church, a rule for the government of other ministers and churches. Still, I conscientiously believe that the time is not far distant when the churches will be united in this expression of abhorrence against this sin. If I do not term slavery by some soft and Christian name, if I call it sin, both consistency and conscience bring us to the inevitable conclusion that while the sin is persevered in, its perpetrators cannot be fit subjects for Christian communion and fellowship.

To this it is objected that there are many ministers in the Presbyterian church who are slaveholders. It is said to be very inconsistent that we should refuse to allow a slaveholder to come to our communion, yet belong to the same church with them, sit with them in ecclesiastical bodies, and acknowledge them as ministers. To this I answer that I do not have the power to deal with those ministers, and certainly I am not to withdraw from the church because some of its ministers or members are slaveholders. My duty is to belong to the church, even if the devil would belong to it. Where I have authority, I exclude slaveholders from the communion, and I always will as long as I live. But where I have no authority, if the table of Christ is spread, I will sit down to it in obedience to His commandment, no matter who else may sit down or stay away.

I do not mean, by any means, to denounce all those slaveholding ministers and professing Christians as hypocrites, and to say that they are not Christians, but I will say that while they continue in that attitude, the cause of Christ and of humanity demands that they should not be recognized as such unless we intend to be partakers of other people's sins. It is no more inconsistent to exclude slaveholders because they belong to the Presbyterian church than it is to exclude people who drink or sell alcohol, for there are a great many rum-sellers who belong to the Presbyterian church.

I believe the time has come, and although I am no prophet, I believe it will be found to have come, that the revival in the United States will continue and prevail no farther and faster than the church takes the right ground upon this subject. The church is God's witness. The fact is that slavery is, preeminently, the sin of the church. It is the very fact that ministers and professing Christians of different denominations hold slaves that sanctifies the whole abomination in the eyes of ungodly people.

Who does not know that on the subject of temperance, every drunkard in the land will hide behind some rum-selling deacon or wine-drinking minister? It is the most common objection and refuge of the intemperate, and of moderate drinkers, that it is practiced by professing Christians. It is this that creates the critical necessity of excluding rum drinkers and traffickers in alcohol from the communion. Let the churches of all denominations speak out on the subject of temperance. Let them close their doors against all who have anything to do with the death-dealing abomination, and the cause of temperance will be triumphant. A few years would annihilate the traffic. It is the same with slavery.

It is the church that mainly supports this sin. Its united testimony upon this subject would settle the question. Let Christians of all denominations meekly but firmly come forth and pronounce their verdict. Let them clear their communions and wash their hands of this thing. Let them give forth and write on the head and front of this great abomination, "Sin!" and in three years a public sentiment would be formed that would carry all before it, and there would not be a shackled slave, nor a raging, cruel slave driver in this land.

Still, it may be said that in many churches, this subject cannot be introduced without creating confusion and ill will. This may be. It has been so upon the subject of temperance, and upon the subject of revivals too. In some churches, neither temperance nor revivals can be introduced without producing dissension. Sunday schools and missionary activities and everything of the kind have been opposed and have produced dissensions in many churches. But is this a sufficient reason for excluding these subjects? And where churches have excluded these subjects for fear of contention, have they been blessed with revivals? Everybody knows that they have not.

However, where churches have taken firm ground on these subjects, although individuals and sometimes numbers have opposed, still they have been blessed with revivals. Where any of these subjects are carefully and prayerfully introduced; where they are brought forward with a right spirit, and the true relative importance is attached to each one of them – if in such cases there are those who will make disturbance and resist, let the blame fall where it should. There are some individuals who are themselves inclined to quarrel about this subject, who are always ready to exclaim, "Do not introduce these things into the church, for they will create opposition." And if the minister and praying people feel it is their duty to bring the matter forward, they will themselves create a disturbance, and then say, "There, I told you so; now see what introducing this subject has done; it will tear the church all to pieces." While they are themselves doing all they can to create division, they are accusing the subject of causing the division, and not themselves. There are some such people in many of our churches. And neither Sunday schools, nor missions, nor revivals, nor anti-slavery movements, nor anything else that honors God or benefits the souls of men will be promoted in the churches without these careful souls being offended by it.

These things, however, have been introduced and carried, one by one, in some churches with more, and others with less, opposition – and perhaps in some churches with no opposition at all. And as true as God is the God of the church, as certain as it is that the world must be converted, this subject must be considered and pronounced sin by the church. It would be infinitely better if there were no church in the world than that it would attempt to remain neutral or give a false testimony on a subject of such importance as slavery, especially since the subject has come up, and it is impossible from the nature of the case that the church's testimony should not be in the scale on the one side or the other.

Do you ask, "What will be done? Will we make it the all-absorbing topic of conversation and divert attention from the all-important subject of the salvation of souls in the midst of us?" I answer, No. Let a church express its opinion upon the subject and be at peace. As far as I know, we are entirely at peace upon this subject. We have expressed our opinion. We have closed our communion against slaveholders and are attending to other things. I am not aware of the least unhealthy excitement among us on this subject. Where it has become an absorbing topic of conversation in a place, in most instances I believe it has been due to the stubborn and unreasonable opposition of a few individuals against even granting the subject a hearing.

6. If the church desires to promote revivals, it must sanctify the Lord's Day. There is a vast deal of Sabbath breaking in the land. Merchants break it, travelers break it, and the government breaks it. A few years ago, an attempt was made in the western part of this state to establish and sustain a Sabbath-keeping line of boats and stages. But it was found that the church would not sustain the enterprise. Many professing Christians would not travel in these stages and would not have their goods forwarded in canal boats that would be detained from traveling on the Lord's Day. At one time, Christians were much engaged in petitioning Congress to suspend the Sunday mail, and now they seem to be ashamed of it.

But one thing is most certain – that unless something is done, and done soon and constructively to promote the sanctification of the Lord's Day by the church, the Lord's Day will go by the board, and we will not only have our mail running on Sundays, and post offices open, but eventually our courts of justice and halls of legislation will be kept open on Sundays. And what can the church do, what will this nation do, without any Sabbath?

7. The church must take right ground on the subject of temperance and moral reform, and all the subjects of practical morality that come up for decision from time to time. There are those in the churches who are standing distant from the subject of moral reform, and who are afraid to have anything said in the pulpit against immorality, profanity, indecency, and so on. On this subject the church does not need to expect to be permitted to take neutral ground. In the providence of God, it is up for discussion. The evils have been displayed, and the call has been made for reform. And what is to reform mankind but the truth? And who will present the truth if not the church and the ministry? Away with the idea that Christians can remain neutral and keep still, yet enjoy the approval and blessing of God.

In all such cases, the minister who holds his peace is counted among those on the other side. Everybody knows that it is so in a revival. It is not necessary for a person to strongly oppose the work. If he only keeps still and takes neutral ground, the enemies of the revival will all consider him as on their side.

It is the same with the subject of temperance. It is not necessary for a person to speak out boldly at the cold-water society in order to be on the best terms with drunkards and moderate drinkers. Only let him plead for the moderate use of wine, only let him continue to drink it as a luxury, and all the drunkards consider him to be on their side. If he refuses to give his influence to the temperance cause, he is claimed, of course, by the other side as a friend.

On all these subjects, when they come up, the churches and ministers must take the right ground, and take it openly, stand by it, and carry it through if they expect to experience the blessing of God in revivals. They must cast out from their communions such members, as in contempt of the light that is shed upon them, who continue to drink or sell alcoholic beverages.

8. There must be more done for all the great objects of Christian benevolence. There must be much greater efforts for the cause of missions, education,

and the Bible, and all the other branches of religious enterprise, or the church will displease God. Look at it. Think of the mercies we have received, of the wealth, numbers, and prosperity of the church. Have we rendered unto God according to the benefits we have received (Psalm 116:12) so as to show that the church is generous and willing to give their money and to work for God? No. Far from it. Have we multiplied our means and enlarged our plans in proportion as the church has increased?

Is God satisfied with what has been done, or has He reason to be? With such a revival as has been enjoyed by the churches of America for the last ten years, we should have done ten times as much as we have for missions, Bibles, education, tracts, free churches, and in all the ways designed to promote true religion and save souls. If the churches do not wake up on this subject and lay themselves out on a larger scale, they may expect the revival in the United States to cease.

9. If Christians in the United States expect revivals to spread and prevail until the world is converted, they must stop writing letters and publishing pieces intended to excite suspicion and jealousy in regard to revivals, and must take hold of the work themselves. If the whole church as a body had gone to work ten years ago, and continued it as a few individuals, whom I could name, have done, there would not now have been an unrepentant sinner in the land. The millennium would have fully come in the United States before this day.

Instead of standing still and writing letters from Berkshire, let ministers who think we are going wrong simply buckle on the harness and go forward and show us a more excellent way. Let them teach us by their example how to do better. I do not deny that we have made mistakes and committed errors. I do not deny that there are many things that are wrong done in revivals by some people. But is that the way to correct them, brethren? Paul did not do so. He corrected his brethren by telling them kindly that he would show them *a more excellent way* (1 Corinthians 12:31). Let our brethren take hold and go forward. Let us hear the cry from all their pulpits: "To the work!" Let them lead on where the Lord will go with them and make bare His arm (Isaiah 52:10), and I, for one, will follow. Only let them go on, and let us have the United States converted to God, and let all minor questions cease.

If not, and if revivals do cease in this land, the ministers and churches will be guilty of all the blood of all the souls that will go to hell in consequence of it. There is no need for the work to cease. If the church will do all its duty, the millennium may come in this country in three years. But if this writing letters is to be kept up, filling the country with suspicions and jealousies, if it is to be always so that two-thirds of the church will hang back and do nothing but find fault in time of revival, the curse of God will be on this nation, and that before long.

Remarks

1. It is time for there to be great searchings of heart among Christians and ministers. Brethren, this is no time to resist the truth or to criticize and find fault because the truth is spoken out plainly. It is no time to berate or to agitate, but we must search our own hearts and humble ourselves before God.

2. We must repent and forsake our sins, and amend our ways and our actions, or the revival will cease. Our ecclesiastical difficulties must cease, and all minor differences must be laid aside and given up, to unite in promoting the great interests of the Christian religion. If not, revivals will cease from among us and the blood of lost millions will be found on our hands.

If the church would do all its duty, it would soon complete the triumph of Christianity in the world. But if this Act and Testimony warfare is to be kept up, and this system of espionage, and insinuation and denunciation, not only will revivals cease, but the blood of millions who will go to hell before the church will get over the shock will be found in the garments of the men who have got up and carried on this dreadful contention.

3. Those who have circulated slanderous reports in regard to revivals must repent. A great deal has been said about heresy, and about some men's denying the Spirit's influence, which is completely groundless and has been made up out of nothing. Those who have made up the reports, and those who have circulated them against their brethren, must repent and pray to God that they may receive His forgiveness.

4. We see the constant tendency there is in Christians to spiritual decline and backsliding. This is true in all converts of all revivals. Look at the revival in President Edwards' day. The work went on until thirty thousand souls had been converted, and by this time so many ministers and Christians got in such a state by writing books and pamphlets on one side and the other that they carried all away and the revival ceased. Those who had opposed the work grew obstinate and aggressive, and those who promoted it lost their meekness and became ill-tempered, and were then driven into the very evils that had been falsely charged upon them.

And now what will we do? This great and glorious work of God seems to be indicating a decline. The revival is not dead – blessed be God for that – it is not dead! No, we hear from all parts of the land that Christians are reading on the subject and inquiring about the revival. In some places there are now powerful revivals. And what will we do to lift up the standard, to move this entire nation and turn all this great people to the Lord? We must do right. We must all have a better spirit. We must get down in the dust, we must act unitedly, and we must take hold of this great work with all our hearts; and then God will bless us and the work will go on.

What is the condition of this nation? Undoubtedly, God is holding the rod of war over the heads of this nation. He is waiting before He lets loose His judgments to see whether the church will do right. The nation is under His displeasure because the church has conducted itself in such a manner with respect to revivals. And now suppose war would come; where would our revivals be? How quickly war would swallow up the revival spirit! The spirit of war is anything but the spirit of revivals. Who will attend to the claims of Christianity when the public mind is engrossed by the all-absorbing topic of war?

See now how this nation is, all at once, brought upon the brink of war. God brandishes His blazing sword over our heads. Will the church repent? It is the church that God primarily has in view. How will we avoid the curse of war? Only by a reformation in the church. It is in vain to look to politicians to avert war. Perhaps they would generally be in favor of war. Very likely the things they would do to avert it would run us right into it. If the church will not feel, will not wake up, will not act, where will we look for help? If the church absolutely will not move, will not tremble in view of the just judgments of God hanging over our heads, we are certainly close to being cursed as a nation.

5. Whatever is done must be done quickly. If we do not go forward, we must go back. Things cannot remain as they are. If the church does not come up, if we do not have a more powerful revival than we have had, very soon we will have none at all. We have had such a great revival that now small revivals do not interest the public mind. You must act as individuals. Do your own duty. You have a responsibility. Repent quickly. Do not wait until another year. Who but God knows what will be the state of these churches if things go on another year without a great and general revival of religion?

6. It is common, when things get all wrong in the church, for each individual to find fault with the church and with his brethren, and overlook his own share of the blame. Do not let anyone spend his time in finding fault with that abstract thing – "the church." But as individual members of the church of Christ, let each one act, and act right, and get down in the dust, and never speak proudly or critically. Go forward. Who would leave such a work, start writing letters, go down into the plain of Ono and see if all these petty disputes can be adjusted, and let the work cease (Nehemiah 6)? Let us mind our work and let the Lord take care of the rest. Do our duty, and leave the matter to God.

*Since these lectures were delivered, great progress has been made in all benevolent enterprises in this country. Time has settled the question of the purity and inestimable value of those revivals, against which so much mistaken opposition existed in the Presbyterian church. It is now known that the great and disastrous reaction predicted by opposers has not been witnessed. It must now be admitted that the converts of those revivals have composed the strength of the churches and that their Christian influence has been felt throughout the land.

This was in 1831. There have been more extensive revivals since. In 1857-58 it was estimated that fifty thousand conversions per week occurred for six or eight weeks in succession in the northern part of the United States.

No revivals have ever existed in which the power and purity have been more thoroughly established by time and experience than that great and blessed work of God against which such a storm of opposition was raised. The opposition was evidently a great mistake. Let it not be said that the opposition was demanded by the great evils attending that work, and that those wrongs and errors were stopped and corrected by the opposition.

The fact is that the supposed errors and wrongs that were made the justification of the opposition never existed to any such extent as to justify alarm or opposition. I have written a narrative of those revivals in which I have considered the question more fully. The churches did take hold of temperance and other branches of reform to such an extent as to avoid those evils against which they were warned. Upon the question of slavery, the church was too late in her testimony to avoid the war, but the slaveholders were much alarmed and exasperated by the constantly growing opposition to their institution throughout all that region of the north where revival influences had been felt. They took up arms to defend and perpetuate the abomination, and by so doing abolished it.

Lecture 16

The Necessity and Effect of Union

Again I say unto you, That if two of you shall agree on earth as touching anything that they shall ask, it shall be done for them of my Father which is in heaven.
—Matthew 18:19

Some weeks ago, I used this text in preaching on the subject of prayer meetings. At present I intend to enter more into the spirit and meaning of the text. The evident design of our Lord in this text was to teach the importance and influence of unity in prayer and effort to promote the Christian religion. He states the strongest possible case by taking the number two, as the least number between whom there can be an agreement, and says that where two of you are agreed on earth, *as touching anything that they shall ask, it shall be done for them of my Father which is in heaven.* It is the fact of their agreement that He emphasizes, and mentioning the number two, appears to have been intended simply to provide encouragement to the smallest number between whom there can be an agreement. But what are we to understand by *agree on earth as touching* the things we shall ask? I will answer this question under the two following headings:

I.   We are to be "agreed" in prayer.

II.   We are to agree in everything that is essential to obtaining the blessing that we seek.

I. We Are to Be Agreed in Prayer

This is specifically taught in the text.

1. We should agree in our desires for the object. It is necessary to have desires for the object, and to be agreed in those desires. Very often individuals pray in words for the same thing, when they are by no means agreed in desiring that thing. Perhaps some of them in their hearts desire the very opposite. People are called on to pray for something, and they all pray for it in words, but God knows that they often do not desire it, and perhaps He sees that the hearts of some may be resisting the prayer the entire time.

2. We must agree in the motive from which we desire the object. It is not enough that our desires for an object should be the same, but the reason why must be the same. An individual may desire a revival for the glory of God and the salvation of sinners. Another member of the church may also desire a revival, but from very different motives. Some might desire a revival in order to have the congregation built up and strengthened so as to make it easier for them to pay their expenses in supporting the gospel. Another person might desire a revival for the sake of having the church increased so as to be more numerous and more respectable. Others might desire a revival because they have been opposed or have been spoken against, and they want to have their enemies know that no matter what they may think or say, God blesses them. Sometimes people desire a revival from mere natural affection, so as to have their friends converted and saved. If they intend to be so united in prayer as to obtain a blessing, they must not only desire the blessing and be agreed in desiring it, but they must also agree in desiring it for the same reasons.

3. We must be agreed in desiring it for good reasons. These desires must not only be united, and from the same motives, but they must be from good motives. The supreme motive must be to honor and glorify God. People may even desire a revival, agree in desiring it, and agree in the motives, yet if these motives are not good, God will not grant their

desires. Thus, parents may be agreed in prayer for the conversion of their children, and may have the same feelings and the same motives, yet if they have no higher motives than because they are their children, their prayers will not be granted. They are agreed in the reason, but it is not the right reason.

In the same way, any number of people might be agreed in their desires and motives, but if their motives are selfish, their being agreed in them will only make them more offensive to God. *How is it that ye have agreed together to tempt the Spirit of the Lord?* (Acts 5:9). I have seen a great deal of this, where churches have been engaged in prayer for a specific purpose, and their motives were evidently selfish. Sometimes they are engaged in praying for a revival, and you would think by their earnestness and unity that they would certainly move God to grant the blessing – until you find out the reason.

And what is the reason? They see that *their* congregation is about to be broken up unless something can be done. Or they see some other denomination gaining ground, and there is no way to counteract them except by having a revival in *their* church. All their praying is only an attempt to get the Almighty in to help them out of their difficulty, and is purely selfish and offensive to God.

A woman in Philadelphia was invited to attend a female prayer meeting at a certain place. She asked what they met there for and what they were going to pray for. She was answered that they were going to pray for the outpouring of the Spirit upon the city. "Well," she said, "I will not go. If they were going to pray for our congregation, I would go; but I am not going there to pray for other churches!" Oh, what a selfish spirit!

I have had many letters and requests for me to visit such and such places, and attempt to promote a revival, and many reasons have been urged why I should go; but when I came to weigh their reasons, I have sometimes found every one of them selfish – and God would look upon every reason with abhorrence.

In prayer meetings, how often do we hear people offer such reasons why they desire such and such blessings that are not right in the sight of God? Such reasons, if they are the true ones, and if Christians are actually motivated by those reasons, would render their prayers not acceptable to God because their motive was not right.

There are a great many things often said in favor of the cause of missions that are of this character of appealing to wrong motives. How often we are told about six hundred million heathens who are in danger of going to hell, yet how little is said of the sin of six hundred million heathens busied and banded together as rebels against God, or of the dishonor and contempt poured upon God our Maker by such a world of outlaws.

I know that God refers to those motives that appeal to our mere natural sympathies and compassion, and uses them, but always in subordination to His glory. If these lower motives are placed foremost, it must always produce a defective piety and zeal, and a great deal that is false. Until the church will look at the dishonor done to God, little will be done. It is this that must be made to stand out before the world, it is this that must be deeply felt by the church, and it is this that must be fully exhibited to sinners before the world can ever be converted.

Parents never agree in praying for the conversion of their children in such a way as to have their prayers answered until they feel that their children are rebels. Parents often pray very earnestly for their children because they want God to save them, and they almost think harshly of God if He does not save their children. But if they want their prayers to prevail, they must come to take God's part against their children, even though for their perverseness and incorrigible wickedness He would be obliged to send them to hell.

I knew a woman who was very concerned for the salvation of her son, and she used to pray for him with agony; but still he remained unrepentant, until at last she became convinced that her prayers and agonies had been nothing but the fond yearnings of parental feeling, and were not dictated at all by a just view of her son's character as a willful and wicked rebel against God. There was never any impression made on his mind until she was made to take strong ground against him as a rebel, and to look on him as deserving to be sent to hell. Then he was converted. The reason was that she was never before influenced by the right motive in prayer, desiring his salvation with a supreme regard to the glory of God.

4. If we want to be so united as to prevail in prayer, we must agree in

faith. That is, we must be in accord in expecting the blessing prayed for. We must understand the reason why it is to be expected, we must see the evidence on which faith should rest, and we must absolutely believe that the blessing will come – or we do not bring ourselves within the promise. Faith is always understood as an indispensable condition of prevailing prayer. If it is not expressed in any particular case, it is always implied, for no prayer can be effectual except that which is offered in faith. In order that united prayer may prevail, there must be united faith.

5. So again, we must be agreed as to the time when we desire the blessing to come. If two or more agree in desiring a particular blessing, and one of them desires to have it come now, while others are not ready to have it quite yet, it is plain they are not agreed. They are not united in regard to one essential point. If the blessing is to come in answer to their united prayer, it must come as they prayed for it. And if it comes, it must be at some time. But if they disagree as to the time when they will have it, then plainly it can never come in answer to their prayer.

Suppose a church would undertake to pray for a revival, and would be all agreed in desiring a revival, but not as to the time when it will be. Suppose some want to have the revival come now, and are all prepared; their hearts are waiting for the Spirit of God to come down, and they are willing to give time and attention and labor to it now. However, others are not quite ready. They have something else to attend to at present, some worldly object they want to accomplish, some piece of business in hand and just want to finish it first, and then – but they cannot possibly find time to attend to it now. They are not prepared to humble themselves, to search their hearts and break up their fallow ground, and to put themselves in a position to receive the blessing. Is it not plain that there is no real union, for they are not agreed in that which is essential? While some are praying that the revival may come now, others are praying with equal earnestness that it may not come now.

Suppose the question were now asked of this church whether you are agreed in praying for a revival of religion here. Do you all desire a revival, and would you all like to have it come now? Would you be wholeheartedly agreed now to break down in the dust and open your hearts to the Holy Spirit if He should come tonight? I do not ask what you would say if I would ask the question. Perhaps if I would ask it to you now, you would all rise up and vote that you were agreed in desiring a revival, and agreed to have it now. You know how you should feel and what you should say, and you know you should be ready for a revival now.

But, I ask, would God see it to be so in your hearts that you are agreed on this point? Has there been a time since I came back from the country that this church was all agreed in desiring and praying for a revival, and in wanting to have it come now? Have any two of you agreed on this point, and prayed accordingly? If not, when will you be agreed to pray for a revival? And if those of this church cannot be agreed among yourselves, how can you expect a revival? It is of no use for you to take the outward attitude and stand up here and say you are agreed, when God reads the heart and sees that you are not agreed.

Here is the promise: *Again I say unto you, That if two of you shall agree on earth as touching anything that they shall ask, it shall be done for them of my Father which is in heaven.* Now this is either true or it is false. Which ground will you take? If it is true, then it is true that you are not agreed, and never have been, except in those cases where you have had a revival.

But we must agree not only upon a time, but it must be the present time, or we are not agreed in everything essential to the work. Unless we agree to have the revival now, we will not now use the means; and until the means are used, it cannot come. It is plain, then, that we must be agreed upon the present time; that is, we are not agreed in the sense of the text until we agree that now we will have the blessing, and will act accordingly. To agree upon a future time is of no use, for when that future time comes, we must then be agreed upon that present time, and use means accordingly, so that you see you are never properly agreed until you agree that now is the time.

II. We Are to Agree in Everything That Is Essential to Obtaining the Blessing That We Seek

You see the language of the text: *If two of you shall agree as touching anything that they shall ask.* Many people seem to read it as if it referred merely to an agreement in asking, and they understand it to promise that whenever two are agreed in asking for any blessing, it will be given. But Christ says there must be an agreement *as touching* the thing prayed for. That is, the agreement or union must comprise everything that is essential to the bestowment and reception of the blessing.

1. If Christians would enjoy the benefits of this promise in praying for a revival, they must be agreed in believing revivals of religion to be a reality. There are many individuals, even in the church, who do not believe in their hearts that the revivals that take place are the work of God. Some of them may pray in words for an outpouring of the Spirit and a revival of religion, while in their hearts they doubt whether there are any such things known in modern times. In united prayer, there must be no hypocrisy.

2. They must agree in feeling the necessity of revivals. There are some who believe in the reality of revivals as a work of God, while at the same time they are undecided as to the necessity of having them for the success of the gospel. They think there is a real work of God in revivals, but after all, perhaps it is just as good to have sinners converted and brought into the church in a more quiet and gradual way, and without so much excitement. Whenever revivals are abroad in the land, and prevail and are popular, they may appear in favor of them and may put up their cold prayers for a revival, while at the same time they would be sorry on the whole to have a revival come among them. They think it is so much safer and better to teach the people, to spread the matter before them in a calm way, and to bring them in gradually without running the risk of having excitement or wildfire in their congregations.

3. They must be agreed in regard to the importance of revivals. People are not blessed with revivals in answer to prayers that are only half sincere. They must feel the infinite importance of a revival before they will pray so as to prevail. Blessings of this kind are not granted except in answer to such prayers as arise from a sense of their importance. As I have shown before, when preaching on the subject of prevailing prayer, it is when people desire the blessing with unutterable agony that they

offer such prayer that will infallibly prevail with God. Those who feel less of the importance of a revival may pray for it in words, but they will never have the blessing. But when a church has been united in prayer, and has really felt the importance of a revival, they have never failed of having one. I do not believe a case can be found of such a church being turned away empty. Such an agreement, when sincere, will secure an agreement also on all other subjects that are indispensable.

4. They must also be agreed in having correct scriptural beliefs about several things connected with revivals.

a) The necessity of divine agency to produce a revival. It is not enough that they all hold this in theory, and pray for it in words, but they must fully understand and deeply feel this necessity. They must realize their entire dependence on the Spirit of God, or it will all fail.

b) Why divine agency is necessary. There must be an agreement on correct principles in regard to the reason why divine agency is so indispensable. If they get wrong ideas on this point, they will be hindered. If Christians get the idea that this necessity of divine influence lies in the inability of sinners, or if they feel as if God was under obligation to give the Holy Spirit in order to make sinners able to obey the gospel, they insult God, and their prayers will not avail. For in that case, they must feel that it is a mere matter of common justice for God to pour out His Spirit before He can justly require Christians to work or sinners to repent.

Suppose a church gets the idea that sinners are poor unfortunate creatures who come into the world with such a nature that they cannot help sinning, and that sinners are just as unable to repent and believe the gospel as they are to fly to the moon. How can they feel that the sinner is a rebel against God and that he deserves to be sent to hell? How can they feel that the sinner is to blame? How can they take God's side when they pray? If they do not take God's side against the sinner, they cannot expect God to regard their prayers, for they do not pray with right motives.

Undoubtedly, one great reason why so many prayers are not answered is that those who pray do in fact take the sinner's side against God. They pray as if the sinner was a poor unfortunate being to be pitied, rather than as if he was a guilty wretch to be blamed. The reason is that they do not believe sinners are able to obey God. If a person does not believe that sinners are able to obey their Maker, and really believes that the Spirit's influences are necessary to make him able, it is impossible, with these views, to offer acceptable and prevailing prayer for the sinner, and it is no wonder that people with these views would not prevail with God and would doubt about the power of the prayer of faith.

How often do you hear people pray for sinners in this way: "O Lord, help this poor soul to do what he is required to do. O Lord, enable him to do so and so"? This kind of language implies that they take the sinner's part, and not God's. If it was understood by those who use it, as it is sometimes explained, and if people meant by it what they should mean when they plead for sinners, I would not find so much fault with it. But the truth is that when people use this language, they often mean just what the language itself would be naturally at first understood to mean, which is just as if they would pray, "Lord, You command these poor sinners to repent, when, O Lord, You know they cannot repent unless You give them Your Spirit to enable them to do it, even though You have declared that You will send them to hell if they do not, whether they ever receive the Spirit or not. Lord, this seems very hard, and we pray that You will have compassion on these poor creatures, and do not deal so harshly with them, for Christ's sake."

Who does not see that such a prayer, or a prayer that means this, whatever language it may be expressed in, is an insult to God, accusing Him of infinite injustice if He continues to exact from sinners a duty that they are unable to perform without that aid that He will not grant. People may pray in this way until the day of judgment, and never obtain a blessing, because they take the sinner's part against God. They cannot pray successfully until they understand that the sinner is a rebel and is obstinate in his rebellion – so obstinate that he will never, without the Holy Spirit, do what he could do as well as not, instantly, and this obstinacy is the reason, and the only reason, why he needs the influence of the Holy Spirit for his conversion.

The only ground on which the sinner needs divine agency is to overcome his obstinacy and to make him willing to do what he can do, and what God justly requires him to do. A church is never in an attitude in which God will hear their united prayers unless they are agreed in understanding their dependence on God so as to feel it in perfect consistency with the sinner's blame. If it is the other way, they are agreed in understanding it wrong, and their prayers for divine help to the unfortunate, instead of divine favor to make a rebel submit, are wide of the mark and are an insult to God, and they will never obtain favor in heaven.

c) They must be agreed in understanding that revivals are not miracles, but that they are brought about by the use of means like other events. It is no wonder that revivals formerly came so seldom and continued so short a time when people generally regarded them as miracles, or like a mere shower of rain that will come on a place and continue a little while, and then blow over – that is, as something over which we have no control. For what can people do to get a shower of rain, or how can they make it rain any longer than it does? It is necessary that those who pray should be agreed in understanding a revival as something to be brought about by means, or they will never be agreed in using them.

d) They must be agreed in understanding that human agency is just as indispensable to a revival as divine agency. Such a thing as a revival of religion, I dare say, never did occur without divine agency, and never did occur without human agency. How often do people say, "If God pleases, He can carry on the work without means." But I have no faith in it, for there is no evidence of it. What is religion? Obedience to God's law. But the law cannot be obeyed unless it is known. And how can God make sinners obey except by making known His commandments? And how can He make them known but by revealing them Himself, or sending them by others – that is, by bringing the truth to bear upon the person's mind until he obeys it?

God never did and never can convert a sinner except with the truth. What is conversion? Obeying the truth. He may communicate it Himself directly to the sinner, but then the sinner's own agency is indispensable, for conversion consists in the right use of the sinner's own agency. Ordinarily, He employs the agency of others also – in printing, writing, conversation, and preaching.

God has put the gospel treasure in earthen vessels. He has seen fit to use men in preaching the Word. That is, He has seen that human agency is that which He can best use in saving sinners. And if there ever was a case (of which we have no evidence), there is not one in a thousand, if one in a million, converted in any way other than through the truth made known and urged by human instrumentality. Just as the church must be united in using those means, it is plainly necessary that they should be united in understanding the true reason why means are to be used, and the true principles on which they are to be governed and applied.

5. It is important that there should be unity in regard to the measures essential to the promotion of a revival. Let individuals agree to do anything whatsoever, and if they are not agreed in their measures, they will run into confusion and counteract one another. Set them to sail a ship, and they can never get along without agreement. If they attempt to do business as merchants when they are not agreed in their measures, what will they do? They will only undo each other's work and thwart the whole business of the concern. All this is preeminently true in regard to the work of promoting a revival. Otherwise, the members of the church will counteract each other's influence, and they do not need to expect a revival.

a) The church must be agreed in regard to the meetings that are held, as to what meeting will be held, and as to how many, where, and when they will be held. Some people always desire to multiply meetings in a revival, as if the more meetings they had, the more religion there is. Others are always opposed to any new meetings in a revival. Some are always in favor of having a protracted meeting, and others are never ready to hold a protracted meeting at all. Whatever difference there may be, it is essential that the church comes to a good understanding on the subject so that they can go on together in harmony, and labor with zeal and effect.

b) They must be agreed as to the manner of conducting meetings. It is necessary for the church to be united and friendly on this subject if they expect to offer united prayer with effect. Sometimes there are individuals who want to adopt every new thing they can hear of or imagine, while others are totally unwilling to have anything changed in regard to the management of the meeting, but want everything done precisely as they are used to. They should be agreed in some way, either to have the meetings changed, or to keep them on in the old way.

The best possible way is for the church to agree that they will let the meetings go on and take their course just as the Spirit of God shapes them, and not even attempt to make two meetings exactly the same. The church will never give the fullest effect to the truth until they are agreed in this principle – that in promoting a revival they will accommodate their measures to circumstances, and not attempt to interrupt the natural course that pious feeling and sound judgment indicate, but cast themselves entirely upon the guidance and direction of the Holy Spirit, introducing any measure, at any time, that will seem called for in the providence of God, without laying any stress upon its being new or old.

6. They must be agreed in the manner of dealing with unrepentant sinners. It is immensely important that the church agrees in its treatment of sinners. Suppose they are not agreed, and one will tell one sinner one thing, and someone else tells another sinner something different. What confusion! How can they agree in prayer when it is plain that they are not agreed as to the things they will pray for?

Go among such a church and hear them pray for sinners. Attend a prayer meeting and listen. Here is one man who prays that the sinners present may repent. Another prays that they may be convicted, and perhaps, if he is very much engaged, will go so far as to pray that they may be deeply convicted. Another prays that sinners may go home solemn, meditative, and silent, contemplating the truths they have heard. Another prays in such a manner that you can see he is afraid to have them converted now. Another prays very solemnly that they may not attempt to do anything in their own strength. And so on. How easy it is to see that the church is not agreed *as touching* the things they ask for, and of course they have no interest in the promise.

If you have them talk with sinners, their ways would be just as inconsistent, for it is plain that they are not agreed and have no clear views in regard to what a sinner must do to be saved, or of what should be said to sinners to bring them to repent. The result is that sinners who are awakened and anxious quickly get confused and do not know what to do – and perhaps give it all up in despair, or conclude that there is in reality nothing rational or consistent in the Christian religion.

One person will tell the sinner he must repent immediately. Another will give him a book such as Doddridge's *Rise and Progress*, and tell him to read that book. Another will tell him he must pray and persevere, and that in God's time he will obtain the blessing. A revival can never go on for any length of time amid such difficulties. If it begins, it will soon end – unless, perhaps, the majority of the church will keep still and say nothing at all and let others carry on the work.

The work there will suffer materially for lack of their cooperation and support. A church should be agreed. Every Christian should have a clear understanding of this subject, with all speaking the same thing and giving the same directions. Then the sinner will find no one to take his part, and can get no relief or comfort until he repents.

7. They must be agreed in removing the impediments to a revival. If a church expects a revival, the stumbling blocks must be taken out of the way.

a) In the exercise of discipline. If there are rotten members in the church, they should be removed, and the church members should all agree to cut them off. If they remain in the church, they are such a reproach to religion as to hinder a revival. Sometimes division is created when an attempt is made to cast them out, and thus the work is stopped. Sometimes the offenders are people of influence, or they have family friends who will take their side and make a faction, and thus create a bad spirit and prevent a revival.

b) In mutual confessions. Whenever wrong has been done to anyone, there should be a full confession. I do not mean a cold and forced acknowledgment, such as saying, "If I have done wrong, I am sorry for it," but a sincere confession, admitting the entirety of the wrong and showing that it comes out of a broken heart.

c) Forgiveness of enemies. A great obstruction to revivals is often found in the fact that active and leading individuals harbor a revengeful and unforgiving spirit toward those who have harmed them, which destroys their spirituality, makes them harsh and disagreeable in their manner, and prevents them from enjoying either communion with God in prayer or the blessing of God to give them success in labor. Instead, let the members of a church be truly agreed in breaking down and confessing their own faults, and in cherishing a tender, merciful, forgiving,

Christlike spirit toward those who they think have done them wrong, and then the Spirit will thoroughly come down upon them.

8. They must be agreed in making all the necessary preparations for a revival. They should be agreed in having all necessary preparations made, and agreed in bearing their part of the labor or the expense of making it. There should be an equality rather than having a few be burdened while the rest do little or nothing, but everyone his proportion, *according to his several ability* (Matthew 25:15). Then there will be no envying or jealousy, nor any of those mutual recriminations and altercations and disrespectful remarks about one another that are so inconsistent with brotherly love, and are such a stumbling block in the way of sinners.

9. They must be agreed in doing wholeheartedly whatever is necessary to be done for the promotion of the revival. Sometimes a slight disagreement about something very little will be allowed to break in and destroy a revival. A minister told me that he once went to labor in a place as an evangelist, and the Spirit of God was evidently present. Sinners began to inquire, and things looked quite favorable until some of the members in the church began to stir up the question as to how they should pay him for his services. They said, "If he stays among us any longer, he will expect us to give him something," and they did not see how they could afford to do it. They talked about it until the minds of the brethren got distracted and divided, and the minister went away.

Look at that! There God stood in the door of that church with His hands full of mercies, but these stingy and wicked professing Christians thought it would cost something to have a revival, and their expenses were about as much as they felt willing or able to bear. So they let the minister depart, and the work ceased. The minister would not have left at the time whether they gave him anything or not, for what he would receive, or whether he would receive anything from them, was a question about which he felt no concern. But the church by their miserly spirit got into such a state as to grieve the Spirit, and the minister saw that to stay longer with them would do no good. Oh, how will those professing Christians feel when they meet sinners from that town in judgment, when it will be revealed that God was ready and waiting to grant them a blessing, but they allowed themselves to get bothered and divided by asking how much they would have to pay!

10. They must be agreed in laboring to carry on the work. It is not enough for them to agree to pray for a revival, but they should also agree in laboring to promote it. They should set themselves to it systematically, and as a matter of business, to visit and converse and pray with their neighbors, to look for opportunities of doing good, to watch the effect of the Word, and to watch the signs of the times so that they may know when anything needs to be done, and do it.

They should be agreed to labor, they should be agreed how to labor, and they should be agreed to live accordingly.

11. They must agree in a determination to persevere. It will not be enough for some members of the church today to begin to move and speak on behalf of the work, and then, as soon as the least thing turns up unfavorable, to get discouraged and faint, and half of them quit the work. They should all be united and agree to persevere, labor, pray, and hold on until the blessing comes.

In a word, if Christians expect to unite in prayer and effort so as to prevail with God, they must be agreed in speaking and doing the same things, in walking by the same rule, in maintaining the same principles, and in persevering until they obtain the blessing so as not to hinder or thwart each other's efforts. All this is evidently implied in being agreed as touching the things for which they are praying.

Remarks

1. We see why it is that so many of the children of parents who profess to be Christians are not converted. It is because the parents have not been agreed as touching the things they should pray for in behalf of their children. Perhaps they never had any kind of agreement respecting them. Maybe they were never agreed even as to what was the very best thing they could ask them. Sometimes parents are not agreed in anything, but their opinions clash and they are always disagreeing. Their children see it, and then it is no wonder that they are not converted.

Perhaps they may not be agreed concerning the salvation of their children. Are they sincere in desiring it? Do they agree to desire their children's salvation, and do they agree from right motives? Do they agree in regard to the importance of it? Are they agreed how their children should be dealt with to bring about their conversion – what will be said to them, how it will be said, when, by whom, etc.? Alas! In how many cases is it evident they are not agreed? Probably few cases will be found where children remain unconverted when it will be seen that the parents were never truly agreed as touching the things they should ask for in regard to the salvation of their children.

Often there is such disagreement that we could not expect any good to result, or anything except ruin to the children. The husband and wife often disagree entirely and fundamentally in regard to the manner of bringing up their children. Perhaps the wife is fond of clothing and display and social visits, while the husband is plain and humble, and is grieved and distressed, and mourns and prays when he sees how his children are puffed up with vanity. Or it may be that the father is controlled by ambition and wants to have his daughters fashionably educated and make a display, and he wants his sons to become great men, so he will send his daughters to a refined boarding school where they may learn anything except their duty to God, and he will be all the time pushing his sons forward and encouraging their ambition. Meanwhile, the mother grieves and weeps in secret to see her dear children hurried on to destruction, and all her own influence counteracted, and her sons and daughters trained up to serve the god of this world and go to hell.

2. We see the hypocrisy of those who profess to be praying for a revival while they are doing nothing to promote it. There are many who appear to be very zealous in praying for a revival, while they are not doing anything at all for one. What do they mean? Are they agreed as touching the things they ask for? Certainly not. They cannot be agreed in offering acceptable prayer for a revival until they are prepared to do what God requires them to do to promote it. What would you think of the farmer who would pray for a crop, and not plow or sow? Would you think that such prayers are pious, or are an insult to God?

3. We see why so many prayers offered in the church are never answered. It is because those who offered them were never agreed as touching the things they asked for. Perhaps the minister never laid the subject before them, never explained what it means to be agreed, never showed them its importance, and never set before them the great encouragement that the promise before us provides to churches that will agree. Maybe the members of the church have never consulted together and compared their views to see whether they understood the subject in the same way, whether they were agreed in regard to the motives, grounds, and importance of being united in prayer and labor for a revival.

Suppose you were to go through the churches in this city and learn the precise views and feelings of the members on this subject. How many would you find who were agreed even in regard to the essential and indispensable things concerning which it is necessary for Christians to be agreed upon in order to unite in prevailing prayer? Perhaps no two could be found who are agreed, and if two were found whose views and desires were similar, it would probably be discovered that they are unacquainted with each other, and of course neither act nor pray together.

4. We see why it is that this text has been generally understood to mean something different from what it says. People have first read it wrong. They have read it as if it said, *If any two of you shall agree to ask anything, it shall be done.* And as they have often agreed to ask for things, and the things were not done, they have said, "The literal meaning of the text cannot be true, for we have tried it and know it is not true. How many prayer meetings have we held, and how many petitions have we put up, in which we have perfectly agreed in asking for blessings, yet they have not been granted?"

The fact is that they have never yet understood what it is to be agreed *as touching* the things they are to ask for. I am sure this is not a stretched construction of the text, but is its true and obvious meaning, as a plain, pious reader would understand it if he inquired seriously and earnestly the true meaning. They must be agreed not only in asking, but in everything else that is indispensable to the existence of the thing prayed for.

Suppose two of you were agreed in desiring to go to London together. If you were not agreed in regard to the means – what route you will take and what ship you will go in – you will never get there together. It is the same in praying for a revival. You must be agreed in regard to the means and circumstances, and everything essential to the existence and progress of a revival.

5. We may ordinarily expect a revival of religion to prevail and extend among those outside the church just in proportion to the unity of prayer and effort within. If there is a general unity within the church, the revival will be general. If the unity continues, the revival will continue. If anything begins to break in upon this perfect unity in prayer and effort, it will begin to limit the revival. How great and powerful would the revival in this city be if all the churches in the city were thus united in promoting it!

There is another fact that I have witnessed that is worthy of notice. I have observed that a revival will prevail out of the church among people in that class of society among whom it prevails in the church. If the females in the church are most awake and prayerful, the work may generally be expected to prevail mostly among females out of the church, and more women will be converted than men. If the youth of either, or of both genders, in the church are most awake, the work is most likely to prevail among youth, male or female, or both, as the work may be in the church in this respect. If the heads of families and the principal men in the church are awake, I have observed that the revival is more likely to prevail among that class out of the church.

I have known a revival mostly confined to females, and few males converted, apparently because the male part of the church did not take hold and work. I have also repeatedly known the greatest number of converts to be among men, apparently due to the fact that the men of the church were the most engaged. When the revival does not reach a particular class of the unrepentant, efforts should be made to stir up that portion of the church who are of their own age and standing, to make more direct efforts for their conversion.

There seems to be a philosophy in this fact that has often been witnessed. Different classes of professing Christians naturally feel a sympathy for the unrepentant of their own gender and age and rank, and more naturally pray for them and have more interaction with them and more influence over them, and this seems to be at least one of the reasons why revivals tend to be the most powerful and general in that class outside the church who are the most awake in the church. Christians should understand this and feel their responsibility.

One main reason why so few of the principal men are sometimes converted in revivals is undoubtedly that that class in the church is often so worldly that they cannot be awakened. The revival will generally prevail mostly in those families where the professing Christians belonging to them are awake, and the unrepentant belonging to those families where the professing Christians are not awake tend to be left unconverted. One main reason obviously is that when the professing Christians in a family or neighborhood are awake, there is not only prayer offered for sinners in the midst of them, but there are corresponding influences acting upon the unrepentant among them. If they are awake, their looks and lives and warnings all tend to promote the conversion of their unrepentant friends. But if they are asleep, all their influences tend to prevent their conversion. Their coldness grieves the Spirit, their worldliness contradicts the gospel, and all their interaction with their unrepentant friends is in favor of impenitence, and calculated to perpetuate it.

6. We see why different denominations have been permitted to spring up in the church, and under the government of God. Christians often see and deplore the evils that have arisen to the church of God from the division of His people into discordant groups. They have wondered and been perplexed to think that God would allow it to be so. But in the light of this subject, we can see that considering what diversities of opinions and feelings and views actually exist in the church, much good results from this division of sects.

Considering this diversity of opinion, many would never agree to pray and labor together so as to do it with success, and so it is better for them to separate and to let those unite who are agreed. In all cases where there cannot be a cordial agreement in labor, it is better that each denomination should labor by themselves, so long as this difference exists. I have sometimes seen revivals broken up by attempting to unite Christians of different denominations in prayer and labor together while they were not agreed as to the principles or measures by which the work was to be promoted. They would then undo each other's work and destroy each other's influence, confuse the anxious, and give occasion to enemies to blaspheme. Soon their feelings would get embittered, the Spirit of God is grieved away, the work stops, and perhaps painful confusion and controversy follow.

7. We see why God sometimes permits churches to be divided. It is because He finds that the members are so much at variance that they will not pray and work together with effect. Sometimes churches that are in such a state will still keep together from worldly considerations and worldly policy because it is so much easier for the whole to support public worship. Perhaps both parties want to keep the meeting house, or both want to retain the minister, and they cannot agree which will go away, so they continue along, jealous and disagreeing for years, accomplishing little or nothing for the salvation of sinners. In such cases, God has often let something turn up among them that would tear them apart, and then each party would go to work in their own way, and perhaps both would prosper.

While they were in the same church, they were always making trouble for each other since they did not think or feel alike, but as soon as they were separated, everything settled down in peace and made it evident that it was better for them to divide. I have known some cases in this state where this has been done with the happiest results, and both churches have been quickly blessed with revivals.

8. It is evident that many more churches need to be divided. How many churches there are that are holding together, yet are doing no good for the simple reason that they are not sufficiently agreed. They do not think alike nor feel alike on the subjects connected with revivals, and while this is so, they can never work together. Unless they can be brought to such a change of views and feelings on the subject that will unite them, they are only a hindrance to each other and to the work of God. In many cases they see and feel that it is so, yet they keep together, conscientiously, for fear that a division would dishonor Christianity, when in fact the division that now exists may be making Christianity

a byword and a reproach (Deuteronomy 28:37). It would be far better if they would just agree to divide amicably, like Abraham and Lot: *If thou wilt take the left hand, I will go to the right; or if thou depart to the right hand, then I will go to the left* (Genesis 13:9). Let them separate and each work in his own way, and they may both enjoy the blessing.

9. We see why a few individuals who are perfectly united may be successful in gathering and building up a new church, and may do so much better than a much larger number who are not agreed among themselves. If I were going to start a new church in this city, I would rather have five people, or three, or even two who were perfectly agreed as touching the things they were to pray for and the manner in which they would labor for them, and in all that is essential to the prosperity of a church, and who would stand by me and stand by each other, than to have a church to begin with, or to have five hundred members who were not agreed.

10. We see what glorious things may be expected for Zion whenever the churches generally are agreed on these subjects. When ministers will lay aside their prejudices, their misconstructions, and their jealousies, and will see eye to eye, and when the churches will understand the Bible in the same way, will see their duty the same, will pray in the same way, and will be agreed as touching the things they will ask for, a nation will be born in a day. Only let them feel as the heart of one man, and be agreed as to what should be done for the salvation of the world, and the millennium will come at once.

11. There is vast ignorance in the churches on the subject of revivals. After all the revivals that have been enjoyed, and all that has been said and written and printed concerning revivals, there are very few who have any real, consistent knowledge on the subject. And when there is a revival, how few there are who can take hold to labor and promote it as if they understood what they were about. How few people are to be found who have ever taken up revivals of religion as a subject to be studied and understood.

Everybody knows that in a revival, Christians must pray and must do some things that they have not been in the habit of doing. But multitudes know nothing of the reason why they should do this, or why one thing is better than another, and of course they have no principles to guide them; and when anything occurs that they did not expect, they are all at a loss and do not know what to do. If men would go to work to build a house of worship, and know as little how to proceed as many ministers and professing Christians know how to build the spiritual temple of God, they would never build a house in the world. Yet people make themselves believe they are building the church of God when they know nothing at all what they are about, and are completely unable to give a reason why they are doing as they do, or why one thing should be done rather than another.

There are multitudes in the church who never seem to suppose that the work of promoting revivals of religion is one that requires study, thought, knowledge of principles, and skill in applying the Word of God so as to give everyone his portion in season. And so they go on, generally doing little or nothing because they are attempting nothing, and if they ever do awake, they go impulsively to work without any system or plan, as if God had left this part of our duty out of the reach of sound judgment and good sense.

12. There is vast ignorance among ministers upon this subject, and one great reason for this ignorance is that many get the idea that they already understand all about revivals, when in reality they know next to nothing about them. I once knew a minister who came in where there was a powerful revival, and he ranted about and found fault with many things, speaking of his knowledge of revivals, that he had been in seventeen of them and so on, when it was evident that he knew nothing as he should know about revivals.

13. How important it is for the church to be trained and instructed so as to know what to do in a revival! They should be trained and disciplined like an army – each one having a place to fill and something to do, and knowing where he belongs and what he is supposed to do, and how to do it. Instead of this, how often you see a church in a time of revival take hold of the work to promote it, just like a group of children taking hold to build a house. How few there are who really know what to

do and how to do it. The very thing for which God permits Christians to live in this world, the very thing for which alone He would ever let them remain away from heaven a day, is the very thing of all others that they do not study and do not try to understand.

14. We see why revivals are often so short and why they so often produce a reaction. It is because the church does not understand the subject. Revivals are short because professing Christians have been stirred up to an unsteady kind of action. They have gone to work by impulse rather than from deliberate conviction of duty, and have been guided by their feelings rather than by a sound understanding of what they should do. The church did not know what to do, what they could do, and what they could not do, nor how to best use their strength, nor what the state of things would bear – and perhaps their zeal led them into some mistakes and they lost their hold on God, and so the enemy prevailed.

The church should be so trained as to know what to do so as never to fail and never to suffer defeat or reaction when they attempt to promote a revival. They should understand all the tactics of the devil and know where to guard against his devices so that they may know him when they see him, and not mistake him for an angel of light who has come to give them lessons of wisdom in promoting the revival, and so they can cooperate wisely with the minister, with one another, and with the Holy Spirit in carrying on the work. No person who has been acquainted with revivals can overlook the fact that the ignorance of professing Christians concerning revivals and their foolish blunders are among the most common things that put revivals down and bring back a fearful reaction upon the church. Brethren, how long will this be so? It should not be so, and it does not need to be so.

15. We see that every church is rightly responsible for the souls that are among them. If God has given such a promise, and if it is true that where two or more are agreed as touching the things they ask for, it will be done, then certainly Christians are responsible; and if sinners are lost, their blood will be found upon the church. If the churches can have what they ask as soon as they are agreed as touching it, then certainly the damnation of the world will be required at the hands of the church.

16. We see the guilt of ministers in not informing themselves, and in not rightly and quickly instructing the churches upon this momentous subject. What is the purpose of the Christian ministry? Is it only to instruct and dispense the sacramental host, and lead them on to conquest? What? Do they let the church remain in ignorance upon the very subject, and the only point of duty, for the performance of which they are in the world – the salvation of sinners? Some ministers have acted as mysteriously about revivals as if they thought Christians were either incapable of understanding how to promote them, or that it was of no importance that they should know. But this is all wrong. No minister has yet begun to understand, or do his duty, if he has neglected to teach his church to work for God in the promotion of revivals. What is he about? What does he mean? Why is he a minister? To what end has he taken the sacred office? Is it that he *may eat a piece of bread* (1 Samuel 2:36)?

17. We see that pious parents can render the salvation of their children certain. Only let them pray in faith and be agreed as touching the things they will ask for, and God has promised them the desire of their hearts. Who can be agreed as well as parents? Let them be agreed in prayer, and agreed in what to do, and agreed in doing all their duty; let them thus train up their children in the way they should go, and when they are old, they *will not depart from it* (Proverbs 22:6).

And now, brethren, do you believe you are agreed according to the meaning of this promise? I know that where a few individuals may be agreed in some things, they may produce some effect; but while the majority of the church is not agreed, there will always be so many things to counteract that they will accomplish but little. The church must be agreed.

Oh, if we could find one church that was perfectly and wholly agreed in all these points so that they could pray and labor together all as one, what good would be done! But now, while things are as they are, we see community after community filling hell because the church is not agreed. Oh, what do Christians think – how can they keep still – when God has brought down His blessings so that if any two were agreed as touching the things they ask for, it would be done? Alas! Alas! How bitter will be the remembrance of this discord in the church when

Christians come to see the crowds of lost souls that have gone down to hell because they were not agreed to labor and pray for their salvation.

Finally, in the light of this promise, we see the awful guilt of the church. God has given it to be the precious inheritance of His people at all times and in all places. If His people agree, their prayers will be answered. We see the awful guilt of this church with many who come here and listen to lectures about revivals and then go away and have no revival, and also the guilt of members of other churches who hear these lectures and go home and refuse to do their duty. How can you meet the thousands of unrepentant sinners now around you at the judgment seat of God and see them sink away into everlasting burnings? Have you been united in heart to pray for them? If you have not, why have you disagreed? Why have you not prayed with this promise until you have prevailed?

You will now either be agreed and pray for the Holy Spirit, and receive Him before you leave, or the anger of the Lord will be upon you. If you would now agree to pray in the sense of this promise for the Spirit of God to come down on this city, the heavenly Dove would fly through the city in the midst of the night and would awaken the consciences and break up the guilty slumbers of the wicked. What then is the crimson guilt of those professing Christians who are sleeping in sight of such a promise? They seem to have skipped over it, or to have entirely forgotten it. Multitudes of sinners are going to hell in all directions, yet this blessed promise is neglected; even more, it is practically despised by the church. There it stands in the solemn record of God's Word, and the church could take hold of it in such a manner that vast numbers might be saved, but they are not agreed. Therefore, souls will perish. And where is the responsibility? Who can take this promise and look the perishing in the face at the day of judgment?

*These lectures were greatly instrumental in reviving religion in the church to which they were preached, and their publication in this country and in Europe has been the means of promoting revivals in very many places. To God belongs all the glory.

Lecture 17

False Comforts for Sinners

How then comfort ye me in vain, seeing in your answers
there remaineth falsehood?
—Job 21:34

Job's three friends insisted that the afflictions he suffered were sent as a punishment for his sins, and were conclusive evidence that he was a hypocrite and not a good man as he professed to be. A lengthy argument ensued in which Job referred to all past experience to prove that men are not dealt with in this world according to their character, that the distinction is not observed in the allotments of providence. His friends maintained the opposite and stated that this world is also a place of rewards and punishments in which people receive good or evil according to their deeds.

In this chapter, Job shows by appealing to common sense, common observation, and experience that this cannot be true, because it is a matter of fact that the wicked are often prosperous in the world and through life, and therefore infers that their judgment and punishment must be reserved for a future state. *The wicked is reserved to the day of destruction*, and *They shall be brought forth to the day of wrath* (Job 21:30). Inasmuch as his friends had come to comfort him, but being in the dark on this fundamental point, had not been able to understand his case and so could not provide him any comfort, but rather aggravated his grief, Job insisted upon it that he would still look to a future state for consolation. He rebuked them by exclaiming, in the bitterness of his soul, *How then comfort ye me in vain, seeing in your answers there remaineth falsehood?* (Job 21:34).

My present purpose is to make some remarks upon the various methods used in comforting anxious sinners. I intend to show the following:

I. The necessity and purpose of instructing anxious sinners.

II. Anxious sinners are always seeking comfort. Their primary desire is to get comfort in their distress.

III. Some of the false comforts often administered.

I. The Necessity and Purpose of Instructing Anxious Sinners

The very idea of anxiety or concern implies some instruction. A sinner would not be anxious at all about his future state unless he had enough light to know that he is a sinner and that he is in danger of punishment and needs forgiveness. But people are to be converted, not by physical force or by a change brought about in their nature or constitution by creative power, but by the truth made effectual by the Holy Spirit. Conversion is yielding to the truth. Therefore, the more that truth can be brought to bear upon the mind, other things being equal, so much the more probable it is that the individual will be converted. Unless the truth is brought to bear upon him, it is certain he will not be converted. If it is brought to bear, it is not absolutely certain that it will be effectual, but the probability is in proportion to the extent to which the truth is brought to bear.

The main purpose of dealing with an anxious sinner is to clear up all his difficulties and darkness, do away with all his errors, drain the foundation of his self-righteous hopes, and sweep away every vestige of comfort that he could find in himself. There is often much difficulty in this, and much instruction is required. Sinners often cling with a death grasp to their false dependences. The last place to which a sinner ever goes for relief is to Jesus Christ. Sinners would rather be saved in any other way in the world. They would rather make any sacrifice, go to any expense, or endure any suffering than just to throw themselves as guilty and lost rebels upon Christ alone for salvation.

This is the very last way in which they are ever willing to be saved. It cuts up all their self-righteousness, and annihilates their pride and self-satisfaction so completely that they are exceedingly unwilling to adopt it. But it is as true in philosophy as it is in fact that this is, after all, the only way in which a sinner could find relief. If God would attempt to free sinners and save them without humbling their pride and turning them from their sins, He could not do it.

The purpose of instructing an anxious sinner should be to lead him by the shortest possible way to do this. It is to bring his mind, by the shortest route, to the practical conclusion that there is, in fact, no other way in which he can be freed and saved except to renounce himself and rest in Christ alone. To do this with effect requires great skill. It requires a thorough knowledge of the human heart, a clear understanding of the plan of salvation, and a precise and definite idea of the very thing that a sinner must do in order to be saved.

To know how to do this successfully is one of the rarest qualifications in the ministry at the present day. It is distressing to see how few ministers and professing Christians there are who have in their own minds that distinct idea of the thing to be done so that they can go to an anxious sinner and tell him exactly what he has to do and how to do it, and can show him clearly that there is no possible way for him to be saved except by doing that very thing that they tell him, and can make him feel the certainty that he must do it, and that unless he does that very thing, he will be damned.

II. Anxious Sinners Are Always Seeking Comfort

Sinners often imagine that they are seeking Jesus Christ and seeking true religion, but this is a mistake. No person ever sought religion and yet remained irreligious. What is religion? It is obeying God. Seeking religion is seeking to obey God. The soul that hungers and thirsts after righteousness is the soul of a Christian. To say that a person can seek to obey God, yet not obey Him, is absurd. For if he is seeking true religion, he is not an unrepentant sinner. To seek religion implies a willingness to obey God, and a willingness to obey God is true religion. It is a contradiction to say that an unrepentant sinner is seeking true religion. It is the same as to say that he seeks and actually desires to obey God, but that God will not let him; or that he longs to embrace Jesus Christ, and Christ will not let him come.

The fact is that the anxious sinner is seeking a hope. He is seeking pardon and comfort and deliverance from hell. He is anxiously looking for someone to comfort him and make him feel better without being required to conform to such humiliating conditions as those of the gospel. His anxiety and distress continue only because he will not yield to the terms. Unfortunately, anxious sinners find comforters enough to their liking. Miserable comforters they all are, too, *seeing in [their] answers there remaineth falsehood*. No doubt, millions and millions are now in hell because there were those around them who gave them false comfort, who had so much false sympathy, or were themselves so much in the dark that they would not let them remain in anxiety until they had submitted their hearts to God, but instead administered falsehood and relieved their distress in this way – and now their souls are lost.

III. Several Ways in Which False Comfort Is Given to Anxious Sinners

I might almost say that there is an endless variety of ways in which this is done. The more experience I have, and the more I observe the ways in which even good people deal with anxious sinners, the more I feel grieved at the endless antics and falsehoods with which they attempt to comfort their anxious friends, and thus, in fact, deceive them and mislead them out of their salvation.

It often reminds me of the manner in which people act when anyone is sick. Let any of you be sick, with almost any disease in the world, and you will find that every person you meet with has a remedy for that disorder, a certain cure, a remedy, a potion; and you will find such a world of pretense all around you, so that if you do not take care and shut it all out, you will certainly lose your life. A man must exercise his own judgment, for he will find as many remedies as he has friends, and each one is certain of his own solution, and perhaps will be annoyed if it is not taken. And no doubt this miserable system of duplicity kills a great many people.

This is true to no greater extent respecting the diseases of the body than respecting the diseases of the mind. People have their remedies and their cures and their potions to comfort distressed souls, and whenever they begin to talk with an anxious sinner, they will bring in their false comforts, so much so that if he does not take care and pay attention to the Word of God, he will infallibly be deceived to his own destruction.

I intend to mention a few of the falsehoods that are often brought forward in attempting to comfort anxious sinners. Time would fail me if I just tried to name them all.

The direct purpose of many people is to comfort sinners, and they are often so intent upon this that they do not stay with specific means or kinds of comfort. They see their friends distressed, and they pity them. They feel very compassionate. "Oh, oh, I cannot bear to see them so distressed. I must comfort them somehow," and so they try one way, and another, and another to comfort them!

God desires them to be comforted. He is benevolent and has kind feelings, and His heart yearns over them when He sees them so distressed. But He sees that there is only one way to give a sinner real comfort. He has more benevolence and compassion than all people, and He wants to comfort them. But He has fixed the terms on which He will give a sinner relief as unyielding as His throne, and He will not change. He knows that nothing else will do the sinner effectual good, for nothing can make him happy until he repents of his sins, forsakes them, and turns to God. Therefore, God will not yield.

Our purpose should be the same as that of God. We should feel compassion and benevolence, just as He does, and be just as ready to give comfort – but we must be sure that it is of the right kind. The fact is that our main purpose should be to persuade the sinner to obey God. His comfort should be with us, and with him, only a secondary object; and while we are more anxious to relieve his distress than to have him cease to reject and dishonor God, we are not likely, by our instructions, to do him any real good. This is a fundamental distinction in dealing with anxious sinners, but it is evidently overlooked by many who seem to have no higher motives than sympathy or compassion for the sinner.

If in preaching the gospel or instructing the anxious, we are not driven by a high regard to the honor of God, and rise no higher than to desire to relieve the distressed, this is going no farther than a natural sympathy or compassion would carry us. Overlooking this principle has often misled professing Christians, and when they have heard others dealing faithfully with anxious sinners, they have accused them of cruelty.

I have often had professing Christians bring anxious sinners to me and beg me to comfort them, and when I have thoroughly probed their consciences, they have shuddered and have sometimes taken the sinners' part. It is sometimes impossible to deal effectively with youth who are anxious, in the presence of their parents, because they have so much more compassion for their children than regard for the honor of God. This is all wrong, and with such views and feelings, you had better hold your tongue than to say anything to the anxious.

1. One of the ways in which people give false comfort to distressed sinners is by saying to them, "What have you done? You are not so bad." They see them distressed, and they cry out, "What have you done?" as if they had never done anything wicked, and had in reality no occasion to feel distressed at all. I have mentioned previously the case of a fashionable lady who was awakened in this city and was going to see a minister to converse with him. However, she was met by a friend who turned her back and drove away her anxiety by the cry, "What have you done to make you feel so? I am sure you have never committed any sin that needs to make you feel so."

I have often met with cases of this kind. A mother will tell her son, who is anxious, what an obedient child he has always been and how good and how kind he is, and she begs him not to carry on so. A husband will tell his wife, or a wife her husband, how good they are, and ask, "What have you done?" When they see them to be in great distress, they begin to comfort them: "You are not so bad. You have been to hear that dreadful minister who frightens people, and you have become excited. Be comforted, for I am sure you have not been bad enough to feel so much distressed."

The truth is, though, that they have been a great deal worse than they think they have been. No sinner ever had an idea that his sins were greater than they are. No sinner ever had an adequate idea of how great a sinner he is. It is not probable that anyone could live under the full sight of his sins. God has, in mercy, spared all His creatures on earth that worst of sights – an unveiled human heart. The sinner's guilt is much deeper and damning than he thinks, and his danger is much greater than he thinks it is. If he would see them as they are, he would probably not live a moment.

A sinner may have some false beliefs on the subject that create distress that have no foundation. He may think he has committed the unpardonable sin, or that he has grieved away the Spirit or has sinned away his day of grace. But to tell the most moral and naturally amiable person in the world that he is good enough, or that he is not as bad as he thinks he is, is not giving him rational comfort, but is deceiving him and is ruining his soul. Let those who do it take care.

2. Others tell awakened sinners that "Conversion is a progressive work," and in this way ease their anxiety. When a person is distressed because he sees himself to be such a sinner, and knows that unless he turns to God, he will be damned, it is a great relief to have some friend hold out the idea that he can get better by degrees, and that he is now advancing little by little. They tell him, "You cannot expect to get there all at once. I do not believe in these sudden conversions. You must wait and let it work. You have begun well, and eventually you will get comfort." All this is as false as the bottomless pit.

The truth is that regeneration, or conversion, is not a progressive work. What is regeneration? It is the beginning of obedience to God. Is the beginning of a thing progressive? It is the first act of genuine obedience to God. The first voluntary action of the mind is what God approves, or that can be regarded as obedience to God. That is conversion. When people talk about conversion as a progressive work, it is absurd. They show that they know just as much about regeneration or conversion as Nicodemus did. They know nothing about it as they should know, and are no more fit to conduct an anxious meeting, or to advise or instruct anxious sinners, than Nicodemus was.

3. Another way in which anxious sinners are deceived with false comfort is by being advised to dismiss the subject for the present time. People who are supposed to be wise and good have assumed to be so much wiser than God that when God is dealing with a sinner by His Spirit, and endeavoring to bring him to an immediate decision, they think God is pushing too hard and that it is necessary for them to interfere. They will advise the person to take a ride, or go into company, or engage in business, or something that will relieve his mind a little, at least for the present. They might just as well say to God, in plain words, "O God, You are too hard. You go too fast. You will make him crazy or kill him. He cannot stand it. Poor creature, if he is so pressed, he will die." So they takes sides against God, and do the same as to tell the sinner himself, "God will make you crazy if you do not dismiss the subject and resist the Spirit, and drive Him away from your mind."

Such advice, if it is truly conviction of sin that distresses the sinner, is in no case either safe or lawful. The strivings of the Spirit to bring a sinner to Himself will never hurt him or drive him crazy. He may make himself deranged by resisting, but it is blasphemous to think that the blessed, wise, and benevolent Spirit of God would ever act with such little care as to derange and destroy the soul He came to sanctify and save. The proper course to take with a sinner, when the striving of the Spirit throws him into distress, is to instruct him, clear up his views, correct his mistakes, and make the way of salvation so plain that he can see it right before him. We are not to dismiss the subject, but should fall in with the Spirit, and thus hush all those dreadful agonies that are produced by resisting the Holy Spirit. Remember that if an awakened sinner voluntarily dismisses the subject once, he will probably never take it up again.

4. Sometimes an awakened sinner is comforted by being told that the Christian religion does not consist in feeling bad. I once heard of a doctor of divinity giving an anxious sinner such counsel, when he was actually writhing under the arrows of the Almighty. He said, "Religion is cheerful. Religion is not gloomy. Do not be distressed. Be comforted. Dismiss your fears. You should not feel so bad," and similar miserable comforts, when in fact, the man had infinite reason to be distressed,

for he was resisting the Holy Spirit and was in danger of grieving Him away forever.

It is true that the Christian religion does not consist in feeling bad, but the sinner has reason to be distressed, because he has no religion. If he had religion, he would not feel this way. If he were a Christian, he would rejoice. But to tell an unrepentant sinner to be cheerful – you might as well preach this doctrine in hell and tell them there, "Cheer up here, cheer up, do not feel so bad!"

The sinner is on the very verge of hell. He is in rebellion against God, and his danger is infinitely greater than he imagines. Oh, what a doctrine of devils it is to tell a rebel against heaven not to be distressed! What is all his distress but rebellion itself? He is not comforted because he refuses to be comforted. God is ready to comfort him. You do not need to think to be more compassionate than God. He will fill him with comfort in an instant if he will submit. But there he stands, struggling against God, against the Holy Spirit, and against conscience until he is distressed almost to death, and still he will not yield; and now someone comes in and says, "Oh, I hate to see you feel so bad. Do not be so distressed. Cheer up, cheer up! Religion does not consist in being gloomy. Be comforted." Horrid!

5. Whatever involves the subject of the Christian religion in mystery is intended to give a sinner false comfort. When a sinner is anxious on the subject of true Christianity, very often, if you obscure it in mystery, he will feel relieved. The sinner's distress arises from the pressure of present obligation. Enlighten him on this point and clear it up, and if he will not yield, it will only increase his distress. But tell him that regeneration is all a mystery, something he cannot understand, and leave him all in a fog of darkness – and you relieve his anxiety.

It is his clear view of the nature and duty of repentance that produces his distress. It is the light that brings agony to his mind while he refuses to obey. It is that which will make up the pains of hell. It will almost make hell in the sinner's heart here, if it is only made clear enough. If you cover up this light, his anxiety will immediately become far less intense and distressing. However, if you lift up a certain and clear light and flash it openly upon his soul, you kindle up the tortures of hell in his heart if he will not yield.

6. Whatever relieves the sinner from a sense of blame is intended to give him false comfort.

The more a person feels himself to blame, the deeper is his distress. But anything that lessens his sense of blame, of course lessens his distress – but it is a comfort full of death. If anything will help him divide the blame and throw off a part of it upon God, it will provide comfort – but it is a relief that will destroy his soul.

7. To tell him of his inability is false comfort. If you tell an anxious sinner, "What can you do? You are a poor, feeble creature. You can do nothing," you will make him feel a kind of despondency. But it is not that intense agony of remorse with which God wrings the soul when He is laboring to cut him down and bring him to repentance.

If you tell him he is unable to comply with the gospel, he naturally falls in with it as a relief. He says to himself, "Yes, I am unable. I am a poor, feeble creature. I cannot do this, and certainly God cannot send me to hell for not doing what I cannot do." If I believed that the sinner was unable, I would tell him plainly, "Do not be afraid. You are not to blame for not complying with the call of the gospel, for you are unable, and God will never send you to hell for not doing what you have no strength to do." *Shall not the Judge of all the earth do right?* (Genesis 18:25). I know it is not common for those who talk about the sinner being unable to be so consistent and to carry out their theory, but the sinner infers all this, and so he feels relieved. It is all false, and all the comfort derived from it is only treasuring up wrath against the day of wrath.

8. Whatever makes the impression on a sinner's mind that he is to be passive in religion is intended to give him false comfort. Give him the idea that he has nothing to do except to wait for God's time. Tell him conversion is the work of God, that he should leave it to Him, and that he must be careful not to try to take the work out of God's hand – and he will infer, as before, that he is not to blame, and he will feel relieved. If he is only to hold still and let God do the work, just as a man holds still to have his arm amputated, he feels relieved. But such instruction as this is all wrong. If the sinner is thus to hold still and let God do it,

he instantly infers that he is not to blame for not doing it himself. And the inference is not only natural, but legitimate, for he is not to blame.

It is true that there is a sense in which conversion is the work of God, but as it is often represented, it is false. It is also true that there is a sense in which conversion is the sinner's own act. It is ridiculous, therefore, to say that a sinner is passive in regeneration, or passive in being converted, for conversion is his own act. The thing to be done is that which cannot be done for him. It is something that he must do, or it will never be done.

9. Telling a sinner to wait for God's time gives him false comfort. Some years ago, I met a woman in Philadelphia who was anxious about her soul, and had been a long time in that condition. I conversed with her and attempted to learn her state. She told me a good many things, and finally said she knew she should be willing to wait on God as long as He had waited upon her. She said that God had waited on her a great many years before she would give any attention to His calls, and now she believed it was her duty to wait on God's time to show mercy and convert her soul. She said that this was the instruction she had received. She must be patient and wait on God's time, and eventually He would give her relief. Oh, amazing foolishness!

Here is the sinner in rebellion. God comes with pardon in one hand and a sword in the other, and tells the sinner to repent and receive pardon, or refuse and perish. Now here comes a minister of the gospel, and he tells the sinner to "wait for God's time." He basically says that God is not ready to have him repent now, and He is not ready to pardon him now, and thus, in fact, throws off the blame of his unrepentance upon God. Instead of pointing out the sinner's guilt in not submitting at once to God, he points out God's supposed insincerity in making the offer when, in fact, God was not ready to grant the blessing, he says.

I have often thought such teachers needed the rebuke of Elijah when he met the priests of Baal: *Cry aloud: for he is a god; either he is talking, or he is pursuing, or he is in a journey; or peradventure he sleepeth, and must be awaked* (1 Kings 18:27). The minister who attempts to imply that God is not ready, and who tells the sinner to wait for God's time, might almost as well tell him that now God is asleep or has gone on a journey and cannot help him now. Miserable comforters indeed! It is little less than outrageous blasphemy of God.

How many people have gone to the judgment, red all over with the blood of souls that they have deceived and destroyed by telling them that God was not ready to save them, and that they must wait for God's time? No doubt, such a doctrine is exceedingly intended to provide present relief to an anxious sinner. It allows him to say, "Oh, yes, God is not ready. I must wait for God's time, so I can live in sin and take it out a while longer, until He gets ready to help me – and then I will get religion."

10. It is false comfort to tell an anxious sinner to do anything for relief that he can do, and not submit his heart to God. An anxious sinner is often willing to do anything else except the very thing that God requires him to do. He is willing to go to the ends of the earth, or to pay his money, or to endure suffering, or anything except full and instantaneous submission to God. If you will compromise the matter with him and tell him of something else that he may do, and yet evade that point, he will be very much comforted. He likes that instruction. He says, "Oh, yes, I will do that. I like that minister. He is not as severe as others. He seems to understand my particular case and knows how to make allowances."

It often reminds me of the conduct of a patient who is very sick, but has a great dislike for a certain physician and a particular medicine; but that is the very physician who alone understands treating his disease, and that is the only remedy for it. The patient is willing to do anything else, and call in any other physician; and he is anxious and in distress and is asking all his friends to tell him what he should do. He will take all the potions and quack medicines in the country before he will submit to the only course that can bring him relief. Eventually, after he has tried everything else without any benefit, if he does not die in the experiment, he gives up his unreasonable opposition, calls in the physician, takes the proper medicine, and is cured. It is the same with sinners. They will eagerly do anything if you will let them off from this intolerable pressure of present obligation to submit to God. I will mention a few of the things that sinners are told to do.

a) Telling a sinner he must use the means. Tell an anxious sinner that he must use the means, and he is relieved. "Oh, yes. I will do that, if that is all. I thought that God required me to repent and submit to Him now. But if using the means will suffice, I will do that with all my heart." He was distressed before because he was cornered up and did not know which way to turn. Conscience had tormented him like a wall of fire and urged him to repent now. But this relieves him at once, and he feels better. He says that he is very thankful that he found such a good adviser in his distress.

He may use the means, as he calls it, until the day of judgment, and not be a bit better for it, but will only hasten his way to death. What is the sinner's use of means but rebellion against God? God uses means. The church uses means to convert and save sinners, to bear down upon them and bring them to submission. But what has the sinner to do with using means? Will you set him to use means back upon God, and so make an offset in the matter? Is he to use means to make himself submit to God? How will he go to work with his means to make himself submit?

It is just telling the sinner, "You do not need to submit to God now, but just use the means awhile, and see if you cannot melt God's heart down to you so that He will yield this point of unconditional submission."

It is a mere delusion to evade the duty of immediate submission to God. It is true that sinners, motivated by a regard to their own happiness, often give attention to the subject of the Christian religion, attend meetings, and pray, read, and many such things. But in all this, they have no regard to the honor of God, nor do they so much as intend to obey Him. Their intention is not obedience, for if it were, they would not be unrepentant sinners. They are not, therefore, using means to be Christians, but to obtain pardon and a hope. It is absurd to say that an unrepentant sinner is using means to repent, for this is the same as to say that he is willing to repent – or in other words, that he does repent, and is not an unrepentant sinner. So to say that an unconverted sinner uses means with the intention of becoming a Christian is a contradiction, for it is saying that he is willing to be a Christian, which is the same as to say that he is a Christian already.

b) Telling the sinner to pray for a new heart. I once heard a celebrated Sunday school teacher do this. He was almost the father of Sunday schools in this country. He called a little girl up to him and began to talk to her. "My little daughter, are you a Christian?"

"No, sir."

"Well, you cannot be a Christian yourself, can you?"

"No, sir."

"No, you cannot be a Christian; you cannot change your heart yourself, but you must pray for a new heart; that is all you can do. Pray to God. God will give you a new heart."

He was an aged and venerable man, but I felt almost disposed to rebuke him openly in the name of the Lord. I could not bear to hear him deceive that child, telling her she could not be a Christian. Does God say, "Pray for a new heart?" Never. He says, "Make you a new heart." And the sinner is not to be told to pray to God to do his duty for him, but to go and do it himself. I know the psalmist, a good man, prayed, *Create in me a clean heart, O God; and renew a right spirit within me* (Psalm 51:10). He had faith and prayed in faith. But that is a very different thing from setting an obstinate rebel to pray for a new heart. Undoubtedly, an anxious sinner will be delighted with such instruction. "Why, I knew I needed a new heart and that I should repent, but I thought I must do it myself. I am very willing to ask God to do it. I hated to do it myself, but have no objection if God should do it, if He will; and I will pray for it, if that is all that is required."

c) Telling the sinner to persevere. Suppose he does persevere. He is as certain to be damned as if he had been in hell ever since the foundation of the world. His anxiety arises only from his resistance, and if he would submit, it would cease. And now, will you tell him to persevere in the very thing that causes his distress? Suppose my child, in a fit of anger, would throw a book or something on the floor. I tell him, "Pick it up," and instead of obeying what I say, he runs off and plays. "Pick it up!" He sees I am sincere, and he begins to look serious. "Pick it up, or I will get a rod" – and I put up my arm to get the rod. He stands still. "Pick it up, or you must be punished."

He comes slowly along to the place, and then begins to weep. "Pick it up, my child, or you will certainly be punished." Now he is in distress, and he sobs and sighs as if his heart would burst, but still remains as stubborn as if he knew I could not punish him. Now I begin to point out reasons for him to submit and obey, but there he stands, in agony, and at last bursts out, "Oh, father, I do feel so bad. I think I am growing better."

Now suppose a neighbor comes in and sees the child standing there in all this agony of stubbornness. The neighbor asks him what he is standing there for, and what he is doing. "Oh, I am using means to pick up that book." If this neighbor would tell the child, "Persevere, persevere, my boy. You will get it eventually," what should I do? I would turn him out of the house. What does he mean by encouraging my child in his rebellion?

God now calls the sinner to repent. He threatens him, He draws the glittering sword, He persuades him, He uses motives; and the sinner is distressed to agony, for he sees himself driven to the dreadful alternative of giving up his sins or going to hell. He should instantly lay down his weapons and break his heart at once. But he resists and struggles against conviction, and that creates his distress. Will you tell him to persevere? Persevere in what? In struggling against God? That is just the instruction the devil would give. All the devil wants is to see him persevere in just the way he is going on, and his destruction is sure. Satan may go to sleep.

d) Telling the sinner to press forward. That is, saying, "You are in a good way; only press forward, and you will get to heaven." This is on the supposition that his face is toward heaven, when in fact his face is toward hell, and he is pressing forward, and never more rapidly than now while he is resisting the Holy Spirit. I have often heard this direction given when the sinner was in as bad a way as he could be. What you should tell him is, "Stop, sinner, stop! Do not take another step that way, for it leads to hell." God tells him to stop, and because he does not want to stop, he is distressed. Now why would you attempt to comfort him in this way?

e) Tell a sinner that he must try to repent and give his heart to God. "Oh, yes," says the sinner, "I am willing to try. I have often tried to do it, and I will try again." Does God tell you to try to repent? All the world would be willing to try to repent – in their way. Giving this advice implies that it is very difficult to repent, and perhaps impossible, and that the best thing a sinner can do is to try and see whether he can do it or not. What is this except substituting your own commandment in the place of God's? God requires nothing short of repentance and a holy heart. Anything short of that is comforting him in vain, *seeing in your answers there remaineth falsehood.*

f) To tell him to pray for repentance. "Oh yes, I will pray for repentance, if that is all. I was distressed because I thought God required me to repent, but if He will do it, I can wait." And so he feels relieved, and is quite comfortable.

g) To tell a sinner to pray for conviction, or pray for the Holy Spirit to show him his sins, or to labor to get more light on the subject of his guilt in order to increase his conviction. All this is just what the sinner wants because it lets him off from the pressure of present obligation. He wants just a little more time. Anything that will defer that present pressure of obligation to repent immediately is a relief. What does he need more conviction for? Does God give any such instruction to an unrepentant sinner? God takes it for granted that he has enough conviction already, and so he has. Do you say he cannot realize all his sins? If he can realize only one of them, let him repent of that one, and he is a Christian. Suppose he could see them all; what reason is there to think he would repent of them all any more than that he would repent of that one that he does see? All this is comforting the sinner by setting him to do that which he can do and will not submit his heart to God.

11. Another way in which false comfort is given to anxious sinners is to tell them that God is trying their faith by keeping them in the furnace, and that they must wait patiently upon the Lord – as if God was at fault or stood in the way of his being a Christian – or as if an unrepentant sinner had faith! What an abomination! Suppose somebody would tell my child, while he was standing by the book as I have described, "Wait patiently, boy; your father is trying your faith." No! The sinner is trying the patience and forbearance of God. God is not setting Himself to torture a sinner and teach him a lesson of patience, but He is waiting upon him and laboring to bring him at once into such a state of mind as will render it consistent to fill his soul with the peace of heaven. Will the sinner be encouraged to resist by the idea that God is bantering? Take care. God has said that His Spirit will not always strive (Genesis 6:3).

12. Another false comfort is telling a sinner, "Do your duty, and leave your conversion with God." I once heard an elder of a church say to an anxious sinner, "Do your duty, and leave your conversion to God. He will do it in His own time and way." That was just the same as telling him that it was not his duty to be converted now. He did not say, "Do your duty, and leave your salvation with God." That would have been proper enough, for it would have been simply telling him to submit to God, and would have included conversion as the first duty of all. But he told him to leave his conversion to God. And this elder who gave such advice was a man of broad education too. How absurd – as if he could do his duty and not be converted! As if God was going to convert a sinner and let the sinner sit calmly under it in the use of means. Horrible! No. God has required him to make him a new heart, and beware how you comfort him with an answer of falsehood.

13. Sometimes professing Christians will try to comfort a sinner by telling him, "Do not be discouraged. I was a long time in this way before I found comfort." They will tell him, "I was under conviction so many weeks, or perhaps so many months, or sometimes years, and have gone through with all this, and I know just how you feel. Your experience is precisely the same as mine, and after so long a time I found relief. I do not doubt you will find it eventually. Do not despair. God will comfort you soon."

Tell a sinner to take courage in his rebellion! How horrible! Such professing Christians should be ashamed. Suppose you were under conviction so many weeks, and afterward found relief. It is the very last thing you should tell to an anxious sinner. What is it but encouraging him to hold on, when his business is to submit. Did you hold out so many weeks while the Spirit was striving with you? You only deserved so much the more to be damned for your obstinacy and foolishness. Sinner! It is no sign that God will spare you so long, or that His Spirit will remain with you to be resisted. And remember, if the Spirit is taken away, you will be sent to hell.

14. "I have faith to believe you will be converted." You have faith to believe! On what does your faith rest? On the promise of God? On

the influences of the Holy Spirit? Then you are counteracting your own faith. The very purpose and object of the Spirit of God is to tear away from the sinner his last vestige of hope while remaining in sin, to annihilate every stone and twig he may cling to. And the purpose of your instruction should be the same. You should fall in with the plan of God. It is only in this way that you can ever do any good – by crowding him right up to the work to submit at once and leave his soul in the hands of God. But when one whom he thinks is a Christian tells him, "I have faith to believe you will be converted," it upholds him in his false expectation. Instead of tearing him away from his false hope and throwing him upon Christ, you just turn him away to depend upon your faith, and to find comfort because you have faith for him. This is all false comfort that works death.

15. "I will pray for you." Sometimes professing Christians try to comfort an anxious sinner in this way, by telling him, "I will pray for you." This is false comfort, for it leads the sinner to trust in those prayers instead of trusting in Christ. The sinner says, "He is a good man, and God hears the prayers of good men. No doubt his prayers will prevail some time, and I will be converted. I do not think I will be lost." And his anxiety, his agony, is all gone. A woman said to a minister, "I have no hope now, but I have faith in your prayers." This is just such faith as the devil wants them to have – faith in prayers instead of faith in Christ.

16. "I rejoice to see you in this way, and I hope you will be faithful and hold out." What is that but rejoicing to see him in rebellion against God? That is precisely the ground on which he stands. He is resisting conviction, resisting conscience, and resisting the Holy Spirit, yet you rejoice to see him in this way and hope he will be faithful and hold out. There is a sense, indeed, in which it may be said that his situation is more hopeful than when he was in ignorance, for God has convinced him, and may succeed in turning and subduing him. But that is not the sense in which the sinner himself will understand it. He will suppose that you think him in a hopeful way because he is doing better than before, when his guilt and danger are, in fact, greater than they ever were before. Instead of rejoicing, you should be distressed and in

agony to see him resisting the Holy Spirit, for every moment he does this, he is in danger of being left by God and given up to hardness of heart and to despair.

17. "You will have your reward for this. Eventually, God will reward you." Yes, sinners, God will reward you. If you continue in this way, He will put you in the fires of hell. Reward for all this distress! Yes, if you are ever rewarded for it, it will be in hell. I once heard a sinner say, "I feel very bad, for I have strong hopes that I will get my reward." But that individual afterward said, "Nowhere can there be found so dark a sinner as I am, and no sin of my life seems so dark and damning as that expression." He was overwhelmed with remorse that he would ever have had such an idea as to think God would reward him for suffering so much distress when he brought it all upon himself, needlessly, by his wicked resistance to the truth. The truth is that what such people want is to comfort the sinner, and being all in the dark themselves on the subject of Christianity, they of course give him false comfort.

18. Another false comfort is to tell the sinner that he has not repented enough. The truth is that he has not repented at all. God always comforts the sinner as soon as he repents. This direction implies that his feelings are right as far as they go. To imply that he has any repentance is to tell him a lie and to cheat him out of his soul.

19. People sometimes comfort a sinner by telling him, "If you are elect, you will be brought in." I once heard of a case where a person under great distress of mind was sent to converse with a neighboring minister. They talked for a long while. As the person went away, the minister said to him, "I would like to write a letter to your father for you to give to him." His father was a pious man. The minister wrote the letter, but forgot to seal it. As the sinner was going home, he saw that the letter was not sealed, and he thought to himself that the minister had probably written about him. His curiosity at last led him to open and read it.

There he found it written something like this: "Dear sir. I find your son under conviction and in great distress, and it seems not easy to say anything to give him relief. But if he is one of the elect, he will surely be brought in." He wanted to say something to comfort the father. But now, notice, that the letter had very nearly ruined his soul. He settled down on the doctrine of election. He said, "If I am elect, I will be brought in," and his conviction was all gone. Years afterward he was awakened and converted, but only after a great struggle, and never until that false impression was obliterated from his mind and he was made to see that he had nothing at all to do with the doctrine of election, but that if he did not repent, he would be damned.

20. It is very common for some people to tell an awakened sinner, "You are in a very prosperous way. I am glad to see you so, and feel encouraged about you." It sometimes seems as if the church was in league with the devil to help sinners resist the Holy Spirit. The thing that the Holy Spirit wants to make the sinner feel is that all his ways are wrong and that they lead to hell, and everybody is conspiring to make the opposite impression. The Spirit is trying to discourage him, and they are trying to encourage him. The Spirit wants to disturb him by showing him he is all wrong, and they try to comfort him by saying he is doing well. Has it come to this, that the worst counteraction to the truth, and the greatest obstacle to the Spirit, will spring from the church? Sinner, do not believe any such thing! You are not in a hopeful way. You are not doing well, but poorly – as poorly as you can do while you are resisting the Holy Spirit.

21. Another very fatal way in which false comfort is given to sinners is by applying certain Scripture promises to them that were intended only for saints. This is a grand device of the devil. It is much practiced by the Universalists, but Christians often do it too. For example:

a) *Blessed are they that mourn: for they shall be comforted* (Matthew 5:4). How often this passage has been applied to anxious sinners who were in distress because they would not submit to God: *Blessed are they that mourn*. Indeed! That is true, where they mourn with godly sorrow, but what is this sinner mourning about? He is mourning because God's law is holy and His terms of salvation are so fixed that he cannot bring them down to his mind. Yet some tell such a rebel, *Blessed are they that mourn*! You might just as well apply it to those who are in hell. There is mourning there too. The sinner is mourning because there is no other way of salvation, because God is so holy that He requires him to give up all his sins, and he feels that the time has come that he must either give them up or be damned. Will we tell him that he will be comforted? Go and tell the devil, "Poor devil, you mourn now, but the Bible says you are blessed if you mourn, and you will be comforted sooner or later."

b) *Seek, and ye shall find* (Matthew 7:7). This is said to sinners in such a way as to imply that the anxious sinner is seeking Christ. This promise was made in reference to Christians who ask in faith and seek to do the will of God, and is not applicable to those who are seeking hope or comfort, but to holy seeking. To apply it to an unrepentant sinner is only to deceive him, for his seeking is not of this character. To tell him, "You are seeking, are you? Well, seek, and you will find," is to cherish a fatal delusion. While he remains unrepentant, he does not have a desire that the devil might not have, and still remain a devil.

If he had desire to do his duty, if he was seeking to do the will of God and give up his sins, he would be a Christian. But to comfort an unrepentant sinner with such a promise – you might just as well comfort Satan.

c) *Let us not be weary in well doing: for in due season we shall reap, if we faint not* (Galatians 6:9). To apply this to a sinner for comfort is absurd, as if he was doing something to please God. He has never done well, and has never done more poorly than now. Suppose my neighbor, who came in while I was trying to correct my child, would say to the child, "In due time you will reap, if you faint not." What should I say? "Reap, yes, you will reap. If you do not give up your obstinacy, you will reap indeed, for I will apply the rod." So the struggling sinner will reap the damnation of hell if he does not give up his sins.

22. Some professing Christians, when attempting to converse with awakened sinners, are very fond of saying, "I will tell you my experience." This is a dangerous snare, and often gives the devil a handle to lead him to hell by trying to copy your experience. If you tell it to him, and he thinks it is a Christian experience, he will almost infallibly be trying to imitate it; and instead of following the gospel or the leadings of the Spirit in his own soul, he is following your example. This is

absurd as well as dangerous. He will never have just the same feelings as you had. No two people's experiences were ever exactly the same. People's experiences are as much unlike as their countenances. Such a course is very likely to mislead him. The intent is often nothing but to encourage him at the very point where he should not be encouraged – before he has submitted to God. It is calculated to impede the work of God in his soul.

23. How many times will people tell an awakened sinner that God has begun a good work in him, and that He will carry it on? I have known parents talk so with their children, and as soon as they saw their children awakened, give up all former concern about them and settle down at their ease, thinking that now God had begun a good work in their children, and He would carry it on.

It would be just as rational for a farmer to say so about his grain, and as soon as it comes up out of the ground, say, "Well, God has begun a good work in my field, and He will carry it on." What would be thought of a farmer who would neglect to put up his fence because God had begun the work of giving him a crop of grain? If you tell a sinner so, and he believes you, it will certainly be his destruction, for it will prevent his doing that which is absolutely indispensable to his being saved. If, as soon as the sinner is awakened, he is taught that now God has begun a good work that only needs to be carried on, and that God will surely carry it on, he sees that he has no further reason to be anxious, for, in fact, he has nothing more to do. And so he will be relieved from that intolerable pressure of his present obligation to repent and submit to God. And if he is relieved from his sense of obligation to do it, he will never do it.

24. Some people will tell the sinner, "Well, you have turned away from your sins, have you?" "Oh, yes," says the sinner – when it is all false. He has never forsaken his sins for a moment. He has only exchanged one form of sin for another. He has only placed himself in a new attitude of resistance. And to tell him that he has left his sins is to give him false comfort.

25. Sometimes this direction is given for the purpose of relieving the agony of an anxious sinner. "Do what you can, and God will do the rest," or "Do what you can, and God will help you." This is the same as telling a sinner, "You cannot do what God requires you to do, but if you will do what you can, God will help you as to the rest." Sinners often get the idea that they have done all they can, when in fact, they have done nothing at all except to resist God with all their might. I have often heard them say, "I have done all I can, and I get no relief. What more can I do?" You can see how comforting it must be to such a person to have a professing Christian come in and say, "If you will do what you can, God will help you with the rest." It relieves all his deep distress at once. He may be uneasy and unhappy, but his agony is gone.

26. Others may say, "You should be thankful for what you have, and hope for more." If the sinner is convicted, they tell him he should be thankful for conviction, and hope for conversion. If he has any feeling, they say that he should be thankful for what feeling he has, just as if his feeling was religious feeling, when he has no more religion than Satan. He has reason to be thankful, indeed. He should be thankful that he is out of hell, and thankful that God is still waiting for him. But it is ridiculous to tell him that he should be thankful in regard to the state of his mind when he is all the while resisting his Maker with all his might.

Errors in Praying for Sinners

I will mention here a few errors in praying for sinners in their presence, by which an unhappy impression is made on their minds, in consequence of which they often obtain false comfort in their distress.

1. People sometimes pray for sinners as if they deserved to be pitied more than blamed. They pray for them as mourners. "Lord help these downhearted mourners," as if they were just mourning, like one who had lost a friend or had met some other calamity, and they could not help it and were very sad about it, but death would come, and so they were greatly to be pitied as they were sitting there, sad, downhearted, and sighing. The Bible never talks in this way. It pities sinners, but it

pities them as foolish and guilty rebels – guilty and deserving to go to hell – not as poor sad mourners who cannot help it, who want to be relieved, but can do nothing except sit and mourn.

2. Praying for them as poor sinners. Does the Bible ever use any such language as this? The Bible never speaks of them as "poor sinners," as if they deserved to be pitied more than blamed. Christ pities sinners in His heart, and so does God pity them. He feels in His heart all the outflow of compassion for them when He sees them going on, obstinate and willful in gratifying their own lusts at the peril of His eternal wrath. However, He never lets an expression escape from Him as if the sinner was just a "poor creature" to be pitied, as if he could not help it. The idea that he is poor rather than wicked, or unfortunate rather than guilty, relieves the sinner greatly.

I have seen the sinner writhe with agony under the truth in a meeting, until somebody began to pray for him as a poor creature. Then he would gush out into tears and weep profusely, and think he was greatly benefited by such a prayer. "Oh, what a good prayer that was!" If you go now and talk with that sinner, you will find that he is pitying himself as a poor unfortunate creature, perhaps weeping over his unhappy condition, but his convictions of sin, his deep impressions of dreadful guilt, are all gone.

3. Praying that God would help the sinner to repent. "O Lord, enable this poor sinner to repent now." This conveys the idea to the sinner's mind that he is now trying with all his might to repent, and that he cannot do it, and therefore Christians are calling on God to help him and to enable him to do it. Most professing Christians pray for sinners, not that God would make them willing to repent, but that He would enable them or make them able. It is no wonder that their prayers are not heard. They relieve the sinner of his sense of responsibility, and that relieves his distress. But it is an insult to God, as if God had commanded a sinner to do what he could not do.

4. People sometimes pray: "Lord, these sinners are seeking You, sorrowing." This language is an allusion to what took place at the time when

Jesus was a little boy and went into the temple to talk with the rabbis and doctors. His parents, you remember, went a day's journey toward home before they missed Him, and then they turned back. After looking all around, they found the little Jesus standing in the temple and disputing with the learned men, and his mother said to Him, *Son, why hast thou thus dealt with us? Behold, thy father and I have sought thee sorrowing* (Luke 2:48).

So this prayer represents sinners as seeking Jesus, and He hides Himself from them. They look all around, and hunt, and try to find Him, and wonder where Jesus is, and say, "Lord, we have sought Jesus these three days sorrowing." It is a lie. No sinner ever sought Jesus with all his heart three days, or three minutes, and could not find Him. There Jesus stands at His door and knocks. There He is right before him pleading with him, and facing him down with all his false pretenses. Seeking Him! The sinner may whine and cry, "Oh, how I am sorrowing and seeking Jesus." It is no such thing; Jesus is seeking you. Yet how many oppressed consciences are relieved and comforted by hearing one of these prayers.

5. "Lord, have mercy on these sinners, who are seeking to know Your love." This is a favorite expression with many, as if sinners were seeking to know the love of Christ and could not. There is no such thing. They are not seeking the love of Christ, but are seeking to get to heaven without Jesus Christ. They speak as if they were seeking it, and He was so hard-hearted that He would not let them have it.

6. "Lord, have mercy on these penitent souls," calling anxious sinners penitent souls. If they are penitent, or repentant, they are Christians. To make an impression on an unconverted sinner that he is repentant is to make him believe a lie. However, it is very comforting to the sinner, and he likes to take it up and pray it over again: "O Lord, I am a poor penitent soul. I am very penitent. I am so distressed. Lord, have mercy on a poor penitent." What a dreadful delusion!

7. Sometimes people pray for anxious sinners as humble souls. "O Lord, these sinners have humbled themselves." That is not true; they

have not humbled themselves. If they had, the Lord would have raised them up and comforted them, as He has promised. There is a hymn of this character that has done great mischief. It begins, "Come, humble sinner, in whose breast a thousand thoughts revolve."

This hymn was once given by a minister to an awakened sinner, as one applicable to his case. He began to read, "Come, humble sinner." He stopped. "Humble sinner – that is not applicable to me. I am not a humble sinner." Ah, how good it was for him that the Holy Spirit had taught him better than the hymn. If the hymn had said, Come anxious sinner, or guilty sinner, or trembling sinner, it would have been good enough, but to call him a humble sinner would not do. There are a vast many hymns of the same character. It is very common to find sinners quoting the false sentiments of some hymn in order to excuse themselves in rebellion against God.

A minister told me he heard a prayer recently in these words: "O Lord, these sinners have humbled themselves, and they come to You as well as they know how. If they knew any better, they would do better, but Lord, as they have come to You in the best manner they can, we pray that You will accept them and show mercy." Horrible!

8. Many people pray, "Father, forgive them; for they know not what they do." This is the prayer that Christ made for His murderers (Luke 23:34), and in that case, it was true. They did not know what they were doing, for they did not believe that Jesus Christ was the Messiah. But it cannot be said of sinners under the gospel that they do not know what they are doing. They do know what they are doing. They do not see the full extent of it, but they do know that they are sinning against God and rejecting Christ, and the difficulty is that they are unwilling to submit to God. But such a prayer is intended to make him feel relieved and to make him say, "Lord, how can You blame me so? I am a poor ignorant creature. I do not know how to do what is required of me. If I knew how, I would do it."

9. Another expression is, "Lord, direct these sinners, who are inquiring the way to Zion with their faces looking toward that place." However, this language is only applicable to Christians. Sinners do not have their

faces toward Zion; their faces are set toward hell. How can a sinner be said to be inquiring the way to Zion when he has no inclination to go there? The real difficulty is that he is unwilling to walk in the way in which he knows he should go.

10. People pray that sinners may have more conviction, or they pray that sinners may go home solemn and tender and take the subject into consideration – instead of praying that they may repent now. Or they pray as if they supposed the sinner was willing to do what is required. All such prayers are just such prayers as the devil wants. He wants to have such prayers, and I dare say he does not care how many such prayers are offered.

Sometimes I have seen the following in an anxious meeting, or when sinners have been called to the anxious seats. The minister has made the way of salvation plain to them, has taken away all the stumbling blocks out of their path, and has removed the darkness of their minds on the various points. When they are just ready to yield, someone will be called on to pray, and instead of praying that they may repent now, he begins to pray, "O Lord, we pray that these sinners may be solemn, that they may have a deep sense of their sinfulness, that they may go home impressed with their lost condition, that they may attempt nothing in their own strength, that they may not lose their convictions, and that, in Your own time and way, they may be brought out into the glorious light and liberty of the sons of God."

Instead of bringing them right up to the point of immediate submission on the spot, it gives them time to breathe. It lets off all the pressure of conviction, and he breathes freely again and feels relieved, and sits down at his ease. Thus, when the sinner is brought up, as it were, and stands at the gate of heaven, such a prayer, instead of pushing him in, pushes him away back again, as if they are told, "There, poor thing. Sit there until God helps you."

11. Christians sometimes pray in such a manner as to make the impression that Christ is the sinner's friend, in a different sense from what God the Father is. They pray to Him, "O, You friend of sinners," as if God was full of wrath and stern vengeance, just going to crush the poor

wretch, until Jesus Christ comes in and takes his side and delivers him. Now this is all wrong. The Father and the Son are perfectly agreed. Their feelings are the same, and both are equally willing to have sinners saved. To make such an impression as described, though, deceives the sinner and leads to wrong feelings toward God. To represent God the Father as standing over him with the sword of justice in His hand, eager to strike the blow until Christ intervenes, is not true. The Father is as much the sinner's friend as the Son. His compassion is equal. But if the sinner gets this unfavorable idea of God the Father, how is he ever to love Him with all his heart so as to say, "Abba, Father"?

12. The impression is often made by the manner of praying that you do not expect sinners to repent now, or that you expect God to do their duty for them, or that you want to encourage them to trust in your prayers – and so sinners are ruined. Never pray so as to make the impression on sinners that you secretly hope they are Christians already, or that you feel a strong confidence they will be eventually, or that you half believe they are converted now. This is always regrettable. Multitudes are deceived with false comfort in this way, and are prevented, just at the critical point, from making the final surrender of themselves to God.

Brethren, I find this field so broad that I cannot possibly mention all I wanted to say. There are many other things that I intended to touch upon, but the time is too far gone.

Remarks

1. Many people who deal in this way with anxious sinners do it from false pity. They feel so much sympathy and compassion that they cannot bear to tell them the truth that is necessary to save them. When a surgeon sees that a man's arm must be amputated or he will die, he might just as well indulge this feeling of false pity, and just put on a bandage and give him a sedative. There is no benevolence in that. True benevolence would lead the surgeon to hide his feelings, to be cool and calm, and with a sharp knife, cut the limb off and save the life. It is false tenderness to do anything short of that.

I once saw a woman under distress of mind who had been nearly driven to despair for months. Her friends had tried all these false comforts without effect, and they brought her to see a minister. The woman was emaciated and worn out with agony. The minister set his eye upon her, poured in the truth upon her mind, and rebuked her in a most direct manner. The woman who was with her interfered. She thought it was cruel, and said, "Oh, please comfort her. She is so distressed. Do not trouble her anymore. She cannot bear it." He turned, rebuked her, sent her away, and then poured in the truth upon the anxious sinner like fire; and in five minutes she was converted and went home full of joy. The plain truth swept all her false beliefs away, and in a few moments she was joyful in God.

2. This treatment of administering false comfort to anxious sinners is, in fact, cruelty. It is as cruel as the grave, as cruel as hell, for it is calculated to send the sinner down to its burning abyss. Christians feel compassion for those who are anxious, and so they should – but the last thing they should do is to flinch right at the point where it comes to a crisis. They should feel compassion, but they should show it just as the surgeon does when he deliberately goes to work in the right and best way and cuts off the man's arm, and thus cures him and saves his life.

In the same way, Christians should let the sinner see their compassion and tenderness, but they should take God's part fully and decidedly. They should lay open to the sinner the worst of his case, expose his sin and danger, and then lead him right up to the cross and insist on instant submission. They must have firmness enough to do this work thoroughly, and if they see the sinner distressed and in agony, still they must press him right on and not give way in the least, no matter how much he may be in agony, but still press on until he yields.

To do this often requires nerve. I have often been placed in circumstances to know this by experience. I have found myself surrounded by anxious sinners who were in such distress as to make every nerve tremble – some overcome with emotion and lying on the floor, some applying camphor to prevent their fainting, and others shrieking out as if they were just going to hell. Now suppose anyone would give false comfort in such a case as this. Suppose he did not have nerve enough to bring them right up to the point of instant and absolute submission. How unfit is such a person to be trusted in a case like this!

3. Sometimes sinners become deranged through despair and anguish of mind. Where this is the case, it is almost always because those who deal with them try to encourage them with false comfort, and thus lead them to such a conflict with the Holy Spirit. They try to hold them up while God is trying to break them down. Eventually, the sinner's mind gets confused with this contrast of influences, and he either becomes deranged or is driven to despair.

4. If you are going to deal with sinners, remember that you are soon to meet them in judgment; be sure to treat them in such a way that if they are lost, it will be their own fault. Do not try to comfort them with false ideas now, and have them reproach you with it then. It is better to suppress your false sympathy and let the simple truth cleave them asunder, joints and marrow, than to sooth them with false comfort and mislead them away from God.

5. Sinner, if you talk with any Christians and they tell you to do anything, first ask, "If I do that, will I be saved?" You may be anxious and not be saved. You may pray and not be saved. You may read your Bible and not be saved. You may use means, in your own way, and not be saved. Whatever they tell you to do, if you can do it and not be saved, do not pay attention to such instructions. They are intended to give you false comfort and divert your attention away from the main thing to be done, and mislead you down to hell. Do not follow any such instructions lest you would die while doing it, and then there is no more opportunity.

Finally, never tell a sinner anything, or give him any advice, that will lead him to stop short, or that does not include absolute submission to God. To let him stop at any point short of this is infinitely dangerous. Suppose you are at an anxious meeting, or a prayer meeting, and tell a sinner to pray or to read a book, or anything short of saving repentance, and he would fall and break his neck that night; of whom would his blood be required?

A youth in New England once met a minister in the street and asked him what he should do to be saved. The minister told him to go home and go into his room, and then kneel down and give his heart to God. "Oh, sir," said the boy, "I feel so bad that I am afraid I will not live to get home."

The minister saw his error and felt the rebuke, thus unconsciously given by a child, and he told him, "Well, then, give your heart to God here, and go home to your room and tell Him of it."

It is enough to make one's heart bleed to see so many miserable comforters for anxious sinners in whose answers there remains false-hood. What a vast amount of spiritual quackery there is in the world, and how many *forgers of lies* there are, *physicians of no value* (Job 13:4), who know no better than to comfort sinners with false hopes and delude them with their *old wives' fables* (1 Timothy 4:7) and nonsense, or who give way to false tenderness and sympathy, until they do not have enough firmness to see the sword of the Spirit applied to cut men to the soul and lay open the sinner's bare heart. It is sad that so many are ever put into the ministry who do not have enough skill to stand by and see the Spirit of God do His work in breaking up the old founda-tions, crushing all the rotten hopes of a sinner, and breaking him all down at the feet of Jesus.

Lecture 18

Instructions to Sinners

What must I do to be saved?
—Acts 16:30

These are the words of the jailor at Philippi, the question that he asked Paul and Silas, who were then under his care as prisoners. Satan had, in many ways, opposed these servants of God in their work of preaching the gospel, and had been as often defeated and disgraced. But here, at Philippi, he devised a new and peculiar project for frustrating their labors. There was a certain woman at Philippi who was *possessed with a spirit of divination* – or in other words, the spirit of the devil – and *brought her masters much gain by soothsaying* (Acts 16:16). The devil set this woman to follow Paul and Silas about the streets, and as soon as they had begun to gain the attention of the people, she would come in and cry, *These men are the servants of the most high God, which show unto us the way of salvation* (Acts 16:17). That is, she undertook to second the exhortations of the preachers, and added her testimony, as if to give additional weight to their instructions.

The effect of it was just what Satan desired. The people all knew that this was a wicked, corrupt woman, and when they heard her attempting to recommend this new preaching, they were disgusted, and concluded it was all the same. The devil knew that it would not do him any good, but would help their cause, to set such a person to oppose the preaching of the apostles, or to speak against it. The time had passed for that to succeed, and therefore he came around the other way and took the opposite ground, and by setting her to praise them as the servants of God and to bear her polluted testimony in favor of their instructions, he led people to suppose the apostles were of the same character with her, and had the same spirit that she had, and thus all their efforts were defeated.

Paul saw that if things continued in this way, he would be totally thwarted and would never succeed in establishing a church at Philippi. So he turned around to her and commanded the evil spirit, in the name of Jesus Christ, to come out of her. *When her masters saw that the hope of their gains was gone* (Acts 16:19), they raised a great persecution, caught Paul and Silas, and made a great fuss. They brought them before the magistrates and raised such a clamor that the magistrates locked them up in prison and *made their feet fast in the stocks* (Acts 16:24).

Thus, they thought they had put down the excitement. But at midnight, Paul and Silas prayed and sang praises, and the prisoners heard them. This old prison that had so long echoed to the voice of blasphemy and oaths now resounded with the praises of God; and these walls that had stood so firm now trembled under the power of prayer. The stocks were unloosed, the gates were thrown open, and everyone's bands were broken. The jailor was awakened from his sleep, and he saw the prison doors open. He knew that if the prisoners had escaped, he must pay for it with his life. He drew his sword and was about to kill himself, but Paul, who had no thought of escaping covertly, cried out to him instantly, *Do thyself no harm: for we are all here* (Acts 16:28). The jailer called for a light, rushed in, and entered trembling. He fell down before his prisoners, Paul and Silas, and brought them out and asked, *Sirs, what must I do to be saved?* (Acts 16:30).

In my last lecture, I spent much time on the false instructions given to sinners under conviction, the false comforts too often administered, and the erroneous instructions that such people receive. It is my intent now to show what instructions should be given to anxious sinners for their timely and effectual conversion. In other words, I want to explain to you what answer should be given to those who ask, *What must I do to be saved?* In doing so, I intend to show the following:

I.   What are not proper instructions to be given to sinners when they ask the question in the text.

II. What is a proper answer to the question.

III. Several errors that anxious sinners tend to fall into.

I. What Are Not Proper Directions to Be Given to Anxious Sinners

No more important question was ever asked than this: *What must I do to be saved?* Mankind is apt enough to ask, "What will I eat, and what will I drink?" Those questions may be answered in various ways with little danger. But when a sinner sincerely asks, *What must I do to be saved?* it is of infinite importance for him to receive the right answer. It is my desire now to tell you professing Christians what to answer to this question, and to tell you, who are sinners, what you must do to be saved.

1. No advice should be given to a sinner that will leave him still in the gall of bitterness and the bonds of iniquity (Acts 8:23). No answer is proper to be given with which, if he complies, he would not go to heaven if he would die the next moment.

2. No advice should be given that does not include a change of heart, a right heart, or wholehearted obedience to Christ. In other words, nothing is proper that does not imply actually becoming a Christian. Any advice that falls short of this is of no use. It will not bring him any nearer to the kingdom. It will do no good, but will only lead him to defer the very thing that he must do in order to be saved. The sinner should be told plainly, at once, what he must do so that he will not die eternally, and he should be told nothing that does not include a right state of heart.

Whatever you may do, sinner, that does not include a right heart, is sin. Whether you read the Bible or not, it is sin as long as you remain in rebellion. Whether you go to a church meeting or stay away, whether you pray or not, it is nothing but rebellion every moment. It is surprising that a sinner would think that he is serving God when he prays and reads his Bible. If a rebel against this government would read the law book while he continues in rebellion, and has no intent to obey; if he would ask for pardon while he holds on to his weapons of resistance and warfare, would you think he is doing his country a service and placing them under obligations to show him favor? No, you would say that all his reading and pleading were only an insult to the majesty both of the lawgiver and the law.

So you, sinner, while you remain unrepentant, are insulting God and setting Him at defiance, whether you read His Word and pray or leave it alone. No matter what place or what attitude your body is in – on your knees or in the house of God – as long as your heart is not right, as long as you resist the Holy Spirit and reject Christ, you are a rebel against your Maker.

II. Proper Answers to the Question in the Text

What must I do to be saved? Generally, you may give the sinner any advice, or tell him to do anything, that includes a right heart; and if you cause him to understand it and do it, he will be saved. The Spirit of God, in striving with sinners, suits His strivings to the state of mind in which He finds them. His great purpose in striving with them is to dislodge them from their hiding places and bring them to submit to God at once. Now these objections and difficulties and states of mind are as various as the circumstances of mankind – as many as there are individuals. The characters of individuals provide an endless diversity. What is to be done with each one, and how he is to be converted, depends on his particular errors. It is necessary to ascertain his errors, to find out what he understands and what he needs to be taught more perfectly, to see what points the Spirit of God is pressing upon his conscience, and to press the same things and thus bring him to Christ. The most common directions are the following:

1. It is generally applicable, and a safe and suitable direction, to tell a sinner to repent. I say "generally," for sometimes the Spirit of God seems not so much to direct the sinner's attention to his own sins as to some other thing. In the days of the apostles, the minds of the people seem to have been agitated mainly on the question of whether Jesus was the

true Messiah. Therefore, the apostles directed much of their teaching to this point, to prove that He was the Christ. Whenever anxious sinners asked them what they must do, they most commonly exhorted them to *believe on the Lord Jesus Christ* (Acts 16:31).

They bore down on this point because this was where the Spirit of God was striving with them, and this was the subject that especially troubled people's minds. Consequently, this would probably be the first thing a person would do on submitting to God. It was the main point at issue between God and the Jew and Gentile of those days – whether Jesus Christ was the Son of God. It was the point in dispute. To bring a sinner to acknowledge the answer to this contended question was the most effective way to bring him to Christ.

At other times, it will be found that the Spirit of God is dealing with sinners primarily in reference to their own sins. Sometimes He deals with them in regard to a particular duty, such as prayer, or perhaps family prayer. The sinner will be found to be contesting that point with God, whether it is right for him to pray, or whether he should pray with his family. I have known remarkable cases of this kind in which the individual was struggling on this point, and as soon as he fell on his knees to pray, he surrendered his heart, showing that this was the very point that the Spirit of God was contesting, and the hinge on which his controversy with God all turned. That was conversion.

The guidance to repent is always proper, but will not always be effectual, for there may be some other thing that the sinner needs to be told also. And where it is the appropriate advice, sinners do not need only to be told to repent, but they also need to have it explained to them what repentance is. Since there has been so much mysticism, false philosophy, and false theology thrown around the subject, it has become necessary to tell sinners not only what you mean by repentance, but also to tell them what you do not mean. Words that used to be plain and easily understood have now become so distorted that they need to be explained to sinners or they will often convey a wrong impression to their minds.

This is the case with the word "repentance." Many people suppose that remorse, or a sense of guilt, is repentance. If so, then hell is full of repentance, for it is full of remorse, unutterable and eternal. Others feel regret that they have done a certain thing, and they call that repenting of it. But they only regret that they have sinned because of the consequences, and not because they abhor sin. This is not repentance. Other people suppose that convictions of sin and strong fears of hell are repentance. Others consider the censures of conscience as repentance. They say, "I never do anything wrong without repenting; I always feel sorry I did it." Still others regard repentance as a feeling of sorrow for sin.

However, repentance is not an involuntary feeling of any kind or degree. Sinners must be shown that all these things are not repentance. They are not only consistent with the utmost wickedness, for the devil might have them all, and doubtless has them all, and yet remains a devil. Repentance is a change of mind in regard to God and toward sin itself. It is not only a change of views, but it is a change of the ultimate preference or choice of the soul. It is a voluntary change, and by consequence involves a change of feeling and of action toward God and toward sin. It is what is naturally understood by a change of mind on any subject of interest and importance.

We hear that such a person has changed his mind on the subject of abolition, for example, or that he has changed his political views. Everybody understands that he has undergone a change in his views, his feelings, and his conduct. This is repentance on that subject. It is a change of mind, but not toward God. Evangelical repentance is a change of will, of feeling, and of life in respect to God.

Repentance always implies abhorrence of sin. It is willing and feeling as God does in respect to sin. Of course, it involves love for God and an abhorrence of sin. It always implies forsaking sin. Sinners should be made to understand this. The sinner who repents does not feel as unrepentant sinners think they should feel at giving up their sins if they would turn to Christ Jesus. Unrepentant sinners look upon Christianity just like this, that if they become pious, they will be required to stay away from balls and parties, and to give up theaters or gambling or other things that they now take delight in. They do not see how they could ever enjoy themselves if they would give up all those things. But this is very far from being a correct view of the matter.

Christianity does not make them unhappy by keeping them away from things in which they delight, because the first step in it is to repent, to change their mind in regard to all these things. They do not seem to realize that the person who has repented has no affection for these things. He has given them up and has turned his mind away from them. Sinners feel as if they would want to go to such places and take part in such things just as much as they do now, and that it will be such a continued sacrifice as to make them unhappy. This is a great mistake.

I know there are some professing Christians who would be very glad to take part in their former practices if they did not feel obligated by fear of losing their reputation or the like. However, if they feel this way, it is because they do not have true religion. They do not hate sin. If they desire their former ways, they have no true religion. They have never repented, for repentance always consists in a change of choice of views and feelings. If they were really converted, instead of choosing such things, they would turn away from them with contempt. Instead of lusting after the fleshpots of Egypt (Exodus 16:3) and desiring to go into their former circles, parties, entertainment, balls, and the like, they find their highest pleasure in obeying God.

2. Sinners should be told to believe the gospel. Here, also, they need to have it explained to them and to be told what is not faith and what is. Nothing is more common than for a sinner, when told to believe the gospel, to say, "I do believe it." The fact is that he has been brought up to admit the fact that the gospel is true, but he does not believe it. He knows nothing about the evidence of it, and all his faith is a mere admission without evidence. He holds it to be true, in a kind of loose, indefinite sense, so that he is always ready to say, "I do believe the Bible." It is strange that they do not see that they are deceived in thinking that they believe, for they must see that they have never acted upon these truths, as they do upon those things that they do believe. Yet it is often quite difficult to convince them that they do not believe.

But the fact is that the careless sinner does not believe the gospel at all. The idea that the careless sinner is an intellectual believer is absurd. The devil is an intellectual believer, and that is what makes him tremble. What makes a sinner troubled is that he begins to be an intellectual believer, and that makes him feel. No being in heaven, earth, or hell can intellectually believe the truths of the gospel and not feel on the subject. The anxious sinner has faith of the same kind with demons, but he does not have as much of it, and therefore, he does not feel as much. The person who does not feel or act at all on the subject of religion is an unbeliever, no matter what he professes to be. He who feels nothing and does nothing believes nothing. This is a philosophical fact.

Faith does not consist in an intellectual conviction that Christ died for you in particular, nor in a belief that you are a Christian, or that you ever will be, or that your sins are forgiven. Rather, faith is that trust or confidence in God, and in Christ, that commits the whole soul to Him in all His dealings with us. It is a voluntary trust in His person, His truth, and His Word.

This was the kind of faith that Abraham had. He had that confidence in what God said that led him to act as if it were true. This is the way the apostle illustrates it in Hebrews 11:1: *Faith is the substance of things hoped for, the evidence of things not seen.* He goes on to illustrate it by various examples. *Through faith we understand that the worlds were framed by the word of God* (Hebrews 11:3); that is, we believe this and act accordingly. Take the case of Noah. Noah was *warned of God of things not seen as yet* (Hebrews 11:7); that is, he was assured that God was going to drown the world, and he believed it and acted accordingly. He prepared an ark to save his family, and by doing so, he condemned the world that would not believe. His actions gave evidence that he was sincere.

Abraham, too, was called by God to leave his country, with the promise that he would gain by it, and he obeyed and went out without knowing where he should go (Hebrews 11:8). Read the whole chapter and you will find many instances of the same kind. The whole intent of the chapter is to illustrate the nature of faith and to show that it invariably results in action. The sinner should have it explained to him and should be made to see that the faith that the gospel requires is simply that confidence in Christ that leads him to act on what he says as a certain fact. This is believing in Christ.

3. Another proper instruction to be given to the sinner is that he should give his heart to God. God says, *My son, give me thine heart* (Proverbs 23:26). But here also there needs to be an explanation to help him understand what that means. It is amazing that there would be

any darkness here. It is the language of common life, in everybody's mouth, and everybody understands just what it means when we use it in regard to anything else. But when it comes to Christianity, they seem to be all in the dark.

Ask a sinner, no matter what his age and education are, what it means to give the heart to God, and as strange as it may seem, he is at a loss for an answer. However, if you ask a woman what it is to give her heart to her husband, or a man what it is to give his heart to his wife, they understand it; but then they are totally blind as to giving their hearts to God.

I suppose I have asked more than a thousand troubled sinners this question. When I have told them that they must give their hearts to God, they would always say they were willing to do it, and sometimes that they were anxious to do it. Some even seemed to be in an agony of desire about it. Then I have asked them what they understood it meant to give their hearts to God since they were so willing to do it. Very seldom have I received a correct or rational answer from a sinner of any age. I have sometimes had the strangest answers that can be imagined – anything except what they should say.

To give your heart to God is the same thing as to give your heart to anybody else – the same as for a woman to give her heart to her husband. Ask that woman if she understands this, and she will say, "Oh, yes, that is plain enough. It is to place my affections on him and to strive to please him in everything." Very well, then. Place your affections on God and strive to please Him in everything. But sadly, when they come to the subject of Christianity, people suppose there is some astonishing mystery about it. Some talk as if they supposed it was to take out this bundle of muscles or fleshy organ in their body and give it to God. Sinner, what God asks of you is for you to love Him supremely.

4. "Submit to God" is also proper instruction to anxious sinners. How ignorant sinners are here too! Scarcely a sinner can be found who will not tell you he is willing to submit to God – but they do not understand it. They need to be told what true submission is. Sometimes they think it means that they should be willing to be damned. Sometimes they place themselves in this attitude and call it submission. They say that

if they are part of the elect, they will be saved, and if not, they will be damned. This is not submission.

True submission is yielding obedience to God. Suppose a rebel, in arms against the government, was called on to submit. What would he understand by it? He would understand that he should acknowledge the point, lay down his arms, and obey the laws. That is just what it means for a sinner to submit to God. He must cease his strife and conflict against his Maker, and must take the attitude of a willing and obedient child, willing to be and do whatever God requires. *Here am I; Lord, what wilt thou have me to do?* (1 Samuel 3:4; Isaiah 6:8; Acts 9:6).

Suppose a company of soldiers had rebelled, and the government had an army to put them down and had driven them into a stronghold where they were out of provisions, had no way to escape, and did not know what to do. Suppose the rebels met together in this extremity to consider what to do, and one man stands up and says, "Well, comrades, I am convinced that we are all wrong from the beginning, and now the reward of our deeds is likely to overtake us. We cannot escape, and as for remaining here to die, I am resolved not to do it. I am going to throw myself on the mercy of the commander in chief."

That man submits. He ceases, from that moment, to be a rebel in his heart, just as soon as he comes to this conclusion. It is the same with the sinner when he acknowledges the point and consents in his heart to do and be whatever God will require. The sinner may be in doubt as to what to do, and may feel afraid to put himself in God's hands, thinking that if he does, perhaps God will send him down to hell as he deserves. But it is his business to leave all that question with God, and not resist his Maker any longer, but to give everything up to God, make no conditions, and trust it wholly to God's benevolence and wisdom to decide what will be done and to appoint his future condition. Until you do this, sinner, you have done nothing to the purpose.

5. Another proper instruction to be given to sinners is to confess and forsake your sins. This means that they should both confess and forsake them. They must confess to God their sins against God, and confess to men their sins against men, and forsake them all. A person does not forsake his sins until he has made all the restitution in his power. If he

has stolen money or defrauded his neighbor out of property, he does not forsake his sins by merely resolving not to steal anymore or not to cheat again, but he must make restitution to the full extent of his ability.

So if he has slandered anyone, he does not forsake his sin by merely saying he will not do so again. He must make things right.

In the same way, if he has robbed God, as all sinners have done, he must make restitution, as far as he has the ability to do so. Suppose a man has made money in rebellion against God, and has withheld from Him his time, talents, and service, has lived and rioted upon the bounties of His providence, and has refused to expend himself for the salvation of the world; he has robbed God. If he would die feeling that this money was his own, and if he would leave it to his heirs without consulting the will of God, he is just as certain to go to hell as the highway robber. He has never made any reparation to God. With all his whining and pious talk, he has never confessed his sin to God, nor forsaken his sin, for he has never felt nor acknowledged himself to be the steward of God. If he refuses to hold the property in his possession as the steward of God, if he considers it his own, and as such gives it to his children, he says, in effect, to God: "That property is not Yours, but it is mine, and I will give it to my children." He has continued to persevere in his sin, for he does not relinquish the ownership of that of which he has robbed God.

What would a merchant think if his hired clerk would take all the capital and set up a store of his own, and die with it in his hands? Will such a man go to heaven? "No," you will all say. "If such a man does not go to hell, there might just as well be no hell. God would prove Himself infinitely unjust to let such a character go unpunished." What, then, will we say of the person who has robbed God all his life? God set him to be His clerk, to manage some of His affairs, and he has gone and stolen all the money, and says it is his, and he keeps it, and dies, and gives it to his children as if it were all his own lawful property. Is that man going to heaven? Has that man forsaken sin? I tell you, no. If he has not surrendered himself and all to God, he has not taken the first step in the way to heaven.

6. Another proper instruction to be given to sinners is: *Choose you this day whom ye will serve* (Joshua 24:15). Under the Old Testament

dispensation, this, or something equivalent to it, was the most common instruction given. It was not common to call on people to believe in Christ until the days of John the Baptist. He baptized those who came to him, with the baptism of repentance, and directed them to believe on Him who would come after him. Under Joshua, the text was something that the people all understood more easily than they would a call to believe on the distant Messiah. It was: *Choose you this day whom ye will serve* (Joshua 24:15).

On another occasion, Moses said to them, *I call heaven and earth to record this day against you, that I have set before you life and death, blessing and cursing: therefore choose life, that both thou and thy seed may live* (Deuteronomy 30:19). The instruction was accommodated to the people's knowledge. It is as good now as it was then. Sinners are called upon to choose – what? They are to choose whether they will serve God or the world – whether they will follow holiness or sin. Let them be made to understand what is meant by choosing, and what is to be chosen, and then if the thing is done from the heart, they will be saved.

Any of these instructions, if complied with, will introduce true conversion. The particular exercises may vary in different cases. Sometimes the first exercise in conversion is submission to God. Sometimes it is repentance, sometimes faith, and sometimes it is the choice of God and His service. Basically, it is whatever their thoughts are taken up with at the time. If their thoughts are directed to Christ at the moment, the first exercise will be faith. If to sin, the first exercise will be repentance. If to their future course of life, it is choosing the service of God. If to the divine governance, it is submission. It is important to find out just where the Holy Spirit is pressing the sinner at the time, and then take care to push that point. If it is in regard to Christ, emphasize that. If it is in regard to his future course of life, push him right up to an immediate choice of obedience to God.

It is a great error to suppose that any one particular exercise is always foremost in conversion, or that every sinner must have faith first or submission first. It is not true, either in philosophy or in fact. There is a great variety in people's experiences. Whatever point is taken hold of between God and the sinner, when the sinner yields that, he is converted. Whatever the particular exercise may be, if it includes obedience of heart to God on any point, it is true conversion. When he yields one point to God's authority, he is ready to yield all. When he changes his mind and obeys in one thing because it is God's will, he will obey in other things, as far as he sees it to be God's will.

Where there is this right choice, then, whenever the mind is directed to any one point of duty, he is ready to follow. It matters very little which of these directions is given, if it is only made plain, and if it is to the point, so as to serve as a test of obedience to God. If it is to the point that the Spirit of God is debating with the sinner's mind so as to fall in with the Spirit's work, and not to divert the sinner's attention from the very point in controversy, let it be made perfectly clear, and then pressed until the sinner yields, and he will be saved.

III. Several Errors That Anxious Sinners Tend to Fall Into in Regard to This Important Question

1. The first error is in supposing that they must make themselves better, or prepare themselves, so as in some way to recommend themselves to the mercy of God. It is astonishing that sinners will not understand that all they have to do is to accept salvation from God, all prepared to their hands. But they all, learned or unlearned, at first pursue a legal course to get relief. This is one main reason why they will not become Christians at once, just as soon as they begin to attend to the subject. They imagine that they must be, in some way or other, prepared to come. They must change their clothing and make themselves look a little better; they are not willing to come just as they are in their rags and poverty. They must have something more on before they can approach God. They should be shown at once that it is impossible for them to be any better until they do what God requires. Every pulse that beats, every breath they draw, they are growing worse because they are standing out in rebellion against God as long as they do not do the very thing that God requires of them as the first thing to be done.

2. Another error is in supposing that they must suffer a considerable time under conviction, as a kind of punishment, before they are ready properly to come to Christ. And so they will pray for conviction. They

think that if they are crushed down to the earth with distress for a sufficient time, then God will pity them and be more ready to help them when He sees them so very miserable.

They should be made to understand clearly that they are unhappy and miserable simply because they refuse to accept the relief that God offers. Take the case of the stubborn child when his parent stands over him with the rod, and the child shudders and screams. Should that child imagine he is gaining anything by his agony? His distress arises from his conviction, and will he pray for more conviction? Does that make him any better? Does his father pity him any more because he cries out? Who does not see that he is all the while growing worse?

3. Sometimes sinners imagine that they must wait for different feelings before they submit to God. They say, "I do not think I feel right yet to accept Christ. I do not think I am prepared to be converted yet." They should be made to see that what God requires of them is to will right. If they obey and submit with the will, the feelings will adjust themselves in due time. It is not a question of feeling, but of will and action.

The feelings are involuntary and have no moral character except what they derive from the action of the will, with which action they sympathize. Before the will is right, the feelings will not be, of course. The sinner should come to Christ by accepting Him at once, and he must do this, not in obedience to his feelings, but in obedience to his conscience. Obey, submit, and trust. Give up all instantly, and your feelings will come right. Do not wait for better feelings, but commit your whole being to God at once, and this will soon result in the feelings for which you are waiting. What God requires of you is the present act of your own mind in turning from sin to holiness and from the service of Satan to the service of the living God.

4. Another error of sinners is to suppose that they must wait until their hearts are changed. "What?" they say. "Am I to believe in Christ before my heart is changed? Do you mean that I am to repent before my heart is changed?" The simple answer to all this is that the change of heart is the very thing in question. God requires sinners to love Him. That is to change their heart. God requires the sinner to believe the gospel. That

is to change his heart. God requires him to repent. That is to change his heart. God does not tell him to wait until his heart is changed, and then repent and believe and love God. The very word itself, "repent," signifies a change of mind or heart. To do either of these things is to change your heart and to make you a new heart, just as God requires.

5. Sinners often get the idea that they are perfectly willing to do what God requires. Tell them to do this thing or that, to repent or believe or give God their hearts, and they say, "Oh, yes, I am perfectly willing to do that. I wish I could do it. I would give anything if I could do it." They should understand that being truly willing is doing it, but there is a difference between willing and desiring. People often desire to be Christians when they are wholly unwilling to be so. When we see anything that appears to us to be something good, we are so made that we desire it. We necessarily desire it when it is before our minds. We cannot help desiring it in proportion as its goodness is presented to our minds. Yet we may not be willing to have it under all the circumstances. It may be that we prefer, in general, that the present possessor should continue to possess it still. Or we may choose to have our friend or child possess it instead of ourselves. A person may desire to go to Philadelphia for many reasons, while for still more important reasons, he chooses not to go there.

In the same way, the sinner may desire to be a Christian. He may see many good things in being a Christian. He may see that if he were a Christian, he would be a great deal happier and that he would go to heaven when he dies, yet he is not willing to be a Christian. Willing to obey Christ is to be a Christian. When an individual actually chooses to obey God, he is a Christian. But all such desires that do not end in actual choice are nothing.

6. The sinner will sometimes say that he offers to give God his heart, but he suggests that God is unwilling. This is absurd. What does God ask? He asks you to love Him. For you to say that you are willing to give God your heart, but that God is unwilling, is the same as saying that you are willing to love God, but God is not willing to be loved by you, and will not permit you to love Him. It is important to clear up

all these points in the sinner's mind so that he may have no dark and mysterious corner to rest in where the truth will not reach him.

7. Sinners sometimes get the idea that they repent when they are only under conviction. Whenever the sinner is found resting in any lie, let the truth sweep it away, no matter how much it may pain and distress him. If he has any error of this kind, you must tear it away from him if you do not intend for him to stumble into the depths of hell.

8. Sinners are often completely taken up with looking at themselves to see if they can find something there – some kind of feeling or other that will recommend them to God. Evidently, for lack of proper instruction, David Brainerd was a long time taken up with this state of mind, looking for some feelings that would recommend him to God. Sometimes he imagined that he had such feelings, and he would tell God in prayer that now he felt as he should in order to receive His mercy. Then he would see that he had been all wrong and would be ashamed that he had told God that he felt right. Thus the poor man, for lack of correct instruction, was driven almost to despair, and it is easy to see that his Christian exercises through life were greatly modified, and his comfort and usefulness much impaired, by the false philosophy he had adopted on this point.

You must turn the sinner away from himself to something else. Suppose he keeps brooding over himself until he is in a state of despair. The proper course, then, is to turn away his attention from looking at himself, and make him look at some duty to be performed, or make him look at Christ – and perhaps, before he is aware, he will find that he has submitted to God. His attention was diverted away from himself in order to contemplate the reasonableness of God's requirements, the sufficiency of Christ's atonement, or something of this kind, and as he dwelled upon it, he just gave up his heart, and the agony was over.

Remarks

1. The labor of ministers is greatly increased, and the difficulties in the way of salvation are greatly multiplied, by the false instructions that

have been given to sinners. The consequence has been that advice that used to be plain is now obscure. People have been taught for so long that there is something awfully mysterious and unintelligible about conversion that they do not try to understand it. Sinners have been taught these false ideas until now they are everywhere entrenched behind these sentiments, such as "cannot repent," "must wait for God," and similar ideas.

It was once sufficient, as we learn from the Bible, to tell sinners to repent, or to tell them to believe on the Lord Jesus Christ. But now faith has been talked about as a principle instead of an act, and repentance as something put into the mind instead of an exercise of the mind – and sinners are perplexed. Ministers are accused of preaching heresy because they dare to teach that faith is an exercise and not a principle, and that sin is an act and not a part of the makeup of man that cannot be avoided. Sinners have become so sophisticated that you have to take much effort to explain not only what you do not mean, but also what you do mean; otherwise they will be almost sure to misunderstand you, and either gain a false relief from their anxiety by throwing their duty off upon God, or else run into despair from the supposed impracticability of doing what is required for their salvation.

It is often the greatest difficulty to lead them out of these theological labyrinths and mazes into which they have been misled, and to lead them along the straight and simple way of the gospel. It seems as if the greatest deceit had been used to mystify the minds of people and weave a most subtle web of false theology that was calculated to involve a sinner in endless darkness.

Who has been in revivals who has not encountered that endless line of foolish ideas that have been taught, until it has become necessary to be as plain as ABC, and the best educated have to be talked to just like children. So much has been done to confuse and mislead people's minds in the simplest matters. Tell a sinner to believe, and he turns around to you and stares and asks, "How do you talk like this? Is not faith a principle implanted in the soul, and how am I to believe until I get this principle?"

So if a minister tells a sinner the very words that the apostles used, in the great revival at the day of Pentecost, *Repent ye therefore, and be converted* (Acts 3:19), they reply as they have been taught: "Oh, I guess you are an Arminian. I do not want any of your Arminian teaching for me. Do you not deny the Spirit's influences?" It is enough to make humanity weep to see the fog and darkness that have been thrown around the plain directions of the gospel until many generations have been emptied into hell.

2. These false instructions to sinners are infinitely worse than none. The Lord Jesus Christ found it more difficult to get the people to give up their false ideas of theology than anything else. This has been the great difficulty with the Jews to this day – that they have received false ideas in theology and have corrupted the truth on certain points, and you cannot make them understand the plainest points of the gospel.

It is the same with sinners. The most difficult thing to be done is to get away from these refuges of lies that they have gotten from false theology. They are so fond of holding on to these refuges, because they are called orthodox and because they excuse the sinner and condemn God, that it is found to be the most troubling, difficult, and discouraging part of a minister's labor to drive them away.

3. It is no wonder that the gospel has taken so little effect since it has been interposed so much with these strange dogmas. The truth is that very little of the gospel has come out upon the world for these hundreds of years without being obstructed and obscured by false theology. People have been told that they must repent, and in the same breath they have been told that they could not repent – until the truth itself has been all mixed up with error so as to produce the same practical effect with error, and the gospel that is preached has been another gospel, or no gospel at all.

4. You can understand what is meant by healing slightly the hurt of the daughter of God's people (Jeremiah 8:11), and the danger of doing it. When sinners are under conviction, it is very easy to say something that will smooth over the case and relieve their anxiety so that they will either get a false hope or will be converted with their views so obscure that they will always be poor, feeble, wavering, doubting, inefficient Christians.

5. Much depends on the manner in which a person is dealt with when under conviction. Much of his future comfort and usefulness depends on the clearness, strength, and firmness with which the directions of the gospel are given when he is under conviction. If those who deal with him are afraid to deal with him thoroughly, he will always be a poor, sickly, doubting Christian. If converted at all, he will never do much good.

The proper way is to deal thoroughly and plainly with a sinner, to tear away every excuse he can produce, and to show him plainly what he is and what he should be, and he will bless God to all eternity that he fell in with those who would be so faithful to his soul. For the lack of this thorough and searching management, many are converted who seem to be stillborn. The reason is that they were never faithfully dealt with. We may graciously hope they are Christians, but still it is uncertain and doubtful. Their conversion seems to be rather a change of opinion than a change of heart. But if, when a sinner is under conviction, you pour in the truth, examine him, break up the old foundations, sweep away his refuges of lies, and use the Word of God like fire and like a hammer, you will find that they will come out with clear views, strong faith, and firm principles – not doubting, wavering, hesitant Christians, but those who follow the Lord wholly.

This is the way to make strong Christians. This has been eminently the case in many revivals of modern days. I have heard old Christians say of the converts, "These converts were born men and women, fully grown. They were never children, but have, at the very beginning, all the clearness of view and strength of faith of old Christians. They seem to understand the doctrines of Christianity and know what to do, how to take hold, and how to promote revivals better than one in a hundred of the old members in the church."

I once knew a young man who was converted away from home. The place where he lived had no minister, no preaching, and no religion. He went home three days after he was converted, and immediately set himself to work to labor for a revival. He set up meetings in his neighborhood, and he prayed and labored, and a revival broke out, of which he had the primary leadership through a powerful work that converted most of the principal people of the place.

The truth was that he had been so dealt with that he knew what he was about. He understood the subject and knew where he stood. He was not all the time troubled with doubts, whether he was himself a Christian. He knew that he was serving God and that God was with him, and so he went boldly and resolutely forward to his object.

However, if you try to make converts without cutting up all their errors and tearing away their false hopes, you may make a host of hypocrites, or of puny, immature Christians who are always doubting and are easily turned back from a revival spirit, and are worth nothing. The right way is to bring them right out to the light. When a person is converted in this way, you can depend on him and know where to find him.

6. Prolonged seasons of conviction are generally due to defective instruction. Wherever clear and faithful instructions are given to sinners, you will generally find that convictions are deep and powerful, but short.

7. Where clear and wise instructions are given to convicted sinners, if they do not soon submit, their convictions will generally leave them. Convictions in such cases are generally short. Where sinners are deceived by false views, they may be kept along for weeks, and perhaps months, and sometimes for years, in a languishing condition, and at last, perhaps, be crowded into the kingdom and saved.

But where the truth is made perfectly clear to the sinner's mind, and all his errors are torn away, if he does not soon submit, his case is hopeless. Where the truth is brought to bear upon his mind, and he directly resists the very truth that must convert him, there is nothing more to be done. The Spirit will soon leave him, for the very weapons He uses are resisted. Where instructions are not clear and are mixed up with errors, the Spirit may strive even for years, in great mercy, to get sinners through the fog of false instruction. But this is not the case where their duty is clearly explained to them and they are brought right up to the single point of immediate submission and have all their false pretenses exposed and the path of duty made perfectly plain. Then, if they do not submit, the Spirit of God forsakes them and their condition is nearly hopeless.

If there are sinners here now, and you see your duty clearly, take care how you delay. If you do not submit, you may expect the Spirit of God to forsake you, and you will remain lost.

8. A vast deal of the instruction given to troubled sinners amounts to little less than the Roman Catholic doctrine of indulgences. The pope used to sell indulgences for sin, and this led to the reformation under Martin Luther. Sometimes people would purchase an indulgence to sin for a certain time, or to commit some particular sin or a number of sins.

There is a vast deal in Protestant churches that is little less than the same thing. What does it differ from this to tell a sinner to wait? This is basically telling him to continue in sin a while longer while he is waiting for God to convert him. And what is that but an indulgence to commit sin? Any instruction given to sinners that does not require them to obey God immediately is an indulgence to sin. It is, in effect, giving them liberty to continue in sin against God. Such advice is not only wicked, but it is also ruinous and cruel. If they do not destroy the soul, as no doubt they often do, they defer, at all events, the sinner's enjoyment of God and of Christ, and he stands a great chance of being lost forever while listening to such instructions. Oh, how dangerous it is to give a sinner reason to think he may wait for a moment before giving his heart to God!

9. As far as I have had opportunity to observe, those conversions that are most sudden have commonly resulted in the best Christians. I know the reverse of this has often been held and maintained, but I am satisfied there is no reason for it, although multitudes, even now, regard it as suspicious if a person has been converted very suddenly. But the Bible gives no justification for this idea. There is not a case of prolonged conviction recorded in the whole Bible. All the conversions recorded there are sudden conversions. I am persuaded there never would have been such multitudes of tedious convictions, and often ending in nothing after all, if it had not been for those theological perversions that have filled the world with "cannot-ism."

In Bible days, they told sinners to repent, and they did it then. Cannot-ism had not been introduced in that day. It is this speculation about the inability of sinners to obey God that lays the foundation for all the prolonged anguish and distress, and perhaps ruin, through which so many are led. When a sinner is brought to see what he has to do, and he takes his stand at once and does it, he generally does so afterward, and you generally find that such a person will hold out so and prove to be a resolute Christian.

You will not find him to be one of those whom you always have to oversee in duty, like a ship that is tied up against wind and tide. Look at those professing Christians who always have to be dragged forward in duty, and you will generally find that they did not have clear and consistent directions when they were converted, and most likely they will be very much afraid of these sudden conversions.

Afraid of sudden conversions! Some of the best Christians I have known were convicted and converted in the space of a few minutes. In one quarter of the time that I have been speaking, many of them were awakened and came right out on the Lord's side, and have been shining lights in the church ever since. They have generally demonstrated the same decision of character in the Christian religion that they did when they first came out and took a stand on the Lord's side.

Lecture 19

Instructions to Converts

Feed my lambs.
—John 21:15

You who read your Bibles will remember the connection in which these words are found and by whom they were spoken. They were addressed by the Lord Jesus Christ to Peter after he had denied his Lord and had professed repentance. Probably one of the intentions that Christ had in view in allowing Peter to sin so dreadfully as to deny his master was to produce a deeper work of grace in him, and thus prepare him for the specific duty to which He intended to call him, in laying the foundations of the Christian church and watching over the spiritual interests of the converts. It needed a special work of grace in his soul to prepare him to lead others through those scenes of trial and temptation to which the early Christians, in particular, were exposed.

It is evident that although Peter had special natural qualifications for such a work, he was still quite a superficial saint. He was probably converted before this, but he was weak, and there was so much of his natural roughness and turbulence of temper left that he was still ready to flare up on any occasion and take offense at everything that crossed him, so that he was still quite unfit for that specific work to which he was destined. Christ designed him for such a distinct service that it seems something was indispensable to prepare him for it and make him such a saint that future opposition would not irritate him, nor difficulties dishearten him, nor success and honor spoil him, by lifting up his heart with pride. Therefore, Christ took the successful method recorded before us of dealing with him once for all to secure a thorough work in his soul.

He asked him this question to remind him, in an affecting manner, at once of his sin and of the love of Christ: *Simon, son of Jonas, lovest thou me more than these?* (John 21:15). This strongly implied a doubt whether he did love Him. Peter answered, *Yea, Lord; thou knowest that I love thee.* He said unto him, *Feed my lambs.* Jesus then repeated the question, as if He would read his inmost soul: *Simon, son of Jonas, lovest thou me?* (John 21:16). Peter was still firm, and promptly answered again, *Yea, Lord; thou knowest that I love thee.* Jesus still asked him the question again, the third time, emphatically. He seemed to urge the point, as if He would search his inmost thoughts, to see whether Peter would ever deny Him again. Peter was touched. He was grieved, it is said. He did not fly into a passion. He did not boast, as he did on a former occasion when he said, *Though I should die with thee, yet will I not deny thee* (Matthew 26:35). However, he was grieved, he was subdued, he spoke tenderly, and he appealed to the Savior Himself, as if he would plead with Him not to doubt his sincerity any longer: *Lord, thou knowest all things; thou knowest that I love thee* (John 21:17). Christ then gave him His final charge: *Feed my sheep.*

By the terms "sheep" and "lambs" here, the Savior undoubtedly designated Christians as members of His church. The lambs probably represent young converts – those who have only a little experience and just a little knowledge of Christianity, and therefore need to have special attention and effort taken with them to guard from harm and to train them for future usefulness. And when our Savior told Peter to feed His sheep, He undoubtedly referred to the important part that Peter was to perform in watching over the newly formed churches in different parts of the world, and in training the young converts and leading them along to usefulness and happiness.

My last lecture was on the subject of giving proper instruction to troubled sinners. This naturally brings me along, in this course of lectures, to consider the manner in which young converts should be treated and the instructions that should be given to them.

Instructions to Young Converts

In speaking on this subject, it is my intent to explain the following:

I.   Several things that should be considered in regard to the hopes of young converts.

II. Several things in regard to their making a profession of Christianity and joining the church.

III. The importance of having correct instruction given to young converts.

IV. What should not be taught to young converts.

V.   What specific things are especially necessary to be taught to young converts.

VI. How young converts should be treated by church members.

I. Several Matters in Regard to the Hopes of Young Converts

1. Nothing should be said to them to create a hope. Nothing should ordinarily be suggested to people under conviction that is intended to make them think they have experienced conversion until they find it out themselves. I do not like the term, "I experienced religion," and I use it only because it is a phrase in common use. It is an absurdity in itself. What is true religion? It is obedience to God. Suppose you hear a good citizen say he had experienced obedience to the government of the country. You see it is nonsense. Or suppose a child should talk about experiencing obedience to his father. If he knew what he was saying, he would say he had obeyed his father, just as the apostle Paul said to the Roman believers, *Ye have obeyed from the heart that form of doctrine which was delivered you* (Romans 6:17).

What I mean to say is that ordinarily it is best to let their hope or belief that they are converted spring up spontaneously in their own minds. Sometimes it will happen that people may be really converted, but because of some ideas that they have been taught about religion, they do not realize it. Their views of what Christianity is, and its effect upon the mind, are so entirely wide of the truth that they do not think that they have it. I will give you an illustration of this point.

Some years ago, I labored in a place where a revival was in progress, and there was in the place a young lady from Boston. She had been brought up as a Unitarian, she had considerable education, and she was intelligent on many subjects – but on the subject of the Christian religion, she was very ignorant. At last she was convicted of sin. She became greatly convinced of her horrible enmity against God. She had been so educated as to have a sense of propriety, but her enmity against God became so great, and broke out so intensely, that it was horrible to hear her talk. She used to come to the anxious meetings, where we talked with each person individually. Her feelings of opposition to God were such that she used to create a disturbance.

By the time I came within two or three seats from her, where she could hear what I said in a low voice to others, she would begin to make remarks in reply so that they could be heard. She would say the most bitter things against God, against His providence, and against His method of dealing with mankind, as if God was an infinite tyrant. She would speak of Him as the most unjust and cruel being in the universe. I would try to quiet her and make her keep still because she distracted the attention of others. Sometimes she would stop and command her temper awhile, and sometimes she would rise and go out.

I have seldom seen a case where the enmity of the heart rose so high against God. One night at the anxious meeting, after she had been very restless, she began to reply as usual as I came toward her. However, I hushed her and told her I could not converse with her there, but I invited her to meet me the next morning, and I said I would talk with her then. She promised to come, but she said, "God is unjust; He is infinitely unjust. Is He not almighty? Why then has He never shown me my enmity before? Why has He let me run on so long? Why does He let my friends in Boston remain in this ignorance? They are the enemies of God as much as I am, and are going to hell. Why does He not show them the truth in regard to their condition?" And in this attitude she left the room.

The next morning she met me, as she had promised. I saw as soon as she came in that her countenance was changed, but I said nothing about it. "Oh," she said, "I have changed my mind as to what I said last night about God. I do not think He has done me any wrong, and I think I will get religion sometime, for now I love to think about God. I have been all wrong. The reason why I had never known my enmity before was that I would not. I used to read the Bible, but I always passed over the passages that would make me feel as if I was a lost sinner, and those passages that spoke of Jesus Christ as God, I passed over without consideration. Now I see that it was my fault, not God's fault, that I did not know any more about myself. I have changed my mind now."

She had no idea that this was religion, but she was encouraged now to expect religion at some future time because she loved God so much. I said nothing to make her imagine that I thought her to be a Christian, but left her to find it out. And for a time, her mind was so entirely occupied with thinking about God that she never seemed to ask whether this was Christianity or not.

It is usually a great evil to encourage people to hope they are Christians. It is very likely that you may judge prematurely. Or if not, it is better for them to find it out for themselves if they do not see it at once. They may break down lower than ever, and then they will come out so clear and decided that they will know where they are.

2. When you see people expressing a hope, yet they express doubts too, it is generally because the work is not thorough. If they are convicted, they need breaking up. They are still lingering around the world, or they have not broken off completely from their sins, and they need to be pushed back rather than urged forward. If you see reason to doubt, or if you find that they have doubts, most probably there is some good reason to doubt.

Sometimes people express a hope in Christ, and afterward remember some sin that needs to be confessed to men, or some case where they have slandered or defrauded, where it is necessary to make satisfaction, and where either their character or their wallet is so deeply implicated that they hesitate and refuse to perform their duty. This grieves the Spirit, brings darkness over their minds, of course, and justly leads them to doubt whether they are truly converted. If a soul is truly converted, it will generally be found that when there are doubts, they are neglecting duty on some point. They should be searched as with a lit candle and brought up to the performance of duty, and not permitted to hope until they do so. Ordinarily it is proper just then to throw in some plain and searching truth that will go through them, something that will diminish their hopes. Do it while the Spirit of God is dealing with them, and do it in the right way, and there is no danger of its doing harm.

To illustrate this, I knew a person who was a member of the church, but a terrible hypocrite, proved to be so by her conduct, and afterward fully confessed to be so. In a revival of Christianity, she was awakened and deeply convicted, and after a while she got a hope. She went to a minister to talk with him about her hope, and he poured in the truth to her mind in such a manner as to annihilate all her hopes. She then remained under conviction many days, and at last she broke out in hope again. The minister knew her temperament, and knew what she needed, and he tore away her hope again. Then she broke down, clear to the ground, so that she could not stand or go. So deeply did the Spirit of God probe her heart that for a time it took away all her bodily strength. Then she came out subdued. Previously, she had been one of the proudest rebels against God's government that ever was, but now she became humbled and was one of the most modest, tender, lovely of Christians. No doubt that was just the way to deal with her. It was just the treatment that her case required.

It is often useful to deal with individuals in this way. Some people are naturally unpleasant in their temper and unlovely in their manner. It is particularly important that such people should be dealt with most thoroughly whenever they first begin to express hope in Christ. Unless the work with them is, in the first place, uncommonly deep and thorough, they will be vastly less useful, interesting, and happy than they would have been if the inquiry had been thoroughly and skillfully applied to their heart. If they are encouraged at first, without being thoroughly dealt with, if they are left to go right along and not sufficiently examined and broken down, these unlovely traits of character will remain unsubdued and will be always breaking out to the great harm both of their personal peace and their general influence and usefulness as Christians.

While such people are in just these circumstances, it is important to take the opportunity to mold them into proper form. Do not spare, even if the person is a child, a brother, a husband, or a wife. Let it be a thorough work. If they express a hope, and you find that they bear the image of Christ, they are Christians. But if that appears doubtful – if they do not appear to be fully changed – just tear away their hope by searching them with the most prudent truth, and let the Spirit do the work more deeply. If the image is still not perfect, do it again; break them down into a childlike spirit, and then let them hope. They will then be clear and thorough Christians.

By such a mode of treatment, I have often known people of the most dishonest and hateful natural character so transformed in a few days that they appear like different beings. You would think that the work of a whole life of Christian cultivation had been done at once.

Undoubtedly this was the intent of our Savior's dealing with Peter. He had been converted, but became puffed up with spiritual pride and self-confidence, and then he fell. After that, Christ broke him down again by three times searching him with the inquiry, *Simon, son of Jonas, lovest thou me?* (John 21), after which he seems to have been a stable and devoted saint the rest of his days.

3. There is no need for young converts to have or express doubts as to their conversion. There is no more need of a person doubting whether he is now in favor of God's government than there is for a person to doubt whether he is in favor of our government or another. In fact, on the face of it, it is absurd for a person to talk of doubting on such a point if he is intelligent and understands what he is talking about.

It has long been supposed to be a virtue and a mark of humility for a person to doubt whether he is a Christian, and this idea that there is virtue in doubting is a device of the devil. "I say, neighbor, are you in favor of our government, or do you prefer that of Russia?"

"Why, I have some hopes that I love our own government, but I have many doubts." Amazing!

"Woman, do you love your children?"

"Why, sir, I sometimes have a trembling hope that I love them, but you know that even the best have doubts."

"Wife, do you love your husband?"

"I do not know. I sometimes think I do, but you know that the heart is deceitful, and we should be careful and not be too confident."

Who would have such a wife?

"Man, do you love your wife; do you love your family?"

"Ah, you know we are poor creatures. We do not know our own hearts. I think I love them, but perhaps I am deceived." Ridiculous!

Ordinarily, the very idea of a person expressing doubts renders his piety truly doubtful. A real Christian has no need to doubt. And when one is full of doubts, ordinarily you should doubt for him and help him doubt. Affection to God is as much a matter of consciousness as any other affection. A woman knows she loves her child. How? By consciousness. She is aware of the exercise of this affection. And then she sees it carried out into action every day. In the same way, a Christian may know that he loves God by his consciousness of this affection, and by seeing that it influences his daily conduct.

In the case of those who are truly young converts, these doubts generally arise from their having been wrongly dealt with, and not sufficiently taught or thoroughly humbled. In any case, they should never be left in such a state, but should be brought, if possible, to such a thorough change that they will doubt no longer. It is inconsistent with the greatest usefulness for a Christian to be always entertaining doubts. It not only makes him gloomy, but it also renders his religion a stumbling block to sinners.

What do sinners think of such religion? They say, "These converts are always afraid to think they have got anything real. They are always trembling and doubting whether it is a reality, and they should know whether there is anything in it or not; for if it is anything, these people seem to have it, and I am inclined to think it is rather doubtful. At any rate, I will let it pass for the present, for I do not believe God will damn me for not attending to what appears so uncertain."

No, a cheerful, settled hope in Christ is indispensable to usefulness, and therefore you should deal so with young converts as to lead them to a consistent, well-grounded, stable hope. Ordinarily this may be done, if pursued wisely, at the proper time, and that is at the beginning of their Christian life. And they should not be left until it is done.

I know there are some exceptions. There are cases where the best instructions will be ineffective, but these generally depend on the state of the health and the condition of the nervous system. Sometimes you find a person incapable of reasoning on a certain topic, and so their errors will not yield to instruction. But most commonly they mistake the state of their own hearts because they judge under the influence of a physical disease. Sometimes people under a nervous depression will go almost into despair. I will not take time now to show the connection, but people who are acquainted with physiology will easily explain the matter, and this will make it plain that the only way to deal with such cases is first to engage their health and get their nervous system in a proper tone, and thus remove the physical cause of their gloom and depression; then they will be able to receive and apply your instructions to the state of their minds. But if you cannot remove their gloom and doubts and fears in this way, you can at least avoid doing any harm by giving them wrong instructions.

I have known even experienced Christians to have the error fastened upon them, thinking it was necessary, or virtuous, or a mark of humility to be always in doubt, and Satan would take advantage of it, and of the state of their health, to drive them almost into despair. You should guard against this by avoiding the error in teaching young converts. Teach them that instead of there being any virtue in doubting, it is a sin to have any reason to doubt, and a sin if they doubt without any reason, and a sin to be gloomy – and disgust sinners with their despondency.

If you teach them thoroughly what true religion is, and make them see clearly what God wants to have them do, and lead them to do it promptly and firmly, ordinarily they will not be harassed with doubts and fears, but will be clear, openhearted, cheerful, and growing Christians – an honor to the religion they profess, and a blessing to the church and the world.

II. Some Things Worthy of Consideration in Regard to Their Making a Profession of Christianity and Joining the Church

1. Young converts should generally offer themselves for admission to some church of Christ immediately. By immediately, I mean that they should do it the first opportunity they have. They should not wait. If they start out in Christianity by waiting, most likely they will always be waiting and will never do anything to much purpose. If they are taught

to wait under conviction before they give themselves up to Christ, or if they are taught to wait after conversion before they give themselves publicly to God by joining the church, they will probably go wavering and stumbling along through life. The first thing they should be taught always is never to wait where God has pointed out their duty. We profess to have given up the waiting system; let us carry it through and be consistent.

2. While I say it is the duty of young converts to offer themselves to the church immediately, I do not say that they should, in all cases, be received immediately. But the church may do so, and have an undoubted right to assume the responsibility of receiving them immediately or not. If the church is not satisfied in the case, they have the power to have candidates wait until they can make inquiries, or in any other way obtain satisfaction as to their character and their sincerity. This is more necessary in large cities than it is in the country, because the church is liable to receive so many applications from people who are complete strangers, where it is necessary to make inquiries before admitting them to communion. But if the church thinks it is necessary to postpone an applicant, the responsibility is not his. He has not postponed obedience to the dying command of Christ, so he has not grieved the Spirit away, and he may not be essentially harmed if he is faithful in other respects. Whereas if he had neglected the duty voluntarily, he would soon get into the dark, and would very likely backslide.

If there is no particular reason for delay, ordinarily the church should receive them when they apply. If they are sufficiently instructed on the subject of the Christian religion to know what they are doing, and if their general character is such that they can be trusted as to their sincerity and honesty in making a profession of faith in Christ, I see no reason why they should delay. But if there are sufficient reasons in the view of the church for making them wait a reasonable time, let them do it, for they are responsible to Jesus Christ. They should, however, remember what the responsibility is that they assume, and that if they keep those out of the church who should be in it, they sin and grieve the Holy Spirit.

It is impossible to lay down particular rules on this subject that are applicable to all cases. There is so great a variety of reasons that may justify keeping people back that no general rules can reach them all. Our practice in this church is to present people for a month after they make application before they are received to full communion. The reason for this is that the Session may have opportunity to inquire respecting individuals who offer themselves, since so many of them are strangers. But in the country, where there are regular congregations, and all the people have been instructed from their youth in the doctrines of Christianity, and where everybody is perfectly known, the case is different, and usually I see no reason why people of good character should not be admitted immediately. If a person has not been a drunkard, or otherwise of bad character, let him be admitted at once, as soon as he can give a rational and satisfactory account of the hope that is in him (1 Peter 3:15).

That is evidently the way the apostles did it. There is not the least evidence in the New Testament that they ever turned aside a person who wanted to be baptized and join the church. I know this does not satisfy some people because they think the situation is different, but I do not see it so. They say the apostles were inspired. That is true; but it does not follow that they were inspired to read the characters of men so as to prevent their making mistakes in this matter.

On the other hand, we know they were not inspired in this way, for we know they did make mistakes, just as ministers may do now, and therefore, it is not true that their being inspired men changes the case on this point. Simon Magus was supposed to be a Christian, and was baptized and admitted to the communion, and remained in good standing until he tried to purchase the Holy Spirit with money (Acts 8). The apostles used to admit converts from heathenism immediately and without delay. If they could receive people who, perhaps, never heard more than one gospel sermon, and who never had a Bible, nor attended a Sunday school or Bible class in their lives, surely it is not necessary to stir up such an outcry and alarm if a church thinks proper to receive people of good character who have had the Bible all their lives, have been trained in Sunday school, and have sat under the preaching of the gospel – and who, therefore, may be supposed to understand what they are about, and not to profess what they do not feel.

415

I know it may be said that people who make a profession of Christianity now are not required to make such sacrifices for their religion as the early believers were, and consequently, people may be more ready to play the hypocrite. To some extent, that is true. But then, on the other hand, it should be remembered that with the instructions that they have on the subject of religion, they are not as easily led to deceive themselves as those who were converted without the previous advantages of a religious education. They may be strongly tempted to deceive others, but I insist upon it that with the instructions they have received, the converts of these great revivals are not half as liable to deceive themselves and take up with a false hope as they were in the days of the apostles. It is on this ground that I believe that those churches that are faithful in dealing with young converts, and that regularly exhibit the power of Christianity, are not likely to receive as many unconverted people as the apostles did.

It is important for the churches to act wisely on this point. Much evil has been done by this practice of keeping people out of the church a long time to see if they were Christians. This is almost as absurd as it would be to throw out a young child into the street to see whether he will live – to say that if he lives and promises to be a healthy child, we will take care of him, when that is the very time he needs to be nursed and taken care of, at the moment when the scale is turning, whether he will live or die.

Is that the way to deal with young converts? Should the church throw its newborn children out to the winds and say that if they live there, let them be raised, but if they die, they should die? I have no doubt that in consequence of this treatment, thousands of converts have gone through life and have never joined any church, but have lingered along full of doubts, fears, and darkness, and have spent their days in this way, going to the grave without the comforts or the usefulness that they could have enjoyed, simply because the church, in its foolishness, has allowed them to wait outside the boundaries of the church to see whether they would grow and thrive, without those ordinances that Jesus Christ established particularly for their benefit.

Jesus Christ says to His church, "Here, take these lambs and feed them, shelter them, watch over them, and protect them." And what does the church do? The church turns them out alone upon the cold mountains, among the wild beasts, to starve or perish, to see whether they are alive or not. This whole system is as unphilosophical as it is unscriptural. Did Jesus Christ tell His churches to do so? Did the God of Abraham teach any such doctrine as this in regard to the children of Abraham? Never. He never taught us to treat young converts in such a barbarous manner. It is the very best way that could be taken to announce it doubtful whether they are converts. The very way to lead them into doubts and darkness is to keep them away from the church, from its fellowship, and from its ordinances.

I understand there is a church not very far from here that has passed a resolution that no young converts will be admitted until they have had a hope for at least six months. Where did they get any such rule? Not from the Bible, nor from the example of the early churches.

3. In examining young converts for admission to the church, their consciences should not be ensnared by examining them too extensively or minutely on doctrinal points. From the manner in which examinations are conducted in some churches, it would seem as if they expected young converts to be immediately acquainted with the whole system of divinity, and able to answer every difficult question in theology. The effect of it is that young converts are perplexed and confused, and give their assent to things they do not understand, and thus their conscience is ensnared and consequently weakened.

One great purpose of receiving young converts into the church is to teach them doctrine, but if they are to be kept out of the church until they understand the whole system of doctrines, this purpose is defeated. Will you keep them out until one main purpose of receiving them is accomplished by other means? It is absurd. There are certain cardinal doctrines of Christianity that are embraced in the experience of every true convert, and young converts will testify to these, on their examination, if they are questioned in such a way as to draw out their knowledge, and not in such a way as to frustrate and confound them.

The questions should be those that are intended to draw out from them what they have learned by experience, and not what they may have got in theory before or since their conversion. The purpose is not to find out how much they know, or how good of students they are in divinity, as you would examine a school or a number of young men striving for a scholarship. It is to find out whether they have a change of heart, to learn whether they have experienced the great truths of Christianity by their power in their own souls. You see therefore how absurd, and harmful too, it must be to examine as is sometimes done, like a lawyer in court cross-examining a suspicious witness. It should rather be like a faithful physician eager to find out his patient's true condition, and therefore leading his mind, by questions and hints, to disclose the real symptoms of his case.

If you ask your questions properly, you will find that real converts will see clearly those great fundamental points, such as the divine authority of the Scriptures, the necessity of the influences of the Holy Spirit, the divinity of Christ, the doctrine of total depravity and regeneration, the necessity of the atonement, justification by faith, and the justice of the eternal punishment of the wicked. By a proper course of questions you will see all these points come out as a part of their experience, if you ask your questions in such a way that they understand them.

I was informed that a church session in this city has passed a vote that no person can join that church until he will give his assent to the whole Presbyterian Confession of Faith and adopt it as his "rule of faith and practice and Christian obedience." That is, they must read the book through, which is about three times as large as this hymnbook, and must understand it and agree to it all before they can be admitted to the church, before they can make a profession of Christianity or obey the command of Christ.

By what authority does a church say that no one can join their communion until he understands all the points and technicalities of this long confession of faith? Is that their charity, to cram this whole confession of faith down the throat of a young convert before they let him so much as come to the communion? He says, "I love the Lord Jesus Christ and want to obey His command."

"Very well, but do you understand and adopt the Confession of Faith?"

He says, "I do not know, for I have never read that, but I have read the Bible, and I love that, and I want to follow the commands in it and to come to the table of the Lord."

"Do you love the Confession of Faith? If not, you cannot come," is the reply of this charitable session. "You will not sit down at the Lord's Table until you have adopted all of the Confession of Faith."

Did Jesus Christ ever authorize a church body to say this – to tell that child of God, who stands there with tears and asks permission to obey his Lord, and who understands the grounds of his faith and can give a satisfactory reason of his hope, to tell him that he cannot join the church until he understands the Confession of Faith? No doubt, Jesus Christ is angry with such a church, and He will show His displeasure in a clear way if they do not repent. Shut the door against young converts until they swallow the Confession of Faith! Will such a church prosper? Never.

No church on earth has a right to impose its extended confession of faith on a young convert who professes the fundamentals of the Christian religion. They may let the young convert know their own faith on many points, and they may examine him, if they think it is necessary, as to his belief; but suppose he has doubts on some points not essential to Christian experience, as the doctrine of infant baptism, or of election, or the perseverance of the saints, and suppose he honestly and directly tells you he has not made up his mind concerning these points. Has any minister or church a right to say that he cannot come to the Lord's Table until he has finished all his research into these subjects – that he cannot obey Jesus Christ until he has fully made up his mind on every such point on which Christians, and devoted ones too, differ among themselves? I would sooner cut off my right hand than exclude a convert under such circumstances.

I would teach a young convert as well as I could in the time before he made his application, and I would examine him plainly as to his views; and after he was in the church, I would attempt to help him grow in knowledge as he grows in grace. And by just as much confidence as I have that my own doctrines are the doctrines of God, I would expect to make him adopt them, if I could have a fair hearing before his mind. But I would never tell someone, whom I openly believed to be a child of God, to stay away from his Father's Table because he did not see all I see, or believe all I believe, through the entire system of divinity. The thing is completely irrational, ridiculous, and wicked.

4. Sometimes people who are known to entertain a hope in Christ dare not make a profession of Christianity for fear they would be deceived. I would always deal actively with such cases. A hope that will not warrant a profession of Christianity is manifestly worse than no hope, and the sooner it is torn away the better. Will a person hope he loves God, yet not dare to obey Jesus Christ? That is absurd! Such a hope should be given up at once.

5. Sometimes people professing to be converts will make an excuse for not joining the church, saying that they can enjoy the Christian religion just as well without it. This is always suspicious. I would look out for such characters. It is almost certain that they have no true religion. Ordinarily, if a person does not desire to be associated with the people of God, he is rotten at the core. It is because he wants to keep away from the responsibilities of a public profession. He has a feeling within him that he would rather be free so that he can eventually go back to the world again if he likes, without the reproach of instability or hypocrisy. Imagine thinking that you can enjoy Christianity just as well without obeying Jesus Christ! It is false on the face of it. He overlooks the fact that true religion consists in obeying Jesus Christ.

III. The Importance of Giving Proper Instruction to Young Converts

Ordinarily, their Christian character through life is molded and fashioned according to the manner in which they are dealt with when first converted. There are many who have been poorly taught at first, but have been afterward taught properly, and if they are then dealt with correctly, they may be made something of. But the proper time to do this is when they are first brought in, when their minds are soft and tender and easily yield to the truth. Then they may be led with a hair, if they think it is the truth of God. Whatever beliefs in religion they get then, they tend to cling to forever afterward. It is almost impossible to get a person's beliefs away from him that he got when he was a young convert. You may reason him down, but he clings to them. How often it is the case where people have been taught certain things when first converted, that if they afterward get a new minister who teaches somewhat differently, they will rise up against him as if he was going to subvert the faith, carry away the church to error, and throw everything into confusion.

Thus you see that young converts are thrown into the hands of the church, and it depends on the church to mold them and form them into Christians of the right stamp. Much of their future comfort and usefulness depends on the manner in which they are instructed at the outset. The future character of the church, the progress of revivals, and the coming of the millennium depend on having proper instruction given and a right direction of thought and life to those who are young converts.

IV. Some Things That Should Not Be Taught to Young Converts

1. "You will not always feel as you do now." When the young convert is rejoicing in his Savior and intending to live for the glory of God and the good of mankind, how often he is met with this reply: "You will not always feel that way." Thus they are preparing his mind to expect to backslide, and not to be much surprised when he does. This is just the way the devil wants young converts dealt with – to have old Christians tell them that their feelings will not last, and that eventually they will be as cold as they are. It has made my heart bleed to see it.

When the young convert has been pouring out his warm heart to some old professing Christian, and expecting to meet the warm bursts of a kindred spirit responding to his own, what does he meet with? He meets with this cold answer, coming like a northern blast over his soul: "You will not always feel so." Shame! They are just preparing the young convert to expect that he will backslide as a matter of course, so that when he begins to decline, as under the very influences of this instruction it is most likely that he will, it produces no surprise or alarm in his mind, but he looks at it as just standard practice, doing as everybody else does.

I have heard it preached as well as prayed that seasons of backsliding are necessary to test the church. They say, "When it rains, you can find water anywhere; it is only in seasons of drought that you can tell where the deep springs are." Wonderful logic! So you would teach that Christians must get cold and careless and backslide from God, and for what reason? Why certainly, to show that they are not hypocrites. Amazing! You would prove that they are hypocrites in order to show that they are not.

Such doctrine as this is the very last that should be taught to young converts. They should be told that now they have only begun the Christian life and that their Christianity is to consist in continuing and progressing in it. They should be taught to go forward all the time and to grow in grace continually. Do not teach them to scrape off their religion and let it grow smaller and smaller until it comes to a point. God says, *The path of the just is as the shining light, that shineth more and more unto the perfect day* (Proverbs 4:18).

Whose path is that which grows dimmer and dimmer until the perfect night? They should be brought to such a state of mind that the first indications of decay in spirituality or zeal will alarm them and motivate them to duty. There is no need for young converts to backslide as they do. Paul did not backslide. I do not doubt that this very doctrine – "You will not always feel so" – is one of the grand devices of Satan to bring about the result that it predicts.

2. "Learn to walk by faith and not by sight." This is sometimes said to young converts in reference to their continuing to demonstrate the power of Christianity, and it is a clear distortion of Scripture. If they begin to lose their faith and zeal, and to get into darkness, some old professing Christian will tell them, "You cannot expect to have the Savior always with you. You have been walking by sight. You must learn to walk by faith and not by sight." That is, you must learn to get as cold as death, and then hang on to the doctrine of the saints' perseverance as your only ground of hope that you will be saved. That is what they mean by walking by faith. Cease to persevere, and then hold on to the doctrine of perseverance. As Edward Young wrote in "Christian Triumph" in his book *Young's Night Thoughts*, "Guilt's blunder! and the loudest laugh of hell." And they call walking by sight living in the enjoyment of God's favor and the comforts of the Holy Spirit!

Do you suppose young converts see the Savior at the time they believe on Him? When they are so full of the enjoyments of heaven, do you suppose they see heaven, and so walk by sight? It is absurd on the face of it. It is not faith, but it is presumption that makes a backslider hold on to the doctrine of perseverance as if that would save him, without any conscious exercise of godliness in his soul. Those who attempt to walk by faith in this way had better take care, or they will walk into hell with their faith. Faith indeed! Faith without works is dead. Can dead faith make the soul live?

3. "Wait until you see whether you can hold out." When a young convert feels zealous and warmhearted and wants to lay himself out for God, some prudent old professing Christian will caution him not to go too fast. He will say, "You had better not be too eager in Christianity until you see whether you can hold out, for if you take this high ground and then fall, you will disgrace the Christian religion." In plain English, that is to say, "Do not do anything that represents Christianity until you see whether you have real religion."

Religion consists in obeying God. These wise teachers tell a young convert, "Do not obey God until you see . . ." – what? – until you see whether you have obeyed Him, or until you see whether you have gotten that substance, that mysterious thing that they imagine is created and put into a person, like a lump of new flesh, and called religion. This waiting system is all alike, and all wrong. There is no biblical justification for telling a person to wait when the command of God is upon him and the path of duty is before him. Let him go along.

Young converts should be fully taught that this is the only consistent way to find out whether they have true religion. The only evidence they can have is to find that they are wholeheartedly engaged in doing the will of God. To tell him to wait, therefore, before he does these things, until he gets his evidence, is reversing the matter, and is absurd.

4. "Wait until you get strength before you take up the cross." This is applied to various Christian duties. Sometimes it is applied to prayer, as if prayer was a cross. I have known young converts who were advised not to attempt to pray in their families, or not to attempt quite yet to pray in meetings and social circles. "Wait until you get strength," they are told, as if they would get strength without exercise.

Strength comes by exercise. You cannot get strength by lying still.

Let a child lie in the cradle all his life, and he would never have any strength. He might grow in size, but he could never be anything more than a great baby. This is a law of nature. There is no substitute for exercise in producing strength. As everyone knows, the body can be strengthened only by exercise. That is true in the nature of things, and it is true with the mind. It is so with the heart, with the judgment, and with the conscience. All the powers of the soul are strengthened by exercise. I do not need to enter into the philosophy of this, for everyone knows it is so. If the mind is not exercised, the brain will not grow, and the person will become dull-minded. If the heart and emotions are not exercised, the person will become a stoic. To talk to a convert about neglecting Christian action until he gets strength is absurd. If he wants to gain strength, let him get to work.

5. Young converts should not be made sectarian or factional in their feelings. They should not be taught to dwell upon denominational distinctions, or to be sticklers about sectarian points. They should examine these points at a proper time and in a proper way, and make up their minds for themselves according to their importance. But they should not be taught to dwell upon them or to make much of them at the beginning of their Christian life. Otherwise there is great danger that their entire religion will run into sectarianism and division.

I have seen some most sad and melancholy demonstrations of the effects of this upon young converts. Whenever I see professed converts taking a strong hold of sectarian specifics, no matter what denomination of Christians, I always feel in doubt about them. I feel sad when I hear them asking, "Do you believe in the doctrine of election?" or "Do you believe in sprinkling?" or "Do you believe in plunging?" I never knew such converts to be worth much. Their sectarian zeal soon sours their feelings, takes all the heart out of their religion, and molds their whole character into sinful sectarian bigotry. They generally become mighty zealous for the traditions of the elders (Mark 7:3), and very little concerned for the salvation of souls.

V. Some Things That It Is Important to Teach to Young Converts

1. One of the first things young converts should be taught is to distinguish between emotion and principle in religion. Do you understand me? I am going to explain what I mean, but I want you to get hold of the words and have them fixed in your mind. What I want is to have you distinguish between emotion and principle.

By emotion, I mean that state of mind of which we are conscious, and which we call feeling – an involuntary state of mind that arises naturally when we are in certain circumstances or under certain influences. There may be elaborate feelings, or they may subside into tranquility, or disappear entirely. But these emotions should be carefully distinguished from religious principle.

By principle, I do not mean any substance or root or seed or sprout implanted in the soul, but I mean the voluntary decision of the mind – the firm determination to act out duty and to obey the will of God, by which a Christian should always be governed. When a person is fully determined to obey God because it is right that he should obey God, I call that principle. Whether he feels any active religious emotion at the time or not, he will do his duty cheerfully, promptly, and wholeheartedly, no matter what the state of his feelings may be. This is acting upon principle and not from emotion.

Many young converts have mistaken views upon this subject, and depend almost entirely upon the state of their feelings to go forward in duty. Some will not lead in a prayer meeting unless they feel as if they could make an eloquent prayer. Multitudes are influenced almost entirely by their emotions, and they give way to this, as if they thought themselves under no obligation to duty unless urged on by some strong emotion. They will be very zealous in religion when they feel like it, when their emotions are warm and lively, but they will not live out the Christian religion consistently and carry it into all the concerns of life. They are religious only as they are impelled by a gush of feeling. But this is not true Christianity.

Young converts should be carefully taught to do their duty when it is before them. No matter how dull their feelings may be, if duty calls, do it. Do not wait for feeling and emotion, but do it. Most likely the very emotions for which you would wait will be called into exercise when you begin to do your duty. If the duty is prayer, for example, and you do not have the feelings you would wish, do not wait for emotions before you pray, but pray, and open your mouth wide. In doing so, you are most likely to have the emotions for which you were inclined to wait and that bring about the conscious happiness of religion.

2. Young converts should be taught that they have renounced the ownership of all their possessions, and of themselves, or if they have not done this, they are not Christians. They should not be left to think that anything is their own – their time, property, influence, abilities, bodies, or souls. *Ye are not your own* (1 Corinthians 6:19). All belongs to God. When they submitted to God, they made a free and full surrender of all to Him, to be ruled and disposed of at His pleasure. They have no right to spend one hour as if their time was their own. They have no right to go anywhere or do anything for themselves, but should hold all at the disposal of God and use all for the glory of God. If they do not, they should not call themselves Christians, for the very idea of being a Christian is to renounce self and become entirely consecrated to God.

A person has no more right to withhold anything from God than he has to rob or steal. It is robbery in the highest sense of the term. It is an infinitely higher crime than it would be for a clerk in a store to go and take the money of his employer and spend it on his own desires and pleasures. For a person to withhold from God is a higher crime against Him than a man can commit against his fellow man, inasmuch as God is the owner of all things in an infinitely higher sense than man can be the owner of anything. If God calls on them to use anything they have – their money, or their time, or to give their children, or to dedicate themselves – in advancing His kingdom, and they refuse because they want to use these things in their own way, or prefer to do something else, it is vastly more reprehensible than for a bookkeeper or an assistant to go and embezzle the money that is entrusted to him by his employer, and spend it for his family, or to spend it on bank stock or in speculation for himself.

In an infinitely higher sense, God is the owner of all, more so than any employer can be said to be the owner of what he has. The church of Christ will never take high ground, will never be disentangled from the world, and will never be able to go forward without these continual declines and backslidings until Christians, and the churches generally, take the ground and hold to it. It is just as much a matter of discipline for a church member practically to deny his stewardship as to deny the divinity of Christ, and covetousness will just as certainly exclude a person from communion as adultery.

The church is mighty orthodox in beliefs, but very heretical in practice. However, the time must come when the church will be just as vigilant in guarding orthodoxy in practice as orthodoxy in doctrine, and just as prompt to expel heretics in practice as heretics who corrupt the doctrines of the gospel. In fact, it is vastly more important. The main purpose of doctrine is to produce practice, and it does not seem to be understood by the church that true faith works by love and purifies the heart, and that heresy in practice is conclusive proof of heresy in belief. The church is very insistent for correct doctrine and very careless about correct living. This is preposterous. Has it come to this, that the church of Jesus Christ is to be satisfied with correct beliefs on some abstract points, and never reduce her orthodoxy to practice? Let it be so no longer.

It is high time these matters were set right, and the only way to set them right is to begin right with those who are just entering upon the Christian religion. Young converts must be told that they are just as worthy of damnation, and that the church cannot and will not hold fellowship with them, if they show a covetous spirit and turn a deaf ear when the whole world is calling for help, as if they were living in adultery or in the daily worship of idols.

3. Teach them how to cultivate a tender conscience. I have often been amazed to find how little conscience there is, even among those who we hope are Christians. We see the reason for it here. Their consciences were never cultivated. They were never taught and told how to cultivate a tender conscience. They do not even have a natural conscience. They have dealt so rudely with their conscience, and have resisted it so often, that it has become dull and does not act.

The usefulness of a Christian greatly depends on his knowing how to cultivate his conscience. Young converts should be taught to keep their conscience just as tender as the apple of the eye. They should watch their conduct and their motives, and should let their motives be so pure and their conduct so just as not to offend or harm or stifle their conscience. They should maintain such a habit of listening to conscience that it will always be ready to give forth a stern verdict on all occasions.

It is astonishing to see how much the conscience may be cultivated by a proper course. If rightly attended to, it may be made so pure and so powerful that it will always respond exactly to the Word of God. Present any duty to such a Christian, or any self-denial or suffering, and only show him the Word of God, and he will do it without hesitation. In a few months, if properly taught and attended to, young converts may have a conscience so delicately poised that the weight of a feather will turn them. Only bring a *Thus saith the* LORD, and they will be always ready to do that, no matter what it is.

4. Young converts should be taught to *pray without ceasing* (1 Thessalonians 5:17). That is, they should always keep a watch over their minds, and all the time be in a prayerful spirit. They should be taught to pray always, no matter what may take place. For the lack of proper instruction on this point, many young converts suffer loss and get far away from God.

For example, sometimes a young convert will fall into some sin, and then he feels as if he could not pray; instead of overcoming this, he feels so distressed that he waits for the sharp edge of his distress to pass away. Instead of going right to Jesus Christ in the midst of his agony, and confessing his sin out of the fulness of his heart and getting a renewed pardon and peace restored, he waits until all the sharpness of his feelings have subsided; then his repentance, if he does repent, is cold and halfhearted. Let me tell you, beloved, never to do this, but when your conscience compels you, go then right to Christ, confess your sin fully, and pour out your heart to God.

Sometimes people will neglect to pray because they are in the dark and feel no desire to pray. But that is the very time when they need prayer. That is the very reason why they should pray. You should go right to God and confess your coldness and darkness of mind. Tell Him just how you feel. Tell Him, "O Lord, I have no desire to pray, but I know I should pray." And the first thing you know, the Spirit may come and lead your heart out in prayer, and all the dark clouds will pass away.

5. Young converts should be faithfully warned against adopting a false standard in religion. They should not be left to fall in behind old professing Christians and keep those Christians before their minds as a standard of holy living. Rather, they should always look at Christ as their model. They should not aim at being as good Christians as the old church members, and think they are doing pretty well because they are as much awake as the old members of the church. But they should aim at being holy, and not rest satisfied until they are as perfect as God. The church has been greatly injured for the lack of attention to this matter.

Young converts have come forward, and their hearts were warm and their zeal ardent enough to aim at a high standard. However, they were not directed properly, and so they soon settle down into the idea that what is good enough for others is good enough for them, and therefore they never aim higher than those who are before them. In this way, instead of the church rising higher and higher in holiness with every revival, it is kept nearly stationary.

6. Young converts should be taught to do all their duty. They should never make a compromise with duty, nor think of saying, "I will do this to make up for neglecting that." They should never rest satisfied until they have done their duty of every kind in relation to their families, the church, Sunday schools, the unrepentant around them, the disposal of their property, the conversion of the world, etc. Let them do their duty as they feel it when their hearts are warm, and never attempt to pick and choose among the commandments of God.

7. They should be made to feel that they have no separate interest or concern. It is time Christians were made to actually feel that they have no interest whatever apart from the interest of Jesus Christ and His kingdom. They should understand that they are incorporated into the family of Jesus Christ, as full members, so that their whole interest is identified with His. They are on board with Him and are to go with

Him wherever He leads. From this time on they have nothing to do, or nothing to say, except as it is connected with this interest and bears on the cause and kingdom of Christ.

8. They should be taught to maintain singleness of motive. Young converts should not begin to have a double mind on any subject, or let selfish motives mingle in with good motives in anything they do. But this can never be as long as Christians are allowed to hold a separate interest of their own, distinct from the interest of Jesus Christ. If they feel that they have a separate interest, it is impossible to keep them from regarding it and having an eye to it as well as to Christ's interest in many things that they do. It is only by becoming entirely consecrated to God, and giving up all to His service, that they can ever keep their eye single and their motives pure.

9. They should set out with a determination to aim at being useful in the highest degree possible. They should not rest satisfied with merely being useful, or remaining in a situation where they can do some good, but if they see an opportunity where they can do more good, they must embrace it, no matter the sacrifice may be to themselves – no matter what it may cost them, no matter what danger or what suffering, no matter what change in their outward circumstances, habits, or employments it may lead to. If they are satisfied that they will on the whole do more good, they should not even hesitate. How else can they be like God? How can they think to bear the image of Jesus Christ if they are not prepared to do all the good that is in their power?

When a person is converted, he comes into a new world and should consider himself as a new man. If he finds he can do the most good by remaining in his old employment, let it be so. But if he can do more good in some other way, he is obligated to change. It is for the lack of attention to this subject, in the beginning, that Christians have got such low ideas on the subject of duty, and that is the reason why there are so many useless members in our churches.

10. They must be taught not to aim at comfort, but at usefulness, in the Christian religion. There are a great many people in the churches who

are all the time seeking to be happy in religion, while they take very little effort to be useful. They would much rather spend their time in singing joyful hymns and in pouring out their happy feelings in a gushing tide of exultation and triumph than to spend it in agonizing prayer for sinners, or in going about and pulling dying people out of the fire. They seem to feel as if they were born to enjoy themselves.

However, I do not think such Christians show such fruit as to make their example one to be imitated. This was not the way of the apostles. They travailed for souls, labored in weariness and pain, and often faced death to save sinners. Nor is it safe. Ordinarily, Christians are not qualified to drink deep at the fountain of joy. In ordinary cases, a deep agony of prayer for souls is more profitable than high flights of joy. Let young converts be plainly taught not to anticipate a life of joy and triumph. They may be called to go through fiery trials. Satan may sift them like wheat. But they must go forward, not planning so much to be happy as to be useful; not talking about comfort but duty; not desiring flights of joy and triumph, but hungering and thirsting after righteousness; not studying how to create new times of delight, but how to know the will of God and do it.

They will be happy enough in heaven. There they may sing the song of Moses and the Lamb. They will, in fact, enjoy a more solid and rational happiness here by thinking nothing about it, but by patiently devoting themselves to do the will of God.

11. They should be taught to have moral courage, and not to be afraid of going forward in duty. The Bible insists fully on Christian boldness and courage in action as a duty. I do not mean that they should indulge in their boldness, like Peter, telling others what they will do, and boasting of their courage. The boaster is generally a coward at heart. Rather, I mean moral courage – a humble and fixed decision of purpose that will go forward in any duty, unangered and unawed, with the meekness and firmness of the Son of God.

12. They should be so instructed as to be sound in the faith. That is, as far as possible, they should early on be made complete and correct in regard to their doctrinal belief. As soon as may be, without turning

their minds off from their practical duties in promoting the glory of God and the salvation of men, they should be taught fully and plainly all the leading doctrines of the Bible.

Doctrinal knowledge is indispensable to growth in grace. Knowledge is the food of the mind. "It is not good for the soul to be without knowledge," says the wise man. The mind cannot grow without knowledge any more than the body can grow without food. Therefore, it is important for young converts to be thoroughly taught and made to understand the Bible. I do not mean teaching them the catechism, but teaching them to draw knowledge from the fountainhead. Create in their minds such an appetite for knowledge that they will eat the Bible up, devour it, and will love it and love it all. *All scripture is given by inspiration of God, and is profitable for doctrine, for reproof, for correction, for instruction in righteousness: that the man of God may be perfect, thoroughly furnished unto all good works* (2 Timothy 3:16-17).

13. Great effort should be taken to guard young converts against criticism. When young converts first come out on the Lord's side, they are all warm and zealous, and sometimes find old professing Christians so cold and dead that they are strongly tempted to be critical. This should be corrected immediately; otherwise the habit will poison their minds and destroy their religion.

14. They must learn to say no. This is a very difficult lesson for many people. See that young woman. Formerly she loved the carefree circle and took delight in its pleasures. She joined the church, and then found herself distant from all her old associates. They do not ask her now to their entertainment and parties because they know she will not join them, and perhaps they completely stay away from her for a time because they are afraid that she might talk with them about their souls. But eventually they grow a little bold, and some of them dare to ask her just to take a ride with a few friends. She does not like to say no. They are her old friends, only a few of them are going, and surely a ride is so innocent a recreation that she accepts the invitation.

But now she has begun to give in. The ice is broken, and they soon have her again as one of them. It goes on, and she begins to attend their social visits – "only a few friends," you know, until soon she goes with them to a dance. Then perhaps she goes out with them on Saturday night and comes home after midnight, and then sleeps all morning on Sunday to make up for it. This is all for the lack of learning to say no.

See that young man. For a time he was always in his place in the Sunday school and in the prayer meeting. But soon his old friends begin to treat him with attention again, and they draw him along step by step. Every step seems to be a very small thing, and it would seem rude to deny so small a thing. He reasons that if he refuses to go with them in things that are innocent, he will lose his influence with them. So he goes on, until the prayer meeting, Bible class, and even his private Bible reading and prayer are neglected.

Ah, young man, stop there! Go only a little farther without learning to say no, and you are gone. If you do not want to hang up the cause of Christ to scorn and contempt, learn to resist the beginnings of temptation. Otherwise it will come upon you in time like the letting out of water.

15. They should be taught what is and what is not Christian experience. It is necessary, both for their comfort and their usefulness, for them to understand this so that they do not need to run themselves into needless distress for the lack of that which is by no means essential to Christian experience, nor flatter themselves that they have more religion than they really exercise. But I cannot dwell on this topic now.

16. Teach them not to consider anything a sacrifice that they do for God. Some people are always talking about the sacrifices they make in the Christian religion. I have no confidence in such piety. They keep talking about their sacrifices as if everything they did for God was a sacrifice. If they loved God, they would not talk so. If they considered their own interests and the interest of Christ identical, they would not talk of making sacrifices for Christ; it would be like talking of making sacrifices for themselves.

17. It is of great importance for young converts to be taught to be especially honest. I mean more by this than perhaps you would think. It is a great thing to be particularly honest. It is being very different from

the world in general, and very different even from the majority of professing Christians. The holiest man I ever knew, and one who had been many years a Christian and a minister, once made the remark to me, "Brother, it is a great thing to be particularly honest, upright, and direct in everything so that God's pure eye can see that the mind is perfectly upright."

It is of the utmost importance for young converts to understand what it means to be particularly honest in everything so that they can maintain a conscience void of offense, both toward God and toward men (Acts 24:16). Alas, how little conscience there is! How little of that real honesty, that pure, simple uprightness, that should mark the life of a child of God! How little do many people regard even a direct promise!

I heard the other day of a number of individuals who subscribed to the Anti-Slavery Society, and half of them will not pay their subscriptions. Their argument is that they signed when they were under excitement, and they do not choose to pay – as if their being excited released them from the obligation to keep their promise. It is just as dishonest as it would be to refuse payment of a promissory note. They promised and signed their names, did they, and now will not pay? And they call that honesty!

I have heard that there are a number of men in the city who have signed for hundreds of dollars for the Oneida Institute, promising to pay the money when called on; and when they were called on, they refused to pay the money. The reason they gave was that everyone in the Institute had become abolitionist. Very well. Suppose they have. Does that change your promise? Did you sign on the condition that if they became abolitionists you would not have to keep your word? If you did, then you are clear. But if you gave your promise without any condition, it is just as dishonest to refuse as if you had given a promissory note. Yet some of you might be almost angry if anyone would accuse you of refusing to pay money when you promised it.

Look at this seriously. Who does God say will go to heaven? Read Psalm 15:4 and see: *He that sweareth to his own hurt, and changeth not.* What do you think of that? If a man has promised anything, except to commit sin, let him keep his promise if he intends to be honest or to go to heaven. But here these people will make promises, and because they cannot be prosecuted, will break them as easily as if they were nothing. They would not let a promissory note be contested at the bank. Why? Because they would lose credit and would be sued. But the Oneida Institute and the Anti-Slavery Society, and other societies, will not sue for the money, and therefore these people take some offense at something and refuse to pay. Is this honest? Will such honesty as this get them into heaven? What? Will you break your promise and go up and carry a lie in your hand before God? If you refuse or neglect to fulfill your promise, you are a liar; and if you persist in this, you will have your part in the lake that burns with fire and brimstone (Revelation 21:8). I would not, for ten thousand worlds, die with money in my hands that I had unrighteously withheld from any other object to which I had promised it. Such money will *eat as doth a canker* (2 Timothy 2:17).

If you are not able to pay the money, that is a good excuse. But then say so. However, if you refuse to pay what you have promised because you have changed your mind, count on it that you are guilty. You cannot pray until you pay that money. What will you pray? "O Lord, I promised to give that money, but I changed my mind and broke my promise; but still, O Lord, I ask You to bless me and forgive my sin, even though I keep my money, and make me happy in Your love." Will such prayers be heard? Never.

Brethren, I find it impossible to discuss all the points I intended to cover, and so I will end here and finish this subject another time.

Lecture 20

Instructions to Converts

Feed my lambs.
—John 21:15

In my last lecture on this text, I remarked that because of lack of time, I had to omit many of the points that I wanted to present in regard to the instruction of young converts.

I intend to continue the subject by discussing the following:

I.   Several other points upon which young converts should be instructed.

II. The manner in which young converts should be treated by the church.

III. Some of the evils that naturally result from defective instructions given in that stage of Christian experience.

I. Further Instructions That Are Important to Be Given to Young Converts

1. It is of great importance that young converts should be made to understand early what true religion consists in. You might be surprised at my mentioning this. "What! Are they converts, and do they not know what true religion consists in?"

I answer that they would know if they would have no instruction other than that which is drawn from the Bible. But multitudes of people have learned such ideas about religion that not only young converts, but a great part of the church, do not know what true religion consists in so as to have a clear and distinct idea of it. There are many ministers who do not. I do not mean to say that they have no religion, for it may be kindly believed they have; but what I mean is that they do not distinguish as to what it consists in, and they cannot give a correct statement of what does and what does not constitute real religion. It is important for young converts to be taught.

Negatively, this is what true religion does not consist in:

a) True religion does not consist in doctrinal knowledge. Knowledge is essential to true religion, but it is not religion. The devil has doctrinal knowledge, but he has no religion. A man may have doctrinal knowledge to any extent without a trace of the Christian religion. Yet some people have very strange ideas on this subject, as though having doctrinal knowledge indicated an increase of piety. I once heard a remark of this kind: in a certain instance, where some young converts had made rapid progress in doctrinal knowledge, a person who saw it said, "How these young converts grow in grace!" Here he confused improvement in knowledge with improvement in piety. The truth was that he had no means of judging of their growth in grace, and it was no evidence of it because they were making progress in doctrinal knowledge.

b) They should be taught that real religion is not a substance. It is not any root, sprout, seed, or anything else in the mind, as a part of the mind itself. People often speak of religion as if it was something that may be covered up in the mind, just as a spark of fire may be covered up in the ashes, which does not show itself, and which produces no effects, yet lives and is ready to act as soon as it is uncovered. In the same way, they think they may have Christianity as something remaining in them, although they do not manifest it by obeying God. But they should be taught that this is not the nature of religion. It is not part of the mind itself, or of the body, nor is it a root, seed, or spark that can exist and yet be hid and produce no effects.

c) Teach them that true religion does not consist in emotion, passion, or high flights of feeling. There may be a great deal of these where there is religion, but it should be understood that they are all involuntary emotions, and may exist in full power where there is no religion. They may be the mere workings of the imagination without any truly religious affection at all. People may have them to such a degree as actually to swoon away with rapture, even on the subject of religion, without having any religion. I knew one person who was almost carried away with rapture by a mere view of the natural attributes of God, His power and wisdom as displayed in the starry heavens, yet the person had no religion. True religion is obedience to God, the voluntary submission of the soul to the will of God.

d) True religion also does not consist in going to church, reading the Bible, praying, or any other of what are commonly called religious duties. The very phrase "religious duties" should be stricken out of the vocabulary of young converts. They should be made to know that these acts are not religion. Many people become very strict in performing certain things, which they call religious duties, and suppose that is being religious, while they are careless about the ordinary duties of life, which in fact constitute a life of piety.

Prayer may be an expression and an act of piety, or it may not be. Going to church or to a prayer meeting may be considered either as a means, an act, or an expression of pious sentiment, but the performance of these does not make a person a Christian, and there may be great strictness and zeal in these without a bit of true religion. If young converts are not taught to differentiate, they may be led to think that there is something special in what are called religious duties, and to imagine they have a great deal of religion because they abound in certain actions that are commonly called religious duties – even though they may at the same time be very deficient in honesty, faithfulness, punctuality, temperance, or any other of what they choose to call their common duties. They may be very particular in some things – they may tithe mint, anise, and cummin, yet neglect the weightier matters of the law, such as justice and the love of God (Matthew 23:23).

e) True religion does not consist in desires to do good actions. Desires that do not result in choice and action are not virtuous, nor are such desires necessarily vicious. They may arise involuntarily in the mind, in view of certain objects, but while they produce no voluntary act, they are no more virtuous or vicious than the beating of the pulse – except in cases where we have indirectly willed them into existence by voluntarily putting ourselves under circumstances to excite them.

The wickedest man on earth may have strong desires after holiness. Did you ever think of that? He may see clearly that holiness is the only and indispensable means of happiness, and he naturally desires it. It is to be feared that multitudes are deceiving themselves with the supposition that a desire for holiness as a means of happiness is religion. Undoubtedly, many people give themselves much credit for desires that never result in choosing right. They feel desires to do their duty, but do not choose to do it, because upon the whole they have still stronger desires not to do it.

In such desires, there is no virtue. In order for an action or desire to be virtuous in the sight of God, it must be an act of the will. People often talk most absurdly on this subject, as though their desires had anything good while they remain mere desires. "I think I desire to do so and so." But do you do it? "Oh, no, but I often feel a desire to do it." This is practical atheism.

No matter what desires a person may have, if they are not carried out into actual choice and action, they are not virtuous. And no degree of desire is itself virtuous. If this idea could be made prominent and fully riveted in the minds of men, it would probably annihilate the hopes of half the church, who are living on their good desires while doing nothing for God.

f) They should be made to understand that nothing that is selfish is true religion. Whatever desires they may have, and whatever choices and actions they may put forth, if the reason for them is selfish, there is no true religion in them. A person may just as well commit sin in praying, reading the Bible, or going to church, as in anything else, if his motive is selfish.

Suppose a person prays simply with a view to promote his own happiness. Is that true religion? What is it other than attempting to make God his almighty servant? It is nothing else but to attempt a great undertaking to put the universe, God and all, under obligation to make him happy. It is a great degree of wickedness. It is so far from being piety that it is in fact immense wickedness.

g) Nothing is acceptable to God, as religion, unless it is performed wholeheartedly to please God. No outward action has anything good, or anything that God approves, unless it is performed from right motives and from the heart. Young converts should be taught fully and positively that all true religion consists in obeying God from the heart. All true religion consists in voluntary action. All that is holy, all that is lovely in the sight of God, all that is properly called religion, consists in voluntary action – in voluntarily obeying the will of God from the heart.

2. Young converts should be taught that the duty of self-denial is one of the leading features of the gospel. They should understand that they are not pious at all, any farther than they are willing to take up the cross daily and deny themselves for Christ. There is very little self-denial in the church, and the reason is that the duty of giving proper instruction to young converts is so much lost sight of. How seldom are they told that self-denial is the leading feature of Christianity. In pleading for benevolent causes, you will often find that ministers and agents do not even ask Christians to deny themselves for the sake of promoting the cause. They only ask them to give what they can spare as well as not, or in other words, to offer unto the Lord that which costs them nothing (see 2 Samuel 24:24). What an abomination! They only ask for the surplus, for what they do not need, for what they can give just as well as not.

There is no religion in this kind of giving. A man may give a hundred thousand dollars to a benevolent cause, and there would be no religion in it if he could give it as well as not, and if there was no self-denial in it. Jesus Christ exercised self-denial to save sinners. God the Father exercised self-denial in giving His Son to die for us, and in sparing us, and in bearing with our stubbornness. The Holy Spirit exercises self-denial in condescending to strive with such unholy beings to bring them to God. The angels exercise self-denial in watching over this world. The apostles planted the Christian religion among the nations by the exercise of self-denial. And are we to think of being religious without any self-denial? Are we to call ourselves Christians, the followers of Christ, the temples of the Holy Spirit, and to claim fellowship with the apostles, when we have never deprived ourselves of anything that would promote our personal enjoyment for the sake of promoting

Christ's kingdom? Young converts should be made to see that unless they are willing to lay themselves out for God and are ready to sacrifice life and everything else for Christ, they do not have the Spirit of Christ and are not His (Romans 8:9).

3. They must be taught what sanctification is. "What!" you will say. "Do not all who are Christians know what sanctification is?" No, many do not. Multitudes would be as much at a loss to tell clearly what sanctification is as they would be to tell what Christianity is. If the question were asked of every professing Christian in this city – What is sanctification? – I doubt if one in ten would give a right answer. They would blunder just as they do when they try to tell what true religion is and speak of it as something dormant in the soul, something that is put in and lies there, something that may be practiced or not, and still be in them.

In the same way, they speak of sanctification as if it were a sort of washing off of some defilement, or a purging out of some physical impurity. Or they will speak of it as if the senses were steeped in sin, and sanctification is taking out the stains. This is the reason why some people will pray for sanctification, yet practice sin, evidently supposing that sanctification is something that precedes obedience. They should be taught that sanctification is not something that precedes obedience, that it is not some change in the nature or the constitution of the soul. Rather, sanctification is obedience, and as a progressive thing, consists in obeying God more and more perfectly and perpetually.

4. Young converts should be taught so as to understand what perseverance is. It is astonishing how people talk about perseverance, as if the doctrine of perseverance was "Once in grace, always in grace," or "Once converted, sure to go to heaven." This is not the idea of perseverance. The true idea is that if a person is truly converted, he will continue to obey God – and as a consequence, he will surely go to heaven. But if a person gets the idea that because he is converted, therefore he will assuredly go to heaven, that person will almost assuredly go to hell, for he likely rests in some "conversion experience" rather than in Christ Jesus.

5. Young converts should be taught to be Christian in everything. They

should aim to be Christian in every department of life and in all that they do. If they do not aim at this, they should understand that they have no religion at all. If they do not intend and aim to keep all the commandments of God, what pretense can they make to piety? *Whosoever shall keep the whole law, and yet offend in one point, he is guilty of all* (James 2:10). He is justly subject to the whole penalty. If he disobeys God habitually in one particular area, he does not in fact obey Him in any particular area.

Obedience to God consists in the state of the heart. It is being willing to obey God. It is being willing for God to rule in all things. However, if a person habitually disobeys God in any one thing, he is in a state of mind that makes obedience in anything else impossible. To say that a person obeys God in some things out of respect to His authority, and that in some other things he refuses obedience, is absurd. The fact is that obedience to God consists in an obedient state of heart – a preference of God's authority and commandments to everything else.

If, therefore, an individual appears to obey in some things, yet perseveringly and knowingly disobeys in any one thing, he is deceived. He offends in one point, and this proves that he is guilty of all (James 2:10). In other words, he does not, from the heart, obey at all. A person may pray half of the time and yet have no religion. If he does not keep the commandments of God, his very prayer will be hateful to God. *He that turneth away his ear from hearing the law, even his prayer shall be abomination* (Proverbs 28:9). Do you hear that? If a person refuses to obey God's law, if he refuses to comply with any one duty, he cannot pray, he has no Christianity, and his very devotions are hateful.

6. By proper instructions, young converts are easily brought to be *temperate in all things* (1 Corinthians 9:25). However, this is a subject greatly neglected in regard to young converts, and almost lost sight of in the churches. There is a vast deal of intemperance in the churches. I do not mean intemperate drinking in particular, but intemperance in eating, and in living generally. There is, in fact, only little conscience about it in the churches. Therefore, the progress of reform in the matter is so slow. Nothing but an enlightened conscience can carry forward a permanent reform.

Ten years ago, most ministers used strong drink, and they kept it in their houses to treat their friends and their ministering brethren with. And the great body of the members in the churches did the same. Now there are only few of either, who are not actual drunkards, who will do it. But still there are many who indulge without hesitation in the use of wine. There are some ministers, and many professing Christians, who will drink down wine that has as much alcohol in it as brandy. This is intemperance.

Chewing and smoking tobacco are mere acts of intemperance. If they use these mere stimulants when there is no necessity for it, what is that but intemperance? That is not being temperate in all things. Until Christians will have a conscience on this subject, and be made to feel that they have no right to be intemperate in anything, they will not make much progress in religion. If the church could be made to know how much they spend for what are mere poisons, and nothing else, they would be amazed. Sit down and talk with many people, and they will strenuously maintain that they cannot get along without these things, these poisons, and they cannot give them up – no, not to redeem the world from eternal damnation. Very often they will absolutely show anger if argued with, just as soon as the argument begins to pinch their consciences.

Oh, how long will the church show her hypocritical face at the prayer meeting and ask God to save the world, while church members are actually throwing away five times as much for sheer intemperance as they will give to save the world? Some of you may think these are little things, and that it is quite beneath the dignity of the pulpit to lecture against wine and other alcohol and similar things. But I tell you it is a great mistake of yours if you think these are little things when they make the church odious in the sight of God by exposing her hypocrisy and lust.

Here is an individual who pretends he has given himself up to serve Jesus Christ, yet he refuses to deny himself any cherished indulgence, and then he will go and pray, "O Lord, save the world; O Lord, Your kingdom come." I tell you it is hypocrisy. Will such prayers be heard? Unless people are willing to deny themselves, I would not give a penny for the prayers of as many such professing Christians as would cover the whole United States.

These things must be taught to young converts. It must come to this point in the church that people will not be called Christians unless they will cut off the right hand and pluck out the right eye and deny themselves for Christ's sake. Is this a little thing? See it poison the spirit of prayer! See it debase and sensualize the soul! Is that a little thing that is beneath the dignity of the pulpit when these intemperate indulgences of one kind and another cost the church five times more, if not fifty times more, than all they do for the salvation of the world?

An estimate has recently been made showing that people in the United States consume seven million dollars' worth of coffee annually, and who does not know that a great part of this is consumed by the church. Yet sincere ministers and members of Christian churches are not ashamed to be seen accepting this enormous waste of money, while at the same time the poor heathen are sending upon every wind of heaven their agonizing wail for help. Heaven calls from above to "Go preach the gospel to every creature." Hell groans from beneath, and ten thousand voices cry out from heaven, earth, and hell, "Do something to save the world!"

Do it now! Oh, do it now, or millions more will be in hell through your neglect. And oh, *tell it not in Gath* (2 Samuel 1:20) that the church, the ministry, will not deny even their lusts to save a world. Is this Christianity? What business do you have to use Christ's money for such a purpose? Are you a steward? Who gave you this liberty? Consider these things lest it should be revealed at last that you have preferred self-gratification to obedience and made a god of your belly (see Philippians 3:19).

The time to teach these things with effect is when they are young converts. If they are not properly taught then, if they get a wrong habit and begin with an easy, self-indulgent mode of living, it is rare that they are ever thoroughly reformed. I have conversed with old professing Christians on these subjects, and have been astonished at their persistent obstinacy in indulging their lusts. I am convinced that the church can never rise out of this sloth until young converts are faithfully taught in the beginning of their religious course to be temperate in all things.

7. They should be taught to have just as much religion in all their business

as they have in prayer or in going to church. They should be just as holy, just as watchful, they should aim just as singly at the glory of God, and be just as sincere and solemn in all their daily work and activities as when they come to the throne of grace. If they are not, their Sunday performances will be an abomination.

8. They should be taught that it is necessary for them to be just as holy as they think ministers should be. For a long time, there has been an idea that ministers should be holy and practice self-denial, and so they should. But it is strange that they should suppose that ministers are obligated to be any more holy than other people. They would be shocked to see a minister show lightheartedness, or following the clothing fashion of the world, or losing his temper, or living in a fancy house, or riding in an expensive car. Oh, that is dreadful to them! It does not look good for a minister. Indeed! For a minister's wife to wear such a fine hat or such a silk shawl – oh, no!

However, they think nothing at all of this in a layman or a layman's wife. That is no offense at all. I am not saying that these things do look good for a minister; I know they do not. But in God's eyes, they look the same in a minister as they do in a layman. You have no more right to indulge in vanity and folly and pride than a minister does. Can you go to heaven without being sanctified? Can you be holy without living for God and doing all that you do to His glory?

I have heard professedly good men speak against ministers having large salaries and living in an expensive style, when they themselves were actually spending a great deal more money for the support of their families than any ministers. What would be thought of a minister living in the style in which many professing Christians and elders of churches are living in this city? Everybody would say that they were hypocrites. However, it is just as much an evidence of hypocrisy in a layman to spend God's money to gratify his lusts or to please the world or his family as it is for a minister to do the same. It is distressing to hear some of our foremost laymen talk of it being dishonorable to the Christian religion to give ministers a large salary and let them live in an expensive style, when it is a fact that their own expenses are, for the number of their families and the company they have, far above that of any minister.

All this arises out of fundamentally wrong ideas taught while they were young converts. Young converts have been taught to expect that ministers will have all the piety, especially all the self-denial; and as long as this continues, there can be no hope that the church will ever do much for the glory of God or for the conversion of the world. There is nothing of all this in the Bible. Where has God said, "You ministers, love God with all your heart and soul and mind and strength," or "You ministers, do all that you do to the glory of God"? This is said to all people, and he who attempts to excuse himself from any duty or self-denial, from any watchfulness or temperance, by putting it off upon ministers, or who ventures to adopt a lower scale of holy living for himself than he thinks is proper for a minister, is in great danger of proving himself a hypocrite and paying the forfeit of his foolishness in hell.

Much depends on the instructions given to young converts. Once they get into the habit of supposing that they may indulge in things that they would condemn in a minister, it is not common for them to ever get out of it.

9. They should aim at being perfect. Every young convert should be taught that if it is not his purpose to live without sin, he has not yet begun to be religious. What is true religion but a supreme love to God and a supreme purpose of heart or disposition to obey God? If there is not this, there is no religion at all. It is one thing to profess to be perfect, and another thing to profess and feel that you should be perfect. It is one thing to say that men should be perfect, and can be if they are so disposed, and another thing to say that they are perfect. If any are prepared to say that they are perfect, all I have to say is to let them prove it. If they are so, I hope they will show it by their actions; otherwise we can never believe they are perfect.

It is the duty of all to be perfect and to intend entire, perpetual, and universal obedience to God. It should be their constant purpose to live wholly to God and obey all His commandments. They should live so that if they do sin, it would be an inconsistency, an exception, an individual case, in which they act contrary to the fixed and general purpose and tenor of their lives. They should not sin at all; they are obligated to be as holy as God is, and young converts should be taught to start out in the right way, or they will never be right.

10. New converts should be taught to exhibit their light. If the young convert does not exhibit his light and hold it up to the world, it will go out. If he does not awaken himself and go forth and try to enlighten those around him, his light will go out and his own soul will soon be in darkness. Sometimes young converts seem inclined to be still and not do anything in public until they get a great deal of light, or a great deal of religion. But this is not the way. Let the convert use what he has. Let him hold up his little twinkling candle of light boldly and honestly, and then God will pour in the oil and make him like a blazing torch. But God will not take the trouble to keep a light burning that is hidden. Why should He? What is the use?

This is the reason why so many people enjoy so little in the Christian religion – they do not exert themselves to honor God. They keep what little they do enjoy so entirely to themselves that there is no good reason why God should bestow blessings and benefits on them.

11. They should be taught how to win souls to Christ. Young converts should be taught specifically what to do for this, and how to do it, and then taught to live for this end as the great leading object of life. How strange has been the course sometimes pursued. These people have been converted, and there they are. They get into the church, and then they are left to go along in their business just as they did before. They do nothing and are taught to do nothing for Christ, and the only change is that they go more regularly to church on Sunday and let the minister feed them, as it is called. But suppose he does feed them; they do not grow strong, for they cannot digest it because they take no exercise. They are unable to digest things spiritually. The great object for which Christians are converted and left in this world is to pull sinners out of the fire. If they do not do this, they might as well be dead. Young converts should be taught this as soon as they are born into the kingdom. The first thing they should do is to go to work for this purpose – to save sinners.

II. How Young Converts Should Be Treated by the Church

1. Old professing Christians should be able to give young converts a great deal of instruction, and they should give it. The truth is, however,

that the majority of professing Christians in the churches do not know how to give good instruction to young converts, and if they attempt to give them instruction, they give only that which is false. The church should be able to teach her children; and when the church receives them, it should be as busy in training them to act as mothers are in teaching their little children those things that they will need to know and do hereafter. But this is far enough from being the case generally. We can never expect to see young converts habitually taking the proper hold of duty, and going straight forward without decline and backsliding, until young converts are intelligently trained by the church.

2. Young converts should not be kept back behind the rest of the church. How often the old professing Christian will keep the young converts back behind the rest of the church and prevent them from taking any active part in religion for fear they would become spiritually proud. Young converts in such churches are rarely or never called on to take a part in meetings, or set to any active duty, or the like, for fear they would become lifted up with spiritual pride. Thus, the church becomes the modest keepers of their humility, and teaches them to file in behind the old, stiff, dry, cold members and elders, for fear that if they are allowed to do anything for Christ, it will make them proud.

In reality, the very way to make young converts humble and keep them so is to put them to their work and keep them there. That is the way to keep God with them, and as long as God is with them, He will take care of their humility. Keep them constantly engaged in religion, and then the Spirit of God will dwell with them, and they will be kept humble by the most helpful process. But if young converts are left to fall in behind the old professing Christians, where they can never do anything, they will never know what spirit they are of – and this is the very way to run them into danger of the worst kind of spiritual pride.

3. They should be watched over by the church and warned of their dangers, just as a tender mother watches over her young children. Young converts do not at all know the dangers by which they are surrounded, such as the devices of the devil, the temptations of the world, the power of their own passions and habits, and the thousand forms of danger

they do not know. If not properly watched and warned, they will run right into danger. See that mother watching her little child. Does she let him put his little hand in the candle, or allow him to crawl where he will get hurt, because his own blindness and ignorance does not prevent him from desiring to do so?

The church should watch over and care for its young children, just as mothers watch their little children in this large city for fear the carts may run over them, or that they may wander away and be lost; or as they watch them while growing up, for fear they may be drawn into the whirlpools of iniquity. The church should watch over all the interests of its young members. The church should know where they are, what their habits, temptations, dangers, and privileges are, what is the state of religion in their hearts, and how their spirit of prayer is.

Look at that anxious mother when she sees paleness gather around the little brow of her child. "What is the matter with you, my child? Have you eaten something improper? Are you getting sick? What is wrong?" Oh, how different it is with the children of the church, the lambs that the Savior has committed to the care of His churches. Alas! Instead of restraining its children and taking care of them, the church lets them go anywhere and look out for themselves.

What would we say about a mother who would knowingly let her little child totter along to the edge of a cliff? Would we not say she was horribly guilty for doing so, and that if the child would fall and die, his blood would rest on the mother's head? What, then, is the guilt of the church in knowingly neglecting its young converts? I have known churches in which young converts were first entirely neglected and regarded with suspicion and jealousy. Nobody went near them to strengthen or encourage or counsel them. Nothing was done to lead them to usefulness, to teach them what to do or how to do it, or to open to them a field of labor. And then, when they find that young converts cannot endure everything, and find them growing cold and backward under their own treatment, they just turn around and belittle them because they did not hold out.

4. Be tender in reproving them. When Christians find it necessary to reprove young converts, they should be exceedingly careful of their

manner of doing so. Young converts should be faithfully watched over by the elder members of the church, and when they begin to lose ground or to turn aside, they should be promptly admonished, and if necessary, reproved. But to do it in a wrong manner is worse than not to do it. It is sometimes done in a manner that is abrupt, harsh, coarse, and apparently critical, more like scolding than like brotherly admonition. Instead of inspiring confidence or leading to reformation, such a manner is simply intended to harden the heart of the young convert and confirm him in his wrong ways, while at the same time it closes his mind against the influence of such condemnatory guardians. The heart of a young convert is tender and easily grieved, and sometimes a single unkind look will set them into such a state of mind as will fasten his errors upon him and make him grow worse and worse.

You who are parents know how important it is when you reprove your children, that they see that you do it from the best of motives – for their benefit – because you want them to be good, and not because you are angry. Otherwise they will soon come to regard you as a tyrant rather than a friend.

It is the same with young converts. Kindness and tenderness, even in reproof, will win their confidence and attach them to you, and will give an influence to your brotherly instructions and counsels so that you can mold them into finished Christians. Instead of this, if you are severe and critical in your manner, you may make them think that you want to lord it over them. Many people, under pretense of being faithful, as they call it, often hurt young converts in such a severe and overbearing manner as to drive them away, or perhaps crush them into despondency and apathy.

Young converts have only a little experience, and they are easily knocked down. They are just like a little child when he first begins to walk. You see him tottering along, and there he stumbles over a straw. You see the mother pick up everything from the floor when her little one is going to try to walk. It is the same with young converts. The church should take up every stumbling block and treat them in such a way as to make them see that if they are reproved, Christ is in it, and then they will receive it as it is meant, and it will do them good.

5. Kindly point out things that are faulty in the young convert that he does not see. He is only a child and knows only a little about true religion. There are a great many things that he needs to learn, and a great many that he should correct. Whatever there is that is wrong in spirit, unlovely in conduct, or uncultivated in manner that will impede his usefulness or impair his influence as a Christian should be kindly pointed out and corrected.

However, to do this in the right way requires great wisdom. Christians should make it a subject of much prayer and reflection so that they may do it right, and not do more harm than good. If you rebuke him merely for the things that he did not see, or did not know to be improper, it will grieve and disgust him. Such instruction should be carefully timed. It is often good to take the opportunity after you have been praying together, or after a kind conversation of religious subjects, calculated to make him feel that you love him, that you seek his good and that you sincerely desire to promote his sanctification, usefulness, and happiness. Then a mere hint will often do the work. Just suggest that "Such a thing in your prayer" or "Your conduct in such a manner did not strike me pleasantly. Maybe you had better consider it, and you may realize that it is better to avoid the same thing again."

Do it right, and you will help and do him good. Do it wrong, and you will do ten times more harm than good. Often young converts will err through ignorance. Their judgment is unripe, and they need time to think and make up an informed judgment on some point that at first appears to them doubtful. In such cases, the church should treat them with great kindness and patience. The older members should instruct them kindly and not denounce them at once for not seeing, at first, what perhaps they did not themselves understand for years after they were converted.

6. Do not speak of the faults of young converts behind their backs. This is quite too common among old professing Christians, and eventually the young converts hear of it. What an influence it must have to destroy the confidence of young converts in their elder brethren, to grieve their hearts and discourage them, and perhaps to drive them away from the good influence of the church.

III. Some of the Evils of Defective Instruction to Young Converts

1. If not fully instructed, young converts will never be fully grounded in right principles. Having right fundamental principles will lead them to adopt a right course of conduct in all particular cases. In forming a Christian character, a great deal depends on establishing those fundamental principles that are correct on all subjects. If you look at the Bible you will see that God teaches right principles that we can carry out in detail in right conduct. If the education of young converts is defective, either in kind or degree, you will see it in the character of their lives. This is the philosophical result, just what might be expected, and must be always so. If I had time, I could show that almost all the practical errors that have prevailed in the church are the natural results of certain false dogmas that have been taught to young converts, and that they have been made to swallow as the truth of God at a time when they were so ignorant as not to know any better.

2. If the instruction given to young converts is not correct and full, they will not grow in grace, but their religion will dwindle away and decay. Instead of being like the path of the just, growing brighter and brighter to the perfect day (Proverbs 4:18), their course will grow dimmer and dimmer and decay, and finally perhaps go out in darkness. Wherever you see young converts let their religion taper off until it comes to nothing, you may understand that it is the proper result of defective instruction. The philosophical result of teaching young converts the truth, and the whole truth, is that they grow stronger and stronger. Truth is the food for the mind; it is what gives the mind strength. Where religious character grows weak, you can rely upon it that in nine cases out of ten, it is due to their being neglected or falsely instructed when they were young converts.

3. They will be understandably left in doubt whether they are Christians. If their early instruction is false or defective, there will be so much inconsistency in their lives, and so little real evidence of real piety, that they themselves will finally doubt whether they have any. They will probably live and die in doubt. You cannot make a little evidence go

a great way. If they do not see clearly, they will not live consistently. If they do not live consistently, they can have only little evidence. If they do not have evidence, they must doubt or live in presumption.

4. If young converts are properly instructed and trained, they will generally take the right side on all great subjects that come before the church. Subjects are continually coming up before the churches on which they have to take ground, and on many of them there is often much difficulty to make all the church take right ground. Take the subject of tracts, missions, Sunday schools, or temperance, for example, and see what criticisms, objections, resistance, and opposition have been encountered from members of the church in different places.

Go through the churches, and where you find that young converts have been well taught, you never find them making difficulty, raising objections, or criticizing. I do not hesitate to place much blame upon pastors and older members of churches that there are so many who have to be dragged up to the right ground on all such subjects. If they had grounded the young converts well in the principles of the gospel at the beginning, when they were first converted, they would have seen the application of their principles to all these things.

It is curious to see, and I have had much opportunity to see, how ready young converts are to take right ground on any subject that may be proposed. See what they are willing to do for the education of ministers, for missions, for moral reform, and for the slaves. If the great body of young converts from the late revivals had been well grounded in gospel principles, you would have found in them, throughout the church, one heart and one soul in regard to every question of duty that occurs. Let their early education be right, and you have got a body of Christians that you can depend on. If it had been general in the church, how much more strength there would have been in all her great movements for the salvation of the world!

5. If young converts are not well instructed, they will inevitably backslide. If their instruction is unsound, they will probably live in such a way as to disgrace Christianity. The truth, kept steadily before the mind of a young convert, in proper proportions, has a natural tendency

to make him grow up into the fullness of the stature of a spiritually mature person in Christ Jesus. If any point is made too prominent in the instruction given, there will probably be just that disproportion in his character. If he is fully instructed on some points and not in others, you will find a corresponding defect in his life and character.

If the instruction of young converts is greatly flawed, they will press on in religion no further than they are strongly propelled by the emotions of their earlier conversion. As soon as that is spent, they will come to a standstill, and then they will decline and backslide. From then on, you will find that they will go forward only when stirred up by some powerful excitement. These are your periodic Christians, who are so apt to wake up in a time of revival and carry on as if they had the zeal of an angel for a few days, and then die away as dead and cold as a northern winter.

Oh, how desirable, how infinitely important it is, that young converts should be so taught that their religion will not depend on impulses and excitements, but that they will go steadily onward in the Christian course, advancing from strength to strength, giving forth a clear and safe and steady light all around.

Remarks

1. The church is truly guilty for its past neglect in regard to the instruction of young converts. Instead of bringing up their young converts to be working Christians, the churches have generally acted as if they did not know how to involve young converts, or what use to make of them. They have acted like a mother who has a large family of daughters and does not know how to set them to work, and so allows them to grow up idle and untaught, useless and despised, and to be the easy prey of every scheming villain.

If the church had only done its duty in training up young converts to work and labor for Christ, the world would have been converted long ago. But instead of this, many churches even oppose young converts when they attempt to set themselves at work for Christ. Multitudes of old professing Christians look with suspicion upon every movement of young converts, and talk against them, and say, "They are too enthusiastic. They should not be so eager, but should wait for those who are older." There is waiting again. Instead of encouraging young converts to do well and cheering them on when they take hold with warm hearts and strong hands, very often they hinder them and might even put them down.

How often young converts have been stopped from going forward, and found themselves behind a formal, lazy, inefficient church until their spirit is crushed and their zeal extinguished; and after a few unsuccessful struggles to throw off the cords, they decide to sit down with the rest and wait. In many places, young converts cannot even attempt to hold a prayer meeting by themselves without the pastor or some of the deacons rebuking them for being so forward and accusing them of spiritual pride. "Oh, you are young converts, are you, and so you want to get together and call all the neighbors together to look at you because you are young converts. You had better become preachers at once."

A well-known doctor of divinity in New England boasted at a public table of his success in keeping all his converts still. He had great difficulty, he said, for they were very eager to do something, to talk or pray or get up meetings, but by the greatest vigilance he had kept it all down, and now his church was just as quiet as it was before the revival. What a wonderful achievement for a minister of Jesus Christ! Was that what the blessed Savior meant when He told Peter, *Feed my lambs* (John 21:15)?

2. Young converts should be trained to labor for Christ just as carefully as young recruits in an army are trained for war. Suppose a captain in the army would take no more effort to teach and train and discipline his company of soldiers than is taken by many pastors to train and lead forward their young converts. The enemy would laugh at such an army. Call them soldiers! Why, as to any effective service, they are in a mere state of infancy. They know nothing about what to do or how to do it, and if you bring them up to the battle, where are they?

Such an army would resemble the church that does not train its young converts. Instead of being trained to stand shoulder to shoulder at the beginning, they feel no practical confidence in their leaders, no confidence in their neighbors, and no confidence in themselves, and they scatter at the first sign of battle.

Look at the church now. Ministers are not agreed as to what should be done, and many of them will turn and fight back against their brethren, quarreling about new measures or a doctrinal statement or something. As for the members, they cannot feel confidence when they see their leaders so divided. Then if they attempt to do anything, what ignorance, what awkwardness, what discord, what weakness, what miserable work they make of it!

And so it must continue until the church will train up young converts to be intelligent, single-hearted, self-denying, working Christians. There is an enterprise now going on in this city that I rejoice to see. I mean the tract enterprise – a blessed work. The plan is to train up a body of devoted Christians to do what? To do what all the church should have been trained to do long ago – to know how to pray, how to converse with people about their soul's salvation, how to attend anxious meetings, how to deal with inquirers, and how to save souls.

3. The church has entirely mistaken the manner in which it is to be sanctified. The experiment has been carried on long enough of trying to sanctify the church without finding anything for them to do. However, holiness consists in obeying God, and sanctification, as a process, means obeying Him more and more perfectly. The way to promote it in the church is to give everyone something to do.

Look at these large churches where they have five hundred or seven hundred members, and get a minister to feed them from Sunday to Sunday. There are so many of them together that the majority of them have nothing at all to do and are never trained to make any direct efforts for the salvation of souls. In that way they are expecting to be sanctified and prepared for heaven. They will never be sanctified in this way. That is not the way God has appointed.

Jesus Christ has made His people coworkers with Him in saving sinners for this very reason – because sanctification consists in doing those things that are required to promote this work. This is one reason why He has not employed angels in the work or carried it on by direct revelation of truth to the minds of men. It is because it is necessary as a means of sanctification that the church should sympathize with Christ in His feelings and His labors for the conversion of sinners. The entire church must move in this way before the world will be converted. When the day comes that everyone in the whole church will realize that they are here on earth as a body of missionaries, and will live and labor accordingly, then will the day of man's redemption draw nigh.

Christian, if you cannot go overseas to labor, why are you not a missionary in your own family? If you are too weak even to leave your room, be a missionary there in your room. How many people are there in your house? Call in your unconverted children, other family members, and friends and be a missionary to them. Think of your physician, perhaps, who is making much effort to save your body, while he is losing his own soul. You receive his kindness, but never make him the greatest return in your power.

It is necessary for the church to take hold of her young converts at the beginning and set them to work, and set them to work right. The hope of the church is in the young converts.

4. We see what a responsibility rests on ministers, elders, and all who have the opportunity to assist in training young converts. How distressing is the picture that often forces itself upon the mind, where multitudes are converted, yet so little effort is taken with the young converts, so that in a single year you cannot tell the young converts from the rest of the church. Then to see the old church members turn around and complain about these young converts, and perhaps slander them, when in truth these old professing Christians themselves are most to blame. Oh, it is too bad.

This reaction that people talk so much about after a revival (as if reaction was the necessary effect of a revival) would never come, young converts never would backslide as they do, if the church was prompt and faithful in attending to their instruction. If they are truly converted, they can be made thorough and energetic Christians; and if they are not such, Jesus Christ will require it at the hands of the church.

Lecture 21

The Backslider in Heart

The backslider in heart shall be filled with his own ways.
—Proverbs 14:14

I cannot conclude this course of lectures without warning converts against backsliding. In discussing this subject, I will state:

    I.   What backsliding in heart is not.

    II.   What backsliding in heart is.

    III. Evidences of backsliding in heart.

    IV. Consequences of backsliding in heart.

    V.   How to recover from this state.

I. What Backsliding in Heart Is Not

It does not consist in the lessening of highly excited religious emotions. The decline of religious feeling may be an evidence of a backslidden heart, but it does not consist in the cooling off of religious feeling.

II. What Backsliding in Heart Is

1. It consists in taking back that consecration to God and His service that constitutes true conversion.

2. It is the leaving, by a Christian, of his first love.

3. It consists in the Christian's withdrawing himself from that state of entire and universal devotion to God that constitutes true religion, and coming again under the control of a self-pleasing spirit.

4. The text implies that there may be a backslidden heart, while the form of religion and obedience to God are maintained. As we know from consciousness that people perform the same or similar acts from widely different motives, and often from opposite motives, we are certain that people may keep up all the outward forms and appearances of religion, when in fact they are backslidden in heart. There is no doubt that the most intense selfishness often takes on a religious type, and there are many considerations that might lead a backslider in heart to keep up the forms while he has lost the power of godliness in his soul.

III. Evidences of a Backslidden Heart

1. Clear formality in religious exercises is evidence of a backslidden heart. There may be a stereotyped formal way of saying and doing things that is clearly the result of habit rather than the outflowing of the religious life. This formality will be emotionless and cold as an iceberg, and will show a total lack of earnestness in the performance of religious duty. In prayer and in religious exercises, the backslider in heart will pray or praise, confess, or give thanks with his lips so that all can hear him, perhaps, but in such a way that no one can feel him. Such a formality would be impossible where there existed a present, living faith and love, and religious zeal.

2. A lack of religious enjoyment is evidence of a backslidden heart. We always enjoy saying and doing those things that please those whom

we most love. Furthermore, when the heart is not backslidden, communion with God is kept up, and therefore all religious duties are not only performed with pleasure, but the communion with God involved in them is a source of rich and continual enjoyment. If we do not enjoy the service of God, it is because we do not truly serve Him. If we love Him supremely, it is impossible that we would not enjoy His service at every step. Always remember then, that whenever you lose your religious enjoyment or the enjoyment of serving God, you may know that you are not serving Him right.

3. Religious bondage is another evidence of a backslidden heart. God has no slaves. He does not accept the service of bondmen, who serve Him because they must. He accepts only the service of love. A backslider in heart finds his religious duties a burden to him. He has promised to serve the Lord. He does not dare to entirely break off from the form of service, and he tries to be dutiful while he has no heart in prayer, praise, worship, devotional duties, or in any of those exercises that are so spontaneous and delightful when there is true love to God.

The backslider in heart is often like a dutiful, but unloving wife. She tries to do her duty to her husband, but fails utterly because she does not love him. Her effort to please her husband is constrained, and is not the spontaneous outburst of a loving heart, and her relation and her duties become the burden of her life. She goes around complaining about the weight of care that is upon her, and will not be likely to advise young ladies to marry. She is committed for life, and must therefore perform the duties of married life, but oh, it is such a bondage!

It is the same with religious bondage. The professing Christian must perform his duty. He shuffles painfully about it, and you will hear him naturally sing backslider's hymns.

> Reason I hear, her counsels weigh,
> And all her words approve;
> And yet I find it hard to obey,
> And harder still, to love.[3]

---

3   This is from a hymn by Samuel Stennett (1727-1795) that begins, "With tears of anguish I lament."

4. An ungoverned temper is another evidence of a backslidden heart. While the heart is full of love, the temper will naturally be subdued and sweet, or at any rate, it will be kept under by the will and not allowed to break out in outrageous abuse; or if at any time it would so far escape from the control of the will as to break loose in hateful words, it will soon be brought under and will by no means be permitted to take control and manifest itself to the annoyance of others. A loving heart will especially confess and break down if at any time a bad temper gets control. Wherever, therefore, there is an irritable, uncontrolled temper allowed to manifest itself to those around the person, you may know there is a backslidden heart.

5. A spirit of unkindness is evidence of a backslidden heart. By this I mean a lack of that disposition that puts the best construction upon everyone's conduct that can be reasonable – a lack of confidence in the good intentions and professions of others. We naturally credit the good professions of those whom we love. We naturally attribute to them right motives and put the best allowable construction upon their words and deeds. Where there is a lack of this, there is clear evidence of a backslidden or unloving heart.

6. A critical spirit is certain evidence of a backslidden heart. This is a spirit of faultfinding, of attacking the motives of others when their conduct allows for a charitable construction. It is a disposition to fasten blame upon others and judge them harshly. It is a spirit of distrust of Christian character and professions. It is a state of mind that reveals itself in harsh judgments, harsh sayings, and the manifestation of uncomfortable feelings toward individuals. This state of mind is entirely incompatible with a loving heart, and wherever a critical spirit is manifested by a professing Christian, you may know there is a backslidden heart.

7. A lack of interest in God's Word is also evidence of a backslidden heart. Perhaps nothing more conclusively proves that a professing Christian has a backslidden heart than his losing his interest in the Bible. While the heart is full of love, no book in the world is as precious as the Bible. But when the love is gone, the Bible becomes not only uninteresting, but

often repulsive. There is no faith to accept its promises, but conviction enough left to dread its threatenings. But in general, the backslider in heart is apathetic as to the Bible. He does not read it much, and when he does read it, he does not have enough interest to understand it. Its pages become dark and uninteresting, and therefore it is neglected.

8. A lack of interest in secret prayer is also evidence of a backslidden heart. Young Christian, if you find yourself losing your interest in the Bible and in secret prayer, stop where you are, return to God, and give yourself no rest until you enjoy the light of His countenance. If you feel disinclined to pray or read your Bible; if, when you do pray and read your Bible, you have no heart in it and no enjoyment; if you are inclined to make your secret devotions short, or are easily induced to neglect them; if your thoughts, affections, and emotions wander and your closet duties become a burden – you may know that you are a backslider in heart, and your first business is to break down and see that your love and zeal are renewed.

9. A lack of interest in the conversion of souls and in efforts to promote revivals of religion reveals a backslidden heart. There is nothing in which a loving heart takes more interest than in the conversion of souls, in revivals of religion, and in efforts to promote them.

10. A lack of interest in published accounts or narratives of revivals of religion is also evidence of a backslidden heart. While one retains his interest in the conversion of souls and in revivals of religion, he will, of course, be interested in all accounts of revivals of religion anywhere. If you find yourself, therefore, disinclined to read such accounts, or find yourself not interested in them, take it for granted that you are backslidden in heart.

11. The same is true of missions and missionary work and operations. If you lose your interest in the work and in the conversion of the heathen, and do not delight to read and hear of the success of missions, you may know that you are backslidden in heart.

12. The loss of interest in benevolent causes generally is an evidence of a backslidden heart. I say the loss of interest, for certainly, if you were ever converted to Christ, you have had an interest in all benevolent causes that came within your knowledge. True religion consists in selfless benevolence. Of course, a converted soul takes the deepest interest in all benevolent efforts to reform and save mankind. In good government, in Christian education, in the cause of temperance, in the abolition of slavery, in provisions for the poor, and in short, in every good word and work, just in proportion as you have lost your interest in these, you have evidence that you are backslidden in heart.

13. The loss of interest in truly spiritual conversation is another evidence of a backslidden heart. *Of the abundance of the heart his mouth speaketh* (Luke 6:45). Our Lord Jesus Christ announced this as a law of our nature. No conversation is so sweet to a truly loving heart as that which relates to Christ and to our living Christian experience. If you find yourself losing interest in conversing about heart religion and of the various and wonderful experiences of Christians, if you ever knew what the true love of God is, you have fallen from it and are a backslider in heart.

14. A loss of interest in the conversation and society of highly spiritual people is evidence of a backslidden heart. We take the greatest delight in the company of those who are most interested in the things that are most dear to us. Therefore, a loving Christian heart will always seek the society of those who are most spiritually minded and whose conversation is most evangelical and spiritual. If you find yourself lacking in this respect, know for certain that you are backslidden in heart.

15. The loss of interest in the question of sanctification is evidence of a backslidden heart. I say again, the loss of interest, for if you ever truly knew the love of God, you must have had a great interest in the question of entire consecration to God, or of entire sanctification. If you are a Christian, you have felt that sin was an abomination to your soul. You have had inexpressible longings to be rid of it forever, and everything that could throw light upon that question of agonizing importance was

most intensely interesting to you. If this question has been dismissed, and you no longer take an interest in it, it is because you are backslidden in heart.

16. The loss of interest in those who are newly converted is also evidence of a backslidden heart. The psalmist says, *They that fear thee will be glad when they see me; because I have hoped in thy word* (Psalm 119:74). He puts this into the mouth of a convert, and who does not know that this is true? *There is joy in the presence of the angels of God over one sinner that repenteth* (Luke 15:10), and is there not joy among the saints on earth over those who come to Christ, and are as infants newly born into the kingdom of heaven? Show me a professing Christian who does not show an absorbing interest in converts to Christ, and I will show you a backslider in heart and a hypocrite; he professes Christianity, but has none.

17. An unkind state of mind in regard to professed converts is also evidence of a backslidden heart. Charity or love hopes all things and believes all things (1 Corinthians 13:7), and is very ready to judge kindly and favorably of those who profess to be converted to Christ. Those who truly love will naturally watch over them with interest, pray for them, instruct them, and have as much confidence in them as it is reasonable to have. A tendency, therefore, to pick at, criticize, and rebuke them is evidence of a backslidden heart.

18. The lack of the spirit of prayer is evidence of a backslidden heart. While the love of Christ remains fresh in the soul, the indwelling spirit of Christ will reveal Himself as the Spirit of grace and supplication. He will produce strong desires in the soul for the salvation of sinners and the sanctification of saints. He will often make intercessions in them with great longings, strong crying, and tears, and with groanings that cannot be uttered in words, for those things that are according to the will of God; or to express it in biblical language, according to Paul, *Likewise the Spirit also helpeth our infirmities: for we know not what we should pray for as we ought: but the Spirit itself maketh intercession for us with groanings which cannot be uttered. And he that searcheth*

the hearts knoweth what is the mind of the Spirit, because he maketh intercession for the saints according to the will of God (Romans 8:26-27). If the spirit of prayer departs, it is a sure indication of a backslidden heart, for while the first love of a Christian continues, he is sure to be drawn by the Holy Spirit to wrestle much in prayer.

19. A backslidden heart often reveals itself by the manner in which people pray. For example, praying as if one was in a state of self-condemnation, or very much like a convicted sinner, is evidence of a backslidden heart. Such a person will reveal the fact that he is not at peace with God. His confessions and self-accusations will show to others what perhaps he does not well understand himself. His manner of praying will reveal the fact that he does not have communion with God, and that instead of being filled with faith and love, he is more or less convicted of sin and is aware that he is not in a state of acceptance with God. He will naturally pray more like a convicted sinner than like a Christian. It will be seen by his prayer that he is not in a state of Christian liberty – that he is having a Romans 7 experience instead of that which is described in Romans 8.

20. A backslidden heart will further reveal itself by praying almost exclusively for self and for those friends who are regarded as parts of self. It is often very astonishing and even shocking to attend a backslider's prayer meeting, and I am very sorry to say that many prayer meetings of the church are little else. Their prayers are timid and hesitating, and they reveal the fact that they have little or no faith. Instead of surrounding the throne of grace and pouring their hearts out for a blessing on those around them, they have to be urged up to duty, to take up their cross.

Their hearts do not and will not spontaneously flow out to God in prayer. They have very little concern for others, and when they do, as they say, take up their cross and do their duty and pretend to lead in prayer, it will be observed that they pray just like a company of convicted sinners, almost entirely for themselves. They will pray for that which, if they would they obtain it, would be true religion, just as a convicted sinner would pray for a new heart, and in praying for Christianity as they do, demonstrate that they have none in their present state of mind.

If you ask them to pray for the conversion of sinners, they will either completely forget it, or just mention them in such a way that will show that they have no heart to pray for them.

I have known professed Christian parents to get into such a state that they had no heart to pray for the conversion of their own children, even when those children were under conviction. They would keep up family prayer and attend a weekly prayer meeting, and never get out of the old rut of praying around and around for themselves.

A few years ago, I was laboring in a revival in a Presbyterian church. At the close of the evening sermon, I found that the daughter of one of the elders of the church was in great distress of mind. I observed that her convictions were very deep. We had been holding a meeting with inquirers in the sanctuary, and I had just dismissed the inquirers, when this young lady came to me in great anxiety and begged me to pray for her. The people had mostly gone, except a few who were waiting for those friends to be dismissed who had attended the inquiry meeting.

I called the father of this young lady into the sanctuary so he could see the very anxious state of his daughter's mind. After a short personal conversation with her in the presence of her father, I called on him to pray for her and said that I would follow him, and urged her to give her heart to Christ. We all knelt, and he went through with his prayer, kneeling by the side of his sobbing daughter without ever mentioning her case. His prayer revealed that he had no more Christianity than she had, and that he was very much in her state of mind – under a dreadful sense of condemnation. He had kept up the appearance of religion. As an elder of the church, he was obligated to keep up appearances. He had gone around and around upon the treadmill of his duties, while his heart was completely backslidden.

It is often almost nauseating to attend a prayer meeting of the backslidden in heart. They will go around and around, one after the other, in reality praying for their own conversion. They do not express it that way, but that is the real meaning of the prayer. They could not make it more evident that they are backsliders in heart, even if everyone were to take his oath of it.

21. Absence from prayer meetings for weak reasons is a sure indication

of a backslidden heart. No meeting is more interesting to a wakeful Christian than the prayer meeting, and while they have any heart to pray, they will not be absent from the prayer meetings unless prevented from attending by the providence of God. If a visit from a friend at the hour of meeting can prevent their attendance, unless the call is made under very unusual circumstances, it is strong evidence that they do not want to attend, and therefore, that they are backsliders in heart.

A visit at such a time would not prevent them from attending a wedding, a party, a picnic, or a game. The fact is that it is hypocrisy for them to pretend that they really want to go while they can be kept away for minor reasons. If it were any place where they much desired to go, they would excuse themselves and say, "I was just going to a game," or "I was just going to such a place," and away they would go.

22. The same is true of the neglect of family prayer for minor reasons. While the heart is engaged in true religion, Christians will not readily neglect family devotions, and whenever they are ready to find an excuse for the neglect, it is sure proof that they are backslidden in heart.

23. When private prayer is regarded more as a duty than as a privilege, it is because the heart is backslidden. It has always appeared to me almost ridiculous to hear Christians speak of prayer as a duty. It is one of the greatest earthly privileges. What would we think of a child coming to his parent for his dinner, not because he was hungry, but as a duty? How it would amaze us to hear a beggar speak of the duty of asking alms from us! It is an infinite privilege to be allowed to come to God and ask for the supply of all our needs. But to pray because we must, rather than because we may, seems unnatural. To ask for what we need, and because we need it, and because God has encouraged us to ask and has promised to answer our request, is natural and reasonable. But to pray as a duty and as if we were accommodating God by our prayer, is quite ridiculous and is a certain indication of a backslidden heart.

24. Pleading for worldly amusements is also an indication of a backslidden heart. To a truly spiritual mind, the most delightful amusements possible are those engagements that bring the soul into the most direct

communion with God. While the heart is full of love and faith, an hour, or an evening, spent alone in communion with God is more delightful than all the amusements that the world can offer. A loving heart is jealous of everything that will break up or interfere with its communion with God. It has no desire for mere worldly amusements. When the soul does not find more delight in God than in all worldly things, the heart is sadly backslidden.

25. Spiritual blindness is another evidence of a backslidden heart. While the eye is single, the whole body will be full of spiritual light; but if the eye is evil (which is a backslidden heart), the whole body will be full of darkness (Matthew 6:22-23).

Spiritual blindness reveals itself in a lack of interest in God's Word, and in religious truth generally. It will also manifest a lack of spiritual discernment, and will be easily imposed upon by the insinuations of Satan. A backslidden heart will lead to the adoption of relaxed principles of morality. It does not discern the spirituality of God's law, and of His requirements generally. When this spiritual blindness is evident, it is a sure indication that the heart is backslidden.

26. Religious apathy, with worldly care and sensibility, is a sure indication of a backslidden heart. We sometimes see people who feel deeply and quickly on worldly subjects, but who cannot be made to feel deeply on religious subjects. This clearly indicates a backslidden state of mind.

27. A self-indulgent spirit is a sure indication of a backslidden heart. By self-indulgence, I mean a tendency to gratify the appetites, passions, and habits in order to fulfill the desires of the flesh and of the mind.

This, in the Bible, is represented as a state of spiritual death. I am convinced that the most common occasion of backsliding in heart is to be found in the desire for indulgence of the various appetites and habits. The appetite for food is frequently, and perhaps more frequently than any other, the occasion of backsliding. Few Christians, I am afraid, perceive any danger in this direction. God's command is, *Whether therefore ye eat, or drink, or whatsoever ye do, do all to the glory of God* (1 Corinthians 10:31).

Christians forget this, and they eat and drink to please themselves. They consult their appetites instead of the laws of life and health. More people are ensnared by their tables than the church is aware of. The table is a snare of death to multitudes that no one can number. A great many people who completely avoid alcoholic drinks will indulge in tea and coffee, and even tobacco, and in food, both in quantity and quality that violates every law of health. They seem to have no other law than that of appetite, and this they so debase by abuse that to indulge it is to ruin body and soul together. Show me a gluttonous professing Christian, and I will show you a backslider.

28. A withered conscience is also evidence of a backslidden heart. While the soul is watchful and loving, the conscience is as tender as the apple of the eye. But when the heart is backslidden, the conscience is silent and dry on many subjects. Such a person will tell you that he is not violating his conscience in eating or drinking, or in self-indulgence of any kind. You will find that a backslider does not have much conscience. The same will be true in regard to sins of omission very generally. Multitudes of duties may be neglected, and a withered conscience will remain silent. Where conscience is not awake, the heart is surely backslidden.

29. Loose moral principles are a sure indication of a backslidden heart, A backslider in heart will not honor the Sabbath, and will engage in secular reading and in much worldly conversation and activity. In business, such a person will take little advantages and use business tricks, conforming to the habits of worldly businessmen in the transaction of business. He will be guilty of deception and misrepresentation in making bargains, will demand exorbitant interest, and will take advantage of the necessities of his fellow men.

30. Prevalence of the fear of man is evidence of a backslidden heart. While the heart is full of the love of God, God is feared, and not man. A desire for the applause of men is kept down, and it is enough for such a person to please God, whether people are pleased or displeased. But when the love of God decreases, the fear of man, which *bringeth a snare* (Proverbs 29:25), gets possession of man. To please man rather than God is then his aim. In such a state he would rather offend God than man.

31. Contending for forms, ceremonies, and non-essentials is evidence of a backslidden heart. A loving heart is particular only about the substance and power of the Christian religion, and will not argue contentiously about its forms.

32. Complaining and faultfinding about measures in promoting revivals of religion is sure evidence of a backslidden heart. Where the heart is fully set upon the conversion of sinners and the sanctification of believers, it will naturally approach the subject in the most direct manner, and by means that are in the highest degree calculated to accomplish the end. It will not object to and stumble at measures that are evidently blessed by God, but will exert its utmost wisdom in devising the most suitable means to accomplish the great end on which the heart is set.

IV. Consequences of Backsliding in Heart

The text says that the backslider in heart will be filled with his own ways.

1. He will be filled with his own works. These are dead works, though. They are not works of faith and love, which are acceptable to God, but are the filthy rags of his own righteousness (Isaiah 64:6). If they are performed as religious services, they are but loathsome hypocrisy and an abomination to God. There is no heart in them, and to such a person God says, *Who hath required this at your hand?* (Isaiah 1:12); *Ye are they which justify yourselves before men; but God knoweth your hearts: for that which is highly esteemed among men is abomination in the sight of God* (Luke 16:15); and *I know you, that ye have not the love of God in you* (John 5:42).

2. He will be filled with his own feelings. Instead of that sweet peace and rest and joy in the Holy Spirit that he once experienced, he will find himself in a state of unrest, dissatisfied with himself and everybody else. His feelings are often painful, humiliating, and as unpleasant and unlovely as can be well conceived. It is often very difficult to live with backsliders. They are often angry, critical, and irritating in all their ways. They have forsaken God, and there is more of hell than heaven in their feelings.

3. They will be filled with their own prejudices. Their willingness to know and do the truth has gone. They will very naturally commit themselves against any truth that bears hard upon their self-indulgent spirit. They will try to justify themselves, they will neither read nor hear that which will rebuke their backslidden state, and they will become deeply prejudiced against everyone who will cross their path. If anyone reproves them, they consider him as an enemy. They hedge themselves in, shut their eyes against the light, stand on the defensive, and criticize everything that would search them out.

4. A backslider in heart will be filled with his own animosities. Such a person will almost surely lay up things against those with whom he has any business or other relations. He will be irritated in almost every relation of life, will allow himself to be bothered and angry, and get into such relations with some, and perhaps many people, that he cannot pray for them honestly, and can hardly treat them with common civility. This is an almost certain result of a backslidden heart.

5. The backslider in heart will be full of his own mistakes. He is not walking with God. He has fallen out of the divine order. He is not led by the Spirit, but is walking in spiritual darkness. In this state he is sure to fall into many serious mistakes, and may get entangled in such a way as to mar his happiness, and possibly destroy his usefulness for life. Mistakes in business, mistakes in forming new relations in life, and mistakes in using his time, his tongue, his money, and his influence – everything will go wrong with him as long as he remains in a backslidden state.

6. The backslider in heart will be filled with his own desires. His appetites and passions, which had been kept under, have now resumed their control, and having been so long suppressed, they will seem to avenge themselves by becoming more demanding and oppressive than ever. The animal appetites and passions will burst forth, to the astonishment of the backslider, who will find himself more under their influence and more enslaved by them than ever before.

7. The backslider in heart will be filled with his own words. While in that state, he will not, and cannot, control his tongue. It will prove itself to be an unruly member, full of deadly poison. It will set on fire the course of nature, and is itself set on fire of hell. By his words he will involve himself in many difficulties and issues from which he can never remove himself until he comes back to God.

8. He will be full of his own trials. Instead of keeping out of temptation, he will run right into temptation. He will bring upon himself multitudes of trials that he never would have had if he had not departed from God. He will complain of his trials, and yet constantly multiply them. A backslider feels his trials sharply, and while he complains of being so tried by everything around him, he is constantly inflaming them. Being the author of them, he seems intent on bringing them upon himself like an avalanche.

9. The backslider in heart will be full of his own foolishness. Having rejected the divine guidance, he will evidently fall into the depths of his own foolishness. He will inevitably say and do multitudes of foolish and ridiculous things. Being a professing Christian, these things will be all the more noticed, and of course will bring him all the more into ridicule and contempt. A backslider is, indeed, the greatest fool in the world. Having experiential knowledge of the true way of life, he has the infinite foolishness to abandon it. Knowing the fountain of living water, he has forsaken it and has hewed out to himself *cisterns, broken cisterns, that can hold no water* (Jeremiah 2:13). Having been guilty of this infinite foolishness, the whole course of his backslidden life must be that of a fool, in the Bible sense of the term.

10. The backslider in heart will be full of his own troubles. God is against him, and he is against himself. He is not at peace with God, with himself, with the church, or with the world. He has no inward rest. Conscience condemns him. God condemns him. All who know his state condemn him. *There is no peace, saith the LORD, unto the wicked* (Isaiah 48:22). There is no position in time or space in which he can be at rest.

11. The backslider in heart will be full of his own cares. He has turned back to selfishness. He considers himself and his possessions as his own. He has everything to care for. He will not hold himself and his possessions as belonging to God, and lay aside the responsibility of taking care of himself and all that he possesses. He does not and will not cast his cares upon the Lord, but tries to manage everything for himself, and in his own wisdom and for his own ends. Consequently, his cares will be multiplied and will come upon him like a flood.

12. The backslider in heart will be full of his own difficulties. Having forsaken God and having fallen out of His order and into the darkness of his own foolishness, he will be filled with difficulties and doubts in regard to what course he will pursue to accomplish his selfish ends. He is not walking with God, but is walking contrary to Him. Therefore, the providence of God will constantly cross his path and frustrate all his plans. God will frown darkness upon his path and will take effort to hinder his projects and blow his schemes to the winds.

13. The backslider in heart will be filled with his own anxieties. He will be anxious about himself, about his business, about his reputation, about everything. He has taken all these things out of the hands of God, and he claims them and treats them as his own. No longer having faith in God, and being unable to control events, he must of necessity be filled with anxiety in regard to the future. These anxieties are the inevitable result of his madness and foolishness in forsaking God.

14. The backslider in heart will be filled with his own disappointments. Having forsaken God and having taken the attitude of self-will before him, God will inevitably disappoint him in pursuing his selfish ends. He will frame his ways to please himself, without consulting God. Of course, God will frame his ways so as to disappoint him. Determined to have his own way, he will be greatly disappointed if his plans are frustrated, and the certain course of events under the government of God must of course bring a series of disappointments upon subjects who have rebelled against Him.

15. The backslider in heart will be full of his own losses. He regards his possessions as his own, his time as his own, his influence as his own, and his reputation as his own. He considers the loss of any of these as his own loss. Having forsaken God, and being unable to control the events upon which the continuance of those things is conditioned, he will find himself suffering losses on every side. He loses his peace. He loses his property. He loses much of his time. He loses his Christian reputation. He loses his Christian influence, and if he persists, he loses his soul.

16. The backslider in heart will be full of his own crosses. All religious duty will be troublesome, and therefore, a cross to him. His state of mind will make multitudes of things crosses that in a Christian state of mind would have been pleasant in a high degree. Having lost all heart in religion, the performance of all religious duties is contrary to his feelings. There is no help for him unless he returns to God. The whole course of divine providence will run across his path, and his whole life will be a series of crosses and trials. He cannot have his own way. He cannot gratify himself by accomplishing his own wishes and desires. He may beat and dash himself against the everlasting rocks of God's will and God's way, but he cannot break through and find victory. He must be crossed and recrossed and crossed again, until he will fall into the divine order and sink into the will of God.

17. The backslider in heart will be filled with his own annoyances. Having forsaken God, he will be sure to have much to irritate him. In a backslidden state, he cannot possess his soul in patience. The issues of his backslidden life will make him nervous and irritable; his temper will become explosive and uncontrollable.

18. The backslider in heart will be full of his own disgraces. He is a professing Christian. The eyes of the world are upon him, and all his inconsistencies, worldly mindedness, foolishness, bad moods, and hateful words and deeds disgrace him in the estimation of all people who know him.

19. The backslider in heart will be full of his own delusions. Having an evil eye, his whole body will be full of darkness. He will almost certainly

fall into delusions in regard to doctrines and in regard to practices. Wandering on in darkness as he does, he will very likely accept the biggest delusions. Spiritism, Mormonism, Universalism, and every other "ism" that is far from the truth will be very likely to gain possession of him. Who has not observed this of backsliders in heart?

20. The backslider in heart will be filled with his own bondage. His profession of religion brings him into bondage to the church. He has no heart to consult the interests of the church, or to labor for its growth, yet he is under covenant obligation to do so, and his reputation is at stake. He must do something to sustain religious institutions, but to do so is a bondage. If he does it, it is because he must and not because he may. Again, he is in bondage to God. If he performs anything that he calls religious duty, it is rather as a slave than as a freeman. He serves from fear or hope, just like a slave, and not from love. Again, he is in bondage to his own conscience. To avoid conviction and remorse, he will do or omit many things, but it is all with reluctance, and not at all of his own sincere goodwill.

21. The backslider in heart is full of his own self-condemnation. Having enjoyed the love of God, and having forsaken Him, he feels condemned for everything. If he attempts religious duty, he knows there is no heart in it, and so condemns himself. If he neglects religious duty, he of course condemns himself. If he reads his Bible, it condemns him. If he does not read it, he feels condemned. If he goes to a church service, the service condemns him, and if he stays away, he is condemned. If he prays in secret, in his family, or in public, he knows he is not sincere, and feels condemned. If he neglects or refuses to pray, he feels condemned. Everything condemns him. His conscience is up in arms against him, and the thunders and lightnings of condemnation follow him wherever he goes.

V. How to Recover from a State of Backsliding

1. Remember from where you are fallen. Take up the question at once, and deliberately contrast your present state with that in which you walked with God.

2. Take home the conviction of your true position. No longer delay to understand the exact situation between God and your soul.

3. Repent at once, and do your first work over again.

4. Do not attempt to get back by reforming your mere outward conduct. Begin with your heart, and set yourself right with God at once.

5. Do not act like a mere convicted sinner and attempt to promote yourself to God by any unrepentant works or prayers. Do not think that you must reform and make yourself better before you can come to Christ, but understand distinctly that only coming to Christ can make you better. No matter how distressed you may feel, know for a certainty that until you repent and accept God's will unconditionally, you are no better, but are constantly growing worse. Until you throw yourself upon His sovereign mercy, and thus return to God, He will accept nothing at your hands.

6. Do not imagine yourself to be in a justified state, for you know you are not. Your conscience condemns you, and you know that God should condemn you; if He justified you in your present state, your conscience could not justify Him. Come, then, to Christ at once, like the guilty, condemned sinner that you are. Accept responsibility for your wayward ways, and take all the shame and blame to yourself. Believe that despite all your wanderings from God, He loves you still – that He has loved you with an everlasting love, and therefore, is drawing you with loving-kindness (Jeremiah 31:3).

Lecture 22

Growth in Grace

But grow in grace, and in the knowledge of our Lord and
Saviour Jesus Christ.
—2 Peter 3:18

I must conclude this course of lectures by giving converts instructions on the subject of growth in grace. I will pursue the following method:

I. What is grace, as the term is used here?

II. What the admonition to *grow in grace* does not mean.

III. What it does mean.

IV. Conditions of growth in grace.

V. What is not proof of growth in grace.

VI. What is proof of growth in grace.

VII. How to grow in grace.

I. What Is Grace, as the Term Is Used Here?

Grace is favor. It is often used in the Bible to signify a free gift. The grace of God is the favor of God, His free gifts.

II. What the Admonition to *Grow in Grace* Does Not Mean

It does not call for the gradual giving up of sin. It is strange to say, but it would seem that some have understood it this way. However, we are nowhere in the Bible commanded to give up sin gradually. We are everywhere commanded to give it up instantly and entirely.

III. What It Does Mean

It urges upon us the duty of growing in the grace of God, of growing in His esteem, in a worthiness of His favor.

IV. Conditions of Growth in Grace

1. Growth or increase in anything implies a beginning. Growth in the grace of God implies that we have already found favor in His sight, that we are already indebted for grace received, and that we are already in grace, in the sense of having a place among His favored ones.

2. Consequently, growth in grace implies that we have already repented of our sin and have actually and practically abandoned all known sin. It cannot be that we are in favor with God if we are still indulging in known sin against Him. Being in favor with God implies, of course, that we are pardoned and favored by Him for the sake of our Lord and Savior Jesus Christ. Pardon is favor, and it implies the renunciation of rebellion against God. The conditions of the divine favor, as revealed in the Bible, are repentance and abandonment of all known sin, and faith in our Lord Jesus Christ.

I said that as a condition of growth in grace, we must have the beginnings of grace. In other words, we must already be Christians, must be in a state of acceptance with God, must have accepted Christ, so far as He is understood, and must be in a state of obedience to all the recognized will of God. Without this, we cannot be in a state of grace or in the favor of God. But being in this state, there is room for everlasting growth. As we know more of God, we will be capable of loving Him more and of having a more universal and complete confidence in

Him. And there can be no end to this while we have any being, either in this or in any other world. Our love and confidence in Him may be complete, so far as we know Him. This love and confidence will secure His favor, but there will be no end to our growth in knowledge of Him, and consequently, there is room for eternal growth in grace. The more we love, the more we believe, and the more we know of God. If we conform to all this knowledge, the more God will be pleased with us, the higher we will stand in His favor, and more and greater gifts He will continue to bestow upon us.

3. Of course, growth in the knowledge of God is a condition of growth in His favor. We might grow in knowledge without growing in His favor because we might not love and trust Him in accordance with this increased knowledge. But we cannot love and trust Him more perfectly unless we become more perfectly acquainted with Him. If our love and faith keep pace with our growing knowledge, we must grow in His favor. But growth in knowledge must be a condition of growth in love and faith.

4. Growth in the knowledge of God, as revealed in Christ Jesus, must be a condition of growth in His favor. It is in and through Christ Jesus that God reveals Himself to man. It is in Christ Jesus that we get the true idea of the personality of the infinite God. That is why the text says, *Grow in grace, and in the knowledge of our Lord and Saviour Jesus Christ.*

5. Growth in grace is conditioned on increased knowledge of what is involved in entire consecration to God. True conversion to God involves the consecration of ourselves and of all that we have to Him, as far as we understand what is implied in this. But at first, converts are by no means aware of all that is involved in the highest forms of consecration. They will soon learn that there are certain things that they did not think of, and that they did not give up to God. At first, perhaps, all that was in their thought was to lay their bare soul upon the altar and give up their whole heart to God. But soon they may learn that they did not think of all their possessions and everything that was dear to them. They did not surrender all, and leave not even a hoof behind (Exodus 10:26).

They surrendered all of which they thought at the time, but they were not fully enlightened. They did not think, nor could they think, at the time, of every appetite, passion, habit, desire, and affection, of everything they call their own and all that is dear to them in the whole creation, to make a thorough surrender and delivery of them all to God. To gain such knowledge is a work of time. Growth in the favor of God is conditioned on making a full surrender and consecration to God of everything we are, have, desire, and love, as quickly as these objects come to mind.

As long as we exist and knowledge increases, there is no doubt that we will be called upon to grow in grace by consecrating to God every new object of knowledge, desire, and affection that we may come to know, desire, and love to all eternity. As you get new light, you must enlarge your consecration from day to day, and from hour to hour, or you will cease to grow in grace. Whenever you stop short and do not place and leave everything that you are, that you possess, or that you love upon the altar of consecration, that moment you cease to grow in grace. I urge you to let this saying sink deep into your hearts.

6. Another condition of growth in grace is intense earnestness and determination in seeking increased religious light by the illumination of the Holy Spirit. You will gain no useful religious light except by the inward showing and teaching of the Holy Spirit. You will not obtain this unless you continue in the true attitude of a disciple of Christ. Remember that He said, *Whosoever he be of you that forsaketh not all that he hath, he cannot be my disciple* (Luke 14:33). He will not, by His Holy Spirit, be your divine teacher unless you renounce self and live in a state of continual consecration to Him. To obtain and preserve the teachings of Christ by His Holy Spirit, you must continually and earnestly pray for His divine teaching, and watch against resisting and grieving Him.

7. Another condition of growth in grace is a constant conformity to all the teachings of the Holy Spirit, keeping up with our convictions of duty and with our growing knowledge of the will of God.

8. A more and more complete faith in God is a condition of growth in grace. By complete, I mean an unreasoning faith, a confidence in God's

character so profound that we trust Him in the dark as well as in the light, as well when we do not understand the reasons of His dealings with us, or of His requirements, as when we do. It is a faith like that of Abraham, who staggered not at a promise through unbelief, although the thing promised seemed most irrational and impossible. A steadfast or complete faith is an unwavering, unquestioning faith, a state of mind that will rest in God, in His promises, in His faithfulness, and in His love no matter how things seem, and no matter how trying and apparently unreasonable His commands or providential dealings may be.

Abraham's faith is often commended in the Bible. God had promised him a son, but did not give him the promised seed until he was a hundred years old, and Sarah was ninety. But even though Sarah was past childbearing age, and he as good as dead, he believed that God was able to fulfill His promise. When Abraham had received his beloved son, with the assurance that this was to be his heir, and that through him the promise was to be fulfilled through all generations, God tried his faith severely by commanding him to offer Isaac as a burnt sacrifice. Without the least hesitation, he obeyed, believing that God was able to raise Isaac from the dead. He made all his arrangements to obey this difficult command with such calmness that neither Sarah nor Isaac suspected that any such thing was in contemplation. This was an instance of the exercise of steadfast faith. Growth in grace, or in the favor of God, is conditioned upon growth in steadfast confidence in Him.

9. A more thoroughly sanctified sensibility is a condition of growth in the favor of God. By the sensibility, I mean that department of our nature that feels and desires and to which belongs all that we call desire, affection, emotion, feeling, appetite, passion, propensity, and lust. The sensibility is an involuntary power, and moral actions and qualities cannot, with strict propriety, be presupposed by it. The states of the sensibility have moral character only as they derive it directly or indirectly from the action of the will. The nature of man, as a whole, in his depraved condition, is in a very unlovely state, and although the will may be given up to God, the sensibility may be in such a state as to be very unlovely in the sight of one who looks directly upon it and who knows perfectly every excited desire, passion, propensity, and lust.

It is mainly through the sensibility that we are assailed with temptations. It is through this that the Christian warfare is kept up. The Christian warfare consists in the battle of the will with these various appetites, passions, propensities, and lusts, to keep them in subjection to the will of God. If the will maintains its integrity and clings to the will of God, the soul does not sin in its battle with the excited states of the sensibility. But these rebellious impulses embarrass the will in the service it renders to God. To keep them under occupies much time, thought, and strength. Therefore, the soul cannot give to God so complete a service, while exerting the full strength of the will to subjugate these impulses, as it otherwise might and would give.

These appetites, passions, and impulses, although not sinful in themselves, have been regarded and spoken of as indwelling sin. Strictly, they cannot be sin because they are involuntary. But they are often a great hindrance to our growth in the favor of God. *For the flesh lusteth against the Spirit, and the Spirit against the flesh: and these are contrary, the one to the other: so that ye cannot do the things that ye would* (Galatians 5:17). This means that we cannot do for God what we otherwise would because we have to battle so much with the states of the sensibility to subdue them. As the sensibility becomes more and more subdued and in harmony with the will's devotion to God, we are left free to give to God a more unembarrassed service. Therefore, the more thorough the sanctification of the sensibility, the more thoroughly we are in favor with God.

10. A growing thoroughness and universality of consecration of spirit, soul, and body is the condition of more and more growth in the favor of God. It is common, at first, for the steadfastness of the will's devotion to God to be overcome by the clamor of the excited appetites, passions, and impulses, or by the various states of the sensibility. Whenever the will yields to these excited states, you sin. But in such cases, the sin is not willful, in the sense of being deliberate and intentional; it is rather a slip, an inadvertency, a momentary yielding under the pressure of highly excited feeling. Nevertheless, this yielding is sin.

No matter how excited the states of the sensibility may be, if the will does not yield, there is strictly no sin. Still, while the will is steadfast, maintaining its consecration and obedience to God, the appetites originating in the body, and the various impulses of the soul (that exist in the sensibility), may be so unsecured and may be in such confusion and in such a state of unhealthy development that the soul may be unfit for the employments and enjoyments of heaven.

11. Therefore, taking on a greater fullness of the divine nature is a condition of growth in the grace of God. Both the will and the sensibility of God must be in a state of utmost perfection and accord. All of His desires and feelings must be in perfect harmony with His intelligence and His will. It is not so with us in our state of physical depravity. The depravity of sensibility must be physical because it is involuntary. Still, it is depravity; it is a lapsed or fallen state of the sensibility. This lapsed area of our nature must be recovered, sanctified, or completely restored to harmony with a consecrated will and an enlightened intelligence, or we are never fit for heaven. As we become more and more the partakers of the divine nature and of the divine holiness, we are more fully sanctified in spirit, soul, and body, and of course grow more and more in the grace of God.

12. A greater and more all-pervading fullness of the Holy Spirit's residence is another condition of growth in the favor of God. You cannot have it too thoroughly impressed upon you that every step in the Christian life is to be taken under the influence of the Holy Spirit. The thing to be attained is the universal teaching and guidance of the Holy Spirit, so that in all things you will be led by the Spirit of God. *Walk in the Spirit, and ye shall not fulfil the lust of the flesh* (Galatians 5:16). *If ye through the Spirit do mortify the deeds of the body, ye shall live* (Romans 8:13). *To be carnally minded is death; but to be spiritually minded is life and peace* (Romans 8:6). Therefore, always remember that to grow in grace, you must grow in the possession of the fullness of the Holy Spirit in your heart.

13. A deeper personal acquaintance with the Lord Jesus Christ in all His official work and relations is a condition of growth in grace. His nature, work, and relations are the theme of the Bible. The Bible presents

Him to us in a great variety of relations. In my *Systematic Theology*, I have considered some sixty or more of these official relations of Christ to the human race, and these are presented rather as examples and illustrations than as covering the whole ground of His relations to us.

It is one thing to know Christ simply on paper, and as spoken of in the Bible, by reading or hearing of Christ, and quite another thing to know Him personally in these relations. The Bible is the means of introduction to Him personally. What is said of Him there is designed to lead us to seek after a personal acquaintance with Him. It is by this personal acquaintance with Him that we are made like Him. It is by direct, personal, individual dealings with His divine mind that we take on His image. *We all, with open face beholding as in a glass the glory of the Lord, are changed into the same image from glory to glory, even as by the Spirit of the Lord* (2 Corinthians 3:18).

Faith cometh by hearing (Romans 10:17), and faith secures for us a personal acquaintance with Christ. Christ has promised to manifest Himself personally to those who love and obey Him. My dear children, do not stop short of securing this personal manifestation of Christ to your souls. Your growth in grace will depend upon this. Do not think of stopping short of personally knowing Christ, not only in all these relations, but in the fullness of these relations. Do not overlook the fact that the appropriation of Christ in each of these relations is a personal act of faith. It is a putting on of the Lord Jesus Christ, taking Him as yours, in each of these relations, as your wisdom, righteousness, sanctification, and redemption (1 Corinthians 1:30) – as your prophet to teach you, your king to govern you, and your high priest to atone for you; as your mediator, your advocate, your strength, your Savior, your hiding place, your high tower, your captain and leader, your shield, your defense, and your exceeding great reward.

In each of these relations, and in all of His other official relations, you need to appropriate Him by faith so as to secure to you personal fellowship with Him in these relations. Remember that growing in a personal acquaintance with Him in these relations is an indispensable condition of growth in His favor.

V. Some Things That Are Not Proof of Growth in Grace

1. Growth in knowledge is not conclusive evidence of growth in grace. Some degree of knowledge is indispensable to our being in favor with God, and growth in knowledge, as I have shown, is a condition of growth in grace – but knowledge is not grace, and growth in knowledge does not constitute growth in grace. A person may grow ever so much in knowledge, and have no grace at all. In hell, they cannot but grow in knowledge as they grow in experience and in the knowledge of God's justice. But there, their growth in knowledge only inflames the guilt and misery of hell. They know more and more of God and His law, and their own sin, and the more they know, the more wretched they are. They never learn piety from their increased knowledge.

2. It is not certain evidence that an individual grows in grace because he grows in gifts. A professing Christian may increase in gifts; that is, he may become more fluent in prayer, more eloquent in preaching, or more tender in exhortation without being any more holy. We naturally increase in that in which we exercise ourselves. If anyone often exercises himself in exhortation, he will naturally, if he makes any effort, increase in fluency and force.

However, he may do all this and yet have no grace at all. He may pray ever so intently, and increase in fluency and apparent zeal, yet have no grace. People who have no grace often do so. It is true that if he has grace and exercises himself in these things, he will grow in gifts as he grows in grace. No person can exercise himself in obeying God without improving in those exercises. If he does not improve in gifts, it is a true sign that he does not grow in grace. On the other hand, it is not sure evidence that he grows in grace because he improves in certain exercises, for he will naturally improve by practice whether he is a Christian or a hypocrite.

3. It is not proof that a person grows in grace because he thinks he is doing so. One may be very favorably impressed in regard to his own progress in religion, when it is evident to others that he is not only making no progress, but is, in fact, declining. An individual who is growing worse and worse is not ordinarily very aware of the fact.

It is not uncommon for both unrepentant sinners and Christians to think they are growing better when they are growing no better. This results from the very nature of the case. If any person is growing worse, his conscience will, for the time being, become more and more withered, and his mind more and more dark, as he suppresses the conscience and resists the light. Then he may think he is growing better, just because he has less sense of sin; and while his conscience continues to sleep, he may continue under a fatal delusion.

A man will judge of his own spiritual state as he compares himself with a high or low standard. If he keeps Christ before him, in His fullness, as his standard, he will undoubtedly always, at least in this state of existence, have a low estimate of his own attainments. While at the same time, if he sets before himself the church, or any of the members of the church as a standard, he will be very likely to form a high estimate of his progress in Christianity, and be very well satisfied with himself.

This is the reason why there is such a difference in people's views of their own state and of the state of the church. They compare themselves and the state of the church by different standards. Therefore, one person has a very humble view of his own state, and complains of that of the church. Another person thinks such complaints of the church are overly critical. To him the church appears to be doing very well. The reason why he does not think the church is cold and in a low state is that Christ is not his standard of comparison. If a man shuts his eyes, he will not see the defilement on him and may think he is clean, while to everyone around him, he appears loathsome.

VI. What Is Proof of Growth in Grace

1. The manifestation of more steadfast and universal trust in God is an evidence of growth in grace. The exercise of greater and more steadfast confidence, as I have said, is the condition of growing in the favor of God. The manifestation of this steadfast and universal confidence is proof that this growing confidence exists, and is, therefore, satisfactory evidence of growth in the favor of God. If you are aware in your own soul that you exercise more steadfast and universal confidence in God, this is conclusive proof to you that you are growing in grace, and as you manifest in your

life, attitude, and spirit this growing confidence, you prove to yourself and to others that you are growing in the grace of God. For as you grow in steadfast confidence in Him, you must grow in His grace.

2. Another evidence of growth in grace is decreasing dependence upon the world. The will may be in an attitude of devotion to God, while the world's seductive charms very much embarrass the healthy action of the Christian life. As the soul becomes crucified and dead to the world, it grows in the grace of God.

3. Less reluctance of feeling when called to the exercise of self-denial is evidence of growth in grace. It shows that the feelings are becoming less and less domineering, that the will is getting more the mastery of them, and that the sensibility is getting more into harmony with the devotion of the will and the dictates of the intelligence.

4. Less temptation to sins of omission is another evidence of growth in grace. For example, less temptation to shun the cross, less temptation to neglect unpleasant duties, less temptation to laziness, less temptation to avoid responsibility, less temptation to neglect prayer, reading the Scriptures, and private and family devotions – basically, less and less temptation to avoid the performance of any duty is evidence of growth in grace. These temptations consist in the excited states of the sensibility. As these become less in strength and frequency, we learn that our sensibility is becoming more completely dominated by the law of the intelligence and the decisions of the will, and consequently, that the work of the sanctification of the spirit, soul, and body is progressing, and that therefore we are growing in the favor of God.

5. A growing intensity and steadiness of zeal in promoting the cause of God is evidence of growth in the favor of God. Sometimes Christian zeal is comparatively cool, and at other times deep and intense. Sometimes it will be steady, and at other times irregular and obscure. As Christians grow in piety, their zeal becomes deep, intense, and steady, and as you are aware of this, and in your life and spirit give evidence of it to others, you have and give proof that you are growing in the grace of God.

6. Losing more and more the consciousness of self, and respect to self, in every action of life, is evidence of growth in the grace of God. Some people have so much consciousness of self in everything, and so much respect to self in everything they say and do, as to be embarrassed in all their Christian life whenever they attempt to act or speak in the presence of others. As they lose this self-consciousness and have less respect to self, their service of God becomes freer and more unembarrassed, and they are all the better servants by how much less they think of self.

Sometimes young converts cannot speak or pray or perform any public duty without being either proud or ashamed, as they think they have performed those duties with more or low acceptance to those around them. While this is so, their piety is in a weak state. They must lose sight of their own glory and have a single eye to the glory of God to find acceptance with Him. As they lose sight of self, and set God always before them, having an eye single to His glory, they grow more and more in His grace.

7. Consequently, a growing deadness to the flattery or the criticism of men is evidence of growth in grace. Paul had grown in grace so much that he considered it a light thing to be judged by man; he only sought to commend himself to God. As you find yourself growing in this state of deadness to the flatteries or criticisms of men, you have evidence that you grow in grace.

8. A growing fondness in the acceptance of the whole will of God is evidence of growth in His grace. Some people rebel against His will as revealed in His Word and in His providence. Other people, under trying circumstances, will barely tolerate His will as revealed in His Word and in His providence. However, those who are growing in grace find it more natural to them to embrace His whole revealed will with greater and greater affection.

9. Increasing calmness and quietness under great afflictions is evidence of growth in the favor of God. This demonstrates a broader and more steadfast faith, a fuller and more heartfelt acceptance of the will of God as revealed in these afflictions, and shows that the soul is more steadily and firmly at anchor upon its rock, Christ.

10. A growing peace under sudden and crushing disasters and bereavements is evidence of growth in grace. The more tranquil the soul can remain when sudden storms of providence come upon it, sweeping away its loved ones and crushing its earthly hopes, the greater is its evidence of being under the particular favor of God. This peacefulness is both a result and an evidence of the grace of God.

11. Growing patience under much provocation is evidence of growth in the grace of God.

12. Patient endurance with joy is evidence of growing in favor with God. When you find that you cannot only tolerate, but can accept the will of God, as revealed in calling you to suffer, and especially when you can accept these sufferings and endure them long and with joyfulness, you have evidence that you are growing in the grace of God.

13. A growing gentleness and joyfulness under crosses and disappointments and severe pain is evidence of growth in the grace of God.

14. An increasing deadness to all that the world has to offer, or to threaten, is evidence of growth in the grace of God.

15. A growing rest in, and satisfaction with, all the dealings of providence is evidence of growth in grace.

16. Less temptation to murmur or complain at any administering of providence is evidence of growth in grace.

17. Less temptation to be troubled when we are crossed or disappointed in any respect is evidence of growth in grace.

18. Less and less temptation to resentment and the spirit of retaliation when we are in any way insulted or mistreated is evidence that the sensibility is becoming more and more thoroughly subdued, and consequently, that we are growing in favor with God.

19. Less temptation to dwell upon and to magnify our trials and troubles, to think of them and speak of them to others, is evidence that we think less and less of self, and accept our trials and troubles with more and more delight in God. It is sad to hear some professedly good people always dwelling upon and magnifying their own troubles and trials. However, if they grow in grace, they will think less and less of these and be more inclined to think of them as "light afflictions" (see 2 Corinthians 4:17). The more we grow in grace, the less stress we lay upon the evils we meet with in the way.

A good man who was really passing through what the world would call very severe trials and afflictions (he had lost a beloved wife, and his children had died one after another) said to me once, "I have many mercies, and few afflictions." When, under such circumstances, a man can say, *The lines are fallen unto me in pleasant places; yea, I have a goodly heritage* (Psalm 16:6), he has the most satisfactory evidence that he is growing in the grace of God, for this state of mind is both a result and an evidence of the grace of God.

20. A growing tendency to make light of our trials and to magnify our blessings is evidence that we are growing in the grace of God.

21. Less and less anxiety and concern about the events of providence, and especially about the things that nearly and deeply affect ourselves, is evidence of growth in grace. This is evidence of a broader and more steadfast faith, of a more submissive will, and of a diminishing tendency to self-seeking. Therefore, it is evidence of growing favor with God.

22. Being less and less disturbed and troubled by the events of life, especially those that go counter to our own plans, hopes, expectations, and desires, and that thwart our most treasured plans, is evidence of growth in grace.

23. A growing and realizing confidence in the wisdom, benevolence, and universality of the providence of God, and a state of mind that sees God in everything, is evidence of growth in grace. Some minds become so spiritual that they hardly seem to reside in the body, and appear

continually to perceive the presence of God in every event, almost as if they were separated from the body and beheld God face to face. They seem to dwell, live, move, and have their being in the spiritual world rather than in the natural world.

They are continually under such a sense of the divine presence, care, and protection that they hardly appear like inhabitants of earth. They are a living, walking mystery to those in the midst of whom they dwell. The springs of their activity are so divine, their life is so much hidden in God, and they act under influences so far above the world that they cannot be judged by the same standards as other people. Carnal minds cannot understand them. Their hidden life is so unknown, and so unknowable to those who are far below them in their spiritual life, that they are necessarily regarded as quite eccentric, as being mystics or zealots, and as having very strange religious views – as being enthusiasts, and perhaps fanatics.

These people are in the world, but they live above the world. They have so far escaped from the pollutions that are in the world (2 Peter 2:20) that they can truly and understandingly say with Paul, in Galatians 6:14, *But God forbid that I should glory, save in the cross of our Lord Jesus Christ, by whom the world is crucified unto me, and I unto the world.* Such people are evidently growing in the grace of God.

24. Being less and less disposed to dwell upon the faults and shortcomings of others is evidence of growth in grace.

25. Being less and less disposed to speak derisively or severely, or to judge uncharitably of others, is evidence of growth in grace. A growing delicacy or tenderness in speaking of their real or supposed faults behind their backs is evidence of growth in grace.

26. An increasing reluctance to regard or treat anyone as an enemy, and an increasing ease and naturalness in treating them kindly and in praying for them sincerely, and in efforts to do them good, is evidence of growing in grace.

27. Less and less temptation to remember an offense, and the decrease of all desire to retaliate when wronged, is evidence of growth in grace.

28. A growing readiness and warmth in forgiving and burying a wrong out of sight, and a kind of moral inability to do otherwise than seek the highest good of those who have harmed us most deeply, is evidence of growth in grace.

29. When we find in our own experience, and demonstrate to others, that it is more and more natural to regard all men as our brethren, especially to drop out of view all denominational distinctions, all ideas and prejudices of class, color, poverty, riches, blood relation, and of natural rather than of spiritual ties, and to make common cause with God in aiming to do good to all people, to enemies and friends alike, we have then ourselves, and give to others, the highest evidence of our growing in the grace of God.

30. It is especially true, when we find ourselves very cheerful and heartfelt in making great sacrifices for those who hate us, and having a willingness to lay down our lives to promote their eternal salvation, that we have evidence of growth in grace.

31. Still more especially, when we find ourselves less and less inclined to consider anything a sacrifice that we can do for God or for the souls of men, when we can consider our lives not dear unto us if called to lay them down to save the souls of enemies, when, for the joy of saving them, we can endure the cross and despise the shame (Hebrews 12:2), or any sacrifice that we are called to make, we have evidence that we are growing in favor with God.

32. Again, when we find ourselves more and more inclined to *count it all joy* when we *fall into divers temptations* (James 1:2), and when we tend to look upon our trials, difficulties, losses, and crosses in such a light as to lay less and less stress upon them, we have evidence that we are growing in patience, and therefore, in favor with God.

33. When we find less and less reluctance to making full confession to those whom we have offended or harmed, when with increasing readiness and gentleness we lay our hearts open to be searched and take

home conviction of wrongdoing, and when, in such cases, we cannot rest until we have made the fullest confession and restoration within our power, and when to acknowledge, confess, and make the fullest satisfaction is a comfort to us rather than a trial and a cross, we have evidence that we are growing in the grace of God.

34. When we are more and more moved and affected by the mercies of God, and by the kindnesses of our fellow men and those around us, when we more deeply and thoroughly appreciate manifestations of kindness in God, or in anyone else, when we are more and more humbled and affected by these kindnesses and find it more and more natural *to do justly, and to love mercy, and to walk humbly* (Micah 6:8) and live gratefully, we have evidence that we are growing in favor with God.

35. When we find ourselves drawn with increasing earnestness to continue to know more of the Lord, we have evidence of growth in grace.

36. When we find ourselves more and more freely moved and affected, quickened and stimulated by religious truth, and when we find an increasing harmony in the action of all our powers – intellectual, voluntary, and sensitive – in accepting and resting in the whole will and providence of God, no matter how unpleasant they may at present be, we have evidence that we are growing in grace.

37. A growing jealousy for the honor of God, for the purity and honor of His church, for the rights of God, and for the rights of all men is evidence of growing in conformity to God, and, of course, of growing in His grace.

VII. How to Grow in Grace

1. Fulfill the conditions noticed under the fourth head of this lecture. I do not need to repeat them.

2. Remember that every step of progress must be made by faith and not by works. The mistake that some good people have made upon

this subject is truly amazing. Dr. Chalmers affirms that the way to be sanctified is to work for it. A few years ago, Dr. Pond published a pamphlet in which he took ground on this subject, with Dr. Chalmers, and affirmed that the idea of being sanctified by faith was an absurdity. Indeed, the custom has been almost universal to represent growth in grace as consisting in the formation of habits of obedience to God. It is quite surprising that so many good men have fallen into this mistake.

The fact is that every step of progress in the Christian life is taken by a fresh and fuller appropriation of Christ by faith, a fuller baptism of the Holy Spirit. As our weaknesses, infirmities, besetting sins, and necessities are revealed to us by the circumstances of temptation through which we pass, our only efficient help is found in Christ, and we grow only as we more fully appropriate Him step-by-step, in one relation or another, and more fully "put Him on" (Romans 13:14).

As we are more and more emptied of self-dependence, as we more and more renounce and discard all expectation of forming holy habits by any obedience of ours, as by faith we are filled more and more by the Holy Spirit and put on the Lord Jesus Christ more and more thoroughly, and in more of His official relations, by just so much the faster do we grow in the grace of God. Nothing can be more erroneous and dangerous than the commonly received idea of growing in grace by the formation of holy habits. By acts of faith alone, we appropriate Christ, and we are as truly sanctified by faith as we are justified by faith.

In my *Systematic Theology*, in pointing out the conditions of entire or permanent sanctification, I have noticed some sixty of the official relations of Christ, as I have said before, and have there insisted, as I here insist, that growth in holiness, and consequently, in the grace of God, is secured only by fresh, fuller, and more thorough appropriations of Christ in all these official relations. If you want to grow in grace, you must do so through faith. You must pray in faith for the Holy Spirit. You must appropriate and put on Christ through the Holy Spirit. At every forward step in your progress, you must have a fresh anointing of the Holy Spirit through faith.

Remarks

1. We see from this subject the vast importance of rightly instructing young converts. In many cases, they have very little instruction suited to their experience and degree of Christian intelligence. By some people, such views are taken of the perseverance of the saints that it is assumed that infants in Christ will grow without nursing, and without that *sincere milk of the word* by means of which they must grow (1 Peter 2:2). Some people, taking it for granted that they need instruction, unintentionally give them false instruction and set them to work outwardly and zealously, without paying much regard to strengthening and developing their inward life.

They do not teach them how to appropriate and live on Christ as their life, but continually push them to do their duty, to labor for God and labor for souls, not sufficiently impressing upon them the idea that their doing is of no account unless it proceeds from the life of God in their own souls. The result of this is a bustling, outward activity, while the inward spiritual life is decaying. This will end in disgust at one's own lack of heart, and settling back into apathy and neglect.

2. Sometimes there is a mistake made in the opposite direction. They are taught to rest in Christ in such a sense as to take on a type of quietism and antinomian inactivity. They are exhorted to exercise faith, but they are not earnestly impressed with the conviction that it must be a faith that works and works by love, that purifies the heart and overcomes the world. The result is that they do nothing in religion. Sinners are allowed to sleep on and go to hell in their midst, and they make no effort to save them.

3. We see the importance of a Holy Spirit anointed ministry. The great need of the church is a ministry so thoroughly anointed by the Holy Spirit as to know how to lead the church onward and upward to the fullest development of Christian piety. In order to instruct converts and keep the church progressing in holiness, the minister must progress himself. He must be a truly living, growing Christian.

I have good reason to know that the churches in many places are deeply hurt by the lack of living piety and growth in their ministers. Their ministers are intellectual, literary, philosophical, and theological in their teaching, but they are sadly deficient in unction. They have but little power with God or with man. They instruct the intellect to a certain extent, but they do not meet the needs of the heart. Converts starve under their preaching. They preach an intellectual, rather than a spiritual, gospel. They preach religion as a theory, a doctrine, or a philosophy, and not as a real living experience.

It is often exceedingly painful to hear ministers preach who clearly do not know what they say or of what they declare. They speak of Christianity as an inward sentiment instead of heart devotion to God, as an emotion or a feeling instead of an all-embracing and efficient love, as a voluntary state and attitude of the mind from which necessarily proceeds a holy life. They speak of faith as a mere intellectual state or conviction, and not as an act of trust and of commitment of the whole being to do and accept all the will of God. They speak of repentance as if it were a mere involuntary sorrow for sin. They do not teach that repentance is a change of mind toward God, a renunciation of the self-seeking spirit, and a turning of the whole mind to God. They speak of holiness as if it were a state utterly unattainable in this life.

Indeed, I say it with sorrow, but I must say it, that the teachings of a great many ministers are simply a stumbling block to the church. Under their instruction, converts do not and cannot get so established in grace as to be greatly useful, or to live lives that are honorable to Christ. Just think that in the nineteenth century, ministers preach to converts that they must grow in grace by works. Heaven and earth must be amazed at this! Such teachers do not know how to grow in grace themselves. Will I be considered harsh if I say, *They be blind leaders of the blind* (Matthew 15:14)?

4. We see the reason of so much backsliding. Converts will of course backslide who are led by false instruction. If, on the one hand, they are set to work out sanctification by works, their works will soon become dead works and will not be the result of that faith that works by love. If, on the other hand, they are filled with abstract beliefs and doctrines, and are taught to rest in an antinomian faith, they will sink

into slothfulness and inactivity. I fully believe that in nearly all cases where there has been a disastrous reaction after a revival, it has been due to the lack of timely and proper instruction. But to be timely and proper, it must be anointed instruction.

5. The theological seminaries need to pay vastly more attention to the growth in grace of their students. They need a professor of experiential religion who has experience and power enough to press them along into those higher regions of Christian experience that are essential to their being able to lead the church on to victory. It is amazing to see how little effort is made to cultivate the hearts of young men studying for the ministry. We must have a change in this respect.

A much higher standard of Christian experience must be required as a condition of ordination. It is painful to see how carefully men will be examined in regard to their intellectual attainments, while the accounts they give of their Christian experience will barely allow us to hope that they have been converted. How sad it is to set such young men to feed the church of God! How must old Christians mourn when they see that the appointed leaders in the church of God are only spiritual infants!

6. I have never been present at the examination of a candidate for ordination where anything more than simple evidence of conversion was required of him. I have never heard them questioned in regard to their progress in Christian experience and in regard to their spiritual ability to lead the flock of God into green pastures and beside the still waters. I never heard them questioned in a manner that manifested the slightest idea of what the indispensable spiritual qualifications of a man are who is to stand forth as the leader and spiritual instructor of the church of God.

More hours are spent in learning the intellectual attainments of a candidate than minutes to discover his spiritual and experiential attainments. The entire examination will plainly indicate that the ordaining body places very little emphasis on this part of a minister's education. Is it any wonder that the church of God is so feeble and inefficient, while so many of its leaders and teachers are mere children in spiritual knowledge and while a mature Christian experience is made no part of the indispensable education of a minister? This is infinitely more dangerous and ridiculous than to entrust men to lead an army in the field while they merely understand mathematics and have never had any training or experience in military matters.

In this respect, too, there must be a great change. Churches should refuse to ordain and receive pastors unless they are fully satisfied of their having made much progress in Christian experience so as to be able to lead on and keep the church awake.

They should insist upon the education of his heart as well as his head, and upon his ability to take young converts and lead them on to those deep experiences that will make them stable and efficient workers in the cause of God. Think of theological seminaries like those over which Dr. Chalmers and Dr. Pond have presided, where the leaders of the church of God are taught that sanctification or growth in grace is attained by works and not by faith. *Tell it not in Gath* (2 Samuel 1:20). Woe to Zion, when her great and good men fall into such mistakes!

Charles G. Finney – A Brief Biography

One of the men most greatly used by God during America's Second Great Awakening was Charles Grandison Finney. He was born in Warren, Connecticut, on August 29, 1792, and died in Oberlin, Ohio, on August 16, 1875. Finney was a devoted evangelist, revivalist, and abolitionist.

Finney, being human, was certainly not perfect, yet he was greatly used by God to lead thousands to the Savior. Those who actually read his writings learn to love and appreciate him as a man surrendered to God and a servant of Jesus Christ.

Charles Finney began his career as a lawyer, but after his conversion on October 10, 1821, he left his law practice and began preaching the gospel of Jesus Christ. He was ordained as a Presbyterian minister in 1824 and began missionary work in western New York. Finney did not usually fit in well with the Old School Presbyterians, but often won his opponents over after discussing his beliefs with them personally and explaining his beliefs from the Bible. As is still true today, many who opposed Finney at first did so based upon hearsay rather than upon actually knowing the man and his teachings.

Charles Finney began preaching and seeing great results. Entire families and communities were changed by the power of God. He often opposed Universalism, which was a common belief of his day. While knowing that salvation comes only through faith in Jesus, Charles Finney preached that people needed to seek God and choose to follow Jesus.

Charles Finney was opposed by many, both sinners and religionists, yet he continued to preach and see spiritual fruit. He was opposed by some of the strict Presbyterians for some of his non-Presbyterian methods, such as allowing women to pray in meetings and adopting the then-Methodist practice of having a bench up front in meetings where those who were concerned about their souls could come up and sit and be dealt with about their souls.

Finney spent much time preaching in towns in western New York. One of his most well-known times of revival occurred in Rochester, New York, in 1830-1831. Finney continued preaching as a traveling revivalist/evangelist, and he saw thousands and thousands of lives changed by God, believers who remained faithful to God even decades later. Finney also preached about social issues, including the evils of alcohol and worldliness. He wrote much against Freemasonry, and he fiercely promoted the abolition of slavery. Finney also travelled to England twice during the 1850s to preach.

He became the minister of a Presbyterian church in New York City for a little while, but then moved on to preach at the Broadway Tabernacle that had been built for him. After about a year, Finney left to become the pastor of a Congregational church in Oberlin, Ohio, as well as to teach theology at Oberlin College. In 1851, Charles Finney became the college's second president, serving in that role until 1866.

Charles Finney was married three times. He married Lydia Root Andrews in 1824, with whom he had six children. After Lydia died in 1847, Charles married Elizabeth Ford Atkinson, who died in 1863. In

1865, he married Rebecca Allen Rayl, who outlived him, dying in 1907. All three of Finney's wives travelled with him as he preached.

Some of Charles Finney's well-known writings include his *Lectures on Systematic Theology, Lectures on Revivals of Religion*, and his *Autobiography*. He has been called the "Father of American Revivalism," and is thought to have led tens of thousands or even hundreds of thousands of people to the Lord Jesus Christ. He is known as one of America's most influential preachers.

Charles Finney did not always fit the traditional religious mold. His past as a lawyer was often seen in his sermons as he reasoned with people and made a case as to why they should follow Christ. He did not just go along with the traditional methods of the strict religionists of his day, but adapted methods to the needs of the people and spoke to them in common language. He did not fit in with the strict Calvinists, nor with the Arminians. Some have referred to his beliefs as "arminianized Calvinism." Nevertheless, he was a man who led many thousands of people from a life of sin to new life in Christ. Charles G. Finney was devoted to God, used by God, and admired and respected by many. He influenced individuals, families, communities, and the entire nation for God.